Chaplin's War Trilogy

Chaplin's War Trilogy
An Evolving Lens in Three Dark Comedies, 1918–1947

Wes D. Gehring

Foreword by Conrad Lane

McFarland & Company, Inc., Publishers
Jefferson, North Carolina

Also by Wes D. Gehring and from McFarland
Will Cuppy, American Satirist: A Biography (2013)
Forties Film Funnymen: The Decade's Great Comedians at Work in the Shadow of War (2010)
Film Clowns of the Depression: Twelve Defining Comic Performances (2007)
Joe E. Brown: Film Comedian and Baseball Buffoon (2006)
Mr. Deeds Goes to Yankee Stadium: Baseball Films in the Capra Tradition (2004)

Frontispiece: Pablo Picasso's 1937 painting *Guernica*, inspired by his outrage over the German bombing of the village of Guernica during the Spanish Civil War (1937–1939), was the catalyst for this book (© 2013 Estate of Pablo Picasso/Artists Rights Society [ARS], New York).

All photographs are from the author's collection unless otherwise noted.

LIBRARY OF CONGRESS CATALOGUING-IN-PUBLICATION DATA

Gehring, Wes D.
Chaplin's war trilogy : an evolving lens in three dark comedies, 1918–1947 / Wes D. Gehring ; foreword by Conrad Lane.
p. cm.
Includes bibliographical references and index.

ISBN 978-0-7864-7465-3 (softcover : acid free paper) ∞
ISBN 978-1-4766-1630-8 (ebook)

1. Chaplin, Charlie, 1889–1977—Criticism and interpretation.
2. Shoulder arms (Motion picture). 3. Great dictator (Motion picture)
4. Monsieur Verdoux (Motion picture) 5. War films—United States—History and criticism. 6. Comedy films—United States—History and criticism. I. Title.
PN2287.C5G375 2014   791.4302'8092—dc23   2014030832

BRITISH LIBRARY CATALOGUING DATA ARE AVAILABLE

© 2014 Wes D. Gehring. All rights reserved

No part of this book may be reproduced or transmitted in any form or by any means, electronic or mechanical, including photocopying or recording, or by any information storage and retrieval system, without permission in writing from the publisher.

On the cover: poster art detail from
The Great Dictator, 1940 (Charles Chaplin/Photofest)

Printed in the United States of America

*McFarland & Company, Inc., Publishers
Box 611, Jefferson, North Carolina 28640
www.mcfarlandpub.com*

To my parents,
from whom ...

Table of Contents

Foreword by Conrad Lane — 1
Preface and Acknowledgments — 3
Prologue — 5

1. Chaplin and the Basic Parameters of Dark Comedy — 9
2. Chaplin's Life and Career to 1918 — 18
3. The War Bond Rallies of 1918: A Neglected Patriot — 31
4. *Shoulder Arms* and War as a Film Topic in 1918 — 49
5. Moving to the Post-War 1920s — 66
6. The 1930s and Gathering War Clouds — 88
7. Napoleon, Hitler and *The Great Dictator* — 101
8. After *The Great Dictator*; Before *Monsieur Verdoux* — 121
9. *Monsieur Verdoux*, Without His "Talisman" Charlie — 139
10. *Monsieur Verdoux* to *Limelight*: From "The Little Tramp" to "The Little Red" — 157
11. Two Bitter Kings, Dark Comedy Reality, and a Lesson from *Monsieur Verdoux* — 168
12. Coming Full Circle: Chaplin's Last Years, an Unrealized Darkly Comic Project, and a Final Macabre Twist — 182

Epilogue — 195
Filmography — 203
Chapter Notes — 205
Bibliography — 219
Index — 229

Foreword by Conrad Lane

"Nothing is permanent in this wicked world. Not even our troubles."—Charlie Chaplin's title character in *Monsieur Verdoux* (1947), rationalizing yet another murder

I first became acquainted with the remarkable Wes Gehring when he came to our university as a fledgling assistant professor. Although we did not teach in the same department, we became aware of each other due to our mutual interest in film history. My first indication that we had attracted someone both unique and knowledgeable was when I learned, early on, that he was familiar with the work of silent comedian John Bunny (1863–1915), America's first international star of movie mirth. Although we were both born well after Bunny's heyday, we enjoyed his anticipation of the often anti-heroic humor of W.C. Fields.

Since our initial meeting over 30 years ago, we have met regularly to share a meal and some movie information. Dr. Gehring's faultless research and sharp memory were always evident in our casual conversations as well as in the 30-plus books that he has written in the intervening years. His first book, published in 1983, was a Charlie Chaplin biography which received a signal honor when he was invited to participate in a tribute to Chaplin at the University of Paris in 1989, the 100th anniversary of Chaplin's birth. By this time his meticulous scholarship was known to all who read him—including Chaplin's oldest daughter, actress Geraldine Chaplin, who personally thanked Wes for his book.

Gehring's passionate interest in the great Mr. Chaplin began when he was but a small lad in Iowa. His Grandpa McIntyre showed him a photo of "The Little Tramp" which immediately piqued his interest. Fortunately, Wes grew up in the fifties when television had access to many prints of old films which cost little or nothing to transmit. Among these were many public domain Chaplin short comedies. (Major Chaplin features such as 1931's *City Lights* were not then available.) Wes also viewed many other comedians in those halcyon days: Laurel and Hardy, the Marx Brothers and W.C. Fields. Abetting the young boy's interest was his father Jerry, who watched and laughed along with Wes. The result of this childhood interest has been our good fortune: an unbroken string of excellent books on comedians famous and not-so-famous. Gehring's books on these individuals have no equal for their quality scholarship.

Gehring's present book deals with Chaplin's changing views on dark comedy in his war trilogy of *Shoulder Arms* (1918), *The Great Dictator* (1940) and *Monsiuer Verdoux* (1947). A further inspiration for the text is Picasso's 1937 painting *Guernica*, which reflects his outrage over the German bombing of the city during the Spanish Civil War.

Prepare to absorb another tour de force by Dr. Wes D. Gehring.

Conrad Lane is a Ball State University emeritus professor who remains active as a film essayist and an Elderhostel movie historian-instructor. He also formerly hosted the PBS film review program Now Showing *on WIPB-TV in Muncie, Indiana.*

Preface and Acknowledgments

In *The Great Dictator* (1940), Charlie Chaplin observes, after yet another death of a war-related guinea pig inventor, "Herring, why do you waste my time like this?"

As a film professor and writer, I attempt to provide my students and readers with an understanding of what parallel events were occurring in the arts when a memorable movie or genre found an audience. Nothing occurs in a vacuum. For instance, a sort of zeitgeist occurred in the 1940s between the paintings of Edward Hopper, particularly his signature café diners in *Nighthawks* (1942), and the birth of film noir. Noir historian Foster Hirsch described a pivotal example of the genre, Fritz Lang's *Scarlet Street* (1945) thus:

> [T]here is no sense of life outside the frame; all exterior scenes are stripped of any sense of the city density and rhythm. The film's unpopulated streets, the elongated shadows, the angular buildings that guard empty space like grim sentinels, recall the eerie night-time cityscapes in the paintings of Edward Hopper.[1]

Director–film historian Martin Scorsese expressed similar thoughts about Robert Wise's *The Set-Up* (1949) and Hopper.[2]

The same connection can be made between the 1930s screwball comedy genre and the Regionalist painters of that era, particularly the canvases of Iowan Grant Wood, most famous for his "American Gothic" (1930, the pitchfork-toting father and daughter in front of their Gothic house), or his senile *Daughters of [the American] Revolution* (1932). Yet at the same time, Wood was painting love letters to the Iowa countryside such as *Young Corn* (1931) and *Spring Turning* (1936). Art historian E.H. Gombrich's description of *Spring Turning* even seems worded with the childlike antihero male of the screwball comedy in mind, with its "charm of a toy landscape."[3] Such idealized country settings are a perfect embodiment of the romantic rural backdrop sometimes used in the screwball genre, such as Leo McCarey's *The Awful Truth* (1937), while simultaneously satirizing its small-town, rural population, best showcased in William Wellman's *Nothing Sacred* (1937).[4]

While the noir world is reflected in Chaplin's *Monsieur Verdoux* (1947), the key art connection to this text is of a different sort: art as a political statement. More specifically, Pablo Picasso's *Guernica* (1937) sparked the writing of this text. Picasso's painting expressed his outrage over Nazi Germany's genocide bombing of the town Guernica (at the behest of the fascist General Francisco Franco) during the Spanish Civil War, the prelude to World War II (1939–1945). Picasso had observed, "What do you think an artist is? An imbecile who has only eyes, if he is a painter? ... No, painting is not done to decorate apartments. It is an instrument of war."[5] Russell Martin's book, *Picasso's War: The Destination of Guernica, and the Masterpiece That Changed the World*, is *the* text on the subject. Thus, Picasso's work triggered thoughts of Charlie Chaplin's decision to wage his own dark comedy on fascism, *à la* Hitler, with *The Great Dictator* three years later. Then I had the epiphany that Chaplin had done two other war-related dark comedies, *Shoulder Arms* (1918) and *Monsieur Verdoux,* yet his perspective had changed on each of the three films. With that, voila, I had a book project.

Oh, of course, there was the research and writing to do, too. My general starting point is the New York Public Library's main branch at Fifth Avenue and Forty-Second Street—the one the librarian comes tearing out of at the beginning of *Ghostbusters* (1984). While nothing like this has occurred to me, my anxiousness to enter the place might clock me at a speed close to that exiting librarian. And though I have never encountered any *paranormal* activities, I do spend all my library time in what researchers call the "tombs," New York's dead newspaper department, looking at microfilm. The other pivotal stop in the city is the Performing Arts Library at Lincoln Center, with its critical period clipping files of film artists and individual movies.

On the West Coast, the key research destination for this text was the Academy of Motion Picture Arts and Sciences' Margaret Herrick Library in Beverly Hills. Since Chaplin and many other early screen subjects have been the focus of my research, both here and in New York, who knows, the chance of paranormal activity might still come my way. Closer to home, Ball State University's interlibrary loan staff—Sandy Duncan, Kerri McClellan, Lisa Johnson, Elaine Nelson, and Karin Kwiatkowski—managed to track down my every research request.

Regardless, I am reminded of a story shared in an earlier preface which is no less true today. That is, I so love these cultural safehouses, cerebral magnets to the scholar turned detective, that I think of legendary basketball player and passionate athlete-writer Bill Russell's comments about departing his creative space: "Whenever I leave the [Boston] Celtics locker room, even heaven wouldn't be good enough because any place else is a step down."[6] As a metaphorical addendum to my scholarly workplaces, each are repositories reminiscent of an autobiographical observation made by novelist Graham Greene concerning long-ago facts as "stray symbols of a dream after the story has sunk back into the unconscious, and they cry for rescue like the survivors of a shipwreck."[7] Thus, while I enjoy the comedy in that old axiom "Writing history is like trying to nail jelly to wall," I refuse to embrace the sentiment.[8]

To change now, however, to a more specific thank you narrative, a great many people helped in the preparation of this book. Beginning with those at the greatest distance, Joe and Marie Pacino have frequently provided research assistance and a place to crash when I am in the Los Angeles area. My Ball State mentor and film scholar Conrad Lane provided both valuable insights and penned the foreword. My department chair, Tim Pollard, has been a supportive friend who also orchestrated university financial support, coupled with a special leave from Ball State. Janet Warrner supplied editorial proofing, while historian Andy Warrner was always available for special questions about the various periods. Kris Scott was responsible for the computer preparation of this manuscript, and Chris Flook helped facilitate the preparation of several stills. The right to reproduce the painting *Guernica* is from the Estate of Pablo Picasso/Artists Rights Society (ARS), New York. The other stills come from the collection of the author.

All projects of this nature are also made possible by the love and support of one's family: my forever nurturing parents; my special muse-partner Cassie, who listened to *so* many passages from the text during its composition; and my film-loving daughters, Sarah and Emily.

Prologue

> The [civil] war in Spain [1936–1939] represents the battle of reactionary forces against the people, against freedom.... In [my painting] *Guernica* [1937] I have clearly expressed my horror of the military group [the Fascist-assisted Nationalists] that has plunged Spain into an ocean of pain and death.—Pablo Picasso[1]

A Pablo Picasso painting might seem an unusual catalyst for a book on Charlie Chaplin. Yet *Guernica,* and Russell Martin's study *Picasso's War: The Destruction of Guernica and the Masterpiece That Changed the World* (2002), had me immediately thinking of Chaplin's *The Great Dictator* (1940), another work of art contemporary to *Guernica,* and drawn from the same war-driven pain which inspired Picasso.[2] For me, always an aficionado of black humor, it then became a tempting task to compare *Dictator* with Chaplin's two other war-driven dark comedies, *Shoulder Arms* (1918) and *Monsieur Verdoux* (1947), and explore how the comedian's relationship with and use of the genre changed through the years.[3] Moreover, each film in this black humor trilogy utilizes its dark comedy in radically *different* ways. Amazingly, no one has studied the evolution of Chaplin's views on this genre. *Shoulder Arms* finds the comedian's Tramp as a World War I soldier on the Western Front. Though groundbreakingly controversial—dark film comedy was just not being done in 1918—Charlie's misadventures are still showcased in a pro-war film.

Dictator came out on the eve of America's entry into World War II, though much of the globe was already engulfed in armed conflict. Its anti-war stance was a plea to stop the insanity. Chaplin plays a dual role, a Jewish barber reminiscent of the Tramp, and the title character who is a take-off on Adolf Hitler. There is a certain continuity with *Shoulder Arms,* in that *Dictator* begins with the barber's service in the First World War. Yet, whereas *Shoulder Arms* is predicated upon the necessity of fighting to defeat Germany, *Dictator* is driven by pacifism. It culminate with the barber's anti-war speech, when he is mistaken for the look-alike dictator. Still, it was seminal dark comedy; no one was cinematically skewering Hitler at this time.

Dictator did provide a compassionate counterbalance with Chaplin's portrayal of the Jewish barber. However, with *Monsieur Verdoux,* Chaplin leaves all semblance of sympathy behind, as he plays a title character Bluebeard who marries and murders wealthy old ladies. So where does the subject of war come in? The movie is a morality play about the murderous war-like inclinations of big business. Chaplin's character paraphrases the famous darkly comic observation made by Prussian general Karl von Clausewitz (1780–1831), "War is the logical extension of diplomacy," by stating, "The logical extension of business is murder." Chaplin suggests that in modern society, in order for the individual to survive, he must emulate the Darwinian tactics of capitalism and/or government in general. The comedian has now taken his lead character to the dark side. I hope this study provides new insights on both cinema's greatest auteur (Chaplin wrote, directed, produced, scored, and starred in his films), as well as chronicling early patterns in the evolution of dark comedy as a genre.

To adequately examine the trilogy necessities studying their placement within the whole of Chaplin's oeuvre. Thus, the first chapter explores the comedian's relationship to the basic perimeters of a genre (dark comedy) he helped to both establish and introduce to mainstream cinema. This section provides a crash course in modern black humor and how Chaplin assisted the industry to get there. Chapter 2 retreats to the comedian's beginnings and his life up until pivotal 1918, the year *Shoulder Arms* was released. What was there about his early years which made him such a seminal figure in the birthing of black cinema humor?

Chapter 3 scrutinizes the intensity with which Chaplin threw himself into the bond rallies for World War I. After discussing his high-profile visits to the White House and Wall Street, with fellow iconic screen stars Mary Pickford and Douglas Fairbanks, the text studies as never before Chaplin's solo tour of countless southern cities drumming up business for bonds. The pages chronicle both the passion of a neglected "American" patriot, despite his British citizenship, and such a unique outpouring of affection for Chaplin that one cannot help thinking of the much later response to four fellow countrymen: the Beatles. Chaplin is *so* immersed in these bond rallies that their culmination with the production of a war-based comedy in *Shoulder Arms* seems inevitable.

Chaplin's southern tour also exposed him to the rabid hatred of a multitude of subjects, including the German Kaiser as the devil incarnate, anyone questioning the war, and the perennial racism of a region still packing movie palaces with D.W. Griffith's inflammatory *Birth of a Nation* (1915). Consequently, this material provides a perfect segue to chapter 4's in-depth look at the groundbreaking *Shoulder Arms*. Given the period's bared hostility, Chaplin had plenty of leeway to break new ground with cinema black comedy and still rein in the incendiary philosophy which continued to run rampant in society.

Chapters 5 and 6 cover the two decades leading up to *Dictator*, and the myriad of events which made it yet again inevitable that Chaplin would tackle dark comedy head-on. First, there is Chaplin's continuing use of black humor in his interim pictures between the world wars. Second, it took nearly a decade but by the late 1920s most of the western world (outside of Germany) had come to feel that the millions of deaths which resulted from the ironically entitled "Great War" had created a "Lost Generation," in which basic human values had died, too, creating a spiritual and emotional wasteland. Consequently, isolationism and appeasement were the law of the land during the 1930s, as a brazen German dictator with a Charlie Chaplin mustache bluffed his goose-stepping soldiers into absolute power in Europe. Neither America nor the continental powers wanted another "Great War." Moreover, *Dictator* came at a time when few could then imagine what horrific acts Hitler was capable of, and the U.S. was not yet in the war. Thus, the year *Dictator* appeared (1940), Chaplin was pushing his dark comedy feature up a steep slippery slope, because most Americans were content to keep their heads in the sand about involvement in another European conflict.

Chapters 7 and 8 examine Chaplin's long gestation period for *Dictator*, as well as the public response to this controversial picture. The latter chapter also sets the scene for Chaplin's largest transition in his dark comedy evolution: *Monsieur Verdoux*. One should add that the three most written-about people in western civilization are Jesus, Napoleon, and Hitler—all individuals Chaplin wanted to play at one time or another. Of the three, he labored longest over a Napoleon film. Yet, with *Dictator* he manages to combine elements of both Napoleon and Hitler, with a touch of Jesus at the end, when the Bible-spouting Jewish barber–Tramp pleads for peace. Though it is well documented that the comedian was truly fascinated by this trio, Chaplin author Julian Smith has puckishly stated that the filmmaker's interest in such parts (Smith also includes Hamlet) was also an "an attention-getting mixture of stubbornness, megalomania, wishful thinking and a playful desire to shock, amuse, and tease his public."[4] Such a suggestion would be equally applicable to a myriad of subjects which interested the complicated comedian ... without making his desire any less true.

Chapter 9 concentrates on *Monsieur Verdoux,* and the comedian finally letting go of his iconic talisman, the Tramp. Much had changed both with Chaplin and the world since the release of *Dictator.* With the Allies' opening of the German concentration camps, the degree to which man's inhumanity to man could be taken had reached horrific heights. Chaplin was now prepared to embrace this shocking development in his art, but the change proved too much for his mainstream American audience, especially as it teetered upon his increasingly messy personal life. *Verdoux* would help jump-start a genre (dark comedy) in the rest of the world, from Britain's Ealing pictures of the late 1940s and 1950s, to Italian Sergio Leone's "Spaghetti Westerns" of the 1960s. But *Verdoux* immediately hit the skids in the U.S. One should never get too far ahead of the typical viewer and expect success. Moreover, *Verdoux* has become more relevant with each passing year, even today considering the ongoing war on terror. For instance, the realpolitik (practical over ethical values) of any confrontation raises the age-old philosophical question: If one embraces the macabre tactics of the enemy, has one not already lost the war by becoming him? Chaplin's film was merely a reminder that the post–World War II moral compass was arguably irrevocably broken.

Chapter 10 charts the nasty fallout from *Verdoux,* and Chaplin's valentine to both himself and America in *Limelight.* Paradoxically, the spectra of the McCarthy witch-hunting years not only negated this amazing olive branch to America (*Limelight*), it essentially banished cinema's greatest auteur from the country. How does the "the little Tramp" become "the little Red" in the course of just a few years? The question is easy: In a blacklisting era in which the fear of anything smacking of communism could even make the major league Cincinnati Reds change their name to the Cincinnati Red Stockings, no one or no thing was too big to be metaphorically crucified by association.

Life imitates art in chapter 11 when Chaplin uses the subterfuge of *Verdoux* to successfully make his very real financial break with America by moving to Switzerland. And not surprisingly, the chapter also chronicles Chaplin's film payback to America in the mild yet very underrated satire *A King in New York* (1957). Though U.S. citizens treated the picture like the joked-about Ford Edsel automobile introduced the following year (1958), *King* was an entertaining satire of everything from CinemaScope to rock 'n' roll. Though hardly in a class with Chaplin's earlier watershed works, it was a picture worth seeing, regardless of one's fondness for Chaplin.

The last chapter documents the highs and lows of Chaplin's final years, from a boatload of honors (including an honorary Oscar and British Knighthood), to a revisionist screwball comedy, *A Countess from Hong Kong* (1967), which was roundly attacked by the critics. Yet, as with *King,* its stock has also gone up with the passing years. Moreover, Chaplin authored a best-selling memoir, *My Autobiography* (1964), whose first half was greatly praised by reviewers.

One might best summarize Chaplin by a comment from his third wife and fellow actor Paulette Goddard. Though it was a performing tip, it easily doubles as a life lesson for success. The actress observed: "Chaplin was a great acting teacher as well as a film creator.... [He told her], 'Baby, don't *play* it, *be* it!'"[5]

Greatness is the product of many ingredients; but "*Be* it!" is certainly a good start.

1

Chaplin and the Basic Parameters of Dark Comedy

"I'm not saying we wouldn't get our hair mussed, but I do say no more than ten to twenty million killed, tops—depending on the breaks."—General Buck Turgidson (George C. Scott) reassuring the president (Peter Sellers) how America would fare in a nuclear war, from *Dr. Strangelove Or: How I Learned to Stop Worrying and Love the Bomb* (1964)

At its most fundamental, black humor is a genre of comic irreverence anchored in three anti-establishment settings (from church and family, to the military, and to government in general): the omnipresence of death, the inherent absurdity of the world, and the tendency of people to be beast-like to their fellow man.[1] George C. Scott's callously casual pitch for a potential nuclear holocaust embraces all three components. Fittingly, this is the film which brought dark comedy to cinematic center stage. Movies down this macabre rabbit hole need not embrace all three themes, yet that is the frequent norm.

Obviously, there is nothing inherently new about dark comedy; it can be found in the work of Aristophanes (448–385 BC), or Jonathan Swift's (1667–1745) Irish baby-eating premise for the celebrated essay "A Modest Proposal" (1729). American literature boasts such pioneer dark humorists as Edgar Allan Poe (1805–1849), Herman Melville (1819–1891), Ambrose Bierce (1842–1914?), and the late work of Mark Twain (1835–1910). Melville's *The Confidence Man* (1857) is the perfect case in point, with its Lucifer-like title character. Scholar Hennig Cohen suggests the novel's ongoing focus is "how to live in a world in which nothing is what it appears to be, in which the only thing knowable is that nothing can be known, and the only thing believable is that nothing can be believed."[2] Cohen might just as well be defining black comedy.

Dark humor also became a more visible topic by the writings of Charles Darwin (1809–1882) and Sigmund Freud (1856–1939). The former's then shocking claims for man's haphazard evolution from lesser beasts derailed the comfortable noble claim of being made in God's image. Darwinism, a still hotly contested subject, reduces mankind's sense of uniqueness to something less than heroic (man as beast and the survival of the fittest and most fierce). Darwin's work still qualifies as the most radical change in image man has ever had to address. Serious doubt was cast upon the comforting religion of your choice—thus, the awful finality of death. As with the later theories of Freud, Darwin's writing might best be labeled naturalism (realism carried to an extreme), in that it leads away from the supernatural. Coupled with another nineteenth-century negation of the uniqueness of the individual (the Industrial Revolution and the oppression which accompanied it), belief in a God-centered rationalism was rapidly failing. Here was fertile ground indeed for dark comedy.

While Darwin shook claims to some heavenly security blanket, Freud's pioneering work in psychoanalysis effectively called into question the possibility of even being in control of one's own mind. Freud's influence on modern "literature" was immense. He was the first guide to the dark chaos of the unconscious, with cinema's various "dream factories" frequently serving up unexpected shocks ... sort of a cling-to-the-wreckage mentality.

During the twentieth century, historian John Keegan drew a provocative analogy between those soldiers who did not survive World War I and the Holocaust victims of World War II—both pivotal tragedies which have had a major impact on the study of black humor. For example, he suggests that the British trenches of the July 1916 first day Somme Offessive (which futilely left twenty thousand dead on both sides) "were the concentration camp [beginnings] of the first World War ... young men plodding forward across a featureless landscape to their own extermination inside the barbed wire."[3]

The student of Holocaust literature has long been aware of dark humor as a Jewish psychological defense against Hitler's "final solution." Radically different approaches to this modern horror story still came back to laughter. Ironically, even the teenager diarist Anne Frank wrote, "There's *one* golden rule to keep before you laugh: laugh about everything and don't bother yourself about the others!"[4] After the war, concentration camp prisoner Dr. Viktor E. Frankl wrote a classic psychiatric text on survival which also counsels laughter: "Humor, more than anything else in the human make-up, can afford an ability to rise above any situation...."[5] But on a more macabre note, he also mentions instances, such as entering a shower room that might be a gas chamber, where black comedy was an automatic reflex: "[M]ost of us were overcome by a grim sense of humor. We knew that we had nothing to lose except our own ridiculously naked lives.... [W]e really tried very hard to make fun." Even before the actual liquidation potential, victims were referring to dark humor as "Jewish novocaine."[6]

With some Holocaust literature, one need not move beyond the title for the dark humor message. The immediate post-war Auschwitz stories of Tadeusz Borowski are entitled *This Way for the Gas, Ladies and Gentleman* (1959).[7] Moreover, the name of Steve Lipman's 1993 study is even more direct: *Laughter in Hell: The Use of Humor During the Holocaust.*[8] Probably the greatest irony of black—so-called sick—humor is that it is *the healthiest survivor outlook to take.*

Not surprisingly, Charlie Chaplin (1889–1977) was in the vanguard of this genre so dark in its humor it is sometimes even described as "anti-comedy." Besides the comedian's ties to many of the aforementioned black humor components, to be expanded upon shortly, he also had a Victorian fascination for the macabre. His 1964 autobiography, while paradoxically telling little about his films, reflects his interest in the grisly tale, including the murder scene of a Japanese prime minister; a clinical examination of what the electric chair does to its victim; often vivid descriptions of the suicides of several friends; a chance meeting with a man condemned to hang; the strange story of a Buddhist monk who, because he had spent a lifetime floating in oil, allegedly had skin so embryonically soft that a finger could be put through it, and so on. Most telling, however, is the Chaplin memoir moment documenting his first realization of the power inherent in the mixing of horror and humor. One of the poverty-stricken flats of his youth was near a slaughterhouse, with sheep routinely being driven past the building. On one occasion a lamb escaped, and people were creating unintentional slapstick as they tripped over themselves trying to capture the creature. Like many, young Charlie had giggled with delight over the misadventure. Yet, when the lamb was caught and carried into the slaughterhouse, the reality of the tragedy made him cry: "[T]hat comedy chase stayed with me ...

and I wonder if that episode did not establish the premise of my future films—the combination of the tragic and the comic."[9]

Charles Chaplin, Jr. (from the comedian's marriage to second wife Lita Grey), suggests in his affectionate biography *My Father, Charlie Chaplin* (1960) that the comedian's interest in dark comedy was very much like that of Charles Dickens; invariably the elder Chaplin's bedtime stories were extracts from the novelist with a "macabre cast to them."[10] A special favorite of his father's was *Oliver Twist* (1837–39), since the hero's experiences in the orphanage reminded Chaplin of a youth spent in and out of orphanage-like workhouses. A popular passage the comedian acted described Oliver's meeting with Fagin:

> "How'd you like to be the little boy just waking up and you see this man with a beard standing there and the knife coming at you?" he would say in that soft, foreboding tone of voice that always ushered us [Charles, Jr., and brother Sydney] into one of his [funny-scary characterizations].[11]

Chaplin's son later theorized that the reason his father's most preferred fiction writers were Dickens and Guy de Maupassant was "because of the peculiar combination of the humorous and macabre in their works."[12] The son knew his father, for when the comedian eventually wrote his memoir, he would describe Fagin as "both humorous and horrific."[13] Many of the other authors favored by his father (such as Poe, Oscar Wilde, and Twain) also specialized in black comedy—though they were seldom initially recognized for that twisted nature to their humor.

These bedtime story observations about Father Chaplin are also consistent with those of the comedian's prodigal son (from his marriage to fourth wife Oona O'Neill) Michael Chaplin, in *I Couldn't Smoke the Grass on My Father's Lawn* (1966), right down to more grisly bedtime stories. Except, now the tales for Chaplin's second young family (he fathered seven children with Oona) were of his own invention and fell under the ironic heading of the "Nice Old Man" stories. One of Michael's favorites ends with a baby falling in the sea and the "Nice Old Man pushed the pram [baby carriage] in after him and went off to spend the money the parents had given him to look after the baby."[14] Consistently, decades before, when Chaplin's Tramp is first saddled with the baby in *The Kid* (1921), he fleetingly considers tossing the child down the sewer grating to the sea.

It seems appropriate, however, that the darkest film-related story in Chaplin's autobiography manages to briefly find its way back to the comedian's celebrated *The Gold Rush* (1925). The tale in question involves the ill-fated Donner Party, a group of mid–nineteenth century American pioneers who resorted to cannibalism when snow stranded them in the mountains. Paradoxically, Chaplin drew heavily upon this real-life tragedy–horror story for a film now labeled one of the greatest of all film comedies. Charlie's Tramp plays a starving miner in the frozen North, trapped in a snowbound cabin with an equally hungry partner (Mack Swain) who periodically hallucinates that the "Little Fellow" is a chicken. Charlie must do comic battle for his life until a passing bear becomes supper.

One of *The Gold Rush*'s signature scenes is also tied to the Donner Party story: the sequences in which hunger forces Charlie and Mack to stew the Tramp's oversized boot for their Thanksgiving meal. Chaplin's catalyst for the scene came from some desperate Donner members attempting to cook and eat their moccasins. The scene also provided the comedian with an excellent opportunity to showcase his inspired metamorphosis abilities—to comically transform inanimate objects into something else, from the basted boot's laces being eaten like so much spaghetti, to nails from the sole being sucked like a wishbone. (For further irony, the boot-eating banquet was also a prime reason for *The Gold Rush* at one time being a TV staple on Christmas Day in Great Britain.)

Though Chaplin's memoir does not belabor the subject of mixing the macabre and comedy, it includes a telling observation which could double as a contemporary definition of black comedy: "[T]ragedy stimulates the spirit of ridicule.... We must laugh in the face of our helplessness ... or go insane."[15] Regardless, one need not focus on high-profile scenes (like the boot-eating routine) to reveal black humor elements in his work. Though the focus of this study is to show how Chaplin applied his use of dark comedy to three different war settings, he liberally peppered elements of the genre throughout much of his work, such as the comic violence of *Easy Street* (1917). Examples would include the exaggerated fight scenes between the police and giant Eric Campbell's street gang, Charlie dropping a small cast iron stove on "Big Eric" from a second story window, and the Tramp using a gas street lamp to anesthetize the oversized bully. (Even what poet Carl Sandburg called Charlie's trademark "east-west" feet was based upon the real-life deformity of a late nineteenth century cabman.[16])

Of course, early non–Chaplin black humor film precedents also exist. To borrow a phrase from dark comedy author Kurt Vonnegut, if one were "unstuck in time" and could travel back through cinema history, there are numerous films with undercurrents of the genre, beginning with pioneer works from Georges Méliès and Mack Sennett.[17] For instance, just think of the latter's Keystone Cops' paddy wagons pinballing through the early streets of Los Angeles, with bodies flying every which way. (Several of these early cinema clowns actually died in the name of comedy.) Moreover, several Chaplin contemporaries had personality comedy personae which sometimes embraced black comedy—cynics like Buster Keaton, W.C. Fields, the Marx Brothers, and even the darkly methodical, "tit-for-tat" violence of Laurel & Hardy. Indeed, the war-related paranoia of *Duck Soup* has direct ties to General Jack

Chaplin's Tramp and the desperation of *The Gold Rush*.

D. Ripper's (Sterling Hayden) psychotic obsession that the Soviets are about to overrun America in *Dr. Strangelove*.[18]

Keaton and Fields had a wonderful way of derailing the normally happily-ever-after endings so synonymous with the other genres of comedy. Black humor tends to squash sweet dream conclusions, for example the mushroom cloud conclusion of *Dr. Strangelove*. While a hydrogen bomb Armageddon was not yet possible during the heyday of either Keaton or Fields, each of them frequently attached a scaled-down yet comparable message to their endings. Keaton was more direct, such as not getting the girl at the close of *Cops* (1922), and then emphasizing the loss by the picture's THE END appearing on a tombstone adorned with Keaton's signature porkpie hat. In contrast, Fields' best films often have such miraculous conclusions, as suggested by the title of his greatest film *It's a Gift* (1934), that one can only "read" them as satirizations of America's Horatio Alger hard work ethic. This darkly comic take on life—that success is completely random—is central to Fields' films, especially such pivotal movies as *It's a Gift* and *The Bank Dick* (1940). Like Chaplin, the self-educated but well-read Fields might have borrowed this basic theme about the significance of chance and circumstances from such literary giants of his youth as Charles Dickens and Leo Tolstoy. Along related lines, Chaplin granting the Tramp sudden millionaire status to close *The Gold Rush* would fall under this same absurdity tenet so near and dear to black humor.[19]

These fantasy finishes also burlesque Hollywood's then traditional happy endings for almost *any* genre. Still, Fields' turnarounds are so entertainingly unlikely they rival director Mike Nichols' brilliant adaptation close to Joseph Heller's *Catch–22* (1970), when Yossarian (Alan Arkin) decides he can escape the war and his conscience by simply rowing a rubber dinghy from Sicily to Scandinavia! Thus, the only upbeat endings in dark comedy, as well as the Fieldsian universe, are comically absurd. But whereas the 1970s film renaissance of black humor as a mainstream genre made such outrageous conclusions acceptably trendy, the pioneering dark comedy of Chaplin, Fields, and the others was not fully embraced at the time.

During Hollywood's golden studio age, from the mid–1920s until the late 1940s, occasional black humor was not limited to the personality comedian world of Chaplin and his fellow clowns. For example, dark comedy had an occasional tendency to surface in the farcical world of screwball comedy, be it Howard Hawks' *His Girl Friday* (1940), which literally incorporated "gallows humor" (the story revolves around an impending execution by hanging), or Frank Capra's *Arsenic and Old Lace* (1944), where Cary Grant's two pleasantly batty elderly aunts poison lonely old gentlemen. Naturally, one must also include Ernst Lubitsch's *To Be or Not to Be* (1942), in which screwball comedy meets Chaplin's *The Great Dictator* (1940).

One need not limit the propensity for dark comedy characteristics to surface early in any one genre. Indeed, Hawks successfully incorporates it into his watershed gangster picture *Scarface* (1932), especially those scenes which highlight the life and death of title figure Paul Muni's private secretary Angela (Vince Barnett). This comically befuddled little man takes one too many phone calls during gun battles. Other major precursor directors of the period whose work (like that of Chaplin and Hawks) often display dark comedy elements (regardless of the genre), were Preston Sturges, Billy Wilder, and Alfred Hitchcock. Still, these are generally macabre undercurrents in films best categorized in other genres, such as Hitchcock's political thriller *The 39 Steps* (1935), which anticipates Chaplin's *Monsieur Verdoux* (1947). Prime examples from this era would include Sturges' screwball comedy *The Miracle of Morgan's Creek* (1944, which borrows a page from Fields in both shish-kabobbing American small town life and having a whopper of a hilariously happy, unbelievable ending), to Wilder's noir classic *Double Indemnity* (1944).

In fact, film noir is such fertile ground for dark comedy that with some modern cinema (post–1965) examples of the genre, such as *Chinatown* (1974), one is tempted to label it equal parts noir and black humor. For instance, in this late 1930s tale of crookedly controlling and expanding the water rights to Los Angeles, the courtly villain is named Noah (John Huston). To make this happen, the water commissioner is drowned during a drought(!), and a central subterfuge occurs at the city's Echo Park Lake. To paraphrase one of its characters, *Chinatown* is a story which has "water on the brain."

Regardless, as noted at the beginning of this chapter, popular culture normally dates the starting point of dark comedy with the release of *Dr. Strangelove*. No little part of that status is provided by a seminal 1965 *Time* magazine article, "The Black Humorists." When it provided dark comedy examples outside of fiction, it started with *Dr. Strangelove*, describing the movie as "treating the hydrogen bomb as a colossal banana peel on which the world slips to annihilations."[20]

There are, however, three earlier Chaplin films which merit prototype status on a level with *Dr. Strangelove*: *Shoulder Arms* (1918), *The Great Dictator,* and *Monsieur Verdoux*. This is a war trilogy, arguably the best setting to examine the trifecta of dark comedy (death, absurdity, and beast-like behavior). These themes might have been summarized by a George Orwell entry from his World War II diary: "As I write, highly civilized human beings are flying overhead, trying to kill me."[21] In any event, each film in this Chaplin dark comedy trilogy utilizes its black humor in radically *different* ways. *Shoulder Arms* chronicles the life and hard times of Chaplin's Tramp as a World War I soldier on the Western Front. His inventive comic depiction of trench warfare represented groundbreaking dark comedy. Though controversial—this genre just was not being done in 1918—the Tramp's misadventures are still showcased in a patriotic pro-war film. Germany and the Kaiser were enemies most Americans could agree upon. This was the idealistically pitched "war to end all wars." Of course, as this text will explore, most-isms, especially nationalism, culminate in various forms of jingoistic inhumanity—killing people for the sake of a misguided idea. Yet, for the time, one might designate *Shoulder Arms* as "dark comedy lite"—black humor used for a traditional cause.

The Great Dictator came out on the eve of the United States' entry into World War II, though much of the globe was already engulfed in armed conflict. Its anti-war stance was a plea to stop the insanity. Chaplin plays a dual role, a Jewish barber reminiscent of the Tramp and a title character take-off on Hitler. There is also a certain continuity with *Shoulder Arms,* in that *Dictator* begins with the barber's service in the first World War (this time he is a German soldier instead of an American doughboy). Moreover, Chaplin's German soldier remains stuck in his World War I mindset, because a head injury has left him in a sanitarium for years—completely oblivious to the rise of Nazism, or what Chaplin so brilliantly puns as the party of the double cross.

However, whereas *Shoulder Arms* is predicated upon the necessity of fighting to defeat Germany, *Dictator* is driven by Chaplin's pacifism—culminating with the barber's anti-war speech, when he is mistaken for the look-alike dictator—though it is really Chaplin stepping out of character to plead for peace in the chaos. Initially, such a personal statement was seen by some as a distractingly self-indulgent action in an otherwise bravely comic picture, but Chaplin's soapboxing seems to successfully resonate with modern audiences. Plus, even at the time, the comic auteur had toned down the scene by discarding previously shot footage of German soldiers literally dropping their weapons and dancing the dance of peace following the Jewish barber-citizen Chaplin's speech.

While *Dictator* shows a Tramp-like character trying to stop the madness, *Monsieur Verdoux* has a title character who has gone over to the other side. The latter picture finds Chaplin playing dapper former bank clerk Verdoux, who marries and murders wealthy old ladies for a profit. The film was inspired, in part, by the "career" of Frenchman Henri Landru, better known as the "modern Bluebeard." The original Bluebeard was guillotined in 1922 for liquidating ten of his girlfriends. Orson Welles (1915–1985) had originally approached Chaplin about playing the Landru role in a series of simulated documentaries that the young director was contemplating. (Consequently, the *Verdoux* credits attribute the original idea to Welles.)

Also keep in mind that *Verdoux* represents a theme of dark comedy, "man as beast," that is not just violence but rather the baser nature of man driven by the sexual card. Verdoux uses the promise of a last chance at lust masquerading as love to marry and murder. Moreover, sex easily dovetails into the genre's sense of absurdity via an absence of control, consistent with man's plight in black humor. As Luis Buñuel (1900–1983), the most acclaimed foreign director of dark comedy, observed in his ironically titled memoir *My Last Sigh* (1982), "[I]n a rigid hierarchical society, sex—which represents no barriers and obeys no laws—can at any moment become an agent of chaos."[22]

Significantly, Chaplin's dark comedy trilogy anticipates key characteristics of the historically pivotal *Dr. Strangelove,* as well as representing polar extremes of the genre. *Shoulder Arms* and *Dictator* foresee the global scaled black humor of *Dr. Strangelove*. Indeed, the latter film's title character (Peter Sellers in one of three roles) is actually a former Nazi whom America has kept around because of his skills in mass destruction, not unlike the true story of how the United States forgave the Nazi V-2 ballistic missile war crimes of Nazi scientist Werner von Braun's (1912–1977) in order that he help American develop a post–World War II rocket program. Accordingly, the big picture extreme of *Shoulder Arms* is tied to Charlie's doughboy helping end the war by capturing Germany's leader, Kaiser Wilhelm. (Though being dark comedy lite, the picture's close reveals Charlie has only dreamed he caught Germany's arch villain.)

Conversely, *Verdoux* departs from the global scope of *Shoulder Arms* and *Dictator* in two ways. It takes place on a much smaller scale, and though the world remains a predatory place, the film's black humor comes from a sympathetic synthesis of a murderer who retains enough of the Tramp's mannerisms to pull the audience in two directions. Moreover, Verdoux is given some justification for his deeds, since he is paying back a harsh world in kind. Instead of either fighting to protect the world from the evil norm (*Shoulder Arms*), or fighting against its renewal (*Dictator*), *Verdoux* merely embraces its Darwinian message. (It is a message with which Hitler had also been most comfortable, even using his regime's designated filmmaker, Leni Riefenstahl, to help prepare the way with the infamous documentary on the 1934 Nuremberg Nazi rallies, *Triumph of the Will* [1935].)

Regardless, though the viewer only "meets" a single Verdoux victim, her less-than-pleasant nature is presented as the norm, especially when coupled with the comically bitchy family of another target (whose members assist in the eventual capture of Verdoux). That one should *not* be concerned about the demise of these women is further underlined by the case of Martha Raye's (1916–1994) character, the only wife Verdoux fails to liquidate. Raye's entertainingly obnoxious nouveau riche loudmouth eventually even has the viewer rooting for her demise, though circumstances always intervene.

Part of the high-profile splash made by *Dr. Strangelove* was the fact that it was unlike the *Verdoux* model, where black humor emanated from a sympathetic character—the pre–1960s norm, which continues to flourish. An early similar follow-up to *Verdoux* was the celebrated British dark comedy *Kind Hearts and Coronets* (1949), from a studio, Ealing, which specialized in the genre, such as their later *The Ladykillers* (1955). *Kind Hearts* follows the *Verdoux* pattern by having a wrongly disenfranchised member (Dennis Price) of a titled family methodically killing with comic coolness eight less-than-sympathetic relatives (all played by Alec Guinness) who stand in his way of becoming a duke. Between the repetitive victimization of so many Guinness figures (more absurdity), including one in drag, and softening the murders by *not* showing them on screen (as was the *Verdoux* norm), such examples of dark comedy lite are made all the more palatable.

Moving to modern examples of dark comedy auteurs who often present a congenial killer and/or criminal, one might best begin with the Coen Brothers, especially since they even remade *The Ladykillers* in 2004. Tom Hanks plays the obsequiously polite mastermind of a heist tripped up by a sweet churchgoing widow from whom he rents a room. Yet, the Coens' most endearing dark comedy players would be a young couple (Nicolas Cage and Holly Hunter) intent on kidnapping their way to parenthood in *Raising Arizona* (1987).

Of the many other contemporary directors fond of sympathetic dark comedy characters, two names immediately come to mind, Quentin Tarantino and Wes Anderson, especially since the duo address the subject from different perspectives. Tarantino manages to make hit men John Travolta and Samuel Jackson likable in *Pulp Fiction* (1994), just as he does with the killing machine Uma Thurman in *Kill Bill Vol. 1* (2003) and *Kill Bill Vol. 2* (2004). In contrast, Anderson's dark comedy antiheroes are absurdly quirky dysfunctional families, best displayed in *The Royal Tenenbaums* (2001) and *Moonrise Kingdom* (2012).

Naturally, today's big picture dark comedies, *à la* the foundation established by Chaplin's *Dictator* and later given mainstream validation by Stanley Kubrick's *Dr. Strangelove,* are equally pervasive in modern cinema, including Kubrick's still entertainingly disturbing *A Clockwork Orange* (1971). Ah, but there is nothing like Nazism for global black humor, and Tarantino's *Inglorious Basterds* (2009) has cartoonishly twisted fun with a unit of Jewish vigilante U.S. soldiers swinging all–American baseball bats against Hitler's team. While *Dr. Strangelove* and *Clockwork* warn us about the future, or our lack thereof, *Basterds* further embraces absurdity by rewriting the past. Another dark comedy auteur comfortable with an epic portrayal of the genre would be Paul Thomas Anderson; his *There Will Be Blood* (2007) is anchored in a bowling ball–killing performance by Daniel Day Lewis.

Most of the modern dark comedy directors have fluctuated between large and intimate depictions of the genre. This flexibility was especially apparent during the heyday of New American Cinema, from the mid–1960s until the late 1970s. Thus, one might begin with two pictures by Hal Ashby, the cult classic *Harold and Maude* (1971) and the savagely witty swipe at American television and national politics, *Being There* (1979, from Jerzy Kosinski's novel). The former chronicles a couple (Ruth Gordon and Bud Cort) drawn together by an obsession with death, despite their sixty-year age difference. The latter picture focuses upon a man-child (Peter Sellers) randomly meeting American powerbrokers who somehow interpret his bewildered minimalism as weighty insight. *Being There* suggests a dumbing down future which makes *Dr. Strangelove*'s mushroom cloud finale seem preferable. Moreover, Sellers' last act in the film, an apparent ability to walk on water, brilliantly adds, via a simple visual, a questioning of the whole concept of New Testament Christianity—what a parting black humor bonus!

Another iconic New American Cinema director capable of broadly diverse explorations of dark comedy would be Robert Altman. In *MASH* (1970) he sideswipes the insanity of the Vietnam War by way of a dark comedy chronicle of the crazy antics of a medical unit during the Korean War. His *Nashville* (1975) is a black humor mosaic of the uneasy marriage of national politics and entertainment, filtered through a political rally. The winningly bizarre *Brewster McCloud* (1970), his cultishly small movie, follows the misadventures of a boy (Bud Cort) determined to fly the old-fashioned way ... in the Houston Astrodome!

A third diverse dark comedy director from this groundbreaking era is Arthur Penn. In *Bonnie and Clyde* (1967) he keys upon two small-time Depression era criminals as a bloody prism of the unraveling of the anti-establishment 1960s. Yet, Penn could move from this poignantly twisted love story to the epic black humor canvas of *Little Big Man* (1970), the sprawling tale of 121-year-old Jack Crabb (Dustin Hoffman), the final survivor of Custer's Last Stand. As with *MASH*, Penn uses another war to attack the absurdity of the Vietnam conflict.

Mike Nichols' large and small dissections of black humor are surprisingly similar to Penn's work. Nichols' landmark film *The Graduate* (1967) is about another twisted love story, and while no banks are robbed or people are killed, à la *Bonnie and Clyde,* it also asks with biting humor, what exactly is going on in the volatile 1960s? Conversely, as with *Little Big Man,* Nichols' aforementioned *Catch–22* embraces yet a different conflict (World War II) to comment upon the surrealistic insanity of Vietnam.

All these varieties of dark comedy films, and many more, would probably have found a way to exist in some form with or without Chaplin, given the long tooth nature of the genre. Yet Chaplin's black humor trilogy was groundbreaking for cinema, establishing strong patterns for the genre which are still in place. Though today's lack of censorship now allows black humor's themes of death, absurdity, and beastliness to embrace such graphicness as to seem almost unrelated to the original genre, the Chaplin foundation remains. After all, what could be a more inherently dark comedy topic than Chaplin's rendering of a global beast-like Hitler in his Hynkel the Dictator, or a based-in-fact Bluebeard like Verdoux? Along similar lines, what conjures up death like the horrific trench warfare of *Shoulder Arms,* or the Holocaust hinted at in *Dictator*? Finally, how better to showcase the absurdity factor than Charlie's doughboy Tramp of *Arms* capturing the Kaiser and ending World War I, or a Jewish barber substituting as war rally speaker for Nazi Hynkel-Hitler, or a sophisticatedly French version of romantic Charlie-Charlot turning into a *Ladykiller*—the working title for *Verdoux*? Thus, one has to say that Chaplin made the difference for this genre ... an ever evolving difference to be fleshed out in the following pages.

2

Chaplin's Life and Career to 1918

So many people have claimed to have given Chaplin his start that pioneer film historian Terry Ramsaye was moved to observe: "The original discoverers of Charlie Chaplin should form an association and hold a convention at the Polo Grounds [stadium in New York], if the seating facilities are adequate."[1]

Charlie Chaplin, cinema's most iconic figure, was allegedly born April 16, 1889, in East Lane, Walworth, London, though in 2012 declassified files from Britain's M15 domestic intelligence service found no records to back up the comedian's claims. The M15 investigation had occurred at the request of United States authorities during the McCarthy communist witch-hunting 1950s, a period which found the leftist Chaplin hounded out of America. (The comedian had lived in the United States for approximately forty years but had remained a British citizen.) When he left America for the London premiere of *Limelight* (1952), his re-entry visa was revoked, and he chose to live in exile for the remainder of his life. He died at his Swiss estate, the Manoir de Ban, in the village of Corsair on Christmas Day 1977.

Though a great hullabaloo was made in 2012 about Chaplin's birthplace stumping British spies, uncertainty has always haunted his origins—a fact the comedian seemed to relish, and even encourage. As Chaplin biographer Denis Gifford sardonically stated, earlier birth site claims have included Paris, Fontainebleau (France), the Bermondsey district of London, and a host of other addresses around the city.[2] While Gifford's book dates from 1974, pop culture entertainer cards from the 1920s (similar to baseball cards and also produced by tobacco companies) sometimes listed his place of birth as Paris.[3] Regardless, such mystery and absurdity, given Chaplin's enjoyment of the vagueness, seems fitting for an artist enamored of dark comedy.

Chaplin's parents, Charles Sr. (1863–1901) and Hannah Chaplin (1865–1928), were music hall performers. They separated in 1891, when Chaplin Jr. was approximately three. Charles Sr. was a successful baritone singer and comedian whose picture occasionally appeared on the covers of popular sheet music, especially during his early 1890s heyday. (His son would later score his own movies and compose such memorable singles as "Smile" and "This Is My Song.") Hannah was a less successful singer and dancer whose stage name was Lillie (sometimes spelled Lilly) Harley.

Hannah had initially jilted Charles Sr. and in 1884 eloped to Cape Town, South Africa, with Sydney Hawkes, a wealthy bookmaker passing himself off as a lord. When that escapade failed, a now pregnant Hannah returned to England and married Chaplin Sr. three months after the birth of her illegitimate son Sydney (sometimes spelled Sidney) on March 16, 1885; Sydney also assumed the Chaplin name. While Hannah's career was somewhat stalled, her husband was in such demand that he signed for an American tour in 1890, including a booking at New York's Union Square Theatre. Hannah was, to use a polite term of the period, a bit of a "rounder" (also the title of an early Chaplin film), and romantically strayed while her husband was abroad. She had an affair with another British music hall star of the 1890s, Leo Dryden (1868–1939), which gave young Charlie a second half brother, Wheeler Dryden (1892–1957). However, this third son was spirited out of Hannah's life after her brief relationship with Dryden ended. Although Charlie, Jr. had little contact with Wheeler until later in their professional careers, half brother Sydney would have a major influence in Charlie's life and film career. They would remain forever close, from the comedian naming his second son (born 1926) after him, to Sydney spending many retirement summers in the 1950s and '60s at his brother's Swiss estate.

Not surprisingly, Hannah's promiscuity essentially ended her marriage to Charles Sr. in 1891, two years after the birth of young Charlie. While her husband essentially abandoned the family, Hannah briefly made do via her own career and possibly some assistance from Dryden. Her professional singing essentially ended in 1894 when her never strong voice failed on stage. She then briefly persevered as a low-paid ballet dancer in London's Katti Lanner Troupe. Hannah's version of babysitting was the free style, with her boys excitedly watching from the wings each night.

When Hannah's career as an entertainer ground to a halt, she attempted to support her boys with work as a seamstress and part-time nurse. She also pawned valuables and sometimes even altered her stage costume to meet the clothes needs of Charlie and Sydney; this guaranteed them a full share of fights with insensitive children in their London district of Kennington. Though they were barely getting by, Hannah attempted to maintain a happy front for the boys. Besides playfully reviving shtick from her days upon the stage, she could perfectly mimic the passing parade of people viewed from their tenement garret window (the addresses often changed as they could afford less and less). Regardless, these ongoing comic tutorials provided invaluable lessons for the future films of cinema's greatest pantomime artist. Chaplin was later most generous in crediting his talent and general mindset to his mother:

> I learned from her everything I know. She was the most astounding mimic I had ever saw.... It was in watching and observing her that I learned not only to translate motions with my hands and features but also to study mankind.[4]

When Chaplin was barely six, Hannah began suffering increasingly from bouts of insanity, which necessitated a sort of revolving door relationship with mental institutions. What had begun in the mid–1890s with severe headaches, reached chronic psychotic dimensions by 1898, when she was admitted to London's Lambeth Infirmary. In a horribly ironic twist upon being a praised mimic, she was eventually diagnosed with "the great mimic" disorder—the 1890s phrase for syphilis, before the Wasserman test was developed.[5] (The medical aphorism came from the fact the disease could imitate other medical problems.) How she contracted syphilis will probably never be known, though the need to provide for her children might have pushed her into part-time prostitution, the Victorian era fate of approximately twenty-five percent of London's female population.

Already like a child from a Dickens novel, young Charlie would now become more than familiar with a series of institutions programmed to care for orphaned or abandoned children. The boy even experienced the wrath of fairy tale literature's proverbial wicked stepmother when Charlie and Sydney briefly stayed with Charles Sr. and his mistress—who, with a child of her own and an increasingly alcoholic mate, had no time or inclination for extra duties. Even then, Charlie seldom saw his father, with Charles Sr. coming home late, if at all, after a music hall night of performing and drinking with the customers—an unfortunate practice strongly encouraged by management. Of course, maybe the mere sight of the boys kept him drinking late, because they reminded him of Hannah, with Sydney even bearing the name of the man who had initially stolen his promiscuous wife away from him. Charles Sr. had drunk himself to death in his thirties (1901).

A basic component of the dark film comedy genre is often a dysfunctional family; the Chaplins could have represented the poster portrait of this phenomenon. No wonder Chaplin would observe late in his life, "[T]o judge the morals of our family by commonplace standards would be as erroneous as putting a thermometer in boiling water."[6] Sympathetic fallen women are often a fixture in Chaplin's movies, including one of this text's focus pictures *Monsieur Verdoux* (1947, with Marilyn Nash playing the streetwalker).

What stability Charlie knew as a boy was provided by older brother Sydney. Their Aunt Mowbrey would later write:

> It seems strange to me that anyone can write about Charlie Chaplin without mentioning his brother Sydney. They had been inseparable all their lives, except when fate intervened [such as being separated at institutions].... Syd, of quiet manner, clever brain and steady nerve, has been father and mother to Charlie.[7]

Sydney would also orchestrate Chaplin's greatest entertainment break prior to the movies: getting his brother into the all-important Fred Karno British comedy hall troupe in 1908. Sydney was first under contract to Karno (1886–1941) in 1906, and had lobbied on behalf of his brother for two years. Charlie would later be discovered by pioneer filmmaker Mack Sennett (1880–1960) during one of Charlie's Karno tours of American during the 1910s.

This is getting ahead of young Chaplin's story. In 1898 he became a member of the Eight Lancaster Lads, a clog-dancing troupe led by a fatherly William Jackson. This position was seemingly orchestrated by Charles Sr.'s friendship with Jackson. The group received major music hall bookings in both London and the provinces. Chaplin toured with the troupe for two years but forever dreamed of becoming an actor and/or performing a solo routine. He soon received his wish, sort of, by playing a cat in a major Hippodrome production of *Cinderella,* which ran from the 1900 Christmas holidays until mid–April 1901. This was also the catalyst for the first on-stage series of comic improvisations by Charlie—acting like the most unusually provocative of cats, from raising a feline leg to simulate peeing upon the stage's proscenium, to sniffing the private parts of a stage dog (another actor). The laughter continued whenever Charlie the cat turned to the audience and winked one of his large eyes, activated from the inside of the costume. Like many of Chaplin's later screen antics, such as using his cane to lift up a woman's dress, the young comedian's spontaneity could be controversial. Thus, while his *Cinderella* bit was a hit with the audience, management immediately made such acts verboten. Though tame by today's dark comedy standards, young Charlie was cutting his teeth upon a basic staple of the genre—surprisingly inappropriate behavior.

There was a turning point in Chaplin's early entertainment career in 1903 when he was booked to play Billy, the detective's pageboy, in a tour of William Gillette's adaptation of *Sherlock Holmes.* Since Charlie's reading skills, for lack of much formal education, were only at an elementary level, Sydney helped the fourteen-year-old learn his lines. Charlie was a hit and even managed to get his brother cast in the play by the end of 1903.

For a short time in early 1904 Hannah had a rare remission in her condition and joined her sons on the *Holmes* tour. That fall Charlie would sign on for another *Holmes* tour, but Sydney's modest role was filled and he scrambled to become an assistant steward on the ship *Dover Castle*. This was not the first time Charlie's industrious brother found work at sea. Fortuitously, as also part of the shipboard entertainment, Sydney discovered he had comic skills, which he later put to use for both Karno and, eventually, the screen. (Not as talented as his brother—but who was?—Sydney would later also become a silent film comedy star, as well as occasionally playing supporting parts in his brother's short subjects.)

Charlie spent over two years as the comic pageboy of *Holmes* before becoming one of the young comedians in a stage revue entitled *Casey's Court Circus* (1906), which specialized in doing parodies of prominent people. Ironically, at the same time Charlie became a professional mimic, his original mimicry tutor (Hannah) had slipped into a permanently clouded condition. In 1907, as if to work harder in order to forget, Charlie attempted to produce a comedy sketch, "The Twelve Just Men," in which he was the writer, director and star. When he couldn't get backing, he joined his brother with the famous Karno troupe in early 1908. Fred Karno, the comedian turned showman-producer, had reservations before Charlie's audition:

> [Chaplin] looked undernourished and frightened, as though he expected me to raise my hand to hit him. I thought he looked much too shy to do any good in the theatre, particularly in the knockabout comedies that were my speciality.[8]

Yet, Britain's comedy Kingpin was soon won over.

Karno's "most vital contribution to British music hall history was the wordless play, the pure story pantomime ... [with] *Mumming Birds* [being one of] the most notable."[9] As a Karno comedy inheritance, such later Chaplin trademarks as the mixing of humor and pathos, the perfectionist attitude about timing, and even a certain proclivity for cruel dark comedy (George De Coulteray's controversial *Sadism in the Movies* devotes nearly an entire chapter to Chaplin[10]) were key elements in the Karno skits. Chaplin "borrowed" most specifically in his later Essanay film *A Night in the Show* (1915), which was drawn directly from the Karno skit *Mumming Birds* (known in the United States as *A Night in an English Music Hall*). *Mumming Birds,* about a disruptive drunk at a show, also has the distinction of being the routine in which Sennett "discovered" Chaplin, while the young Englishman was on his first Karno tour of the United States (1910–1912).[11] However, Sennett did not sign him until 1913, during Chaplin's second American tour for Karno.

As much as Chaplin loved England, he realized there was little chance for advancement there for someone with his limited education. America represented opportunity for the comedian; it was a promised land not unlike the dream world for which his later cinema tramp forever searched. Like the tough little boy who had survived the impoverished childhood, the adult Chaplin was a survivor fighting for more. Stan Laurel, of later Laurel & Hardy fame and Chaplin's understudy for the first American tour, has stated that as their ship approached shore, Charlie ran to the rail and shouted, "America, I am coming to conquer you. Every man, woman and child shall have my name on their lips—Charles Spencer Chaplin!"[12] His boast would be wrong only in its limited geography; by 1915 the comedian was on the verge of conquering the entertainment world. Indeed, a *Variety* review from this first visit produced one of film criticism's greatest understatements: "Chaplin will do all right for America."[13]

Despite this bluster, Chaplin was inherently shy, which made his later (1918) World War

I bond tour activities all the more amazing. (See the following chapter.) A firsthand witness to this withdrawn nature was his understudy Stan Laurel, who was also Chaplin's Karno tour roommate. Laurel described him as a "desperately shy man. He was never able to mix easily unless people came to him and volunteered friendship...."[14] Maybe because of this shyness, Chaplin played up the stereotypical lonely artist image. For example, in his epic-length memoir, he neglects to mention that Laurel was his roommate on that first American tour; Chaplin always suggests he boarded alone. Of course, the omission also subtextually documents the great comedian's ego: Having another comedy giant like Laurel as a roomie might suggest Chaplin's art had been assisted by Oliver Hardy's future partner. Often a biographical subject can be more informative by what s/he decides *not* to tell.

Chaplin quickly became a Karno star, and soon headlined an American tour which crisscrossed the country's many vaudeville houses. In Mack Sennett's later "modestly" titled memoir *King of Comedy* (1954), he chronicles first seeing Chaplin perform at New York's American Theatre at 42nd Street and Eighth Avenue. The pioneering film comedy "King" had come from Hollywood on business, and only caught the Englishman's act by chance in 1912. He was accompanied by his lover and rising film comedy star Mabel Normand. It was near the end of Chaplin's first United States tour, and the comedian presumably by then would have perfectly polished his material for an American audience. As previously noted, the sketch was *A Night in an English Music Hall,* which Sennett found "hilarious":

> A "little Englisher," as Mabel called him, duded up in a frock coat, played the part of a drunken spectator in a [theater] box [seat]. He seemed about forty-five years old [Chaplin was then twenty-three]. He got into the act on stage [this allegedly drunken audience member], of course, and took part in a knockabout comic fight with the other English actors. The most striking effect of his makeup was an enormous red [alcoholic's] nose.[15]

In 1913, Sennett had the New York office of Kessel and Bauman (whose holdings included the producer's Keystone Comedy Company) track down and sign the touring Chaplin. (Sennett could only remember the comedian's moniker to be something like "Chaffin.") A surprised Chaplin had some reservations about signing; he would be trading the security of Karno for this new, not highly respected medium—though the comedian and his American tour manager, Alf Reeves, had flirted with the idea of filming some Karno sketches themselves. Most importantly, however, Chaplin's impoverished childhood had made him rather tightfisted on money matters, with the comedian banking most of his Karno earnings. Thus, a Sennett offer of $150 a week, which would escalate to $175 after three months (more than double his Karno salary), was difficult to resist. A popular syndicated newspaper humorist of the day, Frank "Kin" Hubbard, whose aphorisms appeared under the crackerbarrel name of Abe Martin, summarized Chaplin's money concerns when he observed, "Opportunity only knocks once but th' wolf is liable t' drop around any ole time."[16]

Though the Sennett contract was signed in May, Chaplin's Karno commitment would occupy him through November of 1913. Interestingly, when the comedian arrived in Los Angeles at year's end and finally met Sennett face to face, the producer's initial reaction was not unlike Chaplin's first one-on-one with Karno—professional reservations. The comedian seemed so young! His boyish appearance made the twenty-four-year-old Chaplin look like a teenager; Sennett had been expecting a seasoned, middle-aged performer, based upon the comedian's makeup in the *English Music Hall* sketch. Plus, Chaplin had been brought in to replace a comedian, Ford Sterling (1882–1939), best remembered now as "Chief Teeheezel" in

Sennett's signature Keystone Cop slapstick series, who appeared older than his early thirties age. Of course, as with Karno, Chaplin would more than prove his worth to Sennett ... though some definite differences will soon be explored.

The Canadian-born Sennett was only thirty-three himself and still in the early days of a career that would earn him the title "father of American film comedy." Movie historian David Robinson later called Sennett's Keystone comedies a "monument of twentieth-century popular art [which were] uncompromisingly anarchic ... [and] where authority and dignity counted for nothing."[17] In Sennett's memoir he linked this philosophy of funny to old school burlesque comedians who

> whaled the daylights out of pretension [with bed slats and bladders]. They made fun of themselves and the human race. They reduced convention, dogma, stuffed shirts, and authority to nonsense, and then blossomed into pandemonium.[18]

If I was requested to pinpoint a single example of Sennett's influence on Chaplin in the comedian's post–Keystone career, I would nominate the scene from *The Immigrant* (1917) in which the Tramp kicks a mean-spirited customs official in the backside.

In Chaplin's one year with Sennett, 1914, he made thirty-five short subjects. The period represented an important apprenticeship for the comedian. Besides learning everything he could about movies, he very quickly asserted himself both in front of the camera—an early version of his Tramp actually appears in his second film *Kid Auto Races at Venice*—as well as behind the camera. He was soon writing and directing most of his Sennett films (though at this point "writing" could simply mean being in charge of his own improvisation). After 1914, Chaplin wrote and directed *all* his films, making him one of cinema's first auteurs, and created film's most iconic figure—the Tramp.

Chaplin had growing pains with Sennett, starting with fighting for some creative autonomy. After all, Sennett was a man who considered himself to be *King* of his genre. Moreover, Chaplin was not enamored of Sennett's propensity for comedy mixed with speed, especially the producer's tendency to finish a film with a helter skelter chase sequence. To Chaplin, all this distracted from the key element of comedy, which was based upon personality. For example, Chaplin was a fan of French film comedian Max Linder (1883–1925), arguably the first screen clown with an international following. Linder's screen persona was Max, a wealthy, dapper man-about-town type who, as critic-historian Walter Kerr perfectly describes him, "was essentially an indoor [intimate comedy] man ... insisting on restraint in his gagging ... [and] thoroughly disliking chases."[19] Since Linder's heyday was in the years just prior to Chaplin signing with Sennett, the creator of Charlie might have been all the more influenced by this attitude of restraint, soon to be a hallmark of Chaplin's work. An example would be the comedian's celebrated tabletop dance of the dinner rolls in *The Gold Rush* (1925). Regardless, Chaplin would later seem to be paying homage to his (by then) friend Linder in *The Idle Class* (1921), in which he plays two lookalike characters, the Tramp and a well-dressed, Max-like (including the Linder silk top hat) man of means.

If Chaplin had need of another period example of a funny screen personality with an "intimate" humor style, he might also have looked to America's first internationally popular movie clown, John Bunny (1863–1915). Bunny's persona anticipated the later W.C. Fields: both comedians had an amusingly portly shape and a large, bulbous, veined nose—the result of over-indulging themselves in food and drink. Both were also comedy fifth columnists, generally working behind henpecked matrimonial lines (their own), and attempting manly things with the "boys," like Bunny's card-playing needs in *A Cure for Pokeritus* (1912), or Fields sneaking out to a wrestling match in *The Man on the Flying Trapeze* (1935).[20]

Despite his clownishness, Bunny's acting style was known for its understatement. At the time of his death, no less a publication than the *London Times* praised his comic minimalism: "A twitch of his mouth provided laughter for the nations of the world."[21] Bunny's intimate comedy was something the Sennett Chaplin was only working towards. For instance, a period Bunny career overview in *World's Work* (March 1915) stated that the comedian showed how "a real actor can make an incredible success before this [film] audience without any of the vulgarity or horseplay which used to be considered essential."[22] In contrast, such "vulgarity" might be exemplified by an unidentified Sennett-produced Chaplin short subject which critic James Agee described so entertainingly in his posthumous Pulitzer Prize–winning autobiographical novel *A Death in the Family* (1957):

> Then [Chaplin's Tramp] flicked hold of the straight end of his cane and, with the crooked end, hooked up [a pretty woman's] skirt to the knee, in exactly the way that that disgusted my Mama....[23]

This is the type of action Bunny's screen character might consider but could never do. For instance, in *Stenographer Wanted* (1912), his character was anxious to hire a physically attractive secretary, but his wife decided the position's major prerequisite should be ugliness, and that was the type of applicant hired. As Fields would later do, Bunny found consolation in a stiff drink.

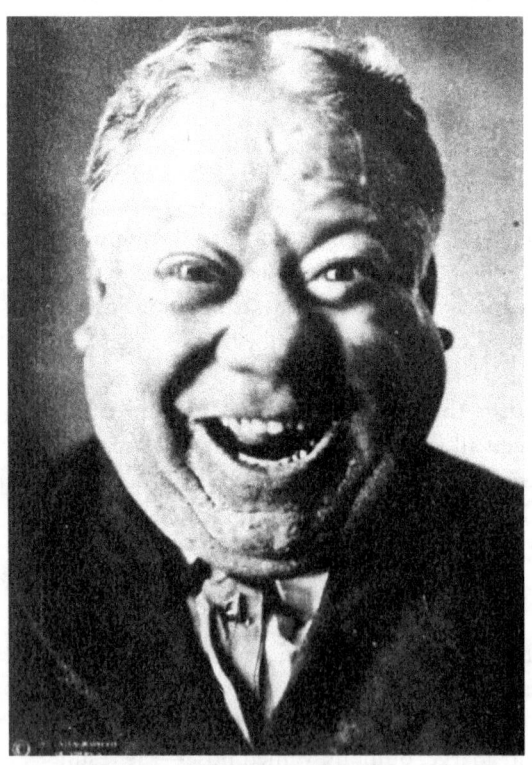

John Bunny, fat, funny, and forgotten, America's first international film star.

I have belabored the Bunny and Linder personae here for two reasons beyond the precedent the duo set for Chaplin creating his own distinctive screen character. First, though his Tramp character was an instant 1914 success with the public, one could argue that the public's embracing of "Charlie" was assisted by the lessening of product from Linder and Bunny. Health issues and the beginning of World War I in Europe effectively derailed Linder's film career for a time, especially when he became a dispatch driver for the French army between Paris and the Western Front. Bunny, who died in April 1915, spent the latter half of 1914 preparing and then touring America in an elaborate stage show compendium of the comedian's entertainment career—a three-hour production entitled *Bunny in Funnyland*. The popular but strenuous tour stretched into 1915 and was considered a contributing factor to his premature death at fifty-two. Regardless, it had kept him off the screen just as the public was discovering Chaplin's Tramp. Second, while Chaplin's thoughts on America's first major screen comedian are unrecorded, there is much evidence of the mutual admiration society which existed between the creators of "Max" and "Charlie." This connection might best be encapsulated in a quote from a 1922 Linder interview: "[Chaplin] calls me his teacher, but, for my part, I have been lucky to get lessons at his [comedy] school."[24]

So how did the creation of Chaplin's seminal cinema clown occur at the dawn of his film career? Chaplin revealed in his memoir that, with encouragement from Sennett to try something new, he had decided on the way to the wardrobe room that

> I wanted everything a contradiction: the baggy pants, the coat tight, the hat small and the shoes large. I was undecided whether to look old or young but remembered Sennett had expected me to be a much older man, [so] I added a small mustache, which, I reasoned, would add age without hiding my expression.[25]

Fittingly, in a democratic borrowing from his fellow Sennett comics, the baggy pants came courtesy of Fatty Arbuckle, while the giant (size 14) shoes belonged to Ford Sterling, with Chaplin having to put the "gunboats" on the wrong feet to keep them on. He then added the undersized derby of comedienne Minta Durfee's father (Minta was the wife of Arbuckle). Chaplin complemented this clothing menagerie with a dandy's cane, a duck's walk, and a toothbrush mustache, scissored down from an oversized one from Mack Swain.

The legendary Tramp beginnings are not without a few footnotes. For example, even as a child Chaplin had dreamed of putting together a comedy tramp act. Plus, Karno music hall comedian Fred Kitchen, whom Chaplin first saw as a child, wore baggy pants and oversized shoes. Moreover, Charles Chaplin, Jr.'s biography of his father has the comedian crediting not that day of inspiration on the Sennett lot but rather a last-minute music hall substitution from his youth.[26] His father had gone on for a much larger comedian and, by way of wearing his oversized costume, happened into the Tramp outfit. Chaplin, who like most artists often borrowed from his life story, does use a similar tale as a subplot in *The Circus* (1928), where Charlie is a spur-of-the-moment fill-in for Rex the tightrope walker, whose costume is much too large. To paraphrase an old axiom, success has many fathers.

The Tramp's signature "east-west feet" gait, like Harpo Marx's famous cross-eyed "gookie" expression, was drawn from a real-life character. Chaplin was reproducing the splay-footed shuffle of an elderly fellow street person from his youth. Indeed, French film theorist André Bazin would later designate this duck walk as another component of Chaplin's realistic style—the either-way shuffle is at the very heart of the ambiguity of life. And Charlie's multi-faceted cane, which encouraged both farce and misplaced dignity, had been a key weapon in Chaplin's comedy costume arsenal for Karno. In a 1918 interview, Chaplin called his decision to use a cane

> perhaps the best piece of [costume] luck I ever had.... I have developed the cane until it has almost a comedy sense of its own. Often, I find it curling itself around someone's leg, or rapping someone on the shoulder and getting a laugh from the audience almost without my knowing that I was diverting the action....[27]

One of the best takes on the Tramp's wardrobe comes from neither a critic nor Chaplin himself but rather a writer born the same year as the Tramp: Budd Schulberg (1914–2009), Oscar-winning screenwriter of *On the Waterfront* (1954). In his watershed autobiographical novel *The Disenchanted* (1950), Schulberg has Manley Halliday, a character based upon F. Scott Fitzgerald, observe:

> Know the secret of Charlie? Not a man at all. [He] sneaks up in [the] attic, puts on [his] father's clothes, pants too big, shoes too big ... anything he happens to find lying around. Then he pretends he's grown up. But it's all a dream ... [for example the girls] he falls in love with, ethereal, too beautiful, [the] way little boys fall in love with grown-up women from a distance.[28]

While Sennett might have encouraged its creation, the seeds of Chaplin's Charlie had no doubt been gestating for years.

Despite Chaplin's disagreement with Sennett over chaotic speed (the eternal chase), versus the power of personality, the comedian's work for the producer found the evolving Tramp to be at his most "tough, obstreperous [and] anarchical" during 1914, their one year together.[29] This is certainly the case with the aforementioned *Kid Auto Races at Venice*, an extremely short picture consisting of various shots of an entertainingly simple one-joke movie: Charlie's constant attempts to get on film while an alleged newsreel cameraman (Henry Lehrman) works at recording an actual soapbox derby competition in Venice, California. (Sennett often took cinema advantage of real area events.) Schulberg's analogy of the Tramp as a child works well here, too, since Charlie's birth on screen is that of an essentially bratty kid, constantly disrupting the efforts of the cameraman in the film within the film, including casually strolling into the shot, backing into camera range, positioning himself dangerously close to the starting ramp, nearly getting hit by one of the miniature cars, and forever being pushed aside by Lehrman's character. The *piece de resistance* for this juvenile delinquent type comes near the close when Charlie gets real close to the camera and proceeds to make faces and hold his nose. Moreover, the mini-movie's closing title includes both a personal introduction by the Tramp to his audience *and* a tongue-in-cheek suggestion that a bad boy film figure has just scaled the walls of Hollywood: "Your ever loving Charlie xxxxx P.S. just heard my picture won't pass the censors."

Yet, for all the rough-housing in Chaplin's pictures for Sennett, there was occasional room for the aforementioned subtle whimsical humor. For instance, in *Those Love Pangs* (1914), Charlie hugs a tree out of jealousy when he sees a couple romantically embracing in the park. The same movie also offers another example of "intimate" humor after Charlie pokes a rival behind a curtain with a fork. Before the Tramp can ditch said "weapon," he is caught with the fork. Charlie immediately brings it to his lips and pretends to play it like a small instrument— a pioneering film demonstration of what has come to be called a Chaplin "metamorphosis." (Because of Chaplin's ongoing popularity but lack of copyright, his early shorts were in almost continual circulation for years, often offered to the public as something new via a changed title. *Those Love Pangs* was reissued as *Rival Mashers*.)

Though Chaplin's Keystone shorts were often rough and crude, the film education *and* opportunities provided by Sennett's funhouse factory helped make possible the Tramp classics to come. And not surprisingly, the huge popularity of *Charlie* after only a year meant Sennett could no longer afford the comedian. In January of 1915 Chaplin signed with the Essanay company for $1,250 a week, roughly ten times his Keystone salary. Nearly a hundred years later, this would be the equivalent of over $28,000 a week. During his equally short period with Essanay, he would make fourteen shorts, fewer than half his Sennett total, yet immeasurably better. With a slower pace both on screen and off, the subtle pantomime quotient greatly increased. Whereas a Sennett short was usually shot in a day or two, at Essanay Chaplin might spend up to three weeks perfecting a picture. Such was the case with his first seminal film, *The Tramp*, released in April 1915. Genuine pathos is introduced when he loses the girl (Edna Purviance) and makes one of his soon to be signature shuffling exits but with a little hitch kick to suggest, "I will get by." Moreover, the picture features moments of metamorphosis, or what one Chaplin biographer has called "comic transpositions," such as Charlie attempting to milk a cow by pumping her tail.[30] *The Police* (1916), the first Essanay short I saw as a child (back in the days of Super–8 collections), includes a much copied metamorphosis scene in which the Tramp opens a stove by working the knob like it is the combination dial of a safe. Chaplin fan Harpo Marx does a variation of the sequence in *Duck Soup* (1933), when he accidently mistakes a large box radio for a safe and twists what appears to be another combination dial; loud music comically surprises both him and the audience.

After *The Tramp,* the other bona fide classic created at Essanay was *The Bank* (1915). Both stories revolve around lost love and a robbery. In the former, Charlie rescues the heroine from a crook and briefly basks in her attention ... until her boyfriend returns. In *The Bank*, Charlie the janitor pines for the lovely stenographer (Purviance) and again seems to save her from robbers, but this time it was a dream. Poor Charlie wakes up kissing his mop instead of his wannabe girl. Worse yet, he then spots the stenographer embracing her true love. The pathos-driven close again finds him defeated and duck walking off, but the hitch kick and shoulder shrug promise he will get by. Sad conclusions were then something novel for the world of slapstick comedy. Though both of these sublime endings elevate the pictures to pantheon status in the Chaplin filmography, they also stand as practice runs for Charlie's most excruciating romantic rejection—the close of 1931's *City Lights*. (To underline again the ongoing popularity of the early Chaplin short subjects, especially *The Bank*, these two-reelers were not only still being shown theatrically well into the 1930s sound era, they often rated full-sheet advertising posters, roughly 40" high to 28" wide, like the ones now only reserved for feature films at your local cinema.)

In February 1916, a year after joining Essanay, Chaplin moved to the Mutual company for $10,000 a week and a signing bonus of $50,000; Chaplin's salary for the year was $670,000, or over fourteen million dollars in today's market. These numbers, like the iconic Tramp, created a global buzz. *Moving Picture World* called the deal the "most gigantic in the history of the film industry," and accented that fact by a four-page color spread.[31] Couple this with Chaplin obtaining his own studio, the Lone Star, formerly the Climax Studios, located in the Colegrave district of Los Angeles. The comedian now had the setting and the carte blanche control most artists only dream of. He did not waste the opportunity.

Over the next eighteen months he made twelve of the most inventively polished short subjects Hollywood had ever seen. Indeed, Chaplin would later describe his Mutual period (February 1916–June 1917) "as the happiest of his life."[32] As with Sennett, a special setting, like the one in *Kid Auto Races at Venice,* or a promising prop was the catalyst for these films. Yet, Chaplin now had ever-increasing time (a month or more) to flesh out each picture. Quite frankly,

> these films were, in a special sense, the prototype of all that was to come from him, and his comedy is increasingly charged with a philosophical significance that lifts it out of farce into satire, and increases its pathos.[33]

Moreover, his first Mutual movie, *The Floor Walker* (1916, which keys upon a department store escalator), even elicited bemused praise from Sennett: "Why the hell didn't we ever think of a running staircase?"[34]

The second Mutual, *The Fireman* (1916), was born, according to a 1918 interview with Chaplin, when he was passing a firehouse one day: "I watched the men sliding down the pole, climbing onto the engine, and rushing off to the fire. At once a train of comic possibilities occurred to me. [For example,] I saw myself sleeping in bed, oblivious to the clanging of the fire bell...."[35] *The Fireman* was followed by the more dramatic *Vagabond* (1916), which has poignant roots in the earlier short *The Bank*. This time Purviance's initial loss of the Tramp produces a hysterical grief which anticipates Jackie Coogan's histrionics in a similar situation in *The Kid* (1921).

The next Mutual short, *One A.M.* (1916), is a tour de force drunk routine which even surpasses Chaplin's brilliant *A Night in the Show*. The former short is essentially a solo performance, other than a brief appearance by a cabbie dropping off the soused Charlie at home. Not only must the dapperly attired comedian (shades of Linder?) navigate about his oddly furnished house and double stairway in a blotto condition, but this nightmare-like dwelling seems to have been designed by Salvador Dali; instead of the painter's melting clocks, there is some pre–Harold Lloyd thrill comedy connected to a huge swinging pendulum. Add a taxidermist special or two, such as a bear rug complete with a stuffed head; one is reminded of drunken Dudley Moore's surprise when confronted with a mounted deer's head in *Arthur* (1981). This striking use of the set, hardly typical of early cinema, is the new norm from Chaplin's Mutual period on—using "the décor of the film to provide an essential part of its atmosphere."[36]

The next picture, *The Count* (1916), doubles up nicely with the final Mutual movie *The Adventurer* (1917): The highlight of both *mis*adventures has Charlie crashing a major social event. In the former film, Chaplin's "little fellow" is a tailor's assistant, persuaded (forced) to attend a reception as the secretary of the giant bullying boss (Eric Campbell), who is pretending to be a Count Brako. In *The Adventurer*, the Tramp is an escaped convict who finds himself at a lah-di-dah party. In both cases, besides helping to comically undermine the elegance, the masquerade quality of people and/or things *not* being what they seem is a telling commentary on life. In fact, the ritzy party from *The Adventurer* later inspired the celebrated masquerade which closes Jean Renoir's *Rules of the Game* (1939), with the French director further embellishing the complexity of the Chaplin model by moving from slapstick farce to an appropriately ironic death-murder conclusion.

Chaplin's other Mutual movies provide thumbnail explanations via their titles, such as *The Pawnshop* (1916), in which the Tramp has a gift for destroying items brought in for appraisal, and *The Cure* (1917), with Charlie as another alcoholic dandy, only this time the goal is to quit. *Behind the Screen* (1916) provides a comic look at period filmmaking, while *The Rink* (1916) allows the Tramp to show off his dancer-like grace on roller skates—which Chaplin will flesh out further in the later *Modern Times* (1936). Keep in mind that beginning with Max Linder's *The Skater's Debut* (1907), being physically awkward on any sort of skates still remains the clown standard. No wonder a jealous W.C. Fields was fond of calling Chaplin "a goddamn ballet dancer."[37]

Extending the dance analogy, the way in which Chaplin choreographs the action scenes in Mutual's *Easy Street* (1917), where the Tramp becomes a cop on an anything but "easy street," is nothing short of brilliant for the 1910s—fitting for a filmmaker who greatly admired the legendary ballet dancer Nijinsky (1890–1950). For example, Eric Campbell is the giant bully who rules the street. After Eric and his gang have routed an army of policeman, throwing the cops around like so many rag dolls, he further asserts his dominance by walking up the center of the street *alone*. As Eric jauntily struts, the gang members on the right side of the street venture out in an orchestrated cadence; when he turns in their direction, they dive back in rhythm. Then the neighborhood people on the left replicate this timed movement, only to have Eric's pivot in their direction repeat the same diving ballet of fear.

Easy Street's slum setting backdrop is also another example of Chaplin's use of décor enhancing the satirical atmosphere of the movie. One could even argue that this is Chaplin's greatest use of a Mutual backdrop, *other* than the disturbing irony to be found in *The Immigrant* scene in which, just as Charlie's ship passes the Statue of Liberty, the hoping-to-become-citizens passengers are herded about like cattle. In Richard Attenborough's underrated biography film *Chaplin* (1992, with Robert Downey, Jr. in the title role), the inclusion of that scene is given added resonance in four ways. First, Chaplin's ability to have the Tramp kick the insensitive custom office in the rump without censorship is a visual demonstration of America's freedom of speech—something that Downey's Chaplin and his brother Sydney (Paul Rhys) also discuss at that point in the biography. Second, Attenborough later demonstrates the creeping loss of such freedom during the McCarthy era by staging the sequence in which Chaplin discovers his U.S. re-entry visa will be denied just as his vacationing ocean liner exits New York Harbor and passes Lady Liberty. Besides these more prominent *Chaplin* examples of hypocrisy connected to the statue, the film features two more fleeting but pertinent references to the monument. The first occurs with Chaplin's initial arrival in America in 1910, and the promise of this new country—so amazingly realized by the comedian—is symbolized with his ship passing the statue. The second takes place just after World War I and Chaplin is at a victory gathering which includes a young J. Edgar Hoover, soon to be the longtime FBI chief. Hoover's after-dinner speech briefly notes the inappropriateness of comedy mocking government officials, which Chaplin rebukes. While this no doubt entails some poetic license on Attenborough's part, the spirit of their differences was true, as the FBI's large damning files on Chaplin will later prove. Moreover, the comedian does reference having dinner with Hoover very early in the filmmaker's career.[38] Thus, at least from the perspective of Attenborough's biography, this sequence from *The Immigrant* is Chaplin's most memorable Mutual scene. The ironic use of the statue still resonates with filmmakers such as writer-director Tom McCarthy: his *The Visitor* (2007) movingly tells the story of an illegal immigrant couple living in New York. The duo's favorite activity is taking the Staten Island Ferry past the statue. One of them, without warning, will be summarily deported.

The Mutual films appeared at the culmination of America's Progressive Era (1897–1920), a time of great reform and change, such as women getting the right to vote.[39] In eleven of the twelve Mutual films, Chaplin places the Tramp in situations that focus on, and possibly in the case of alcohol capitalize on, Progressive issues. The films are best divided into five social areas: (1) urban corruption, *The Floorwalker* and *The Fireman*; (2) the plight of the urban poor, *The Pawnshop, Easy Street* and *The Immigrant*; (3) the idle rich (not a specific concern of Progressives but a tangential area to both urban poverty and corruption, especially when contrasted with Chaplin's portrayal of the poor), *The Count, The Rink,* and *The Adventure*; (4) elitism, *Behind the Screen,* which endorsed the anti-strike stance of the Progressive in a time of violent anarchist activities for the common worker; and (5) alcoholism, *One A.M.* and *The Cure.*

The Mutual movies were Chaplin's springboard to even greater success, as he became his own producer by signing a special distribution deal with the newly created First National Exhibitors' Circuit, which guaranteed the comedian more than a million dollars. Chaplin would now also own his films outright. Add to this the groundbreaking for a new Chaplin studio, on the corner of Sunset Boulevard and La Brea Avenue (then still in the heart of orchard territory), and the promise of 1918 loomed large—a gateway to unprecedented cinematic greatness.

3

The War Bond Rallies of 1918: A Neglected Patriot

> During a April 8, 1918, New York City war bond rally Chaplin would yell out over a crowd of human pavement, "Although British-born I am 144 percent American and would be in the trenches if it were not for a physical disability."[1]

By 1918 Chaplin had come an unbelievable distance from his Dickensian childhood. Critic-historian Richard Schickel has suggested that from about 1918 through the late 1930s, he was the most famous man in the world.[2] What makes this cinema-based achievement all the more remarkable is to understand a singular point about Chaplin's youth: "how lonely it must have been, how surviving on these [London] streets made him into the radically self-sufficient man he became. Aside from his half-brother Sidney [only intermittently present, Chaplin] lived by his own wits."[3]

The year 1918 was crammed with much activity, from one of this text's focus films (*Shoulder Arms*) to his brief marriage to actress Mildred Harris (1901–1944); his new studio was even completed in January of that year. Yet much of his 1918 activity was shaped by his whirlwind war bond tour in April. This was the United States' third bond rally since entering World War I on April 6, and it was America's most significant and successful effort because the country was not a factor in the conflict until 1918. Though much of the world had been at war since 1914, the United States needed an extensive period (1917) to train and mobilize its forces. Thus, with American soldiers about to see extended action in 1918, with all the accompanying expenditures, funding of the country's involvement was of paramount importance.

The previous chapter noted that the star ascendancy of Chaplin's Tramp persona had been assisted by the vacuum created by both the 1915 death of America's first international film comedy star, John Bunny, and French cinema clown Max Linder volunteering for service in the French army in 1914 at the outbreak of World War I. Yet the first wave of Chaplin's popularity has also been linked to the special comedy needs of humanity while suffering through the darkness of the war. The argument is analogous to the case made for the unprecedented popularity of the Beatles in 1964 and 1965 following a period of global crisis ranging from the Cuban Missile Crisis (October 1962), to the assassination of President John F. Kennedy (November 22, 1963)—as if to say, America was looking for something to be happy about again. In Philip Norman's biography of John Lennon, he wrote that the Beatles phenomenon "signaled the end of mourning for JFK, through an event as hugely harmless [a boys' band] as the November 22 had been hugely horrible."[4] The world's seemingly sudden case of Chaplinitis is best described to a more modern audience as not unlike the Beatlemania of the 1960s.

While the public continued to line up for Chaplin's films, Allied soldiers often showed their appreciation by using the Tramp as a mascot and/or having an impersonator in each of their companies. Thus, children of the period played a game where they bounced a ball against a wall to the refrain of:

> One, two, three, four,
> Charlie Chaplin went to war,
> He taught the nurses how to dance,
> And this is what he taught them:
> Heel toe, over we go.
> Heel toe, over we go.
> Salute to the King
> And bow to the Queen
> And turn your back on the Kaiserin.[5]

Along similar lines, British soldiers were said to often affectionately march to a song which also subtextually suggested some resentment for his not being in uniform:

> For the Moon shines bright on Charlie Chaplin,
> His shoes are cracking,
> For want of blacking,
> And his little baggy trousers want mendin'
> Before they send him
> To the Dardanelles [where there were high losses].[6]

In fact, Chaplin's first reaction to the song was said to be fear: "I really thought they were coming to get me. It scared the daylights out of me."[7] The song was loosely based upon an old soldier's song with provocative language, which is touched upon in T. S. Eliot's later watershed poem with the apt title for the war: "The Waste Land" (1922).

Thus, whatever positive impact the war had on Chaplin's burgeoning career, it was not without some negatives. Because he was still a British citizen of military age, a number of individuals in the United Kingdom felt he was shirking his duty by not enlisting. Legendary British film historian Kevin Brownlow now suggests that when Chaplin signed his $670,000-a-year contract with Mutual, the fact that it included a clause not allowing him to leave the country probably meant a sizable piece went to the British government, "for such a clause would not have been legally binding without their assurances."[8] Regardless, like many other young men not in uniform, he received white feathers (symbolic of being a coward) in the mail. Later the correspondence would contain threats, particularly after the United States entered the war in 1917. Consequently, while he also received countless letters of thanks for movies that helped keep morale up, that viewpoint more and more became a defensive posture to explain why he was not in uniform instead of simply the artistry of his work. For the record, whether the comedian ever took an army physical remains a question.

Chaplin's war detractors were given added ammunition by Max Linder's much-publicized involvement in the conflict, especially when he was said to be severely wounded (initially reported as dead) in action. Two excellent period articles with titles reflecting the patriotic celebration of Linder are Clement F. Chandler's "Max Linder Comes Back!" in *Motion Pictures* (February and March, 1917), and Rhea Irene Kimball's "Max Linder, Soldier, Actor, Gentleman" in *Motion Picture Classic* (April 4, 1917).[9] It was later revealed that Linder had also flunked his army physical, but he volunteered to work as a dispatch driver between Paris and the Western Front. Conflicting stories abound why his military involvement ended, but it appears the comedian's dispatch vehicle (his own private car) was struck by enemy fire. His companion was killed and Linder was either wounded and/or then contracted pneumonia after hiding in icy

3. The War Bond Rallies of 1918

waters for hours in order to avoid patrolling German soldiers. Linder returned to making films and entertaining troops before the conflict's end but his war-related experiences were the beginning of an ongoingly serious condition of chronic depression which tragically resulted in his 1925 suicide.

Just when Chaplin failed a physical is unclear. Chaplin biographer Robert F. Moss vaguely suggests the comedian made an attempt to enlist in 1917 and was turned down because of his small stature (barely five feet four) and being underweight.[10] The April 8, 1918, quote which opens the chapter implies a failed military physical had already occurred. Yet a *Los Angeles Times* article from April 15, 1918, "Charlie Chaplin Will Soon Don Khaki Garb," stated:

> Yes, Charlie is to take off those funny shoes of his, he'll lay aside his queer old derby, he'll park his comical cane, he'll give his sloppy clothes to the poor, and he'll don the neat British uniform, for Uncle Sam's khaki ... to march away with the rank and file.[11]

Chaplin, then on his war bond tour through the South, states in the same article: "I've always been ready and am still ready to serve my country and the cause of liberty whenever it was necessary for me to go."[12] Interestingly, this quote also reads like an excerpt from an earlier letter to a British correspondent which posits a different perspective on being in uniform: In *Pictures and Picturegoer* (February 23, 1918), Chaplin states:

> I only wish that I could join the English army and fight for my mother country. But I have received so many letters from soldiers at the front, as well as civilians, asking me to continue making pictures that I have come to the conclusion that my work lies here in Los Angeles. At the time, if any country thinks it needs me in the trenches more than soldiers need my pictures, I am ready to go.[13]

Before this letter was published, "his brother [Sydney] set about gathering a list of famous and influential signatures supporting Chaplin's position as a non-combatant and managed to acquire more than a hundred."[14] Finally, a *Photoplay* interview from September 1918 muddies the military physical waters by suggesting that one never took place. Interviewer Julian Johnson states:

> Chaplin's one bitterness is that covert, sneering accusation that he is a draft dodger. As a matter of fact, he stands ready for any service but has never been called and is of such physical fragility that he would probably be rejected by the first board that looked him over.[15]

The value of Chaplin as a soldier, especially when linked to the millions of dollars he raised on his extended war bond tour, was probably most artfully stated in William Dodgson Bowman's 1931 biography of Chaplin:

> Had [Chaplin] gone to the front the British Army would have gained a recruit of indifferent physique and doubtful value, but it would have lost one of the few cheering influences that relieved the misery and wretchedness of those nightmare days.[16]

To properly gauge the carefulness of Chaplin's position or participation in the war, one must be aware of the extreme furor and fear over the Kaiser's Germany in America in 1918. With the collapse of Russia in 1917, Germany no longer had to fight a two-front war; they could now transfer tens of thousands of troops to the Western front and break a stalemate which had cost millions of lives since 1914. Some politicians were projecting that the war, which supposedly was going to last a few weeks, would continue into 1919. In fact, former President William Taft said, "We must count on three more years of war."[17] And the commander-in-chief prior to Taft, "Rough Rider" Theodore Roosevelt, went so far as to suggest, "If we do not win now, fighting abroad beside our allies, then sooner or later our sons or

A 1918 newspaper cartoonist's version of the Tramp unleashed upon the enemy.

grandsons will have to fight here at home, without allies, for their homes, their wives and their little ones."[18]

An ugly vigilante mentality gripped the nation. In Collinsville, Illinois, a mob of 350 people hung Robert Praeger for being "accused of making disloyal remarks in a recent address to miners at Maryville, Illinois."[19] In New Jersey a near-lynching produced the newspaper headline "Mobs Try to Hang 3 in Comden for Disparaging [War Bond] Loan Drive," while in

Birmingham, Alabama, the KKK was given the power to find "disloyal [unpatriotic] people."[20] In Wichita Falls, Texas, when George G. Napulos

> refused to buy Liberty Bonds or assist the Red Cross ... [he] was taken to the edge of town by 200 business men, tarred and feathered, and after being paraded through the main street, released. He left town on foot.—Buy Liberty Bonds—[21]

Besides numerous stories along these lines, just anything German was under attack, such as the *Los Angeles Times* story entitled "Teaching of Enemy Speech in American Schools Roundly Denounced."[22] Plus, true or not, there was a paranoia about foreign disruption of the war loan drives themselves. Another *Los Angeles Times* articles claimed, "German Propagandists Attack Liberty Loan."[23] Whatever the reality of German fifth columnists in the country, it was becoming fodder for jokes: Ziegfeld Follies star Will Rogers observed on stage, "Mr. [Eddie] Cantor and myself have been selling Liberty bonds, and if this [next] song doesn't go well we attribute it to German propaganda."[24]

Emotions were also fanned by cartoon art, usually directed at the Kaiser, in newspapers and other publications. For example a national print ad for the movie *The Kaiser: "The Beast of Berlin"* depicted the German leader strangling a young girl.[25] Yet frequently, as Chaplin would later do with *Shoulder Arms*, the caricature material would be couched in dark comedy, such as a political cartoon of a golfing Uncle Sam hitting the Kaiser with a tee shot ball labeled "3d Liberty Loan," or the cartoon of a frightened Kaiser on the Western Front watching a bomb go off which is captioned "85,000 U.S. Soldiers Every Month."[26] However, the best example of such dark comedy came courtesy of a poster from the United States' National War Garden Commission reading: "CAN Vegetables, Fruit and the Kaiser, too."[27] Beneath the caption were three fruit jars. The one on the left was labeled "Tomatoes," the one to the right was inscribed "Peas" but the oversized jar in the middle contained the Kaiser's head and was labeled "Kaiser Brand Unsweetened."[28]

Besides such inflammatory acts and the aforementioned stories of disturbing war-related vigilante violence, horrific acts were routinely reported in newspapers covering the southern portion of Chaplin's bond tour. The *Atlanta Constitution* carried the two following features on the front page of its April 23, 1918, issue: "Mob Lynches Negro in Courthouse Yard" and "Negro Lynched in Louisiana."[29] Earlier that week the *Constitution* also published a rave review of the reissuing of D.W. Griffith's racist 1915 film epic *Birth of a Nation,* noting in part:

> Probably the greatest of all scenes [is] that showing the gathering of the [KKK], when the moment comes to strike the final blow, which will rid the state of the clutch of negro domination.[30]

One might almost call it fitting that Chaplin was selling *war* bonds in such a powderkeg section of the country.

Regardless, Chaplin's trip to Washington, D.C., to kick off the bond tour was described in the *Los Angeles Times* in a manner befitting a star of slapstick films. The article also managed to suggest a true patriot doing his duty despite iffy health (indirectly reinforcing his explanation about why he was not in uniform): it describes a physician finding the film star at his Athletic Club apartment, so ill that the doctor "commanded the comedian to take to his bed and remain there, giving up his trip East [for the bond tour]."[31] Said doctor had Chaplin's assistant lock the entertainer in his bedroom and remain outside if needed. However,

> everybody forgot ... that Charlie is an athlete ... and this morning ... he was gone ... Charlie had descended the fire escape, called a taxi, beat it out to [his brother] Sid's house and ... col-

In 1918, the U.S.A.'s National War Garden Commission produced this darkly comic poster for the war effort.

lected a sufficient wardrobe with which to depart on his journey ... bound on a patriot mission.... [He] departed by the same train for Washington [as fellow bond selling stars Douglas Fairbanks and Mary Pickford].[32]

If indeed Chaplin had been ill when he exited Los Angeles, it might have been from pure exhaustion over just completing the picture *A Dog's Life* (1918; see the following chapter), which would be released during the April bond tour. Of the argument that keeping Chaplin a civilian allowed him to better entertain the soldiers and war-related industry workers, *A Dog's Life* was seminal evidence. The picture would receive the best reviews yet of Chaplin's career, with pioneering French film critic Louis Delluc calling it "cinema's first total work of art."[33] Whether exhausted or ill, the comedian slept much of the first two days on the train. However, nervousness over the speeches he would be expected to deliver at the bond rallies soon had him, at Fairbanks' suggestion, practicing on film fans who would gather at the train's brief whistle stops in order to catch sight and, as it turned out, the sound of these patriotic movie stars.

Still, Chaplin was not that comfortable with either the press or the public when it came time to just be himself. Little had changed from an interview comment he had made in 1915: "You [the reporter] have an awful job on your hands if you expect to make this interesting reading matter, for there are thousands of other players whose experiences have been far more exciting than mine."[34] In the year following his April 1918 visit to the White House, it was revealed he had ducked a press conference there after meeting with President Woodrow Wilson: "Charlie stuck his head in the door, took one look, said he 'had to have some air,' and 'ditched' them all—went out for an auto ride!"[35]

After Chaplin, Fairbanks and Pickford, dubbed the "Three Star Special" by the press, had launched the bond tour in the capital, they moved the event to New York City. After that, they split up to cover a series of eastern and southern states.

While these events are noted briefly in Chaplin texts, they invariably get short shrift; a closer examination of period publications provides a vivid account of these rallies and how passionately Chaplin, a native of England, embraced his adopted country, and how American citizens reciprocated these nationalistic feelings. When coupled with Charlie's later single-handed cinematic capture of the Kaiser in the groundbreaking dark comedy *Shoulder Arms,* one has quite the patriotic portfolio for World War I. Moreover, they represent such a paradox when juxtaposed with the "un–American" label given Chaplin during the reactionary period now known as the witch-hunting Joseph McCarthy era of the 1950s. This travesty resulted in Chaplin being hounded from the country in 1952. Thus, when Chaplin's patriotic World War I actions are refracted through McCarthyism, one experiences a poignant lesson in the inherent history-impaired nature of humanity. Not since Thomas Paine had there been such a misunderstood American patriot.

The third and largest war bond campaign began in early April 1918 to mark the first anniversary of America's entrance into the war. And by far the greatest splash occurred when Chaplin and Fairbanks appeared at a rally on April 8, 1918, before a Gotham crowd estimated by the *New York Sun* to be 50,000 to 100,000.[36] People began to gather early on Wall Street (from Broadway to William Street) and on Broad Street (from Wall Street to the Exchange). The *New York Telegram* went on to report:

> There was a roar as Charlie Chaplin ... mounted the platform to announce that he had just come from addressing a Liberty Loan meeting in Washington, and that his "British heart was

100 percent American today [differing from the 144 percent reported by the *New York Sun* to open the chapter]." He wore his trick derby and with the aid of a cane did the celebrated Chaplin walk.[37]

The *New York Herald Tribune* keyed upon the entrances of the stars, with Chaplin appearing first:

There was a mighty howl of delight when Chaplin, with his mincing dance steps, bounded into view from the interior of the [Federal Reserve Bank] and pranced to the front of the

Chaplin selling war bonds in 1918 New York.

Washington statue. "Charlie" was not in costume. Grabbing a megaphone, the little comedian, looking smaller than ever beside the heroic statue of [George] Washington ... led his admirers in three cheers for the Army and Navy and three more for the Liberty Loan.[38]

The *New York American* focused upon an artist initially stunned by the crowd's size: "Charlie, sans cane and mustache, was obviously suffering from stage fright. He was vociferously cheered."[39] The *Wall Street Journal* provided a lengthy sound byte from the comic patriot's speech; it read, in part:

> Don't think of the percentage of the loan; think of the lives that are being sacrificed. America's richest blood is now being given up for democracy. The Germans are now in an advantageous position and we must get them out of it.[40]

The *New York Tribune* expanded even further on Chaplin's comments:

> Money is needed—money to support the great army and navy of Uncle Sam. This very minute the Germans occupy a position of advantage, and we have got to get the dollars. It ought to go over so that we can drive that old devil, the Kaiser, out of France. [interruption from cheers] How many of you men—how many of you boys out there have bought or are willing to buy Liberty bonds?[41]

The most entertainingly detailed of all the print coverage came from the *New York Sun,* especially in its winning description of Fairbanks' acrobatic treatment of his close friend. Just after Chaplin said he was "144 percent American,"

> Doug reached for the slim wasted little Charley [sic] and gripped him below the belt on the East River side while Charley was facing the Hudson [River]. Then the muscular Doug held Charley high in the air with one hand and jiggled him above the roaring crowd.[42]

Chaplin's greatest friend, and one of his few true friends, during a long life was Fairbanks. The comedian greatly admired the charm and off-the-cuff humor of his swashbuckling colleague. Nowhere was this more apparent than in the coverage of the bond tour. For example, during Fairbanks' comments, he asked the crowd, "How did you like Chaplin's speech?" There were cries of "Great!" "I wrote it!"[43] This produced a wave of laughter, according to the *New York Telegram.* More humor followed the rally when Chaplin and Fairbanks were invited to a tour of a sub–Treasury Building vault. Shortly after being shown its millions of dollars,

> Doug called Charley's attention to the fact that he was hatless. "Sure enough!" cried Charley, with every semblance of surprise. "Yes, I must have left the little old trick hat back there in the vault room. Doug ... and all you guards go on right up to the main floor and I'll join you as soon as I've found my hat. Go on—all the guards and everybody; don't wait for me—I couldn't think of detaining you gentleman." But they wouldn't let Chaplin go back. [A tongue-in-cheek Fairbanks later told the press] he had seen Charley deliberately place the trick hat on top of $85,000,000—in a dark corner of the vault room when no one was looking.[44]

This entertaining *New York Sun* coverage continued by adding that three days earlier, Fairbanks' humorous savoir faire took center stage when the members of the Three Star Special were honored guests at the White House, but the trio initially struggled in their response to President Wilson's question about what they were going to say in their speeches about the Third Liberty Loan. At last Fairbanks responded:

> Mr. President, the only general scheme I've got for a speech is to mention your name whenever I get stuck. That'll get a cheer every time, and while the crowd is making a lot of noise I'll keep waving my arms and working my lips as if I'm saying something. And when the noise

dies down again I'll shout, "And fellow citizens, this great, great president, Woodrow Wilson..." Bingo, they'll begin to cheer again. [The *Sun* concluded this coverage by adding:] "All of which the Hon. Woodrow Wilson enjoyed immensely."[45]

Maybe Fairbanks was also doubling up on the Wilson compliments to make amends for his Hollywood ego on the earlier trip east to the capital. That is, the *Los Angeles Times* had satirically reported (under the title "Illiteracy Note"):

> Evidently they don't know who Bennie Ziedman [Fairbanks' publicist] is, in benighted Washington ... Bennie telegraphed ahead of himself and Fairbanks [and Chaplin and Pickford] ... requesting that President Wilson meet Mr. Fairbanks [and company] at the train and that Mrs. Wilson give a reception—and those mean old authorities at Washington never even answered![46]

Be that as it may, before addressing Chaplin's subsequent bond tour in the American South, some additional factors about this epic World War I fund-raising steamroller merit noting. On April 10, Pickford (dressed in blue, with a purple orchid corsage) also generated a large Wall Street turnout, just two days after Chaplin and Fairbanks. The *New York Tribune's* article "Mary Pickford Convinces 20,000 in Wall St. Loan Should Succeed" quoted the actress extensively, including the following:

> I have come 3,500 miles to talk Liberty Bonds to you.... Do you know why Germany is as hard to lick? ... It is because ... they all stand and fight as one. My own brother has enlisted [in the navy]. Jack's some boy. He gave up a mighty good job [film actor] to go to war. I would rather go hungry all my life than see one of my brother's arms or legs cut off in the war. You girls out there, you have brothers, I know you feel the same way.[47]

Interestingly, one of the preliminary speakers that day, German-born American businessman Jacob H. Schiff, reinforced the earlier statements about the conflict possibly going beyond 1918:

> I am frequently asked about the probable duration of the war.... It may be that this war will last so long that we shall become impoverished, both in material resources and, in what would be worse, our young manhood. But, be it so if it must; it will be better if we give up everything to succeed....[48]

A second basic war bond factor would be to underline that the dangerous jingoistic spirit noted in other parts of the country was also alive and well in Gotham. In a *New York Herald* article covering a later Pickford Liberty Loan speech in the Bronx, the newspaper reported:

> "Isn't she an innocent thing," is all that Dennie Joseph ... says he said about Pickford as she spoke.... Yet, Mrs. Charlotte Pickford, Mary's mother, had him arrested for making "an insulting remark about her daughter." ... Policeman Flannagan arrested the youth upon her complaint. The [Hungarian-born] prisoner denied making an insulting remark but when Mrs. Pickford's allegation was corroborated by two ... reporters, the policeman took them all to the ... station house. There Mrs. Pickford pressed her charge.... When arraigned ... [he pled guilty] to a charge of disorderly conduct....[49]

One of Germany's World War I Central Powers' allies was the Austria-Hungary Empire, a multi-national realm which was dissolved into many separate nations after the conflict. (Less than a week after this incident, the *Tribune* ran the article "Booklet of Hate Issued to Help America Win."[50] Truly, these were patriotically dangerous times.)

Besides the bond activities of Chaplin, Fairbanks, and Pickford, several other screen personalities were part of the campaign. For instance, in New York, after the Three Star Special,

Marie Dressler (1868–1934) was the most prominent. Dressler periodically appeared at bond rallies with Pickford; she was primarily known at that time for her stage work and for appearing with Chaplin in Mack Sennett's pioneering feature *Tillie's Punctured Romance* (1914, based upon Dressler's stage hit *Tillie's Nightmare*). She would later win a Best Actress Oscar for *Min and Bill* (1930). Dressler was arguably the most entertaining performer stumping for bond sales. To illustrate, in her appearance at New York's City Hall Park, the fifty-year-old actress introduced herself by saying, "I'm an immigrant. My mother was German and my father English. I came here as a child many years ago—it's nobody's business how many years ago. But I am an American now."[51]

The beloved early cinema cowboy William S. Hart was another of "the few great stars selected by the government to tour the United States on behalf of the third big Liberty Loan drive, and who recently eclipsed all previous records held by photoplay [film] artists by purchasing $105,000 worth of Liberty Bonds...."[52] Unlike the Three Star Special, Hart started his tour from the West Coast.

Hart was just one of many touring stars who donated generously. Pickford gave $100,000 and Fairbanks $15,000—equivalent to over $2,200,000 and $330,000 today."[53] But keep in mind, these numbers are for the third bond drive. Pickford had already given $300,000 for the first two drives![54] At Chaplin's bond rally in Richmond, Virginia, he stated, "It's a good investment. I am buying $100,000 worth myself, and I am some businessman." Plus, if the aforementioned suggestion by film historian Brownlow is correct, the comedian would undoubtedly also have made an under-the-table donation to the British war effort in excess of $100,000.[55] Fatty Arbuckle is on record as having given $50,000 to the war effort.[56]

Fittingly, Pickford would pen an 1918 article, "The 'Movies' in War Time," which championed the extensive effort being made for the conflict by Hollywood. She wrote:

> Perhaps the cinema has given more to the Liberty Loan campaigns than to anything else. At any rate, this was one of the first ways in which we were able to help. Pictures were made in which the best known stars of the industry appeared, giving their time and labor, and these were distributed free of charge to the exhibitors throughout the county.... Besides large personal subscriptions to the Liberty Loan, our personal services in the way of leading parades, speaking at ... rallies, Red Cross drives and, whenever possible, have been freely given.[57]

While Pickford's comments might strike some as self-serving, no less a historian than Brownlow would write that film, even at its most basic level, made all the difference in the First World War:

> More than any general or politician, it was a motion picture star who raised morale. Charlie Chaplin was a true war hero, for his films did nothing but good. Other players, too, were held in high regard. [Poet-painter-novelist-filmmaker] Jean Cocteau recalled his surprise at finding in a [war-]ruined French village a cellar where people huddled together to watch [melodramatic] Pearl White in an [American serial] episode of *The Exploits of Elaine*.[58]

With all these rallies for the drive, which had raised in New York City alone, after the Chaplin, Fairbanks, Pickford, and Dressler appearances, $180,239,000 (nearly four billion dollars in today's currency), what would these bonds buy in 1918? All the following statistics come from the *New York Sun* article "Thousand Pulpits Urge Liberty Loan"[59]: A $100 bond would clothe and feed a soldier for eight months, or pay for five rifles, or 30 rifle grenades, or 42 hand grenades, or 23 pounds of ether, or 145 hot water bottles, or 2,000 surgical needles. Two $100 bonds would purchase a horse or a mule for the cavalry, artillery or other war services. Three

$100 bonds would clothe a soldier and feed him for one year in France, or would buy a motorcycle for a machine-gun company. Four $100 bonds would pay for a complete x-ray outfit. One $500 bond would supply bicycles for the headquarters company of an infantry regiment.

Chaplin as demonstrated by his aforementioned speeches, had come a long way from the shy overnight movie star. Still, he maintained a low profile in New York when not appearing at bond-related functions. This is demonstrated in a reluctant impromptu interview published

Charlie models some war supplies in *Shoulder Arms*.

in May 1918, after his southern sales tour. In "Capturing Charlie Chaplin," *New York Tribune* critic Harriette Underhill randomly runs into the comedian who "has the whitest teeth we ever saw, the bluest eyes and the blackest eyelashes."[60] When she begged for an interview, his initially reluctant reply made her a Chaplin fan for the first time:

> "If you'll promise not to say anything about my work for the government why—all right." He looked terribly suspicious. Just as though we were not taking more of a chance than he was. Hadn't we seen him drop ice cream down a lady's neck [in *The Adventurer*, 1917] and get her [Edna Purviance] involved in a revolving door [*The Cure*, 1917]...? We talked to Mr. Chaplin for an hour, and then he suddenly remembered that he had to go out and make a speech on the subject which we promised not to mention....[61]

Underhill's interview also stated that Chaplin was seeing few people after his return from his southern bond tour. Besides the implied sense of shyness, the comedian was also undoubtedly suffering from sheer fatigue. For instance, what follows is just a partial peek at the comedian's early fast-forward southern itinerary:

> The Chaplin party will be in Richmond [Virginia] on Thursday, the 11th [of April], leaving there at midnight for Rocky Mount [Virginia]. Mr. Chaplin is scheduled to speak in Rocky Mount at 10:30 a.m. on Friday, immediately afterward leaving by automobile for Wilson [North Carolina], where he will speak at 1 p.m. From Wilson he will journey to Raleigh [North Carolina] by train, arriving at 4:05 p.m.... [Chaplin] will speak in the auditorium Friday night.... It is very probable that Mr. Chaplin will make a public appearance on the streets of Raleigh during the afternoon.[62]

Period accounts of Chaplin's southern bond tour have it starting in Petersburg, Virginia (April 11, 1918), and culminating in a mass rally in New Orleans on April 23. As the previous quote documents, the comedian often spoke at multiple sites each day. Chaplin had so pushed his patriotic tour that his health was weakened; with the *New Orleans Times-Picayune* reporting, "His work was all the more commendable when it is realized he really was a sick man."[63] His weakened condition had also caused a large Liberty Bond parade to be cancelled preceding his rally at New Orleans' largest arena, the Palm Garden at the city fairgrounds.[64] Chaplin's tour entourage included Charles Lapworth, former associate editor of the *London Daily Mail*; J.R. Murphy, custodian of alien enemy property in Washington, D. C.; and Chaplin's friend Rob Wagner, a writer and teacher of Greek and art who was fascinated by the comedian's cinematic gifts. Members of this party, as well as local leaders, acted as warm-up speakers before the headlining Chaplin appeared. There was, however, one snobbish exception to these proceedings in New Orleans. Leslie M. Shaw, former secretary of the treasury, and ex-governor of Iowa, did not feel the country should use actors and actresses on the bond drive. Consequently, Chaplin was not on the stage during Shaw's speech.

Front-page news nearly everywhere he went, the comedian received daily on-the-job training and became an effective bond salesman. What follows are some of the memorable moments from his campaign. In Richmond, he learned the dangers of wading into the crowd:

> [In a loud voice which was] 100-proof Bill Sunday [famous period preacher] style ... Chaplin spent some twenty or thirty minutes in the "great [bond] revival." ... [Then] he "swiped" the cap of a policeman ... and leaping from the stage, shouted to the audience ... "Look out! I'm going through you [to collect subscription cards]!" ... Chaplin, with Boy Scouts, pretty girls and sober men spilling after him and calling, "Here Charlie," started through the crowd to collect the cards.... Over benches he jumped to get to the women who waved and shouted to the movie "nut" ... "Sing something" and such remarks as those ... [were shouted by a local spokesman] calling at the top of his voice to prevent a "stampede."[65]

A more subdued Chaplin spoke for twenty minutes the following day in Wilson:

> After smiling himself into increased favor with "Howdy Wilson," the movie celebrity ... said, "I know not what your allotment is in this drive but whatever it is don't only subscribe it but double it, triple it, fourth it, yes, fifth it."[66]

The same day (April 12) in Raleigh, his animation was more controlled, and he borrowed some New York bond rally material from his friend Douglas Fairbanks. Following Charles Lapworth's

Charlie Chaplin
(Himself)

Will sell Liberty Bonds at the big patriotic meeting to be held **Tuesday** evening at 8 o'clock at the Fair Grounds in the Palm Garden. Everyone buying a Bond at this meeting will get a receipt right there, signed by Charlie Chaplin, and later an autographed photo will be sent the purchaser from Los Angeles, California. All that is necessary is to pay one dollar down—at the meeting—and a dollar a week at a bank until Bond is paid for.

Among the Other Speakers Will Be

Hon. Leslie M. Shaw
Former Secretary of the Treasury.

Music by Tosso's Band

Doors Open	7:00 P. M.
Band Concert	7:15 P. M.
Meeting Opens	8:00 P. M.

This will be the largest patriotic meeting ever held in New Orleans. The Palm Garden at the Fair Grounds is the only auditorium large enough to hold the crowd. The meeting is indoors and will be held rain or shine. Extra street car service will be furnished and the grounds and approaches will be unusually well lighted. It will be perfectly safe for women and chidren. Let everyone come, see the world's greatest comedian, and get his autograph by paying down at least one dollar towards a Liberty Bond.

ADMISSION FREE

In the Palm Garden, Fair Grounds, Tuesday Evening

A Chaplin war bond newspaper ad for the comedian's tour of the southern states.

speech, Chaplin asked the gathering, "Did you like Lapworth's speech?" The crowd gave its assent. "Well, I wrote it," said the comedian, generating the same response Fairbanks' claim to have authored Chaplin's New York remarks had elicited.[67] Then, borrowing from the acrobatic antics of Fairbanks, Chaplin "swung himself out over the crowd from the flag-decorated speakers' stand."[68] The *Raleigh News and Observer* also chronicled the comedian's folksy banter with the crowd: "'Hullo Folks! Howdy do, Raleigh! I've just had a fine dinner,' he continued, when the round of greeting had died down, 'and if you can't hear me, you may know it's the peach pie that's stopping it.'"[69]

The comedian was also realizing and becoming resigned to the fact that everywhere he appeared Chaplin-mania broke out. The press coverage hyped the hysteria, too. A Rocky Mount correspondent set the stage for the comedian's visit:

> The greatest patriotic demonstration in the history of Rocky Mount will be staged here ... when Charlie Chaplin, the great screen comedian, will be here ... [It includes a] monster parade [and] school children will be given a half holiday [and] will take part in the event....[70]

Even prior to each speaking event, Chaplin was an affectionately hunted man. For example, a "howling mob of boys" who swarmed Raleigh's Yarborough Hotel was a problem which challenged the manager and the local bond committee:

> The comedian was served with supper in a room on the second floor of the hotel to protect him from the crowd which overflowed from the lobby of the hotel to the hall leading to the main dining room. Even with this precaution ... boys collected in numbers on the second floor looking for the room where Charlie was supposed to be.[71]

Several plans were considered before Chaplin was smuggled into a freight elevator and then taken into the nearby auditorium by way of a side stage entrance while a large crowd "was waiting to see him emerge from the front door of the hotel...."[72]

A few days later in Atlanta, Chaplin was in more of a comfort zone, even before an audience of 8,000. He opened the gathering by saying, "Gee whiz, this is some crowd!" "[But to] thousands of eager Atlanta kiddies the famous comedian was not Charlie Chaplin at all until he warmed up."[73] Then, after a short speech, he again borrowed some shtick from friend Fairbanks who, during their White House visit, told the president that all a speaker had to do was use Wilson's name to get a positive response from an audience. Thus, Chaplin called for three cheers for the president and the flag and the audience came alive. Next, aping the physical Fairbanks, he leaped upon a table and led the band in some patriotic songs. "He was Charlie Chaplin, now, without doubt—the same Chaplin smile, the funny Chaplin hair, the Chaplin antics."[74] Once he had the audience going, he promised certain signature Tramp antics, such as his east-west shuffle, when each ever-rising bond subscription goal was met.

While no specific totals are noted in the *Atlanta Constitution* coverage of their rally (with monetary amounts varying, of course, based upon the city's size), the *New Orleans Times-Picayune* documented the fiscal incentives Chaplin offered their city, via his "Charlie" persona, concluding with the newspaper's own comic embellishment:

> If he sells bonds to the extent of $25,000 he will do his funny walk across the stage. If the amount goes to $50,000 he will execute his funny derby tricks. Should the total reach $100,000 he will stand on his head, and if the sum goes above that amount, there is no telling what he will do.[75]

Just for the record, Chaplin sold $227,000 worth of bonds in New Orleans—but no one seems to have recorded just what the "no telling what he will do" craziness represented.[76]

This represents a rare omission by New Orleans' *Times-Picayune,* since their coverage of Chaplin's first visit to the city (which was added late at the comedian's request) was one of the most thorough of any newspaper on the bond campaign. One could break these added insights into five categories. First, there is the documentation of how difficult it was to precede Chaplin on the stage. For example, the aforementioned Leslie M. Shaw "had a hard time getting the crowd [of 10,000—not the sometimes reported 40,000] to listen to him. But he fought the crowd, finally conquered it, although those close up were probably the only ones who could hear him [in the days of megaphones]...."[77] Of course, the audience's response might have been a partial response to his aforementioned uppity attitude towards performers. (However, as this report documents, at least Shaw appeared on the same bill as Chaplin.)

Second, the newspaper directly addressed Chaplin's draft status at length, something conspicuously missing in earlier press coverage of the bond tour. Consequently, New Orleans' premier paper noted, "The several thousand young men of New Orleans subject to [the] draft probably will be interested to know Chaplin has been placed in Class 1-A by a local board in California. He has entered no claim for exception."[78] As a side note, with regard to Chaplin's place of birth, in the draft status information he shared, the comedian claimed to have been born in "Fontainebleau, France, of English parents, who were traveling show people."[79] Third, another *Times-Picayune* article played up the luxuriousness of Chaplin's accommodations during his New Orleans stay, which could have been a pin prick about his sudden cancelling of an elaborate parade in which he was to have been the main attraction: "Chaplin Parade to Boom Liberty Loan Called Off."[80]

Fourth, the last component to be limited to the New Orleans portion of the tour involved references to Chaplin's next film, *A Dog's Life* (1918), completed on April 18, just days before he left Hollywood for the bond campaign. The *Times-Picayune* stated, "He has not seen it since it was assembled and at 11 o'clock Tuesday [April 23, the day of his arrival, Chaplin] will review it in a private showing in the Strand Theatre."[81]

One could also credit the *Times-Picayune*'s Chaplin reporting for fleshing out details only cited briefly in earlier articles on his southern rallies. For example, the newspaper expanded upon the fact that the children forever swarming around Chaplin were frequently outfitted as pint-sized versions of Charlie the Tramp—sort of surrealism meets early cinema idolatry. Yet, this was a phenomenon which had been going on since the 1914 inception of the Tramp look-alike contests—one of which put a young Bob Hope on stage for the first time. Another period story, probably hyperbole, had Chaplin entering one such competition in costume ... and finishing third! Thus, to paraphrase an equally common 1910s joke, "There's nothing worse than visiting friends and having their children either entertain by way of piano playing or doing imitations of the Tramp."

The *Times-Picayune* also brought more detail to what might be called "Chaplin's propensity for the campaign 'kiss'": He frequently blew them to the crowd when on stage. The comedian's kisses were sometimes used as a perk to sell the bonds themselves. For instance:

> Little girls came and were kissed. One elderly woman brought in a subscription [card] for $1,000. She drew a kiss and became the happiest woman in the building. She brought her two little daughters [granddaughters?] up to meet Chaplin. He kissed the youngest one and started to kiss the other. She appeared older than she really is, and the comedian hesitated but recovered quickly and delivered the kiss.[82]

A "regular riot ensued" as Chaplin attempted to leave the New Orleans arena Palm Garden, with policeman fighting for a passageway for him as "a mob of people surged to the plat-

3. The War Bond Rallies of 1918

During the Chaplin phenomenon of the 1910s, children dressed as the Tramp was a norm.

form." As a result, the comedian's doctor attempted to change the film star's travel plans.[83] Chaplin had intended to remain in the city for two weeks. However, his doctor ordered him to take a complete rest, which he said that the actor "cannot obtain anywhere except in Los Angeles, where the people are so accustomed to movie folk they do not crowd around him."[84] Yet, once again Chaplin did not abide by the medical advice (earlier this chapter chronicled how Chaplin left for the bond tour despite a *Los Angeles Times* headline declaring "CHAPLIN DEPARTS: Doctor Said He Mustn't But He Did"[85]). How fitting, therefore, that by his tour's conclusion, Chaplin would come full circle and once again defy his physician. Yes, he left New Orleans but his destination was New York, as previously noted in the May 12, 1918, interview "Capturing Charlie Chaplin."[86] Traditional accounts, including classic Chaplin biographies by Theodore Huff and David Robinson, have the comedian returning directly to California.[87] But the "Capturing" article proves otherwise. For those who might suggest the interview had simply been delayed in its publication from the comedian's earlier bond stop in New York, the essay offers two irrefutable facts that it occurred *after* his New Orleans finale on April 24— with one representing a sad twist related to 1918's *A Dog's Life*. First, and most poignant, it reveals that "Mutt," Chaplin's co-star in the aforementioned picture, had died and been buried on the 29th of April.[88] Second, the interviewer, *New York Herald* critic Harriette Underhill, states that the impromptu Chaplin session had taken place just "four days" prior to the May 12 publication date.[89] Of course, what would have been the most telling proof of Underhill's article, related to the whereabouts of Chaplin, was negated by her promise *not* to ask the comedian about his current bond-selling activities. Had she done so, Chaplin would have mentioned leading a final New York rally at City Hall Park, and then finished his bond duties with a short talk at the Astor Hotel on May 1. He did not leave for Hollywood until later that week.[90]

On the train home, Chaplin must have felt invincible, given the cinema royalty receptions he received. His automobile entrance into Nashville, Tennessee, was typical:

> Men, women and children, all ages and sizes, surged around the Chaplin party to get a look at "Charlie." Women threw flowers ... men waved their hats and "the kids" simply swarmed and scrambled over each other in their effort to get a glimpse of the popular little actor.[91]

He was even introduced to bond crowds in the following manner:

> When Secretary [of Treasury] McAdoo ... looked around for speakers that would reach the heart of the people ... he sent for Charlie Chaplin as the man who was nearer and dearer to the people as a whole than any other man in the country.[92]

Is it any wonder that he would be emboldened to mix comedy and war in his next project?

4

Shoulder Arms and War as a Film Topic in 1918

No less a pioneering filmmaker than director Cecil B. DeMille suggested to Chaplin he delay the release of the dark comedy *Shoulder Arms* (1918) because of "its bad taste."[1]

Today if a fan of dark comedy was confronted with criticism of the genre, s/he would be in the minority. Yet, a black humor advocate might be moved to define/defend a genre once also disparagingly described as "sick humor" by asking what one can expect of a world so succinctly clarified with this line from Stanley Kubrick's sardonic *Eyes Wide Shut* (1999): "Life goes on. It always does, until it doesn't." If the currency of death has been cheapened, is there not comfort in oblivion?

Regardless, as the previous chapter noted, World War I–era pop culture sometimes toyed with dark comedy, often at the expense of Germany's Kaiser ... a macabre foreshadowing of how the genre used Hitler as a pivotal target before, during, and after the Second World War. Yet in both wars Chaplin would lead the way in bringing meaningful black humor to cinema.

Before addressing the focus film of this chapter, *Shoulder Arms,* it is necessary to briefly sketch how America's Central Powers enemy, Germany, was portrayed by period cinema. Though the majority of the picture product then available to the general public was not unlike any previous era (largely forgettable mind-candy), there were several movies, often masquerading as quasi-documentaries, which were inflammatorily ugly about the brutality of the German soldiers and the Kaiser.

In a survey of period literature from 1918, one such picture easily stands out as generating the most critical and commercial success, as well as promises of gripping war authenticity: D. W. Griffith's *Hearts of the World*. The director who had given cinema the groundbreaking yet provocative racist epic *Birth of a Nation* (1915) now used that picture as a loose blueprint for *Hearts*. The *New York Tribune* ad for the film is typical of its 1918 marketing:

> D.W. GRIFFITH'S
> Supreme Triumph
> *HEARTS of the WORLD*
> See:
> One Million Fighting Men
> Twenty Thousand Horses
> Miles of Artillery
> March of Legions
> Squadrons of Airplanes
> Fleets of Zeppelins
> The Destruction of Cities
> The Charge of Tanks[2]

The only problem with these details was that the movie was largely shot in California, with the European war scenes recreated thousands of miles away from the actual events. Yes, Griffith had briefly visited England and France, with a modest amount of footage being shot. Plus, some stock documentary material was peppered throughout the epic. Yet, what the British War Office Cinematographic Committee (the organization which was the catalyst for *Hearts of the World* being made) had in mind, according to Griffith's definitive biographer Richard Schickel, was for the director

> to make a picture that would aid their extensive efforts to draw America into the war, a picture that would stress the sadistic brutality of the German enemy but would not, of course, hint at the mass stupidity and unredeemed horror of trench warfare.[3]

Though released after America's 1917 declaration of war, *Hearts* undoubtedly aided the ardor of the United States to defeat this alleged beast of an enemy, from boosts in military recruitment and bond sales, to simply fanning the frighteningly frenzied jingoism which then gripped the nation. What Griffith created with *Hearts,* to continue the racist *Birth of a Nation* analogy, was to essentially portray the Germans along the lines of the earlier picture's sadistic blacks and mulattoes, with the Americans saving the day in the finale, just as the Ku Klux Klan rode to the rescue to conclude *Birth*. Both pictures key upon two families caught in the horrors of war, with Griffith's signature actress, Lillian Gish (forever the virginal heroine in distress), again used as the focal point of the suffering. Even noted silent film historian William K. Everson has remarked upon the plot similarities to *Birth*: "[They] have the same family structure, the same separations, and reunions, the same editing patterns...."[4]

Hearts proved such a success that upon Griffith's return to California after the movie's New York opening, the *Los Angeles Times* proclaimed, under the conquering hero–type headline "Griffith Returns":

> Something in the nature of a triumph was the return to this city yesterday of D.W. Griffith ... who comes from New York, where his great war photodrama, presented at the 44th Street Theatre, is breaking not only all picture records but even nearly every theatrical record ever established in the metropolis.[5]

Despite these kudos, Gish, normally Griffith's greatest advocate, would much later observe, "The movie's depiction of German brutality bordered on the absurd. Whenever a German came near me, he beat me.... I don't think dear Mr. Griffith ever forgave himself for making the picture. He would later say, 'War is the villain, not any one people.'"[6]

Of the many other World War I propaganda films of 1918, period accounts suggest *Hearts* received its greatest competition from *The Kaiser, the Beast of Berlin*—a title which perfectly represents its German-baiting tendencies. The ad campaign for this movie proclaimed:

> "The HIM of Hate"
> gets a hard poke on the jaw
> at every performance of
> *THE KAISER*
> *The Beast of Berlin*
> and the audience stands up
> and cheers like mad![7]

The film played at two major New York theaters simultaneously, and Universal, its distributor, boasted that the huge lines to see the film "blocked traffic on Broadway."[8] An *Atlanta Constitution* article entitled "Great Picture Still Turning Away Thousands in New York" summarized some of the Gotham hosannas:

4. Shoulder Arms and War as a Film Topic in 1918

Said the *New York American*: "Should be shown to every one of our two hundred million citizens." Said the *Tribune*: "If there is anyone who doubts that we are going to win the war, let him visit the Broadway theaters [where *The Kaiser* is playing]." Said the *Telegraph*: "A remarkable and wonderful picture; conveys a powerful message for every true American...."[9]

Some middle America reviews even placed it ahead of Griffith's *Hearts*. For example, the *New Orleans Times-Picayune* said of *The Kaiser*:

> [Audiences have been able] to witness what has been declared throughout America to be the most effective production of all times, standing comparison only with that other big epic of the screen world—*The Birth of a Nation*.... It was left for [director and title character] Rupert Julian [to take] as his subject the most detested of all human beings [and create] a positively fixed masterpiece that will stand the test of time.[10]

German hate propaganda not only helped get the United States into World War I, it was later a blueprint for Hitler's hate propaganda against the Jews.

The Kaiser, the Beast of Berlin is now one of cinema's lost films. Significantly, however, as it relates to Chaplin's later *Shoulder Arms*, the culmination of both pictures is the capturing of the Kaiser, though the antiheroic "Charlie" the doughboy's accomplishment turns out to be a dream.

While one could go on *ad nauseam* with these forgettable propaganda films, with such telling titles as *To Hell with the Kaiser!* and *The German Curse in Russia* (both 1918), one final unique cinematic slant on the sadistic Hun merits noting: cartoonist and pioneering animator Winsor McCoy's film *The Sinking of the Lusitania* (1918). The *Lusitania* was the luxurious British ocean liner sunk off the coast of Ireland on May 7, 1915, by a German U-boat. Germany's justification for an attack was that the ship was secretly transporting war material, which much later was proven to be true. Ironically, the second *Lusitania* explosion, which caused the ship to sink, was possibly the result of war-bound ammunition igniting in the cargo hold. Moreover, Germany had been running warning ads in New York newspapers about just this sort of danger to potential passengers sailing to Europe. Over half of the nearly 2000 people on board died, including 128 Americans. Given the toll of civilians lost, the sinking shocked the world. More than any other single event, the *Lusitania* disaster helped change American opinion in favor of war with Germany. Indeed, in Chaplin's memoir he suggests that prior to the sinking, one might have defined American's war perspective from the song "I Didn't Raise My Boy to Be a

Soldier." The *Lusitania* incident, to Chaplin, cued the country for another song, "Over There" (with the telling lyric "The Yanks are coming").[11] Public opinion against Germany turned so quickly after the sinking that Groucho Marx dropped overnight the German accent he had been using in the Marx Brothers' vaudeville act.

McCay's amazingly ambitions *Sinking of the Lusitania* took him two years to draw "on 25,000 sheets of celluloid."[12] The creator of such groundbreaking cartoons as *Little Nemo* (1911) and *Gertie the Dinosaur* (1914) had once again drawn a visually arresting animated film of greater cartoon length (12 minutes) than the period norm. Yet McCay's animation then slips into this standard inflammatory propaganda sub-genre which had sprung up in 1918. Thus, one of his *Lusitania* titles reads:

> Germany, which had already benumbed the world with its wholesale killing, then sent its instrument of crime [the U-boat] to perform a more treacherous and cowardly offense.

The finale ratcheted the propaganda quotient to the max: A mother holds her baby above the waves as she sinks below them. For a one-two propaganda punch, this image is coupled with the title: "The man who fired the shot [launched the torpedo] was decorated by the Kaiser. AND THEY TELL US NOT TO HATE THE HUN!" In 1919, despising all things German even contributed to the passing of the eighteenth amendment to the Constitution, which outlawed the manufacture, transportation, and consumption of alcoholic beverages by 1920. (The overwhelming majority of all breweries in this country were then owned and operated by German-Americans.)

Given this level of hate towards Germany and the Kaiser, is it any wonder that many Hollywood insiders, with the exception of Chaplin's close friend Douglas Fairbanks, felt the comedian was taking quite the risk in making a dark *comedy* about World War I? Moreover, *Shoulder Arms* was also well outside the wheelhouse of what the public had grown to expect from its three greatest cinema stars, Chaplin, Fairbanks, and Pickford. For instance, at the time of the April 1918 bond tours, Pickford could be seen on screen in *Amarilly of Clothesline Alley,* a comedy-drama which suggested that the working poor could neither mix with the upper class, nor be happy doing so. One period critic summarized the stereotypical child-woman Pickford part in the picture thus: "Mary invests the role of scrub-girl with all the sympathetic tenderness for which she is famed...."[13]

The Fairbanks picture playing during the bond tour, the comedy-drama *Mr. Fix-It*, anticipates Will Smith's date doctor coach from *Hitch* (2005) by nearly nine decades. Yet, whereas Smith was helping romance to happen, Fairbanks was fixing matrimonial difficulties. *Mr. Fix-It* was a commercial and critical success, from the title of the *New Orleans Times-Picayune*'s review, "Fairbanks Brings Joy to the Strand," to the *New York Tribune* critic opining,

> The next time someone says to us (which someone does nearly every day): "Isn't it a crime that these movie actors get so much money when they hardly do a thing to earn it?" we are going to say, "Yes, except Douglas Fairbanks."[14]

The Fairbanks trademark athleticism suggested in this review is more fully fleshed out in a rave review in the *Atlanta Constitution*:

> An exciting scene in the picture is a battle between "Mr. Fix-It" and several gangsters in the slums. Mr. Fairbanks climbs down the side of the house on a clothesline and swings across a street on an election banner. This is said to be one of the most thrilling stunts Mr. Fairbanks ever has performed.[15]

4. Shoulder Arms *and War as a Film Topic in 1918*

Indeed, Fairbanks' swashbuckling persona (accented more after World War I) was also frequently on display at public events, such as lifting Chaplin over his head at the New York bond rally. Fairbanks even enjoyed comically injecting his athleticism into the most surprising situations. For example, when the Three Star Special (Chaplin, Fairbanks, and Pickford) lunched with President Woodrow Wilson at the White House on April 6, 1918, to kick off the third war bond rally, Fairbanks' ice-breaking small talk with Wilson was often action-related. Thus, the *Los Angeles Times* reported Fairbanks bet "he could climb the side of the Capitol quicker than the president, and the president smiled and said, yes, he guessed so."[16]

Before leaving this action-driven comedy *Mr. Fix-It,* one ironic footnote related to both the film and the bond tour merits noting. Despite Fairbanks' cinematic skills at correcting marital messes, in real life his own marriage was publicly failing during this patriotic sales tour of the country. Moreover, while seemingly not impacting his "Everybody's Hero" popularity status, the catalyst for his problem was loving "America's Sweetheart" (Pickford). A further war-related comic paradox was how the public became aware of the situation. What follows is the lead to a *Los Angeles Times* article from April 13, 1918:

> Douglas Fairbanks' statement, made in Detroit [on his war bond tour], that the story of an estrangement between himself and his wife was "German propaganda," and entirely false, and stung [the actor's estranged wife] Mrs. [Anna Beth] Fairbanks into naming names and threatening to reconsider her first attitude of quiet self-effacement when she was interviewed in her apartment at [New York's] Hotel Algonquin today [April 12]. [She] intimated very broadly that if Fairbanks and the popular idol ... whom she named [but goes unnoted in the article] as the present possessor of Fairbanks' heart do not admit their love for one another and cease "denying the obvious" ... she will not be content to sacrifice herself further for their sakes.[17]

Though Pickford is not named, her husband Owen Moore, from whom she had long been estranged, responded to Mrs. Fairbanks' comments the following day in another *Los Angeles Times* article. In a rambling statement to the press he stated:

> The "other woman" [his wife Pickford] is now ill and under great nervous stress and I feel it to be obligatory upon myself to make a statement to save her the humiliation of making any public statement.[18]

This Douglas Fairbanks still from *The Thief of Bagdad* (1924) captures the muscular athleticism of which he was so proud.

Moore goes on to admit surprise over Mrs. Fairbanks' revelation, given that Pickford had life-threatening health issues which necessitated her avoiding any shock. Then he moved from this subtextual attack upon Fairbanks to a direct offense:

> Mr. Fairbanks possesses a peculiar and complex personality that has a strong fascination for women.... I have hesitated to take action ... because I did not wish to interfere in any way with the Liberty Loan campaign.... I wish it to be distinctly understood that in my opinion there is only one aggressor.... The "other woman" [Pickford] has been as much victimized as the rest [other Fairbanks conquests], not wholly blameless perhaps but imposed upon.[19]

These comments about the affair speak volumes about the war paranoia then gripping America, from Fairbanks alibi-ing that his marital "estrangement was a German plot to destroy the value of the work" he was doing for the Liberty Loan campaign, to a knowingly cuckolded husband (Moore) hiding behind patriotic bond rallies.[20]

For the record, this potential scandal had little impact upon Fairbanks and Pickford—the distraction of the war and the duo's huge popularity made them Teflon celebs, with the two becoming even bigger stars in the 1920s. Indeed, no small part of their later growing global stardom was the eventual shedding of their spouses and a 1920 marriage which made them Hollywood royalty and arguably still filmland's most celebrated couple.

That being said, just as Pickford's aforementioned *Amarilly of Clothesline Alley* and Fair-

Fairbanks and his wife Mary Pickford at their legendary Hollywood home, "Pickfair," circa 1925.

banks' *Mr. Fix-It* were what one expected of these performers, the Chaplin film in release during the bond tour, *A Dog's Life,* also showcased the star's standard persona—"Charlie," the underdog Tramp. Also, like *Amarilly* and *Mr. Fix-It, Life* was popular with both critics and audiences alike. This combination of praise is amusingly demonstrated in the *New York Herald*'s review, which noted:

> Charlie Chaplin's position in motion pictures as an eccentric and highly original comedian was demonstrated yesterday in the Strand Theatre, when *A Dog's Life* was shown.... The theater was packed, and when the film was on, if a man rose to take off his overcoat fifty other persons instantly stood up behind him so they would not miss a single move of the comedian....[21]

The *New Orleans Times-Picayune*'s *Life* critique stated, "Chaplin—idol of America's millions—by reason of his original and infectious comedy ... shows Charlie as the inseparable pal of a street mongrel, that will make the family of American screen fans roar with delight."[22]

The difference between these business-as-usual Pickford and Fairbanks pictures, versus Chaplin's *Life,* is that while *Amarilly* and *Mr. Fix-It* have now slipped through the cracks of time, forgotten by all but the most dedicated silent film aficionados, *Life* "remains one of [Chaplin's] most perfect films."[23] Fittingly, the latter quote is from the comedian's definitive later biographer, David Robinson. Yet, even at the time, as previously noted, pioneering French film critic Louis Delluc called *Life* "cinema's first total work of art."[24]

The title character of *Life* generated a great deal of human interest in 1918. Even before the movie was released, the Chaplin studio credited the random arrival of a dog, which came to be called Scraps, as the catalyst for the picture (in which he was named Mutt):

> Charlie himself had hit upon the idea of utilizing as his chief support a homeless, unkempt white mongrel that had sought refuge in the studio one day.... [The dog] furnished the novel note of pathos that the comedian believes is absolutely essential to the type of screen humor that he has made all his own; so a story was built about the pair....[25]

Then, after the film was in release and Chaplin was on his southern bond tour, Scraps' death generated a new round of press attention, especially as it was suggested by Chaplin and his staff that the dog "could never get used to Charlie's absence ... [and died]" ... or as another article title suggested, "Dog Gone, Sad Story of Grief."[26] Consequently, combine an artist at the top of his game, easily inspired by the day-to-day events around him and just coming off a month of day-to-day patriotic war bond events, is it any wonder that Chaplin would soon both tackle and accomplish an inspired war-related dark comedy?

Chaplin had been off the screen for a year, and as previously noted, his antiheroic Tramp was someone with whom antiheroic-feeling soldiers could identify. As Paul Fussell states in *The Great War and Modern Memory,* "In the ironic phase of the literary cycle, a standard character is the man whom things are done to ... [such as] Charlie Chaplin."[27] Fussell goes on to state that "the man whom things are done to" also perfectly describes the life of most soldiers. Thus, a new picture from their fellow sufferer ("Charlie") would undoubtedly be as wildly welcomed as those previously noted civilian fans at New York's Strand Theatre.

Second, a film entitled *A Dog's Life* would certainly resonate with soldiers stuck in the rat-infested muddy trenches of the Western Front. Third, in Chaplin's film the dog provides both companionship to Charlie as well as coming to his rescue by digging up a billfold full of cash. This perfectly dovetails into a fact largely forgotten about the First World War, a fact which would further draw fighting men to *A Dog's Life*: canines played a vital part on World

War I's Western Front, starting with companionship and various forms of rescue and/or comfort duties. A more detailed duty résumé of the conflict's 50,000-plus military dogs included: acting as messengers, carrying everything from ammunition and food to cigarettes, acting as scouts, equipment-pulling sled dogs, Red Cross assisting casualty mutts known as "Mercy Dogs," terrier "ratters" killings the rats which were everywhere in the trenches and the "No Man's Land" between said trenches (lured by decaying bodies), sentry dogs, guard dogs, mascots, and warning devices—their sensitive hearing could pick up the whine of incoming artillery shells well before their human counterparts' ears.

One of America's first war dogs of the time was the decorated pit bull Stubby, promoted to sergeant for a rescue mission in which he was wounded. Moreover, silent cinema's later canine star Rin Tin Tin was originally a World War I mascot dog. Articles such as "[Cigarette] Dog Scorns Shells to Help Soldiers," from the *Richmond [Virginia] Times-Dispatch,* were common in period publications.[28] In *no* war, before or since, have canines played such an integral part. Yet, coming back full circle to Chaplin's *A Dog's Life,* the psychological comfort "Mutt" provided to "Charlie" undoubtedly matched the greatest good (companionship) these war dogs gave to the fighting men of World War I. (As a dog-related footnote, U.S. government personnel I.D.s for servicemen, "dog tags," were a product of World War I. In earlier American conflicts, going back to the Civil War, any type of individual I.D. was left up to the man in uniform. Chaplin was well aware of this development, since soldier Charlie's dog tag is, fittingly, number 13.)

Chaplin and friend on the set of *A Dog's Life*.

Shoulder Arms, Chaplin's follow-up to *A Dog's Life,* began production in late May (1918), shortly after he returned to Hollywood from New York. A long three-reeler (44 minutes), it focuses entirely upon Charlie's days in the army, from basic training to the apparent capturing of the Kaiser. Originally, Chaplin had planned a five-reel picture in three acts. The first section would address his pre-war civilian life. Shot but not used in the finished film is footage in which Charlie is seen as the father of three boys, likes beer, and is saddled with a large, henpecking, frying pan-toting wife—though she remains an off-screen presence. (Chaplin would briefly return to the theme of the female-dominated working man, later a popular scenario for Laurel & Hardy, with *Pay Day* in 1922.) Not surprisingly, the *Shoulder Arms* Charlie is not unhappy to receive his draft notice. This portion of act one concludes with him going for his military examination.

The second act eventually becomes the entire film: the Charlie-in-uniform overview previously noted, and soon to be fully sketched out. The third act, which was never shot, was to have the little fellow on a victory banquet tour of Europe, with all of its leaders celebrating the man who captured the Kaiser. This sequence of the proposed picture was undoubtedly inspired, at least in part, by the rock star–like reception Chaplin had just received on his recently concluded war bond tour. The only idea from this act which was retained for the movie was the Charlie-waking-from-a-dream conclusion, never to have been a hero. (Interestingly, given the catalyst the bond tour had given to making *Shoulder Arms,* the only interruption in its production was the time Chaplin took to make a short ten-minute film for the government entitled *Charles Chaplin in a Liberty Loan Appeal,* later retitled *The Bond,* which was widely distributed in the autumn of 1918.)

A thorough examination of *Shoulder Arms* is best broken down into three parts—two perspectives upon Chaplin's use of dark comedy, and a general overview of inspired comic material not directly tied to the genre. Keep in mind that Chaplin's use of black humor in *Shoulder Arms* is as an unfortunate extension of concluding what was then perceived to be a necessary conflict. First, after basic training, the film showcases Charlie as an anxious soldier new to the Western Front. In a very realistic trench, he walks by a sign proclaiming "Broadway and Rotten Row." An ironic title card announces, "A Quiet Lunch," as Charlie and his sergeant (Sydney Chaplin) attempt to eat, but the little fellow is ever more comically fearful as the shells bursting behind them come increasingly closer. Soon Sydney says, via another ironic title card, "Make Yourself at Home," and the bombs again begin to burst even closer. Now Charlie's big-eyed expression is heightened by his helmet rattling more with each explosion ... until it almost pops off his head. Each of these examples represents one of dark comedy's basic components, the constant presence of death.

Second, and most pervasively central to *Shoulder Arms,* is the dark comedy attached to the more seasoned Charlie the soldier—a nonchalant business-as-usual behavior which anticipates the casual callousness to life's horrors condensed to the aforementioned expression from Kurt Vonnegut's *Slaughterhouse-Five* (1969): "So it goes."[29] Thus, a blasé Charlie, originally so worried about death at meal time, is later casually capable of opening a bottle of beer by merely lifting it slightly above trench level so that an enemy sniper opens it with a shot. Then Charlie performs a variation of the same trick by lighting his cigarette in this manner.

Consequently, a second basic dark comedy element joins death: the absurdity of the situation. Along similarly absurd but more practical lines, Charlie attempts to use his gas mask, a device to protect a soldier from a grisly new weapon (chemical warfare), in order to eat some extremely odorous Limburger cheese. When this proves too difficult, he pitches the cheese into a nearby German trench and momentarily disables an enemy officer.

Charlie the soldier is equally blasé about the absurdly filthy conditions in the trenches. For example, in one scene, using his ability to metamorphosize an object into something else, he attaches a cheese grater to the wall of his dugout (a cave-like room dug inside the trenches), converting the grater into a back scratcher to combat the constant lice-induced itching. An even more ingenious Chaplin transformation, though on a risky topic for period comedy, is inspired by the flooding of his dugout. (Keep in mind that thousands of real Western Front soldiers forced to stand for hours in waterlogged trenches without being able to remove wet socks and boots often came down with "trench foot." Planks put down to help minimize the problem were referred to as "duckboards." Yet, when feet were left untreated, gangrene could set in and necessitate amputation.) As noted in Chapter 1, the catalyst for Chaplin comedy often came from the most macabre realities. Regardless, the water is so high in Charlie's dugout that his bunk is submerged, necessitating another metamorphosis in order to sleep underwater. The sequence is entertainingly described by pioneering Chaplin biographer Theodore Huff: "With the help of a phonograph horn as a breathing tube [Charlie] settles down to a submarine snooze."[30]

The prelude to the flood sequence starts out innocently enough with Charlie on duty during a rainstorm. As he is relieved of duty, yet another cynical film title reveals the password phrase: "It's wet." Chaplin cannot resist milking the lake-like dugout for as much absurd comedy as possible, from Charlie fluffing a soaked pillow before lying down in his submerged bunk, to finding it easier to subdue a snoring fellow soldier (Sydney Chaplin) whose head is barely above water: Just create a wave in his direction and the half-drowned fellow will snore no more. The following morning, upright Charlie, still half-submerged, has no feeling in his feet. After

Three Allied soldiers in their Western Front bunker in *Shoulder Arms*: Chaplin's Charlie (center), his sergeant (Sydney Chaplin, right), and, fittingly for a war that was the first to give recognition to unknown soldiers, an unidentified actor on the left.

rubbing the circulation back into one foot he has lifted out of the drink, the same procedure does not seem to be working on his other foot ... until he realizes he has fished out one of Sydney's feet.

Another basic dark comedy component—man as beast—is also brilliantly presented by Charlie the veteran. With the bored demeanor of a board game player keeping score, the little fellow briefly but methodically plays at being a sniper. After each of his casual pop-up rifle shots above the trench, he chalks up an enemy kill with a single perpendicular line. After the fourth seemingly deadeye shot, however, when he peers over the trench top his helmet is shot off by an unseen German; Charlie ever so manner-of-factly erases one of his kill lines. Yet, he immediately returns to the business at hand, and the fourth kill line is soon back on his chalkboard. In addition, he also manages to shoot down an off-screen enemy plane, which he documents simply by his eyes gradually panning down to ground (crash) level. As in most early examples of dark comedy, particularly with the "man as beast" element, the dark nature of the deed is made more palatable by *not* showing the victim.

A modest exception to this tendency occurs late in the film, when Charlie, disguised as a German officer, is on the verge of kidnapping the Kaiser back to Allied lines. Suddenly, a captured Sydney is brought into Charlie's presence, and as the prisoner starts to happily greet his comrade, the little fellow immediately starts to beat on Sydney in order to protect his cover. Though it's necessary, Charlie seems to overly enjoy roughing him up, a task he relishes repeating later even when it is not necessary. Maybe there was just something about wearing a German uniform which set him off. (During production of *The Great Dictator*, 1940, Chaplin claimed he acted more brusque, on camera and off, when attired in the quasi–Nazi uniform.)

However, of the three key themes of dark comedy, it is the sense of absurdity which surfaces most frequently in *Shoulder Arms*. Easily the most surreal of scenes occurs when Charlie goes on a secret mission behind enemy lines disguised as a tree. It was probably the signature sequence for Chaplin, too, since one of the film's working titles was *Camouflage*. Not surprisingly, it was singled out as a special highlight by many critics. For instance, *Variety*'s review stated, "His camouflage as a small tree, during which he runs through a wood to escape from a German, is one of the best and most original pieces of comedy work ever put on screen—and perhaps anywhere else."[31] The *New York Tribune* critic was in total agreement about the tree scene, and even celebrated its dark comedy elements:

> The funniest thing in the picture is where Charlie is sent as a spy behind German lines and camouflages himself as a tree. Never has anything like this been seen on the screen. He kills dozens [exaggerated] of Huns by ... letting the branch [with his arm in it] fall on their helmets.[32]

When smaller publications only had space for a pocket review of the picture, this segment was the one often accented, which is what occurred in the *Richmond Times-Dispatch* critique: "[A]s a tree stump ... he starts on a spying trip into enemy territory only to be met by a small party of Huns seeking firewood, who promptly decide to chop down the human stump...."[33]

Regardless, *Variety*'s perspective on Charlie the tree (maybe the variety called a "lancewood," since he sometimes uses his branch-arm like a poking stick) is the most spot-on about the surreal nature of the sequence. That is, instead of other publications focusing on his direct confrontation with the enemy, *Variety* keys upon his flight through the forest pursued by a single fat German soldier (Chaplin regular Henry Bergman). What gives it such a peculiarly funny tone is that Charlie is running through a real—on-location—forest, and when, in long

Chaplin's Charlie, masquerading as a German officer (center), almost has his cover blown by an American prisoner (Sydney Chaplin) in *Shoulder Arms*. Frequent Chaplin co-star Edna Purviance looks on.

shot, he assumes a tree-like pose, the audience is as mystified as Bergman's Hun as to just which trunk contains the comedian.

Other examples of dark comedy absurdity in *Shoulder Arms* would range from little fellow number 13 capturing the Kaiser, to the bombed-out building which symbolizes poor France. There he meets the beautiful peasant girl (Chaplin regular Edna Purviance) on his mission. While the first is self-explanatory, the building merits an explanation. The house is so damaged, with most of its walls gone, it only seems to be standing from force of habit. Yet the door remains intact, and Charlie, still behind enemy lines but *sans* his tree costume, always enters and exit said house by way of the entrance—though he could do his duck-walk through any wall-less side. Along similar lines, the building's second floor interior is equally open to view, excepting for part of a wall with a window and shade miraculously still standing. Incongruously, Charlie opens the window to look out of an essentially open-air second floor. Then he tops this absurdity by pulling the shade down, as if that will keep the war out and render him invisible. One is reminded of a comparable sequence in Leo McCarey's *Duck Soup* (1933), in which the Marx Brothers are caught in another war-ravaged building, and Groucho also pulls down a window blind—as if, like Charlie, he is taking the phrase literally.[34] McCarey, who had teamed and molded Laurel & Hardy in the 1920s, and later won Oscars for *The Awful Truth* (1937,

Best Director) and *Going My Way* (1944, Best Director and Story), was a longtime Chaplin fan.[35]

One final bit of *Shoulder Arms* absurdity is tied to its title cards which, as a whole, are arguably the best of Chaplin's oeuvre. Somehow, on an earlier mission into No Man's Land, the bombed-out lunar landscape–like territory between the warring trenches—a theater of absurd all its own—Charlie single-handedly brings back a platoon of enemy prisoners. When asked by an officer how he managed such a feat, he answers via a title card, "I surrounded them."

These then have been some of the seminal examples of Chaplin's groundbreaking application of dark comedy to *Shoulder Arms,* even though they are all anchored in a war which seemed to have a purpose at the time. Thus, long before Joseph Heller or Kurt Vonnegut, Chaplin helped transform an early cinema form of this genre of absurdity and the grotesque, so often spawned by conflict, into a mass-market American reflex. And perversely appropriate for dark comedy, sometimes awful things (such as World War I) can inspire an artistic gift like *Shoulder Arms.*

One cannot leave the film without documenting some traditional Chaplin touches he wove into his black humor war narrative, without necessarily being tied to armed conflict and/or the dark comedy genre. The best such routine opens the movie and follows Charlie's inability to follow drill commands involving marching, holding his rifle, and pivoting in the opposite direction, all of which are borrowed by Abbott & Costello in the basic training portion of their *Buck Privates* (1941, which opened on the eve of America's entry into World War II). However, one aspect of Charlie's shtick was non-transferable: his inability to keep those "east-west feet" pointed straight ahead, either while marching or just at ease in rank. This straight toes-feet misadventure ranks with the best of Chaplin's career laugh-out-loud filmography.

Initially, Charlie also had such comic difficulty entering the small dugout entrance, weighed down by his knapsacks, rifle, blankets, and kitchen utensils, that Sergeant Sydney literally had to push him through. Later, when duty called, Chaplin reworked a variation of this slapstick by having Charlie attempt to exit said dugout holding his rifle horizontally, and bouncing back on his keister.

In addition, *Shoulder Arms* includes a signature example of Chaplin pathos: At mail call he receives nothing. Crushed, he leaves the dugout and spots another soldier reading a letter from home. Charlie edges close behind him to read and experience the second-hand joy of being remembered. As Chaplin biographer Robert F. Moss touchingly describes the scene, "The eye movements and facial expressions of Charlie and the other soldier are as expertly synchronized as two sets of electronic scanners. It is a thumbnail sketch of truly desperate vicariousness."[36] Charlie's fleeting happiness is soon ended when the soldier senses his presence and stomps off. Eventually, out of pity Charlie is gifted with an unclaimed parcel containing the aforementioned Limburger cheese. Some gift!

Also, many of the chase sequences between Charlie and the Germans are reminiscent of earlier Chaplin short subjects, particularly when some of his regular film troupe play the enemy soldiers. The most obvious such parallel would be with *Easy Street* (1917), in which Charlie is chased by a street gang leader through a two-level cold water flat not unlike the bombed-out French house in *Shoulder Arms.* In both cases, he falsely assumes the chase is over, only to be comically hunted again.

Making Charlie's ultimately heroic war efforts a dream immediately brings to mind two other Chaplin pathos-driven pictures. First, in *The Bank* (1915), Charlie plays a janitor in love with a young stenographer (Edna again) and dreams of saving her from bank robbers ... only to wake up and find himself kissing a mop. Conversely, the *Shoulder Arms* ending is later reworked for *The Kid* (1921), when the desperate Tramp wanders the street looking for the missing boy and falls asleep dreaming of a heavenly reunion, only to have a celestial cop shoot him from the sky just after he gets his wings. As the policeman starts to pick him up, the scene switches back to reality, with a real cop shaking the Tramp to inform him the boy is okay. In the earlier *Shoulder Arms,* celebrating soldiers have lifted Charlie onto their shoulders after the little fellow catches the Kaiser, but the scene irises out and closes with affectionate soldiers shaking Charlie awake after his exhausting post-drill nap.

Finally, Chaplin periodically has Charlie smoothly moving between conflicting comic personae (bravado to comic cowardice), something later synonymous with Bob Hope and Woody Allen—both huge fans of Chaplin. With sound, Hope and Allen could accent even more this fluctuation between the most cowardly, incompetent of comic antiheroes and the cool, egotistical wise guy.[37] The phenomenon is best demonstrated in *Shoulder Arms* when Chaplin is disguised as a German officer about to kidnap the Kaiser and the leader's own command car. Waiting outside an impromptu German headquarters for the Kaiser (Sydney Chaplin in a second role), Field Marshal von Hindenburg (Henry Bergman also in another role), and the country's crown prince (Jack Wilson), a cocky, German-uniformed Charlie shows his disdain for the danger around him by brashly lighting a match for his cigarette on the polished surface of the Kaiser's car. Yet, seconds before, Charlie had jumped with startled fear twice when a platoon of nearby German soldiers routinely came to attention each time he passed.

Paradoxically, for all of Chaplin's effective mix of dark comedy and his standard shtick, maybe his greatest *Shoulder Arms* accomplishment was to *not* make the picture a rabid anti–German diatribe, like the Hun hysteria then gripping the nation, best exemplified by the aforementioned *The Kaiser, the Beast of Berlin.* Chaplin would later describe 1918 America as a dangerous period when "every thought was secondary to the religion of war."[38] While he had worked hard to help defeat Germany and the Central Powers through his bond rallies, he abhorred the vindictiveness already chronicled in this text, such as tar and feathering or even lynching people deemed less than patriotic. Ultimately, the only link *Shoulder Arms* had with the ugly anti–German propaganda film was that Charlie also captures the Kaiser, as was often the finale to these movies. Yet, even here the effect is softened, since it is only a Charlie dream.

So how did Chaplin's *Shoulder Arms* balance his dark comedy with a more reasonable look at the enemy? First, the catalyst for much of the black humor either came from Charlie himself (like being a sniper), or was simply a generic product of war, such as the flooded trenches. Second, when there was a direct dark comedy jab at the enemy, as in making the German trench commander a dwarf-sized individual, the officer's abusive actions toward his own soldiers (intermittently hitting and kicking them), even generated sympathy for the rank and file enemy, especially with their appreciation of Charlie punishing this pint-sized meanie by bending him over his knee and spanking him! (Jean Vigo would later borrow Chaplin's idea of making a small-minded authority figure equally diminutive in size in his classic 1933 picture *Zero for Conduct,* in which the principal of a French boarding school is a dwarf.) Third, as suggested earlier in reference to *Easy Street,* many of the confrontations between Charlie and the enemy are little different than any slapstick neighborhood nemesis in a Chaplin short subject. Fourth, some comic sequences with the enemy just play upon the fundamentals of funny, such as Bergman's fat German soldier getting stuck in a narrow drain culvert when he attempts to follow Charlie through this escape route.

Fifth, harkening back to softening the enemy's image to something child-like is the scene in which the Kaiser, the crown prince, and the field marshal are huddled over a battle map. One of these subordinates to the Kaiser, like a child playing with a less than focused playmate, admonishes the other, "Pay attention to the war!" Sixth, Chaplin sometimes has the Germans being dimwittedly comic to each other. For instance, when Bergman becomes stuck in the culvert, a fellow German soldier (Chaplin stock company regular Albert Austin) attempts to "help" by smacking the flat side of his axe (the one almost used to chop down Charlie the tree) against said culvert. It is funny enough that Chaplin recycled a variation of the same gag in *The Idle Class* (1921), when Charlie attempts to also "help" someone with a blunt object (banging a hammer against an inhabited suit of armor) to assist in freeing someone.

While all of these factors came together to complement the pioneering dark comedy status of *Shoulder Arms,* one final wild card further put mid–1910s viewers in the mood for a cinema service comedy: period comic strips. Most significant was British cartoonist Bruce Bairnsfather's strip character "Old Bill," a veteran English soldier with a walrus moustache and a younger troopmate, little Alphie. It was created in 1914 at the beginning of the war; by 1917 he was the centerpiece of a hit London play called *The Better 'Ole,* which came to Broadway around the time of the opening of *Shoulder Arms.* Thus, while not initially as well known to American viewers as to British fans, Old Bill still had enough stateside recognition that Sydney Chaplin reported to friends and contacts during the production of *Shoulder Arms* "that Charlie was intent on showing the humorous side of war ... [as] demonstrated by [comic] commentators such as Captain Bruce Bairnsfather...."[39]

Moreover, Sydney's walrus moustache–wearing *Shoulder Arms* character is obviously inspired by Old Bill, right down to playing the "pops" character to the young sidekick—— though naturally the focus is more on Charlie. Fittingly, Sydney would go on to play Old Bill in the later hit film *The Better 'Ole* (1926). Sydney would also have a hand in the American cartoon strip *Charlie Chaplin's Comic Capers,* syndicated from 1915 to 1917. Though Sydney was not there at its inception for the *Chicago Record-Herald and Inter-Ocean* (later the *Chicago Herald*), which was made possible by an arrangement with Chaplin's then production company Essanay, the comedian's older brother made sure the strip continued even after Chaplin moved to the Mutual Company. Unlike Old Bill, however, the Chaplin strip did not put Charlie into the European war until mid–1917. Still, of the numerous comic book compilations of recycled *Charlie Chaplin's Comic Capers,* two popular editions played upon the World War I theme with their titles and cover art. One was called *Charlie Chaplin in the Army* (1917) and featured a cartoon of him in uniform.[40] Another comic book, *Charlie Chaplin Up in the Air* (1917), had the little fellow falling from the sky surrounded by biplanes.[41]

Consequently, all the comedy stars seemed to be aligned for the critical and commercial success of *Shoulder Arms,* and the picture did not disappoint. Review after review shouted its hosannas. For example, the *New York Tribune* stated:

> Charlie Chaplin's new picture at the Strand is twice as funny and twice as long as any of his previous productions, which really makes it four times as amusing ... he is a great artist. He could, we are sure, do Hamlet as well, if he chose.[42]

A 1917 book cover of collected Charlie newspaper cartoon strips already had the Tramp in uniform, though of a more Napoleonic style.

The critique's title said it all: "Charlie Chaplin Surpassed All Former Fun Making Marks in *Shoulder Arms*."[43] Significantly, critics also noted and praised the groundbreaking darker tone to the comedy. *Variety* acknowledged:

> [H]ad Chaplin held back the subject [black humor about war] until after victory [the following month] it would have been even a bigger comedy, although one must still laugh heartily notwithstanding what the subject matter forces into memory, but it's never mournful fun. Chaplin has done his biggest and best with *Shoulder Arms*.[44]

The *New York American* observed:

> Now that Chaplin has discovered the trenches, the war may be said to have been immortalized.... The best of the picture is that it is not simply old slapstick tricks transferred to the trench background but it is Chaplin satire on the life of a soldier ... it is uproariously funny....[45]

Kenneth Macgowan's *New York Tribune* think piece on the comedian, "Charlie Chaplin and the Pure Idea," published in November 1918 shortly after the end of the war, both praises and elevates *Shoulder Arms*' tone of black humor even more, such as the critic's enjoyment of Charlie the sniper: "Chaplin makes it a ludicrously businesslike matter of aim, recall, inspect and chalk 'em up [dead]."[46] After much more general praise of the movie, Macgowan further fleshes out the importance of the picture's dark comedy:

> There is real substance in [Chaplin's] anecdotage. Much of the humors of the drenched trench strike home with disturbing reality. *Shoulder Arms* takes place in the Valhalla of veritable warcomedy, which—but for ... Bairnsfather's [comic strip turned play] *Better 'Ole*—is distressingly empty.[47]

So ended 1918, Chaplin's most acclaimed year as both a filmmaker and patriot ... or did it? The twenty-nine-year-old comedian would marry the seventeen-year-old former child

4. Shoulder Arms *and War as a Film Topic in 1918*

actress Mildred Harris on September 23; the impetus for the union was Harris' alleged pregnancy. Yet surprisingly, or maybe not so surprisingly, an additional catalyst for marriage had been planted during Chaplin's war bond tour. In the comedian's memoir, he recalls taking a respite during the Augusta leg of his seemingly non-stop rallies and befriending a fascinated man named Judge Henshaw, who had organized the local bond activities. During a most pleasant mint julep–assisted conversation, covering many topics, Henshaw eventually got around to the subject of marriage, given that Chaplin was still single. The older crackerbarrel-like judge was unattached; he said, "If I were young again I'd marry; it's lonely being a bachelor."[48]

Shotgun marriage, or not, the close proximity in Chaplin's autobiography between the judge's advice and the comedian painting a not unromantic courtship of Harris, suggest the union did not begin without some hope. Unfortunately, however, this marriage, born of a war year, would soon take on those dimensions itself. (Over time, Chaplin only seemed to fully comprehend the first part of Oscar Wilde's famous axiom about romance: "One should always be in love. That is the reason one should never marry.")

5

Moving to the Post-War 1920s

> Late in his career Chaplin closed an interview with this comment about his intensity of involvement in film comedy: "And so this thing that I've got, whatever it is, whether it's creativeness or whatever it is, I care. I really care."[1]

In 1918, the war inspired Chaplin to the critical and commercial heights with *Shoulder Arms*. If genius amounts to thinking outside the box, Chaplin was capable of comedy even outside *that* box—such as the groundbreaking black humor of his war film. Yet Chaplin's late 1918 wedding to Mildred Harris seemed to lessen the magic of his next two productions, *Sunnyside* and *A Day's Pleasure* (both 1919). Chaplin himself later observed that the unfortunate union seemed to dry up his comedy ideas.[2] *Sunnyside* mirrors the lyrical praise of the critics too closely—Chaplin even includes a dance to Pan, the Greek god of the forest. *A Day's Pleasure* finds him miscast in a domestic comedy about the frustrations of a short holiday with a wife and children (reminiscent of later W.C. Fields territory).

The failure of Chaplin's first marriage was more complicated than simply a mismatch of character types, a great artist and a child bride. One imagines conversations, when there were conversations, so awkwardly uneasy they would be triple-spaced if recorded on the printed page. Chaplin's fascination with the image of the Victorian child-woman would frequently prove disruptive to his personal professional career. The Harris marriage was merely the first chapter of a repetitive story that might be labeled "The Search for Hetty Kelly"—Kelly was a fifteen-year-old idealized beauty of Chaplin's youth who died before the comedian could establish a relationship. As critic Ricky Moody has noted, "The beloved dead girl is recurring poltergeist in American narrative art," such as Laura Palmer in David Lynch's *Twin Peaks* (1992).[3] The seemingly impossible correction to this sorry situation would be to have known the person better while she was alive. Still, Chaplin would spend years trying to excise the pain, both personally and professionally, until he met his Hetty Kelly–like fourth wife Oona O'Neill. To emphasize the comedian's eventual success in solving this "beloved dead girl" dilemma, Richard Attenborough's biography film *Chaplin* (1992) cast the same actress, Moira Kelly, as both Hetty Kelly and Oona O'Neill.

However, the lovely teenage blue-eyed blonde Harris completely captivated the comedian ... for a time. But, Chaplin's nineteenth-century romanticism was equally matched with that century's propensity for linear thought, and he was soon too involved in his work for the success of any relationship, especially when one partner is so young. Hetty's death would forever freeze her in the idealized perfection of a fairy tale Sleeping Beauty, yet prevent her from making any demands for time on the workaholic comedian; the very much alive, continued presence of Harris represented more responsibility than Chaplin was then capable of shouldering.

The marriage was also doomed by its forced nature, and then the suggestions of trickery, when Harris later proved to not be pregnant. (Her mother moving in, hardly helped the situation.) Just as Chaplin the artist was ill-prepared for marriage, so was Harris the child. Whereas the comedian entered the union already heavy of heart, Harris was like a little girl about to play house, as misguided by her own sense of romanticism as was Chaplin.

Further cracks in the marriage were provided by the loss, on July 10, 1919, of their three-day-old malformed baby, Norman Spencer Chaplin (whose grave marker bore Harris' childishly touching nickname for the youngster, "The Little Mouse"), and also by professional friction over her attempt to continue a film career. Chaplin's Victorian belief that a woman's place was in the home was hardly lessened by Louis B. Mayer's attempt to capitalize on the comedian's name when he signed Mildred Harris *Chaplin* to a large film contract. Consequently, Chaplin was soon even more livid when *Shoulder Arms* was later sometimes double-billed with his wife's work. For example a movie ad from the *New York Sun*, dated November 17, 1918, for the Broadway Theatre double-billed *Borrowed Clothes* (starring "Mrs. Charles") and *Shoulder Arms* (starring "Mr. Charles") and played up their newlywed status.

The ad began with "Just Married" and above that line were interlocking iris shots (circular photos) of each performer.[4] (Chaplin and Mayer would come to blows during a chance meeting at Los Angeles' Alexandria Hotel's restaurant in early 1920, when an "old school" Chaplin challenged the producer to a fight.) Given Chaplin's frequent Victorian tendencies, one might say living in the past was frequently the comedian's future. Of course, as this text documents, the comedian's evolving perspective on dark comedy would be the exception to that rule.

Even when Harris tried to please Chaplin, she had a tendency to upset him, such as her thoughts on *Shoulder Arms*. She praised the picture in a letter to her new husband. However, there was one note of criticism: "I did not like especially where the German shook your hand in the trenches and you accepted it…. [This] might not be liked in foreign countries."[5] (Chaplin had defended some enemy soldiers against their mean commander.) Harris' perspective reflected the rabid hatred drummed up against World War I Germany (see previous chapter), a perspective Chaplin deplored. Moreover, like many great artists, he did not take criticism kindly, especially from someone he described as "no mental heavyweight."[6]

While the marriage had been acrimonious and professionally disruptive, its dissolution was even more so—reducing the mini-scandal of the Douglas Fairbanks-Mary Pickford war bond tour to back burner status. After a separation of several months, during which time Chaplin moved back to the Los Angeles Athletic Club (where he had lived for most of his early years in filmland), Harris first made accusations about desertion which soon escalated to mental cruelty. This quickly became newspaper headline material—an ugly proceeding about which Chaplin would learn all too much in the coming years.

The observations of popular period humorists helped soften such scandal, both then and later. For example, Kin Hubbard's widely syndicated crackerbarrel character Abe Martin reported, "Mr. an' Mrs. Charley [sic] Chaplin have split up. Charley is like a whole lot o' other fellers—he kin make ever' buddy laugh but his wife."[7] Getting a comedy pass from Hubbard on the scandal was no small PR assist, given that even the celebrated Will Rogers later wrote, "No man in our generation was within a [comedy] mile of [Hubbard] … I have said it from the stage and in print for twenty years."[8] Even after Hubbard's death in 1930, comedians of the stature of W.C. Fields would sometimes "borrow" Hubbard material. For instance, one Hubbard line later recycled by Fields would even have been good advice for the eventually much married Chaplin, despite its chauvinistic slant: "Women are like elephants to me; they're nice to look at but I wouldn't want to own one."⁹ Of the several messy divorce and/or sexual scandals which would plague Chaplin's life, his career would only suffer *after* the 1940s retirement of the Tramp, when a variation of the character would last appear in the guise of the little Jewish barber in *The Great Dictator* (1940). Prior to that, the public seemed to forgive any indiscretion. One could have substituted the Tramp for the durable Model-T Ford in a popular joke of the time, in which a farmer requests he be buried in this pioneering automobile. When asked why, the farmer responds, "I've never been in a hole yet it couldn't get me out of!"

Prior to Chaplin's divorce from Harris on November 19, 1920, for which she received $100,000 (the equivalent of well over $2,000,000 today) and a share of the community property, the comedian had completed three films, the aforementioned *Sunnyside, A Day's Pleasure,* and the yet-to-be released *The Kid* (1921). While art, like life, runs in cycles, with the former two pictures representing Chaplin catching the down-ride on the Ferris wheel, *Sunnyside* still had bellwether ties to dark comedy. The earliest example of a macabre tone occurs when Charlie, a hired hand, is attempting to court the village beauty (Edna Purviance). When a local simpleton cramps his style, he blindfolds the youth, as if to play hide-and-seek, and then, with perverse gentleness, moves him to the middle of a busy road. One is reminded of a routine by Richard Pryor (a comedian whose persona critic Pauline Kael likened to a modern Charlie Tramp-street character), in which he describes the alleged gallows humor of a martinet father on the subject of punishment: "Go stand in the street while I start the car." Charlie performs this black humor task with the casualness of his *Shoulder Arms* sniper, yet there is not the patriotic excuse of being at war.

While this potential road kill example occurs early in the ironically titled *Sunnyside,* the *pièce de resistance* example of dark comedy is planted at the picture's conclusion. After Charlie has seemingly lost Edna to a city slicker passing through the village, the distraught little fellow attempts suicide by planting himself in front of an oncoming car on the same busy road where he had placed the village idiot. Artistically, he has come full circle and given a narrative reason for the opening danger of the road. Yet, once again, the apparent dramatic climax of a Chaplin film, like capturing the Kaiser in *Shoulder Arms,* turns out to be a dream. Or is it? The ending is most enigmatic. As Chaplin biographer David Robinson wrote in 1985, "In sixty-five years, critics have failed to agree whether it is the suicide itself which is the dream, or whether the happy end is itself the wish-dream of the dying suicide."¹⁰ Thus, even in a film considered one of his lesser works, Chaplin is capable of applying thought-provoked black humor in a manner decades ahead of dark comedy as the new normal.

Artistically, the up-ride on the metaphorical Ferris wheel would begin again with Chaplin's *The Kid*. Interestingly, the picture's backstory rivals the seminal film itself, from spiriting the unedited movie out of Los Angeles to Salt Lake City as a possible attachment to all of Chaplin's assets during the messy divorce from Harris, to simply the amazing discovery of its mesmerizing instant child star, Jackie Coogan (1914–1984).

Before examining the ongoing dark comedy components of *The Kid,* one needs to backtrack to Chaplin's watershed dual focus narrative *A Dog's Life* (1918). The comedian is arguably at his best when he creates a variation of himself in what is essentially a co-starring role. The relationship between Charlie and the dog Scraps in *A Dog's Life* represents a dress rehearsal for the more celebrated dual focus camaraderie between Charlie and Coogan in *The Kid.*

Chaplin's anthropomorphizing of the dog, attributing human characteristics to the animal, further demonstrates the Victorian roots of his art. Anthropomorphism reached its zenith in

Victorian Great Britain, especially in the paintings of Edwin Landseer. His most celebrated work, a stone copy of which now covers his grave, was *Old Shepherd's Chief Mourner,* which movingly details a bereaved collie with its head on his master's coffin. Paintings such as this made Landseer a nineteenth-century cultural hero among people not normally familiar with the arts, the same people who would so often be early motion picture patrons.

A more specific comparison between a Landseer canvas and Chaplin's *A Dog's Life* might be made with the painting *Dignity and Impudence,* in which a small terrier comically tries to measure up to a hunting dog. It is amusingly moving, both because it deposits the human fragility of delusions of grandeur (like the Tramp playing at being a dandy with his hat and cane) on the canine corps, and because it undercuts the trait, since the subject is, after all, merely two dogs. Still, as James Thurber later suggested, he found pooches more sensible and sane than humans, because they "tried patiently at all times to understand Man's way of life ... a sound creature in a crazy world."[11] Also, in the world according to Thurber, since dogs had been domesticated the longest of all animals, the poor things had assumed more of man's basic antiheroic fears and frustrations than any other creature. Such are the rewards(?) of being "man's best friend."

Additional links between *A Dog's Life* and *The Kid* occur when Edna Purviance's character gifts Coogan's waif with a toy dog. As Chaplin biographer Julian Smith notes:

> The toy dog, which is replaced by an angelic puppy [with wings] in the final dream sequence, also connects ... the Coogan character to Scraps. The similarities seem to have been intentional, for Chaplin posed for a still showing him sitting with Coogan in a pose similar to an earlier publicity still with Scraps.[12]

A further Scraps-Kid parallel soon occurs when the toy Scraps is taken from Coogan's character, just as the Kid will soon be taken from Charlie by the city officials. To paraphrase a frequently cited Orson Welles observation, great directors often make variations of the same movie over and over again. (Interestingly, along related lines, the cop who awakens the Tramp from his dream sequence in *The Kid* is played by the same actor, Tom Wilson, who shakes Charlie out of his dream at the close of *Shoulder Arms.*)

Yet, as poignantly funny and sad as Scraps is as a surrogate Charlie, the dual focus play is even more effective in *The Kid,* with soon-to-be child star Coogan more obviously a miniature Tramp figure. Not surprisingly, one catalyst for *The Kid* was the then four-year-old Coogan, whom Chaplin had seen perform as part of his parents' vaudeville act. The comedian acted more quickly in signing the boy than Sennett had after seeing Chaplin on stage. Still, there was some lag time, and for a short period Chaplin feared he had lost young Coogan to comedy screen rival Fatty Arbuckle. When Chaplin realized that it was the boy's *father* Arbuckle had placed under contract, he wasted no time in signing young Jackie. (Chaplin would first use Coogan in a small role in *A Day's Pleasure.*)

At their first meeting, Chaplin and Coogan are said to have played and chatted at length like two children at recess. Poignantly and paradoxically, this "play" session occurred less than two weeks after the death of Chaplin's boy Norman Spencer, and at a time when Chaplin was already, presumably with some difficulty, auditioning babies to play the Coogan character at a young age. The creative touch which had presumably abandoned him on his two previous productions, came roaring back on *The Kid*. Coupled with the fortuitous discovery of Coogan, it hardly seems coincidental that Chaplin began making a picture about rearing a baby boy shortly after losing his own. Moreover, Lita Grey further suggests the link between the comedian's loss and a great compassion for children at this time. In her memoir, besides suggesting the death of Chaplin's child ending any hope of the Harris marriage surviving, she fondly remembers the time he took with the picture's children:

> After a tense hour or two on the set ... it wasn't unusual for him to call the kids together for a game of hide-and-seek. He would play vigorously, with genuine and passionate abandon, and when he was tagged "it" his loud groan was sincere. He ... seemed to give every bit as much concentration to hide-and-seek as he did to filming his movie. We adored him because he was at once one of us and an all-knowing father.[13]

The opening for *The Kid,* involving a young unwed mother (Edna Purviance), suggests other ties to the comedian's life. That is, Purviance's character's pregnancy is the result of a liaison with an artist who abandons her. Just the year before, another artist (Chaplin) had found himself in a similar situation with Harris *but* despite his lack of real love for the young girl, he had done the proverbial "right thing" and married her. It had resulted in a train wreck of a union, but the parallels are unmistakable.

A final direct link between *The Kid* and Chaplin is suggested by Stephen Weissman's *Chaplin: A Life* (2008), a biography endorsed by the comedian's family. Keep in mind, *The Kid* opens with footage of an unwed mother and baby intercut with a still shot of Christ on the Cross—introduced by a title card stating, "The woman whose sin was motherhood." Now link these images with Chaplin's following vivid memories from childhood:

> [My mother] gave the most luminous and appealing interpretations of Christ I have ever heard or seen. She spoke of His tolerant understanding; of the woman who had sinned and was to be stoned by the mob, and of His words to them: "He that is without sin among you, let him first cast a stone at her...." As she continued, tears welled up in her eyes ... and we both wept.[14]

Moreover, given the promiscuous nature of Chaplin's mother noted earlier, Weissman makes a compelling case for the comedian's ongoing sympathetic portrayal of fallen women and/or prostitutes. Moreover, at the time Chaplin started production on *The Kid* (1919), the comedian's mother was again on his mind, because he and his brother Sydney had initially planned to bring her to America that year. (Eventually they did this in 1921.)

The Kid, Chaplin's first personally produced feature, was peppered with dark comedy, though the comedian makes it palatable by the poignant balancing act he maintains with the dual focus personality comedy of the Tramp-Kid duo. Chaplin was literally a genre-bending genius. For instance, while Charlie's first thought of what to do with the abandoned baby is simple black humor—toss it down into a sewer—the unwilling guardian of the mislaid tyke comes to lovingly raise him. And we anticipate the transition based upon a past Tramp persona anchored in nurturing. A more modern variation of this phenomenon would be a Bill Cosby theater of the real story about one of his kids being such a brat, he "was looking forward to seeing his child's picture on a milk carton [for missing kids]." The dark comedy is softened by the viewer knowing, as they did with Charlie, that the Cosby persona is inherently loving.

Arguably, *The Kid*'s best example of this constantly shifting kaleidoscope of comedy occurs in its seemingly tacked-on Heaven dream sequence, in which the mean streets of Chaplin's Dickenseque ghetto setting are transformed into a papier-mâché paradise. Yet, even here, "sin creeps in," and a less-than-dreamland cop shoots down dead an airborne Tramp just after Charlie has been fitted for his cardboard wings. Unlike the careening pin ball Keystone Cops of a Mack Sennett short, who do not even seem capable of hurting themselves, or the gullibly sweet policemen in Laurel & Hardy Land (especially Tiny Sanford in 1929's *Big Business*), the hardtack realism of a Chaplin cop is potential death ... a most fitting atmosphere for dark comedy. Plus, period *Kid* critics were aware and appreciative of Chaplin's ability to suddenly sandwich in black humor, such as the *Exceptional Photoplays*' winning description of Charlie's perverse heaven

> [where] the people fight and envy just as before, and a policeman with wings has to enforce brotherly love with his pistol! What an ingenious travesty on our easy beatitudes.[15]

The *New Republic*'s Francis Hackett even defines Chaplin's new growth as an artist via the comedian's easy assurance with dark comedy:

> Chaplin's relations to his audience may once have been deferential. Now he is an artist who uses his medium as he wills. When he opens the sewer-trap and debates whether to slip the baby into it, he gains the credence which is only won by complete expressiveness.[16]

The phenomenal critical and commercial success of *The Kid* (second at the 1921 box office to *The Four Horsemen of the Apocalypse*) also has a subtextual link to the somber dark comedy of *Shoulder Arms*. Chaplin was convinced that the universal appeal of the world's first true child star, Jackie Coogan, went beyond the youngster's brilliant talent, as amazing as he was in the title role. Chaplin felt Jackie's poignant character also functioned as a "symbol of all the orphans of the recent war"—a global catharsis which the world needed.[17] (This perspective was reinforced in 1924, when Coogan was the centerpiece of a world "Children's Crusade" which raised more than a million dollars' worth of aid for a still destitute post–World War I Europe.) War orphan–related poignancy and/or artistic expression of personal grief *à la* the 1992 Eric Clapton song "Tears in Heaven" (about the death of his young son), *The Kid* was certainly a celebration of children, as poet Carl Sandburg wrote in a Chaplin article the year of the film's release:

> I have heard children four or five years old bubble and ripple with laughter in the course of a Chaplin film. They answer to the child in him. *The Kid* is a masterpiece of love for the child heart—love and understanding.[18]

Chaplin and little Jackie Coogan, a symbol for World War I orphans in *The Kid*.

Paradoxically, from a historical perspective, I find the most provocative child-related scene in *The Kid* does not even involve Coogan. The sequence occurs just after Purviance's character has had a great success on the stage but is still searching for the child (Coogan) she had reluctantly given up. One of her fans has sent a large congratulatory wreath of flowers to her dressing room, and it is delivered by the cutest bellhop-like uniformed black youngster. His acting is entertainingly natural in this brief scene, especially his smiling pleasure at receiving a large tip. Besides being a narrative reminder of the lost child for which Purviance would immediately trade any theatrical glory, African-American performers were just not seen in mainstream movies of that era. If such an ethnic part was called for, it was invariably derogatory in nature, and was played by a Caucasian in black face, *à la Birth of a Nation* (1915). Such racist traditions would be the norm during the silent era, be it the joke at the expense of a black mother and baby in Harold Lloyd's *The Freshman* (1925), or Buster Keaton actually appearing in blackface for the sake of another joke in *College* (1927).

The forever liberal Chaplin was colorblind along racial lines, and never stooped to such racist period tendencies. Thus, the aforementioned scene with the young flower-delivering youngster simply playing a part instead of a joke remains refreshingly modern today. Sadly, it is quite possible that the short sequence was later deleted by Southern state censors, which was the norm well into the 1940s. Regardless, the seeming incongruity of Chaplin's fascination with *Birth of a Nation* is easily explained away by a basic truism penned by Griffith's definitive biographer, Richard Schickel: "[I]f our century has taught us anything it is that high artistic vision does not necessarily correlate with a similarly elevated social vision."[19] That is, Chaplin was inspired by Griffith's technique, while abhorring his racism. Thus, *The Kid* showcases both racial tolerance while still footnoting a central artistic scene from the first half of *Birth of a Nation*. That is, when the Little Colonel (Henry B. Walthall) returns from the Civil War, the *mise-en-scène* of a family-laden doorway symbolizes literally an embrace from hearth and home not unlike a similar cinematic closure to *The Kid*. Chaplin's Tramp is ushered to the doorway of a pleasantly oversized bungalow. The door opens and the Kid and his biological mother (Purviance), now reunited, welcome Charlie to a new home and life in a manner reminiscent of Griffith's starting-over signature scene from *Birth*.

Chaplin, moreover, was obviously aware of the still lingering racism during his Southern bond tour. The newspaper coverage of his patriotic march across a less than new Dixie also regularly reported both ugly acts of vigilante violence and the return engagements of the still passionately praised *Birth of a Nation*, three years after its initial release (see chapter 3). One would assume Chaplin also had to deal with segregated audiences during said tour, though the comedian made every effort to meet with African-American groups, too. For example, the front page coverage of his Memphis visit in the city's *Commerce-Appeal* (April 20, 1918) had the comedian leading a rally in Overton Park at 4 p.m. after which "Chaplin will speak to the negroes of Memphis at Church's Park at 6 p.m. He will be introduced by Roscoe C. Simmons, an energetic Liberty Loan worker among the negroes."[20]

Given Chaplin's established sensitivity to inequality—what else would one expect of the man who created the underdog Tramp?—the racial content of *The Kid* has to also be placed in a historical context. World War I labor shortages had resulted in several hundred thousand African-Americans moving from the South to northern industrial centers. Seeming opportunity was soured by being forced to live in segregated slums, not to mention being the object of further racial hatred fueled by unskilled laborers resentful of blacks competing for jobs. Even more significantly, an increasing number of African Americans, educated by the experience of military service, the war's avowedly democratic aims, and by the inequities they met in the North, began to demand the rights long denied them.... Yet while supremacists were determined to keep the Negro in their place.... Turning to terrorism, lynch mobs in the South made victims of more than seventy Negroes in 1919, ten of them veterans in uniforms.[21]

In addition to these factors, Chaplin's newest critical champion, poet Carl Sandburg, wrote an acclaimed series of articles on the Chicago race riots of 1919 (a year in which twenty-five major riots occurred across the country). "Published as *Chicago Race Riots: July 1919* [in which thirty-eight people died], the work was praised by a contemporary critic as a 'serious and intelligent investigation into conditions which made the race riots possible.'"[22] The tragedy also resulted in two powerful Sandburg poems about lynching, "Man, the Man-Hunter" and "I Should Like to Be Hanged on a Summer Afternoon"; the latter went unpublished during the poet's lifetime. This was the 1919 backdrop in which Chaplin broke precedent by casting a sympathetic young black character in *The Kid*. For this writer, such a brave action was as war-relatedly relevant to the significance of the movie as the aforementioned Coogan–war orphans phenomenon.

As if 1919 had not been busy enough, from movies to marriage to social unrest, Chaplin had become one of the founding members, with Douglas Fairbanks, Mary Pickford, and D.W. Griffith, of a new distribution company appropriately called United Artists. Once again, just as the bond tour had impacted Chaplin in so many ways, it was also a factor in the formation of United Artists. When Chaplin and company had met Oscar Price, the press agent for Secretary of the Treasury William Gibbs McAdoo in the capital, Price had suggested how much more lucrative it would be for the artists if they banded together and distributed their own pictures. With strong encouragement and leg work from Sydney Chaplin, United Artists would soon come into existence.

Ironically for Chaplin, however, he still had contractual obligations with First National Films for three additional pictures, which ultimately resulted in *The Idle Class* (1921), *Pay Day*, and *The Pilgrim* (both 1922). Between *The Idle Class* and the latter two films, Chaplin, with customary impulsiveness, decided to make a homecoming visit to England. Though the recently finished *Idle Class* was yet to be released, and he had begun production on *Pay Day*, as well as pre-production work on a never-realized film about wealthy plumbers, Chaplin suddenly felt himself in need of a holiday.

There was at least one additional factor in his decision to visit England, but it varies depending upon which of the comedian's books is consulted. In *My Trip Abroad* (1922) he mentions having received a cablegram from London noting the upcoming premiere of the already celebrated *The Kid* and suggesting this to be an opportune time for a return visit, one Chaplin had been promising himself for a year.[23] *My Autobiography* (1964) points toward an "insatiable desire" to return to England which had been growing throughout the summer of 1921.[24] His nostalgia was also heightened by letters he had received during this time from H.G. Wells, with whom he would stay for a portion of his visit.

Regardless of just what the inspiration was, Chaplin closed down his current production and made travel arrangements almost immediately, leaving the film capital the following evening. The quick exit, forever linked with Sydney Chaplin's parting instructions to a member of his brother's party, "For God's sake, don't let him get married," reveals more than an impulsive nature—it shows someone who enjoyed surprising people. Chaplin underlined this in *My Trip*

Abroad when he observed, "Everyone was shocked [by my quick departure]. I was glad of it. I wanted to shock everyone."[25] Such a tendency is at the heart of dark comedy. Is it any wonder that an artist with this predisposition would be a cinema pioneer of the genre? Throughout his life he enjoyed saying and doing the controversial. Though this "keep them guessing" trait would soon be as much associated with his political comments as his dark comedy, the pleasure he derived from jolting people with his sudden 1921 departure for Europe is commentary enough on what a basic Chaplin component this was. Neither dark comedy nor artists of the genre like Chaplin have any understanding of what it is to dial it down a notch. The comedian would have been in total agreement with a signature line from the later dark comedy *Heathers* (1989): "The extreme always seems to make an impression."

One of the best examples of an early shocking Chaplin political comment occurred on his 1921 trip, before he even left the United States. Upon arriving in New York he was asked by a reporter whether he was a Bolshevik. His reply was the provocative, "I am an artist. I am interested in life. Bolshevism is a new phase of life. I must be interested in it."[26] Chaplin's comment came little more than a year after the Red scare in late 1919 and 1920, when U.S. Attorney General A. Mitchell Palmer took it upon himself to conduct his own witch-hunting campaign against an almost entirely imagined domestic threat (foreshadowing the McCarthy Era). Yet Chaplin, for all the trouble this might have caused him, most certainly was playing for effect. In fact, only the day before, upon his arrival in Chicago, he had answered no to the very same question from the press.[27] As it was, with Chaplin's embarking, many Americans believed the comedian was a Bolshevik and was traveling to the Soviet Union.

Regardless, there was much about his visit to Europe which still resonated about World War I. The trip convinced him of the aforementioned Coogan–war orphan connection to the immense popularity of *The Kid*. And while this was the Chaplin movie of the moment, the groundbreaking dark comedy *Shoulder Arms* was still being praised, and even continued to play in some venues. (This ongoing interest in *Shoulder Arms* possibly contributed to its elaborate New York revival in 1922, complete with program notes and a full "grand orchestra."[28]) Moreover, the crowds that turned out to greet Chaplin in London and Paris reached such frightening proportions, one newspaper could only describe it in a war-related headline, "Homecoming of Comedian to Rival Armistice Day."[29]

A comic side to Chaplin's European visit might have further fueled a basic component of his later black humor: absurdity. For example, in one three-day period in London he received 73,000 pieces of mail; nearly 700 people claimed to be related, and nine imaginative women alleged that they were his long-lost mother, all of them asserting that little Chaplin was stolen away as a baby.[30] Not surprisingly, most of the "relations" were requesting financial assistance. Film theorist and Chaplin aficionado André Bazin has labeled the ability of an artist to bring personal reality (however absurd) to his work as an "example of transposed autobiography."[31] In Chaplin's case the application of the phenomenon seems to have been a major element of his success. Fittingly, the picture Chaplin completed upon his return to America, *Pay Day*, which depicted him as a hen pecked husband, obviously reflected both the lingering absurdity of the media-circus which surrounded his recent divorce, as well as the sudden Chaplin "family" which surfaced in Europe.

Yet if there was to be any absurdity factor in his art inspired by the craziness of the European trip, it appeared in Chaplin's inspired conclusion to his final First National obligation: *The Pilgrim*. But even prior to this finale, the picture had been given a dark comedy moniker by way of Charlie playing an escaped convict masquerading as a minister. Though hardly black humor territory today, it was provocative enough then to result in the picture being banned by Pennsylvania censors. Regardless, the absurd scene in question involves a benevolent sheriff (Tom Murray), aware of Charlie's background, allowing the pretend pastor to escape after the Tramp has redeemed himself. Taking his prisoner to the Texas-Mexico border, the marshal orders Charlie to pick some flowers across the border ... and a gift of freedom. Yet, the naively honest Tramp picks a bouquet *and* brings it back to the incredulous sheriff. Since subtlety is lost on Charlie, the marshal literally kicks him across the border.

Though the freedom factor finally dawns upon the little fellow, he is immediately blindsided by several Mexican bandits suddenly materializing out of the sagebrush and engaging in a gun battle. Thus, Charlie is confronted with a dilemma: Mexican freedom and the possibility of being collateral damage versus potential arrest in the United States. The Tramp does

Even before the border conclusion of *The Pilgrim*, Chaplin's character found many reasons to be surprised.

a running two-step along the border between the countries, straddling the boundary with one foot on either side. Chaplin biographer Theodore Huff noted, "In this humorous and eloquent ending some have seen a symbol of the eternal pilgrim on the tragic roads of the world."[32] Moreover, this arbitrary man-made invisible line also doubles as a darkly comic commentary on the human condition. As cartoonist Walt Kelly's (1913–1973) most famous creation, Pogo, so insightfully stated, "We have met the enemy and he is us."

Charlie facing conflicting dangers waddling along the Mexican-U.S. border was certainly the inspiration for Jean Renoir's pivotal black humor close to his anti-war film about the First World War, *Grand Illusion* (1937), whose very title tells the ironic story of most conflicts. Renoir's finale follows two escaping prisoners of war as the rifle fire from their German pursuers suddenly stops when the duo crosses another arbitrary boundary: the border between Germany and neutral Switzerland. Talk about the human absurdity of war *games?*! Fittingly, as with so many other World War I veterans, Renoir's service had been made more palatable by Chaplin. Indeed, in Renoir's memoir, he states:

> I saw every film of his that was shown in Paris again and again, and my love of him did not grow less [over the years]. The master of masters, the film-maker of film-makers, for me is still Charlie Chaplin. He has done everything in his films—script, direction, setting, production, performance and even the music. We are far removed [in talent] from that sliced melon [genius].[33]

Naturally, Chaplin's influence is also prominently cited in Renoir's *Grand Illusion* chapter.[34] Moreover, coming full circle back to *The Pilgrim*, one could apply an observation by critic-historian Leo Braudy about the ambiguity of *Grand Illusion*'s close which is equally applicable to Chaplin's picture. The films "are inconclusive statements about the nature of society, because there is no clear future indicated for the characters."³⁵ Ambiguity is at the heart of both filmmakers' realism, which also parallels the naked truth (reality) of dark comedy: "The message is, there isn't any message." Ultimately, black humor tries to be honest—life's a bitch and then you die. In movie terms, life's a rough cut, with no chance at a polished final print.

Speaking of these various arbitrary boundaries and equally arbitrary rules of nations reminds me of my own ethnic heritage and an axiom I was made well aware of as a child: "To be Irish is to know that sooner or later the world will break your heart." Dark comedy essentially appropriates that maxim as, "To be *human* is to know that sooner or later the world will break your heart."

The release of *The Pilgrim* completed Chaplin's ties to First National Films, and allowed him to finally contribute to the coffers of United Artists—that revolutionary new studio of independent artists—satirically described around Hollywood as the place "where the inmates [actors] were running the asylum." Ironically, given his United Artists partners' anxiousness over Chaplin contributing a box office smash to their risky enterprise, the comedian's first project had them feeling like maybe he *needed* to be in an asylum. The time was the fall of 1922 (United Artists was created in early 1919), and the world's biggest cinema star (Chaplin) "decided to scratch a long-standing itch and direct a movie in which he would not appear."³⁶ What's more, the planet's funniest funnyman was making a drama! This would be the perfect time to repeat the aforementioned Chaplin mantra, "I wanted to shock everyone."

However, the good news for this study is that the picture, *A Woman of Paris* (1923), is a satirically ironic romance with dark comedy overtones. And as referenced earlier with Bazin, while Chaplin has not been an autobiographical filmmaker in the strictest sense, certain themes and patterns in his movies more or less parallel the trajectory of his life. For instance,

Peggy Hopkins Joyce, pictured here in the later film *International House* (1933), was a major factor behind the making of *A Woman of Paris*.

Chaplin had just returned from Europe, where he both examined and partook of sophisticated Parisian society. He was also then involved in a brief but intense lust affair with Peggy Hopkins Joyce, the woman who first inspired the term "gold digger." Joyce married and lucratively discarded millionaire husbands like some women cut coupons. Yet despite her flamboyant costumes and exotic ways, Joyce also played at being a simple country girl ... while she regaled Chaplin with the legion of broken hearts and even suicides her cavalier attitude towards love had recently caused around the French capital. Now add to this picture Chaplin's desire to launch his longtime leading lady and former mistress Edna Purviance into an independent dramatic career—because both their professional and private lives had reached an impasse—and one had the foundation for making *A Woman of Paris*.

The dramatic film stars Purviance as Maria, a French girl living with a controlling father in a village outside Paris. With her boyfriend Jean (Carl Miller) she plans an elopement to the capital, yet the sudden death of his father makes Jean a no-show at the train depot; Maria leaves anyway. Within a year she has become the mistress of the wealthy, sophisticated Parisian Pierre Revel (Adolphe Menjou, in a career-making role). Unhappy in her situation, Maria, by chance, meets Miller in Paris. He is now a struggling artist living with his mother, and Maria has commissioned a portrait of herself. Naturally, Maria and Jean again fall in love and make wedding plans ... until Maria overhears her lover telling his mother he is not serious about the proposal. Angry, Maria returns to the worldly Revel, refusing to see Jean, who proves he really was serious about marriage by committing suicide.

Jean's mother plans revenge, but when she discovers a distraught Maria weeping over her son's body, the women reconcile and return to the country. In a masterful close, Maria is seen caring for a child in the back of a haywagon. An expensive town car speeds by, carrying Revel and his manservant—with neither Maria nor Revel aware of the other. Revel's secretary-assistant randomly asks whatever became of Maria, and Revel provides an uninterested shrug.

So where is the comedy, dark or otherwise, in *A Woman of Paris?* Chaplin was fond of an axiom which, paraphrased, reads, "Life is a tragedy in close-up, and a comedy in long shot." In other words, the inherent comic absurdity of the human condition. The ironic restrained details of the picture essentially "introduced the comedy of manners to the screen, and showcased how to circumvent the censors by subtleties and laconic touches."[37] It is the gift for showing *little* of a physical object but revealing *much* about a character or characters by so doing. The signature *Woman of Paris* example of this phenomenon was how Chaplin got across to audiences during a censorship era that Maria was Revel's mistress. He comes to her very upscale apartment and is admitted by a maid. Who is this stranger to her? A man who appears to be a date for dinner casually pours himself a drink from the liquor cabinet, and then just as casually enters her bedroom, where Maria, is still primping. With neither party paying attention to the other, Revel nonchalantly pulls a handkerchief from a bureau and exits the room. With that subtle touch, the viewer knows she is a kept woman. On a broader, darkly comic scale, there is another Maria-Revel scene in which she attempts to demonstrate how little his expensive pay-for-sex gifts means to her by tossing a diamond necklace out the window. Yet, when it seems likely a tramp will pick it up, she asks Revel to retrieve the jewelry. When he calmly ignores her, Maria dashes to get the necklace. Revel is amused by the power of money for sexual pleasure. Yet, his man-as-beast nature is best demonstrated at the picture's close, when he reveals how little Maria's existence ever meant to him.

Fittingly, the director now most associated with this provocative light touch, Ernst

78   Chaplin's War Trilogy

Lubitsch (1892–1947), was bowled over by the picture. Lubitsch biographer Herman G. Weinberg described *A Woman of Paris*' influence: "[Lubitsch] learned from it how to utilize in the domain of comedy the allusive art of nuances and subtle indications."[38] At the time, Lubitsch told the *New York Times,* "I like [Chaplin's film] because I feel that an intelligent man speaks to me and nobody's intelligence is insulted in the picture."[39] In retrospect, Lubitsch's special assistant Henry Blanke later added, "[The film] influenced Lubitsch's entire life from then on

Ernst Lubitsch (in the well), with Chaplin to the left, athletic Fairbanks on top, and Mary Pickford.

... from being very spectacular [with] big crowds ... he became very simple, and discovered wonderful American actors that he picked himself."[40]

Pivotal Soviet film artists were equally impressed by *A Woman of Paris*. For example, "To Eisenstein [soon to give the world his montage masterpiece *Potemkin*, 1925], *Paris* was the most remarkable production of the motion pictures up to that time. He found it to be highly significant in its power to stimulate."[41] In Eisenstein's later theoretical writing, he applied *A Woman of Paris*' much praised minimalism to Chaplin's Tramp, too, by way of quoting actor George Arliss: "The art of restraint and suggestion on the screen may any time be studied by watching the acting of the inimitable Charlie Chaplin."[42] Soviet Futurist and poet of the revolution, Vladimir Mayakovsky, said the film's "'organization of simple little facts' leading to the 'greatest emotion saturation' signaled a new storytelling and cultural sophistication."[43] The opinion of the global film community might have best been summed up by the critic of Britain's *Manchester Guardian*, who called *A Woman of Paris* "the greatest modern story that the screen has yet seen...."[44]

There was a downside to all these hosannas. The general public was not interested in a sophisticated drama-farce, with dark comedy overtones. Chaplin had been afraid of this development, and had even prepared a special program note for the October 1, 1923, New York premiere of this picture, almost nervously noting *Paris*' more somber tone. Though considered a box office failure, worldwide it would generate a slight profit. Nevertheless, Chaplin would quickly withdraw the picture from circulation and it would be lost to the general public for over fifty years.

A less immediate disappointment for *Paris* was its failure to launch Purviance's career as a dramatic actress. Chaplin's relationship with his former lover and co-star of 35 films (the majority of which were short subjects, including the comedian's Liberty Bond drive split-reel *The Bond*, 1918) was nearly over. The qualifier is Chaplin producing one final Purviance picture to jump-start things by starring her in *The Sea Gull* (1926), later given a title similar to *A Woman of Paris*: *A Woman of the Sea*. Written and directed by Josef von Sternberg, prior to his signature 1930s screen successes with Marlene Dietrich, *The Sea Gull* has become a mystery film. Chaplin never released the picture, and later had the print destroyed, a rather extreme measure for an artist who seemingly saved everything he shot, including his own unused footage. Many theories exist as to why *The Sea Gull* was jettisoned, ranging from Chaplin's jealousy at its greatness, to the comedian questioning the quality of the movie and/or Purviance's performance. The first explanation is ludicrous, especially since Chaplin had just released arguably his greatest film, *The Gold Rush* (1925), the previous year—*the* picture for which he always said he wished to be remembered. The latter perspective has more credence, given that von Sternberg was just beginning, and Purviance's inactivity since *Paris*, mixed with a drinking problem, had made *Sea Gull* a challenging shoot. Still, in von Sternberg's whimsically entitled memoir *Fun in a Chinese Laundry* (1965), he praises the actress' performance.[45] That it was a lesser picture is also given more credence by Chaplin allegedly telling someone privately (no name is ever attached) that the movie was merely not good enough.[46] Unlike Menjou's character in *Paris*, Chaplin continued to care about his mistress, whom he had once affectionately kidded as having an unpronounceable name and suggested she should change it to Edna Pollolobus. Though she never worked for Chaplin again, she remained on his payroll until her 1958 death, well over thirty years.

As sometimes happens, when a groundbreaking picture like *Paris* is not fully appreciated by the general public, the artist's next effort is a commercial smash. Examples would include Keaton's classic *The General* (1926, a misunderstood, darkly comic reaffirmation parody), followed by a popular mainstream comedy, *College* (1927), or the Marx Brothers' seminal dark comedy *Duck Soup* (1933, another commercial disappointment) followed by the cash cow *A Night at the Opera* (1935). The iconic HOLLYWOODLAND sign, which was created the same year (1923) as *A Woman of Paris*, might just as well have had stenciled on its backside, "You're only as good as your last picture." Yet, while Keaton and the Marxes had to compromise artistically for their comeback pictures, Chaplin merely had to return to what he did best—The Tramp.[47]

Chaplin's first picture after *Paris* was the aforementioned *Gold Rush*, which had the perfect title to describe how audiences responded at the box office. During a time when ticket prices were well under a quarter, it grossed over $4,500,000, or $100,000,000-plus in today's dollars. When the change in ticket prices is factored in, the gross jumps to *several* hundred million dollars.[48] *The Gold Rush* was the most commercially successful comedy film in the history of silent cinema, as well as being Chaplin's most critically acclaimed. *Variety* called it "the greatest and most elaborate comedy ever filmed ... [transcending] everything that has ever gone before in comedy production...."[49] And the *New York Times* said it was "the outstanding gem of all Chaplin's pictures ... [with] more originality than even such masterpieces as *The Kid* and *Shoulder Arms*."[50]

The movie's pivotal importance in this text is that, after the book's focus war trilogy, *The Gold Rush* represents Chaplin's most frequent and creative depictions of dark comedy. As briefly noted in Chapter 1, the very inspiration for the film was cannibalism—American pioneer style. Moreover, of equal importance, the tone of the *Gold Rush* black humor begins to change, working towards the harsher indictment of humanity to be found in *The Great Dictator* (1940) and *Monsieur Verdoux* (1947). That is, in *Shoulder Arms* Charlie the soldier, for the most part, found dark comedy in situations *expected* on the World War I Western Front, from constant shelling to the wet and/or flooded trenches. In contrast, wagon train pilgrims *never* counted cannibalism as one of the basic dangers of heading west. In his memoir, Chaplin notes reading a book about the Donner Party settlers snowbound in the Sierra Nevadas, who resorted to this grisly tactic to survive.[51] The same passage notes these homesteaders cooking their moccasins for food. Consequently, and paradoxically, a comic highlight of *The Gold Rush* finds starving Charlie and Big Jim McKay (Mack Swain) snowbound in the Yukon, with the latter prospector having designs on eating the Tramp. Though McKay's perspective is softened by periodically seeing his hallucinated image of Charlie as a giant chicken ... it is still humor anchored in cannibalism.

In more dark comedy homage to Chaplin's Donner research, another memorable sequence has Charlie boiling his boot for the most unconventional of holiday dinners. Ironic metamorphism includes shoelaces eaten as so much spaghetti, and boot nails doubling as wish bones. To underline the black humor realism inherent to the *Gold Rush* world, Charlie's new bootless foot is wrapped in rags for the remainder of the movie. One could count a similar ongoing reminder of an ugly genre environment in film noir's *Chinatown* (1974), in which nosy detective Jack Nicholson has his schnozzle sliced, necessitating he wear a comic collage of bandages for much of the movie.

Befitting the fundamentals of dark comedy, Chaplin is that rare personality comedian whose stories are comfortable with including death, or the threat thereof. In *The Gold Rush*,

Big Jim (Mack Swain) hunts Charlie for supper in *The Gold Rush*.

Black Larson (Tom Murray), the owner of the snowbound cabin in which Charlie and Big Jim find shelter, will later shoot and kill two Canadian Mounties. Larson also makes no attempt to get food back to Charlie and Big Jim, even though he was the one designated to go for help. Thus, Larson is a solid example of the genre's "man as beast" component. Of course, other than Charlie, there are few *Gold Rush* characters who are not self-centered. Even Big Jim only has time for the Tramp when it is in his own interests.

From a historical criticism perspective, Erich von Stroheim's epic drama *Greed* (1924), released the year prior to *The Gold Rush,* is a one-word Rosetta Stone to why the cast of Chaplin's film would seem to prove Darwin wrong: Have these people really evolved from animals? Their mining town greed for gold showcases so directly the thin veneer of civilization which separates us from the beasts. Of equal time capsule interest is another period picture which also speaks to *The Gold Rush,* but from both the setting and the fundamental goodness of Charlie: Robert Flaherty's pioneering documentary *Nanook of the North* (1922). A huge commercial hit, it chronicled the life and challenging times of the Eskimo title character and his family in the frozen white north of Canada's Hudson Bay area. Like *The Gold Rush*'s Charlie, Nanook is a charismatic figure in a harsh landscape more entertainingly interested in the joys of basic survival than self-centered inhumanity to his fellow man. Though never acknowledged as such, the blockbuster critical and commercial success of *Nanook* (pop culture items capitalizing on the documentary even included the "Eskimo Pie" dessert) might also have been a subliminal catalyst for Chaplin placing Charlie in a world of white. Though the comedian never mentioned the connection, period comics recognized the obvious link. For instance, Will Rogers called *The Gold Rush* a "snow picture," with Charlie being "as busy as an Eskimo trying to keep warm with a Palm Beach suit on."[52] Moreover, the joke's summer suit reference in that top-of-the-world frozen setting produces humor theory's perfect example of comic incongruity: an urban misfit Tramp shuffling along a glacier. Plus, we have come back full circle to dark comedy. What is the life expectancy of the Tramp in his worn thin and tattered signature costume in Eskimo land?

Continuing with the basic dark comedy components of *The Gold Rush*, one should examine a key scene seldom mentioned in chronicles of the film: Black Larson and Big Jim fighting over the life-and-death control of a large shotgun. As their clash takes them to every nook and cranny of the cabin, the weapon's barrel is constantly moving—up and down and all around. The black humor comes from the fact that no matter where Charlie moves, the long barrel is *forever* pointed at him. Chaplin's inspired choreography of this trio's movement makes Ingmar Bergman's dance of death at the conclusion of the rightfully celebrated *The Seventh Seal* (1957) seem like so much child's play. What better demonstrates one of black humor's pivotal elements—the constant presence of death—than this *Gold Rush* sequence! (It also anticipates the aborted shell which forever points Charlie's way in *The Great Dictator*.)

Near the film's end, a storm in the night has blown Charlie and Big Jim's cabin halfway off a high cliff. They wake up unaware of their precarious position; the "thrill comedy" which follows is based upon the teeter-totter–like effect produced by their random movements about the cabin. Initially blaming their uneven gait upon alcohol from the evening before, the men soon realize their danger. As *Variety* noted, this black humor balancing act and their struggles to escape before the cabin goes over the cliff provided "more than a [film] reel of solid laughs that do not cease until [they are safe]."[53] Besides showcasing a fundamental component of dark comedy—laughter from death, or its possibility—another of the genre's basics, man as beast, is present, too. Big Jim is most interested in rescuing himself. Once safe, saving Charlie is an afterthought.

In his movies, Chaplin's timing was impeccable; in his private life, it was the opposite. As with his messy marriage to Mildred Harris, during *Gold Rush* production the comedian would metaphorically crash and burn in his next union, to teenage Lita Grey, the girl who fittingly played "temptation" in the dream sequence from *The Kid*. One should remember how that dream-nightmare ended: a flying-high Charlie is shot down dead. Grey was originally cast in *The Gold Rush* as the saloon girl love interest Georgia (ultimately played by Georgia Hale); early in the production, Grey became pregnant and Chaplin found himself in another shotgun marriage. On-location in Nevada's snow-covered mountains, which doubled as Alaska's Chilkout Pass (more connection to the documentary *Nanook?*), the production soon switched to a studio Klondike, after a quickie Mexico marriage on November 24, 1924, to Grey.

This union eliminated a full-blown scandal, though there were snickering comments privately and publicly about the incident and age difference (nineteen years), especially after a Los Angeles court order that the new Mrs. Chaplin was still too young to drop out of school. Yet it was not a career-threatening scenario, with folksy man-of-the-people humorist Will

Rogers putting it all into defusing comic perspective: "This girl don't need to go to school. Any girl smart enough to marry Charlie Chaplin should be lecturing at Vassar College on 'Taking advantage of your opportunities.'"[54] Yet the eventual happy ending of Chaplin's greatest professional triumph, *The Gold Rush,* would soon (1927) be followed by a long, scandalous divorce from Lita Grey. Because the action followed the famous film, Grey's lawyer (her uncle, Edwin McMurray) was able to obtain the then largest divorce settlement in history, $625,000. The proceedings became known as the second "Gold Rush."

Several items increased the sensationalism of the case. First and foremost was a 42-page divorce complaint which "extended sensationally from 'cruel and inhuman treatment' and infidelity to every sin she, or her legal advisers, cared to devise."[55] There was no denying Chaplin was an often difficult, often contradictory person with whom to live. Yet at the same time there was little denying that her divorce "brief" was, in the language of the streets through which she and McMurray dragged it, a hatchet job. Even Grey, in her much later memoir, was moved to confess the document went beyond "just asking for support. I was smearing Charlie's name, maybe beyond repair."[56] The atypical nature of the divorce complaint was further accented when within two days of its January 1927 submission to the court, some enterprising duplicating insider turned it into an underground Los Angeles bestseller.

Chaplin was the target of countless newspaper attacks, though even then there were many who felt the case to be rather one-sided. Probably the most celebrated observation to come out of the situation was that of acid-tongued humorist H.L. Mencken: "The very morons who worshipped Charlie Chaplin six weeks ago now prepare to dance around the stake while he is burned; he is learning something of the psychology of the mob."[57] A cynic like Mencken could hardly be expected to celebrate Chaplin's romantically sentimental art. His defense of Chaplin allowed him another shot at the people, of whom he had a low view and whom he often labeled "homo boobiens."

Mencken's comments anticipate the message of Nathanael West's novel *The Day of the Locust* (1939), a once obscure book now routinely included among the best English-language novels of the 20th century. B-movie scriptwriter West put together a cast of Hollywood outcasts who want what the cinema stars seem to have—fulfillment. Yet, as stated by Mencken, they are just as happy to periodically destroy movie gods as to worship them—thus the use of *Locust* in the title. West's book ends with a riot at a film premiere.

The love-hate trajectory of Mencken's "homo boobiens" might be further fleshed out by noting a comment associated with the aptly named movie whose production was interrupted by the ugly Grey divorce: Chaplin's *The Circus* (1928). After all the scandalous hullabaloo associated with their parting, the finished film proved another huge critical and commercial success. Alexander Woollcott, critic and commentator for *The New Yorker* and normally not a movie fan, noted the irony in the picture's production being delayed by what he vaguely recalled as the "witless clumsiness ... of our civilization, someone (a wife I think it was ...) was actually permitted to have the law on Chaplin as though he were ... not such a bearer of healing laughter as the world had never known."[58] Besides being an inspired dissection of the inherent "locus" nature of so many "fans," it was fittingly uttered by a raconteur whose many quotes included his description of Hollywood as "Seven suburbs in search of a city." Nathanael West could not have said it better. In 1942, an appreciative Chaplin would later dedicate the reissued, re-edited *The Gold Rush* to Woollcott.

With *The Circus*, Chaplin was still fascinated with dark comedy. Indeed, his initial idea for a new picture was an adaptation of Robert Louis Stevenson's *The Club of Suicides*. This was a collection of three 19th-century detective short stories, set in London and Paris, which dovetail into a single tale about the investigation of a suicide club. It represents just the sort of macabre Victorian material to which Chaplin was drawn and was addressed in this book's Chapter 1. However, after *The Gold Rush* made Chaplin the darling of the critics with comparisons to such great stage clowns as Grock and Grimaldi, it only seems natural he would gravitate to a subject like the circus. Though Chaplin hardly mentions the picture in his memoir, it is understandable given the painful period through which he was then going, including the Grey divorce, his nervous breakdown, the death of his mother (1865–1928), whom he had relocated to California in 1921, and a fire which destroyed the initial *Circus* sets. Though not his greatest film, and suffering from being produced between his two most acclaimed pictures *The Gold Rush* and *City Lights* (1921), *The Circus* is arguably his funniest film (*no* small accomplishment!), with a lineage often tied to the more broad comedy of his best short subjects of the 1910s.

Before we wring the dark comedy components out of *The Circus*, one might pause to note that later students of black humor and/or theater of the absurd often used signature items of Charlie's Tramp costume as defining touchstones or symbols of their own depictions of the genre—an immediate communication to the modern audience's senses. For example, in J.L. Styan's book *The Dark Comedy*, he discusses the potential meaning behind Samuel Beckett's attiring his *Waiting for Godot* duo with bowler hats:

> The bowlers not only transform the actor, again like a comic mask, but also give him a second [mask], a bizarre tongue, as they have done for ... Chaplin.... The language of the bowlers is extensive. Their tilt can suggest amazement, indifference ... knockabout ... [which could imply a devious] "thinking" hat.[59]

This *ambiguity* of the bowler (a trait film theorist Andre Bazin also attributes to Charlie's cane), when reinforced by mockery, as is the case in *Waiting for Godot*, can assist in the loss of man's masquerade at dignity—the façade of the short-lived folly known as life. After all, *Godot*'s theme is "[Samuel] Beckett's old tune—man is born astride of a grave."[60] Along similar absurdity lines, though nothing is more absurd than death, award-winning contemporary author Susan Kinsolving also sees Charlie's cane as having *thinking* abilities in her poem "Without," observing in one stanza the cane moving along "without connection."[61] The poem's narrator follows said cane through the snow (a refuge from *The Gold Rush?*) but can never grasp it. Ultimately, it simply goes away—"an immaculate line of idea" on which no one will be able to lean ... symbolizing yet another mystery in the human comedy?[62] There is no fleeting moment of clarity here. Indeed, one is tempted to recycle the pocket definition of the genre, "The meaning of dark comedy is that there is no meaning."[63]

Bowler hat and cane are certainly very much a part of Chaplin's misadventures in *The Circus*. Whether or not they have individual thinking abilities here is open to debate. Charlie does use his talisman cane to rescue his magic hat in a watershed *Circus* scene of comic absurdity. The Tramp is trapped in the fun house Mirror Maze, this sudden comic cloning, like multiple masks, representing all one's many identities. Charlie cannot decide which reflection is both the one most conducive to helping him exit the maze, as well as retrieve his dropped hat. After painfully smacking into one of his mirror images, he realizes a safe departure plan simply involves inverting his cane at floor level and hooking the elusive hat.

Charlie also has company in the Mirror Maze on two occasions—one with a pickpocket (who has inadvertently involved the Tramp in a theft) and the other with a pursuing policeman. In each case, however, the Tramp, like Alice going through the looking glass, is now more knowledgeable about mirrors and false reflections and manages to lose his pursuers. Charlie is luckier than the ultimately dead duo caught in Orson Welles' riveting hall of mirrors in *The Lady from Shanghai* (1948), a scene as logically inspired by Chaplin as Jean Vigo's use of a midget principal in *Zero for Conduct* (1933) is a dark comedy homage to the midget German commander in *Shoulder Arms*.

One might draw a black humor analogy between Chaplin's Mirror Maze sequences in *The Circus* with the figure of death following the disillusioned knight in Ingmar Bergman's *The Seventh Seal* (1957). That is, acknowledged or not, we are all being stalked by the shroud, just as movie mirrors remind us to forever question reality. Ironically, sometimes the fun house looking glass can even reveal a reality which will never be. For instance, Peter Bogdanovich's biography film *Mask* (1985) takes a carnival distortion poignantly to peek at normalcy. That is, a teenage boy whose face has been disfigured by a rare disease has a brief glance at what might have been, courtesy of a now not-so-crazy mirror.

Ultimately, many mirror movies are like an ironic reading of life. If an individual has been blessed with many years, is there not an element of surrealism in watching one's reflected image change over time? Like Groucho seeing his reflection as Harpo in the mirror scene of the Chaplin-influenced *Duck Soup* (1933), passing years create similar-looking imposters for us all.[64] Thus, as in most art, mirror movies like *The Circus* are often absurd lies which tell the truth.

From such absurdities, *The Circus* is also rich with other components of dark comedy, including two variations upon the use of death. The first and most famous involves Charlie being accidently locked in a cage with a lion. The comedian improves upon the black humor thrill comedy of *The Gold Rush*'s cabin on the cliff by what Bazin calls "comedy of space":

> If slapstick comedy succeeded before the days of [D.W.] Griffith and montage, it is because most of its gags derived from a comedy of space, from the relation of man to things and to the surrounding world. In *The Circus* Chaplin is truly in the lion's cage and both are enclosed within the framework of the screen.[65]

The dark comedy is heightened because we know Charlie is performing the routine or actually taking the risk, as in entering the cage. Edited together, solo shots of Charlie and the lion would have made viewers question the reality and danger of the situation. Besides making for more effective dark comedy, Bazin successfully argues that Chaplin's decision to film in long shot and long take was technically wise. Consequently, Bazin reversed a then long-held theoretical view: to applaud Chaplin's comedy despite his seemingly primitive technical approach (realism at its most fundamental level).

The Circus, however, does not just register dark comedy with the Tramp as the potential victim. For instance, Charlie is in love with the circus' bareback rider (Merna Kennedy), and she with him ... until the tall, handsome Rex, the tightrope walker (Harry Crocker), arrives. Charlie's immediate response to his rival has filmmaker Chaplin performing a double-exposure daydream sequence in which Charlie steps out of himself and flattens Rex with a punch Jack Dempsey would have been proud of. (In this era, Chaplin and much of Hollywood were professional fight fans.) Unfortunately, to paraphrase one of Preston Sturges' later quips, "Usually those people most in need of a thrashing are quite large." The Tramp must hope that fate will lend a hand. Consequently, when Charlie and the girl first watch Rex perform his highwire act with its built-in thrills and chills, Merna is frightened and the Tramp cannot contain his glee over the possibility of Rex falling to his death. Indeed, a seated Charlie, facing the viewer, proceeds to extend both of his legs straight out and attempts to emulate the tightrope walker's footwork—underlining its difficulty and the excellent chance for a fatality. When Rex successfully completes his act, the girl's joy comically contrasts with Charlie's disappointment.

The highwire act provides *The Circus* with one final extended sequence of dark comedy, but this time the movie again makes Charlie the person at risk. Rex does not show up for a per-

The Circus' Charlie locked in a cage with a lion—the "comedy of space."

formance, and the jealous Tramp—who has been practicing the act—volunteers to replace him. Though Charlie is not ready for such a challenge, the melodramatically evil circus owner is happy to see Charlie try; a death would make for great "theater." In fact, as the Tramp struggles through the routine, filmmaker Chaplin frequently cuts to one oversized audience member gobbling up his popcorn as he excitedly waits for a Charlie miscue. Nothing underscores dark comedy more than eating with death in the air. One is reminded of Robert Wise's black humor depiction of a fight crowd in his noir masterpiece, *The Set-Up* (1949), which includes a glutton whose nonstop eating is never deterred by the ring violence.

Despite the Tramp's need to impress Merna by playing at being Rex—the man's oversized clothing on Charlie is reminiscent of an earlier description of Chaplin's persona being a boy in his father's clothing—the wannabe tightrope walker eliminates all risk by paying the prop man to fasten him to a halter and wire. The Tramp now can be recklessly inspired in the highwire stunts he attempts. Halfway into the act, the halter becomes detached; the false bravado of the oblivious Charlie comically carries him for a while, as if he has acquired the dumb luck safety sometimes attributed to drunks and little children. The Tramp then sees the halter dangling above him, and suddenly his thoughts turn to the opposite direction.

Charlie's thrill comedy adventures in highwire black humor are increased by the talent which the well-trained Chaplin brought to the part. One plus to a drawn-out production schedule is the chance for added practice. Though there was always a natural grace to Charlie's physical movement, one also needs great skill to appear unskilled. The Tramp on the highwire is a combination of both, especially when some uninvited circus monkeys join the act. With Charlie's hands desperately gripping the balancing pole as he walks the wire, the monkeys do everything from pull down his pants to bite Charlie's nose and somehow lodge a wayward tail in his mouth. The threat of dying has never been so funny. That last *pièce de resistance* even tops any of the distractions encountered by Harold Lloyd in his groundbreaking thrill comedy *Safety Last* (1923).

Besides the dark comedy which enhances Chaplin's last film released in the 1920s, the movie's bittersweet conclusion, with Charlie staying behind as the circus moves on, can be "read" along several metaphorical lines. At the time it was perceived to be Chaplin going arty for deep-dish admirers and critics wanting Charlie to embrace tragic overtones. Given that *The Jazz Singer* (1927) had opened the year before *The Circus,* with the sound revolution already overrunning Hollywood, Chaplin's finale now also feels like an artist letting the talkie parade pass him by; he would resist making a conventional sound film until 1940. Of course, given that the movie's production had almost been derailed by an ugly divorce, there is also a certain real-life logic in Chaplin having the Tramp realize Merna would be better off with Rex and the departing circus. Still, Charlie's sacrifice is consistent with how the Tramp usually behaved after the early short subjects: doing the right thing, even if there was a risk of loss. That philosophy is at the heart of his next picture *City Lights* (1931), in which he does everything to make it possible for the blind girl to see ... even though it undoubtedly means she will reject him.

For the purpose of this text, however, *The Circus*' sad conclusion coincidentally seems like a decade-closing dark harbinger to the shape of things to come—the Great Depression and a time ripe for the rise of dictators. Plus, as the following chapter chronicles, the end of the 1920s was when the artistic community began to more fully articulate the waste and horror of the First World War.

6

The 1930s and Gathering War Clouds

"The situation right now is not promising. The Germans are advancing and we must realize the seriousness of the situation. Never mind the reason we are in the war. We are in it and must get out successfully...."—Charlie Chaplin World War I bond rally comment[1]

By the late 1920s a growing amount of literature was beginning to address statements like, "Never mind the reason we are in the war." In Adam Hochschild's seminal, ironically titled study *To End All Wars* (2011), he notes, "Within a decade after its end, the war had already come to be seen by many as a needless tragedy...."[2] Why did it take so long? At the conflict's end in 1918, every literate person was aware that approximately ten million soldiers had died, with an additional twenty million wounded—many so disfigured they were forced to permanently wear masks. Prominent intellectuals from most of the warring countries, such as Bertrand Russell in Britain and Eugene Debs in the United States, had even been imprisoned for protesting their countries' involvement in the war. Another pivotal historian of the war, Hew Strachan, further explains that there were initially "many interpretations [of the war] and that until at least the late 1920s those different meanings co-existed with each other."[3]

What would some of these other meanings be? First, many of the mourning millions needed reassurance that such sacrifices had not been in vain. Second, it took time for the realization to sink in that "The extraordinary carnage of World War I did not just kill men. The violence destroyed accepted ideas about valor, duty, class, human behavior and whether the future even mattered."[4] Third, the victims who had somehow survived did not, at least for a time, want to relive the horrors of the war. For example, in Erich Maria Remarque's *All Quiet on the Western Front* (1928), the greatest anti-war novel of the conflict (and arguably any war), the author poignantly addresses the topic:

> There is nothing [my father] likes more than just hearing about [the war]. I realize he does not know that a man cannot talk of things; I would do it willingly but it is too dangerous for me to put these things into words. I am afraid they might then become gigantic and [I'd] be no longer able to master them. What would become of us if everything that happens out there [in the war] were quite clear to us?[5]

Remarque (1898–1970), a German soldier in World War I, eventually spoke out for the war dead, including his alter ego narrator, who ironically falls at the novel's end on a day so serene that the army report confined itself to the single sentence: "All quiet on the Western Front."[6] Yet, this narrator-victim had best articulated a soldier's plight by confessing:

> The terror of the front sinks deep.... [W]e make grim, coarse jests about it; that keeps us from going mad.... If it were not so we could not hold out.... Our humor becomes more bitter every month.[7]

One might also read Ernest Hemingway's *A Farewell to Arms* (1929), British Robert Graves' memoir *Good-Bye to All That* (1929), and Italian-American Humphrey Cobb's novel

Paths of Glory (1935). A teenage Hemingway (1899–1961) volunteered to be an ambulance driver on the Italian front, where a mortar shell left 200-plus shrapnel fragments in his legs. Graves (1895–1985) fought in France on the Western Front. Cobb, enlisted with Canadian forces in 1916 and served on the Western Front. His text chronicles the drastic actions devised by the French military to curb mutiny among their troops. A man randomly chosen from each company would be run through a rubber stamp court-martial for cowardice and executed.

Remarque, Hemingway, Graves, and Cobb represent a multinational cast of writing veterans; each text resonates with the war-related ironies which often double as dark comedy. For instance, Graves' war philosophy anticipates Joseph Heller's *Catch-22* (1961): "I took the line that everyone was mad except ourselves and one or two others, and that no good could come of offering common sense to the insane."[8] Hemingway's soldier is decorated for a wound he received while "eating cheese."[9] Again, one is reminded of *Catch-22*—the scene in which the central character Yossarian and his bombing squadron are decorated for killing fish. Returning to Graves, other absurd and/or darkly comic observations range from the Chaplinesque comment "Our machine-gun crew boil their [cooking] hot water by firing off belt after belt of ammunition at no particular target," to what passed for trench humor: A new soldier turned in for the night and "heard a scuffling, shone his [flashlight] on the bed, and found two rats on his blankets tussling for the possession of a severed hand. The story circulated as a great joke."[10] Yet, maybe the most absurd passage generated by any of these anti-war texts involves a dialogue about the aforementioned French plan to discourage mutiny by the French command:

> One man's got to be shot for a [mutiny] he didn't commit, which nobody committed. Do you call that justice?
> Who said anything about justice? There's no such thing. But injustice is as much a part of life as the weather. And you're getting away from the point again. He isn't being shot for a crime he didn't commit. He's being shot as an example. That's his contribution to the winning of the war. A heroic one, too, if you like.[11]

Such are the "paths of glory." (Also see Frenchman G. Chevallier's *Fear.*)

These works and many more begin to address this chapter's pure patriotism opening of "Never mind the reason we are in the war." One feels awkward, of course, noting it is a Chaplin quote, given that the comedian never embraced the rabid anti–German propaganda of that period. While addressed earlier in the text, there is a point to mentioning a final 1918 bond tour example of Chaplin civility. During a large rally in Nashville, one of the preliminary speakers was Captain I.S. Rossiter, a Canadian officer who was a prisoner in a German prison camp for nearly a year. In an impromptu opening he observed:

> I was passing by a picture show this afternoon and noticed that there was a picture in this town called *The Kaiser, the Beast of Berlin*. Don't insult a beast by comparing a German to it; call them Huns, that is what we are fighting.[12]

Paradoxically, at a Nashville dinner for Chaplin just hours before the rally and Rossiter's comments, the comedian had limited his remarks to the following joke:

> A young Irishman was captured by the Germans and was put in a German prison camp. Every time the German soldier who was on guard passed by the Irishman he would call out, "Wasn't that a terrible licking that the Irish gave the Germans at the [Battle of] the Marne?" The German soldier became tired of hearing this and at last said to the Irishman, "The next time that you say that you will be shot." The Irishman made the statement again and was taken out to

be shot but was given his choice of becoming a German subject or being shot. Thinking that a live German was better than a dead Irishman, he chose to be a German. The next time the Irishman saw his former German guard he said, "Say, Boche, that was a terrible licking that we Germans got at the hands of the Irish, wasn't it?"[13]

This belaboring of his balance, Chaplin's conscious effort not to demonize the enemy yet still feel the need for the blind allegiance of "never mind the reason," fully demonstrates why it took a decade for attitudes to change about the war. Interestingly, the opening to *City Lights* (1931), Chaplin's first film after *The Circus* (1928), represents a sort of summing-up of the ten-year period prior to the anti-war awakening. To set the scene, city officials and a large crowd have gathered for the unveiling of a three-figure monument entitled "Peace and Prosperity," which is what the 1920s were supposed to be about—President Warren Harding had even campaigned on the slogan, "A return to normalcy." Whether one embraced the Jazz Age partying of a "lost generation," or the small town provincialism of a million and one "Babbitt"-villes, the end result were similar: Memories were for mausoleums and statues.

Granted, Chaplin's chief satirical target for the opening of *City Lights* was the poor sound quality of early talkies. Thus, two local dignitaries, a rotund mayoral type (played by longtime Chaplin regular Henry Bergman) and a stereotypical pompous clubwoman, proceed with the standard boring political-civic chatter associated with these events. What Chaplin does next is brilliant: He uses the synchronized distorted sounds of a saxophone to double as a gibberish take on such talks. In this simple act the comedian produces a double satirical whammy, undercutting both early sound films and mind-numbing political prattle.

The opening was a hit with the public and the press. The *Hollywood Reporter* observed, "Chaplin has opened the picture with a knockout blow. The first gag is the best and takes an awful sock at the talkies."[14] The *New York Sun* described the scene as a "devastating gag showing Mr. Chaplin's opinion of the talkies as a succession of impressionistic noises."[15] Yet, there is an old axiom of "Trust the tale, not the teller": Whatever the artist's intentions, the viewer also brings his own particular angle of vision. And from the vantage point of this study, *City Lights*' opening now also acts as an unintended jab at the lip-service granted a world war guaranteed to cause another world war. Moreover, all movies eventually act as time capsules of the times in which they were made. Consequently, at the very least, Chaplin's unveiling of a three-figure tribute to "Peace and Prosperity" was mirroring a "blinders about war" phenomenon then being acted out all over America.

The beauty of this unfolding situation is that Chaplin has not yet revealed his comic coup de grace. This arrives with the unveiling of the three-figure statue configuration: a seated maiden perhaps symbolic of justice, with two standing males—one implying peace by way of an extended hand, the other a defensive warrior brandishing a sword. Where's the satirical topper? Charlie is asleep in the motherly lap of justice! As film historian Gerald Mast amusingly noted, the iconoclastic Charlie "doesn't break the idol but he does sit on it."[16] Angry dignitaries and the crowd demand Charlie's exit from his makeshift bed; the filmmaker has created a scenario which can be deciphered as a darkly comic commentary on the ease with which wars occur. This can be explained by a further description of the scene. Everything Charlie does to get out of the spotlight is a further affront to the dignity of the situation, such as planting his keister against the feminine nose of justice's extended hand. Most symbolically, the aforementioned sword of peace manages to get entangled in those Charlie-defining baggy pants. It is as if to say, "We vacuously talk about peace while war stealthily slips up on us every time." This interpretation of the sequence is reinforced by the skewering sword literally hanging Charlie up like a flag.

The analogy is appropriate, since Chaplin tops the Tramp's comic attempts to extricate himself from this dilemma by then introducing "The Star-Spangled Banner" on the soundtrack, a fitting number for a civic unveiling. It ironically interjects what comedy theorist Henri Bergson has described as "mechanical inelasticity," the funny phenomenon where other actions are called for, but prior conditioning causes one to respond in the most predictable of ways.[17] Consequently, though Charlie should continue to work at getting his trousers loose from said sword, the national anthem has him attempting to come to attention while he literally dangles in the wind. Along similar lines, the officials and audience members upset over Charlie's disruption of the ceremony spring to attention, too. Knee-jerk patriotism has never been more darkly comic ... and disturbing, in the context of this book. Moreover, given how easy this mechanism converts an audience to a mob mentality represents another variation on the dangers of blindly accepting any "never mind the reason" cause.

One could also argue that the burlesqued sound effects of *City Lights*' opening—reducing pompous public figures to clowns—were the seeds of a pivotal black humor sequence in *The Great Dictator* (1940). The scene in question is the film's initial presentation of the title character, Hynkel (Chaplin). Anchored in dark comedy's frequent portrayal of man as beast, the scene is a delicious travesty of Hitler as an orator, with its "Demokratien shtunk!" and "Frei Sprecken Shtunk!" allowing Chaplin to showcase exceptional talents for both verbal mimicry and black humor. This acclaimed performance of German gibberish (echoed in the full name Chaplin gives the dictator—Adenoid Hynkel) is complimented by the comedian's ongoing ability to give his work numerous levels of comedy richness. While one first laughs at Chaplin's parody of German guttural sounds (reminiscent of Mark Twain's essay "That Awful German Language"), the speech disintegrates into an angry tirade of an incoherent scene which manages to be simultaneously funny and frightening.

In a period article from the *New York World Telegram,* Chaplin said, "I listen to Hitler on the radio. The mad, bitter voice I listened [to] only a few times. Then I had it, and we worked out some ordinary German words every American could understand. The rest was gibberish."[18] As if playing off his comments on the nonsense speech, the comedian later insightfully observed, "Mine made just as much sense as his do. It's not the words, it's the tone. [This] makes for complete mass hysteria. That voice bangs on your brain, and before you know it, you're cheering."[19] Chaplin's comments here also bring one full circle back to the opening of *City Lights*. While the comedian was not suggesting these dignitaries were evil by way of their distorted gobbledygook speech, Chaplin's observation about "It's not the words, it's the tone" would still apply. That is, their saxophone-generated mumbo-jumbo about a "Peace and Prosperity" monument could stand in for all the 1920s misdirected rhetoric which lulled the masses into not asking hard questions about the *why* of World War I.

While *City Lights*' opening plays with dark comedy's sense of the absurd, a second key component of the genre—possible death by suicide—is central to the storyline. At the heart of *City Lights* is the odd sometimes-friendship between the Tramp and an alcoholic millionaire (Harry Myers), who only acknowledges Charlie when he is drunk (more absurdity!). The relationship begins when Charlie prevents Myers' manic-depressive character from drowning himself. The setting is under a bridge by a river (the studio pool), and the drunken millionaire is preparing to tie a weighted-with-a-rock rope around his neck. The Tramp, about to bed down on a nearby bench, rushes to the rescue. Through mime and titles like, "Be brave, face life!," Charlie does his best to dissuade the depressed drunk. Unfortunately on two counts, the suicidal figure is not brave, and in attempting to put the rope around his neck, *only* the Tramp ends up in the noose. Thus, when the rock is tossed into the stream, Charlie follows. Now the millionaire plays rescuer by attempting to pull Charlie out but he ends up in the water too. As the sequence progresses, the duo record several entertaining variations upon this in-out routine before they both are finally safe at river's edge. At the millionaire's mansion, there's a comic drinking session in which the unsteady drunk pours nearly a bottle of brandy down Charlie's pants; then Myers' depression returns. His millionaire suddenly puts a gun to his head, and again the Tramp steps in. (In the 1920s Chaplin had flirted with the idea of adapting Robert Louis Stevenson's *Suicide Club* [1878] to the screen.)

Just as Chaplin was a pioneer in the cinematic use of dark comedy, mixing the genre with *City Lights*' suicide attempts was also groundbreaking. Since black humor begins with the omnipresence of death, it is a natural genre progression. That is, suicide is that rare activity in which a dark comedy character can initiate the event instead of being the random recipient. How ironically fitting for the genre that this act results in the total negation of the individual. Later classic dark comedies will be peppered with the component, such as Harold's (Bud Cort) multiple staged suicides in *Harold and Maude* (1972) and a *MASH* (1970) theme song entitled "Suicide Is Painless," with another elaborate mock suicide.

On a metaphorical level, suicide is also an apt phrase for the literal implementation of the death wish–like tendency of modern man to seemingly rush toward an apocalypse of his own making, such as the inevitable mushroom cloud conclusion of *Dr. Strangelove* (1964). Suicide is a modest example of something black comedy frequently showcases on a broader and more terrible scale: man playing an Old Testament God. The cinema road to this phenomenon so associated with *Dr. Strangelove* begins with Chaplin's *The Great Dictator. City Lights*' baby suicide steps are the comedian just warming up. Yet even the brief attempts by the drunken millionaire underline a key point of suicide's place in any dark comedy: the pure randomness of the act and/or death in general. Thus, in Charlie's first rescue of the troubled rich man, it is suddenly the Tramp in the noose and in the river. Dark comedy often suggests, like film noir, that it is safer not to get involved.

When the millionaire is not attempting suicide, he provides Charlie with a zany backdrop for more absurdity: Chaplin's love of visual puns, mistaking one look-alike object for another. For example, during a party at the millionaire's mansion the Tramp mistakes a guest's bald head for a melon being served during the festivities. When this apparent culinary treat turns out to be someone's noggin, Charlie has the most surreal of moments, like dinner turning into a Dali painting.

If Chaplin's belief that the success of *The Kid* (1921) was built, in part, upon the connection between the title character and the countless war orphans created by World War I, possibly having a blind *City Lights* heroine (Virginia Cherrill) had a link to the conflict, too. Keep in mind that a large number of the war's twenty million casualties involved temporary or permanent blindness (often from chemical warfare), and that the film's original scenario had the Tramp being blind. Chaplin's continuing fondness for the comic contrast of teaming a big man (Myers) with a little one (Charlie) also allows the filmmaker's story to have a feasible financial explanation for how the blind girl gets her operation: The big man is wealthy.

While the rich drunk makes the miracle possible, Charlie goes to prison for stealing, since Myers' sober self again neither recognizes the Tramp nor remembers providing him with the life-changing cash. Ultimately, this leads to an ending often hailed as cinema's greatest sequence. America's cornerstone critic James Agee called it "the greatest piece of acting and the highest moment in the movies."[20] What is the movie magic behind the moment? Charlie, just out of jail, happens upon Cherrill in her new florist shop, and is frozen in place. He is overjoyed that she can see, yet overwhelmed about what this means for them, since she thinks he is rich. Unfortunately, while the Tramp sees yet another Chaplin idealized heroine, Cherrill only sees a laughable hobo apparently smitten by her beauty. Cherrill and an assistant even kid about a "conquest." Worse yet, Cherrill expresses her pity by offering Charlie a coin and a fresh flower—a frequent Chaplin symbol for the fragility of life and love. Embarrassed, the Tramp shakes off his shock and starts to move away. However, when Cherrill comes into the street and places the coin in his hand, it is her turn to be shocked. With that single touch, the once blind girl realizes the Tramp is her benefactor.

"You?" she hesitantly asks. Giving her a humiliated smile, Charlie answers with a nod.

Still finding the situation hard to comprehend, the Tramp has to ask via a title, "You can see now?"

Responding as if in one of the millionaire's stupors, yet looking directly into Charlie's sad eyes, she dully states, by way of a title, "Yes, I can see now."

After a series of close-ups between the two, the camera ultimately stays on the Tramp. The haunting image of this face is the picture of pathos—the difficult smile that somehow acknowledges that this Charlie wannabe romance is certainly at the end. As Agee wrote, "It is enough to shrivel the heart...."[21] And one is reminded of a D.W. Griffith title for a movie Chaplin admired, *Broken Blossoms* (1919). While Chaplin's arguably greatest of all cinema closes is not dark comedy, it embraces the ethos of that genre: Harsh reality is seldom happy.

Unlike many initially neglected masterworks, *City Lights* immediately lit up the critical and commercial world of film. The *New York Sun* stated, "The genius of the [Greta] Garbos and [Jack] Oakies may be disputed, but the genius of Chaplin is admitted—now that *City Lights* ... has opened in our town...."[22] The *New York Post* added:

> [O]nce again Chaplin's consummate artistry is put forth with that earthy simplicity which is the touchstone of his genius, so that it is impossible not to share keenly in the tribulations which beset the friendly figure in the shabby hat and baggy trousers.[23]

The term "genius" was not good enough for the *New York World*, which preferred the description "cosmic rightness!"[24] Even the sedate *New York Times* produced a mini-headline for its review of "cosmic rightness" proportions:

Charlie in the finale of *City Lights*—the scene which is "enough to shrivel the heart."

"Pathos Is Mingled with Mirth in a Production of Admirable Artistry."[25] The *New York Herald Tribune* (the *Times*' greatest literacy criticism rival in that period's sea of Gotham City newspapers) had no such restraint. Reviewer Richard Watts, Jr., opened his critique with the suggestion that if *City Lights* did not result in "dancing in the streets, ringing of bells and awarding of the city's keys ... then something has gone wrong with New York's power of appreciation."[26] (When the film opened in London, no less an artist than George Bernard Shaw said, "The little fellow is a genius [that word again] whom none of us has properly appreciated."[27])

Chaplin would turn his decision to attend the New York and London premieres of *City Lights* into an around-the-world trip lasting over a year. Though the making of *The Great Dictator* was more than eight years away, two events on the comedian's extended 1931–1932 holiday would foreshadow his dark comedy on Hitler. First, as the European portion of his travels wound down, he realized another world war was inevitable:

> Patriotism is the greatest insanity the world has ever suffered. I have been all over Europe in the past few months. Patriotism is rampant everywhere, and the result is going to be another war. I hope they send the old men to the front the next time, for it is the old men who are the real criminals in Europe today.[28]

Second, arguably his greatest reception on the continent was in Berlin. The Nazi party, yet to consolidate their power, was less than pleased. But their displeasure with the German hosannas given Chaplin would later surface in assorted ways, one of which might have contributed to the comedian making *The Great Dictator*: largely because of that warm German welcome, which even included being entertained by Reichstag members, Chaplin was included in the anti–Semitic text *The Jews Are Looking at You* (1934) by Nazi propaganda ministry official Johann von Leers. Chaplin's friend Ivor Montagu (1904–1984), the British filmmaker and movie critic, came across this book and sent a copy to the comedian. A seminal 1980 interview with Montagu on the subject is included in Kevin Brownlow's documentary *The Tramp and the Dictator* (2001, a comparison of Chaplin and Hitler anchored in *The Great Dictator*). As with most of Chaplin's friends, the comedian had kept in touch with Montagu through the years by cards, telegrams, and phone calls, but

> he only sent me one letter and it was ... thanking me for that book [in which Chaplin is described as "a disgusting Jewish acrobat"]. And I always think it may have contributed to his resolve to make *The Great Dictator*.[29]

(Chaplin composed few letters, feeling extended writing should be limited to scripts.[30])

Newsreel footage of Chaplin's triumphant 1931 German visit would later turn up in the Nazi propaganda film *The Eternal Jew* (1940), with voice-over narration explaining how citizens were duped: "The Jew Chaplin was enthusiastically welcomed on his first visit to Berlin. One cannot deny that many Germans unsuspectively applauded the foreign Jews who had come to Germany, the deadly foes of their race."[31] Paradoxically, beyond the racism, while Chaplin was always proud to be called Jewish, he was not of that faith ... though his half-brother Sydney was. On the flip side, Chaplin aficionados often observe that Charlie resembles a Jewish stereotypical character ... an ostracized outsider, the eternal wandering outcast. (The classy showcasing of the black child in *The Kid* is another outsider.)

While Chaplin's early 1930s world tour was seemingly a backburner catalyst for eventually making *The Great Dictator,* the immediate creative inspiration from the trip was to make a picture addressing the Great Depression: *Modern Times* (1936). The movie would also represent an important transition in his evolution on dark comedy. Before this picture, "modern times" had never before intruded so strongly into the Tramp's world; for the first time his ongoing existence seemed threatened by change.[32] As pop culture pioneer Robert Warshaw has suggested, prior to *Modern Times,* Charlie and society were often at odds, but there seemed to be no real threat to the continued independence of a professional free spirit like the Tramp. With the 1930s, however, changes in society had created a condition that represented an ongoing menace to mankind, individual by individual.[33] Thus, unlike *Shoulder Arms'* use of dark comedy for an established cause, both *Modern Times* and *The Great Dictator* showcased black humor as a warning that the new machine and/or the fascist society of the day literally threatened the life of Chaplin's underdog alter ego ... and the Everyman everywhere.

Before the next project (*Modern Times*) came to fruition, Chaplin continued to ponder an assortment of other film subjects, including his longtime interest in playing Napoleon, which is addressed in the next chapter. Even as Chaplin flirted with a picture about the French emperor, a front page August 1932 *Hollywood Reporter* article stated that the comedian would write and direct a serious screen drama—but would not star. The newspaper added that just as Chaplin had written and directed the innovative *A Woman of Paris* (1923), he was "anxious to make the 'perfect talking picture'—one which will carry his own ideas of new technique and methods for handling sound with dramatic action."[34] A year later, in August 1933, the comedian's business manager Alf Reeves stated that Chaplin soon would begin production on what sounds like the eventual *Modern Times.* Paulette Goddard, Chaplin's new protégé and future wife, was to play "a tomboy character in the picture, which will be laid in the lower part of any big city with factories."[35]

Even with *Modern Times* technically starting production in September 1933, another front page *Hollywood Reporter* news item (January 26, 1934) revealed that the comedian had continued to toy with a third picture project before presumably returning to *Modern Times:*

> Latest from the Charlie Chaplin front is that the comedian has decided to make his new picture entirely silent, with synchronized music and effects. Chaplin has abandoned the idea of making a talkie in which he would himself play the role of a deaf mute.[36]

There were other publication headlines about a different Chaplin film between September 1933 and January 1934 but these examples should suffice.[37] Ultimately, Chaplin's stop-start creative antics prior to the opening of *Modern Times* were later affectionately kidded in early 1936 in the beginning of Robert Forsythe's positive *New Masses* review of the film: "If you have had fears, prepare to shed them.... After years of rumors, charges and counter-charges, reports of censorship and hints of disaster, his new film ... had its [successful] world premiere...."[38] (Forsythe was the pseudonym used by the scholar and sometimes journal editor Kyle Crichton when critiquing for Communist publications like the *New Masses.*)

So what are the dark comedy elements of *Modern Times,* which was originally entitled *The Masses?* They are present from the first scene, with sheep hurrying through a gate, quickly followed by workers rushing out of a subway late for work. This is what Soviet filmmaker Sergei Eisenstein, the master of montage, editing would call an "intellectual" transition, since one must make a metaphorical leap—workers are like sheep to the slaughter. This was an atypical technique for Chaplin, as it then was for the most of Hollywood, where "invisible editing" was the norm—narrative cuts and/or transitions which do *not* call attention to themselves. Possibly Chaplin was footnoting his awareness of Eisenstein's work; Eisenstein was best known for the "Odessa Steps" montage sequence from *Battleship Potemkin* (1925). Moreover, when the Soviet filmmaker came to Hollywood in the early 1930s with the aforementioned Ivor Montagu as his filmland guide, Chaplin's residence became like their second home.

Regardless of the catalyst, the message of the opening is textbook dark comedy—the negation of the individual. Charlie is one of these new age victims. His job is to tighten nuts on an assembly line—a line whose speed is constantly being increased, as if in reference to the ever-changing clock face over which the opening title (*Modern Times*) is superimposed. Eventually Charlie's enslavement to a conveyor belt (he misses tightening a nut, and proceeds to go after it) causes him to be swallowed by the machine—an industrial age Jonah. This is the picture's signature scene, the "money shot." The maddening institutionalism of the modern age will eat the worker alive ... and when it spits him out, his mind will be so much mush. Indeed, as the pioneering Chaplin biographer Theodore Huff has amusingly put it, "The endless nut tightening finally drives Charlie nuts."[39] Yet this comic breakdown (equipped with two wrenches, he tries to tighten everything in sight, including some provocatively placed buttons on a woman's blouse) represents a defeat over Charlie to which no other living antagonist has ever come close. Eventually as self-defense, this debilitating development is moving Chaplin towards the eventual philosophy of turnabout is fair play—where the comedian's title character in *Monsieur Verdoux* (1947) adopts a defensive, deadly policy toward unleashing dark comedy on society. To paraphrase Oscar Wilde, "In creating man God overestimated his abilities."

Interestingly, two pioneering American authors of dark comedy, Edgar Allan Poe and Mark Twain, have also used mechanical devices for dire human effect. However, for these writers, the negligence of the individual is at fault, not the machine. For example, in Poe's "A Predicament," originally titled "The Scythe of Time" (from his *Tales of the Grotesque and Arabesque,* 1840), a female narrator explores a cathedral. In the steeple she sees a small opening and in placing her head through the space discovers she is in the face of a giant clock. Unfortunately, the minute hand begins to dig into her neck and eventually decapitates her. Yet the central character is merely annoyed ... and ponders which is the real her, the headless body or the severed head. The head then launches into a heroic speech but alas, her body has no ears with which to hear. (The tale has the surreal quality of Nikolai Gogol's 1836 short story "The Nose," in which the nose of a St. Petersburg official leaves his face and assumes a life of its own.) Twain's comic piece of mechanical macabre merit is "The Story of the Old Ram," drawn from his 1872 novel *Roughing It*. William Wheeler visits a carpet factory and manages to get caught in the works. In less than a quarter of a minute he is woven into fourteen yards of three-ply carpet. At the funeral his widow refuses to bury him rolled up; instead, he is planted as if standing. Again, the surreal rules, and the machine age is not yet at fault.

Regardless, Charlie's *Modern Times* road to the sanitarium is also assisted by other (so-called) "progressive" elements in the factory. There are large monitors placed in strategic places, so Charlie cannot even steal a quick smoke in the washroom without being reprimanded by a big screen boss. This black humor totalitarian touch from Chaplin was the later inspiration for George Orwell's "Big Brother is watching you" telescreens in the renowned novel *1984*.[40] (Orwell was a big fan of Chaplin's *The Great Dictator,* and he called for the British government "to subsidize showings of it so it could be seen by poor people who could not afford seats."[41]) And the aforementioned Brownlow documentary *The Tramp and the Dictator* suggests that it was no accident that the *Modern Times* big screen factory boss (Allan Garcia) resembles Henry Ford—this was black humor directed at the industrialist who invented the debilitating mass market assembly line, as well as being a homegrown American fascist in his written and verbal

6. The 1930s and Gathering War Clouds   97

anti–Jewish diatribes. Indeed, the greater Detroit area (home to the Ford auto industry) was a hotbed of anti–Semitism given that the famous (infamous) "radio priest"–political power broker Charles E. Coughlin operated out of Royal Oak, Michigan, and was equally down on the Jews. (It must have given anti–Semitics like Ford and Coughlin fits that even before Chaplin went to bat for the Jews, the greatest Jewish baseball player in history, Hank Greenberg, was starring for the 1930s Detroit Tigers.[42]) The period's elephant in the room (the Jewish people) will be addressed further in the text, especially as it applies to Ford.

Returning to Chaplin's machine age Jonah scene: inspired creative endeavors usually have many fathers, and such was the case here. Thus, the seeming epiphany for the film and its defining sequence occurred when the comedian drove past "a mass of people coming out of a factory ... and was overwhelmed with the knowledge that the theme ... of modern times was mass production."[43] Yet the gestation period for any idea is invariably longer than it seems. For example, as a boy the comedian had briefly worked as a printer's assistant and he was terrified of this large machine—"I thought it was going to devour me."[44] Then flash forward several decades, and Chaplin recalls an early 1930s conversation he had with a *New York World* reporter on the topic. After hearing that the comedian was visiting Detroit, the journalist told Chaplin a disturbing story of "big industry luring healthy young men off the farms who, after four or five years at the [factory] belt system, became nervous wrecks."[45]

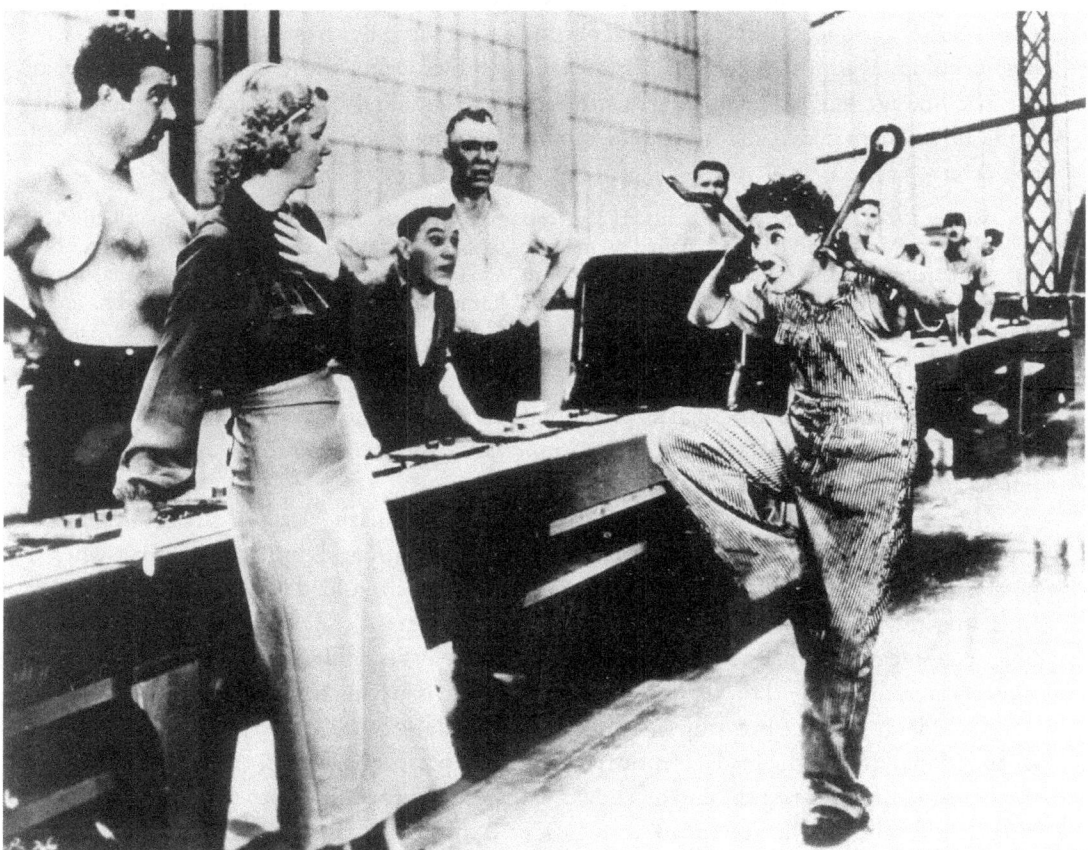

Modern Times' "endless nut tightening finally drives Charlie nuts."

Even before the machine swallows Charlie, the speed and unnatural physical demands of his twisting, retracting, twisting again on the conveyor belt job have made his actions mechanical and reduced him to a description not unlike the title of Anthony Burgess' 1962 dark comedy novel *A Clockwork Orange*. That is, a man reduced to a mix of the mechanical (clockwork) and the living (orange). The novel became a 1971 Stanley Kubrick movie, and all this plays into one of Kubrick's central themes: Man is easily conditioned (dehumanized) into something else ... often involving a seminal black humor element of man as beast. Kubrick's bookend examples of the phenomenon are *A Clockwork Orange* (violence to passivity ... and back again) and *Full Metal Jacket* (1987, particularly the Marine basic training first half of the picture), where the kindly are conditioned to kill.

Granted, Chaplin plays *Modern Times*' dehumanization with more gentle slapstick. For instance, shortly before the Tramp's nervous breakdown, a bell sounds for a lunch break. As Charlie tries to eat, he is still twitching so much that when a colleague (Stanley Sanford) asks the Tramp to pass a bowl of soup, our antihero's machine-produced jerkiness means *none* of the soup survives the bowl passing. Yet, in Charlie's embarrassment over this lack of control rests his lingering humanity.

One might also link man, machines, and *Modern Times* to another novelist even more synonymous with dark comedy—Kurt Vonnegut, author of *Slaughterhouse-Five* (1969). In a January 12, 1983, letter to filmmaker Robert Weide, the novelist observes, "[My novel] *Player Piano* [1952] gets more timely with each passing day. It could be an up-to-date *Modern Times*, if you could find another Chaplin."[46] *Player Piano* provides an additional warning sign about the machine age, and believing an industrial society would know what was best for mankind. Ironically, modern man is also incapable of comprehending this absurdity. *Player Piano*'s central character

> wondered at what thorough believers in mechanization most Americans were, even when their lives had been badly damaged by mechanization. The [train] conductor's plaint, like the lament of so many, wasn't that it was unjust to take jobs from men and give them to machines, but that the machines didn't do nearly as many human things as good designers could have made them do.[47]

This insight brings one full circle back to another fundamental Kubrick theme: If something is planned by man it will fail, such as a seemingly *perfect* heist (*The Killing*, 1956), a *safeguard* doomsday device that ends the world (*Dr. Strangelove*), and the *advanced* Hal the killing computer (*2001: A Space Odyssey*, 1968).

Another dark comedy scene in *Modern Times* finds Charlie accidentally leading a disgruntled crowd of Marxist workers. The Tramp is innocently walking down a street when a passing flatbed truck loses its red warning flag for an oversized load. Charlie picks it up and runs after the truck to return the flag, which is also a sign of the communist party. At this precise moment the aforementioned band of striking workers fall in behind the Tramp from a street intersecting the thoroughfare on which Charlie is waving his red flag. Thus, when the police suddenly arrive to break up this Marxist demonstration, the Tramp seems to be the "red" leader. Moreover, Charlie inadvertently reinforces that perspective when, in backing away from the riot squad, he steps on the end of a board which catapults a brick onto the noggin of a cop. Not surprisingly, Charlie, the apparent ringleader, is thrown into prison. Again unlike the dark comedy of *Shoulder Arms*—suffered willingly by the Tramp for a cause perceived to be just—*Modern Times* once more seems randomly out to negate the individual, aka Charlie.

More disturbing for students of the Tramp, the *Modern Times* prison stretch reveals the extent to which an institutionalizing contemporary scene has changed him: Charlie does not want to leave prison, even after he is pardoned. Times must really have changed when a "Tramp" cannot get along in the outside world, especially one who has formerly been so fiercely independent. As if to underline this disturbing change, not long after his release from his security blanket haven in prison, Charlie dines on a huge restaurant feast for which he has no money—in order to return to prison.

Though *Modern Times*' signature eating-machine sequence has led to the Tramp's fall from independence and individuality, an earlier comparable scene was more favored by period critics: Charlie's boss wants to streamline productivity by strapping workers into an automatic feeding device that will allow them to work through lunch. Charlie gets to be the guinea pig for this culinary torture apparatus, which begins to malfunction early in the demonstration. Thus, the machine attacks the defenseless Tramp with everything from a renegade revolving ear of corn (which he can only stop at the risk of losing his nose), to a blotter-like metal napkin that keeps smacking him in the face. Fittingly, for a mechanical device, it even attempts to force-feed him some steel nuts mistakenly placed on his dessert dish. The sequence makes a perfect transition to a crazed Charlie becoming a voluntary cog in the factory machine when he follows an unscrewed nut into the mechanized belly of this industrial age behemoth. Like the protagonist of Orwell's *1984,* Charlie is not only asked to accept the new order, he is expected to like it.

Returning to the much-praised eating-machine scene, *New York Evening Journal* reviewer Rose Pelswick observed, "The best of the [*Modern Times*] gags is one in which Chaplin is fed by a mechanical food server that goes out of commission with riotous results."[48] The *London Daily Telegraph*'s Campbell Dixon elevated the routine to cinema pantheon status: "I laughed at this sequence till I cried. If only 200 feet [of film] in all of film history could be preserved, this is what I choose."[49] Seconding this notion, variations of this sketch would later surface in numerous comedies, including Bob Hope and Bing Crosby's *Road to Hong Kong* (1962) and Woody Allen's *Bananas* (1971).

Besides these institutionalized dehumanizing examples of *Modern Times*' dark comedy, the picture occasionally gifts the viewer with conventional instances of the genre. The most artfully ballet-like involves mixing Charlie on roller skates with thrill comedy. During the course of the picture he attempts an assortment of jobs. One of the more promising involves being a department store night watchmen. Since it is a large multi-level building, with punch-in time clocks scattered throughout the premises (to prove the watchman is making regular security sweeps), Charlie finds skates to be a more efficient way to make his rounds. Yet, the initial catalyst was simply to have some fun with his gamine companion (Paulette Goddard) in the store's toy department. Lacing on skates, the gamine provides the traditional humor expected in this situation: She can barely stand up. (One is reminded of the pivotal pioneering French film comedian Max Linder's short subject *The Unskilled Skater,* 1907.) In contrast, the Tramp is a regular Baryshnikov on wheels, and shows off further by blindfolding himself. The dark thrill comedy soon surfaces when the camera reveals that his skating area is an invitation for disaster—its unfinished balcony-like setting is without protective railings. Each of Charlie's graceful circular movements has him on the verge of going into an abyss *à la The Gold Rush*'s (1925) cabin cliffhanger. Only the skating dilemma of this man-child is more mesmerizing, given both his skills (W.C. Fields called him a "god-damned ballet dancer") and the fact that he egotistically brought the situation on himself—dark comedy is often driven by feelings of superiority.

As Chaplin had done after the completion of *City Lights,* he took an extended vacation following the February 17, 1936, premiere of *Modern Times.* Fittingly, given the location of the opening, Grauman's Chinese Theatre, the comedian, Goddard, and her mother spent three months in the Far East. Honolulu was their original destination, but upon arrival, Chaplin suddenly decided they should go to Hong Kong. As with many of the comedian's trips, it was often a working holiday. He began writing a story for Goddard tentatively called *Stowaway*, essentially a farce set in Asia. Though nothing would come of the project for decades, it was later the basis for Chaplin's last film *A Countess from Hong Kong* (1967, with Sophia Loren and Marlon Brando).

Of more immediate interest were two diverse developments. First, Chaplin and Goddard were married on the trip, though there was no public acknowledgment at the time. Second, as with his 1931 holiday in Europe, when his comments on the region's disjointed patriotism had him predicting the inevitability of another world war, Chaplin saw the same shadow of global conflict in Japan's already open aggression against China. Ironically, just as the Nazis had been upset with the 1931 Berlin crowds celebrating Chaplin's arrival, there were ultra-rightist groups upset with the comedian's popularity in Japan. Just such a group, the Black Dragon Society, had even considered assassinating Chaplin during his 1931 visit.

As was Chaplin's standard M.O., his return from Asia had the comedian considering several projects. Chaplin's social consciousness had him moving towards a controversial dark comedy about a chap with a Charlie mustache who also doubled as the world's most hated man. A man created in part by Ambrose Bierce's celebrated pocket definition of war: "A by-product of the arts of peace"—the overly harsh peace imposed upon Germany at the end of World War I.

7

Napoleon, Hitler and *The Great Dictator*

"I thought *The Great Dictator* was a marvelous film. I thought it was a remarkable combination of comedy and outrage."—historian Arthur Schlesinger, Jr.[1]

The three most written-about people in Western Civilization are Jesus, Napoleon, and Hitler. At one time or another, Chaplin seriously wished to play each of these individuals in a movie. Technically he only assumed the role of one member of the trio—Hynkel, his dark comedy title character take on Hitler in *The Great Dictator* (1940)—but one could argue there are elements of all three in this picture. In the controversial close to the movie, when he steps out of character to plead for peace as citizen Chaplin, his speech is Christ-like, including the quoting of scriptures. Moreover, for much of the 1930s, he expended a great deal of time and effort on a Napoleon script. Thus, before examining *The Great Dictator* in detail, Chaplin's fascination with Napoleon bears fleshing out.

One could argue that Chaplin's most researched and worked upon unrealized project was a Napoleon movie. For Chaplin, the Napoleon implanting began very early. On three different instances early in his memoir he recalls the dictator being significantly referenced in his childhood. His beloved mother often described Charlie's largely absentee father as looking like Napoleon, and she also enjoyed acting out a comic anecdote about the actual dictator being indignant about his short height.[2] In 1897, a young Chaplin's last moving visit with his suddenly demonstrative father had the boy describing him as "Napoleon-like."[3] Chaplin scholar Eric L. Flom has added:

> [The comedian] was hard-pressed to shake his Napoleon fascination through the succeeding years. At one of William Randolph Hearst's lavish costume balls, during the period of [Chaplin's] marriage to Lita Grey, Chaplin was photographed in full Bonaparte splendor, complete with hand tucked into the waistcoat and a conqueror's scowl.... The costume also came in handy for a few undated test photographs for the proposed Napoleon [1930s film] project with Harry Crocker....[4]

Throughout the 1920s Chaplin flirted with making a picture which would focus on Napoleon *and* his first wife Josephine. For instance, before he fashioned *A Woman of Paris* (1923) as a last Chaplin-produced vehicle for Edna Purviance (see Chapter 5), the comedian considered teaming them as Napoleon and Josephine. This idea then became a leading lady pattern for Chaplin for much of the decade. Prior to marrying actress Lita Grey, he had suggested the same scenario to her. (In the aforementioned reference to the Hearst costume party where Chaplin appeared as Napoleon, the accompanying Grey was lavishly dressed as Josephine.) Chaplin had also pondered using the Spanish singer Raquel Meller as a cinematic Josephine, as well as offering the part to his romantic co-star from *The Circus* (1928), Merna Kennedy.

Not surprisingly, during Chaplin's around-the-world tour following the completion of

City Lights (1931), he would discuss his Napoleon film idea with prominent Europeans, including Winston Churchill, who encouraged the project and even suggested comic bits, such as a sequence with the dictator in a bathtub. The Chaplin-Churchill conversations on Napoleon made such an impression on the British leader that possibly the topic was also pursued at a later date, given a 1935 article the future prime minister wrote on the comedian. Churchill frequently noted Chaplin's interest in a Napoleon film; one Churchill comment actually links itself to *Shoulder Arms:*

> It is Mr. Chaplin's dream to play tragic roles as well as comic ones. The man whose glorious fooling made *Shoulder Arms* a favorite with war-weary veterans of the trenches wants to reinterpret Napoleon to the world.[5]

Given Churchill's prodigious and varied reading habits, one also wonders if the British statesman had alerted Chaplin that Napoleon, appropriately enough, had some insightful comments on comedy, too. For example, in Nobel Prize–winning philosopher Henri Bergson's study *Laughter* (1900), he describes a situation where Napoleon confesses to being verbally abused by the queen of Prussia. In order to defuse a difficult situation with some tact, Napoleon, "who was a psychologist when he wished to be," observed:

> To make her change her [aggressive] style, I requested her to take a seat. This is the best method for cutting short a tragic scene, for as soon as you are seated it all becomes comedy.[6]

Regardless, Chaplin visited Napoleon's tomb during his 1931 tour, which also fascinated Hitler during his 1939 victory visit to Paris. In describing the experience, the comedian stated:

> One can hardly realize that in that marble casket lies the most dramatic mortal that ever lived. I think for sheer drama Napoleon comes first. As I glance over the balcony, I am reminded of the line in [Thomas] Gray's "Elegy" [1750]—"The paths of glory lead to the grave" [and from which Humphrey Cobb draws his title for the aforementioned anti-war novel, *Paths of Glory,* 1935].[7]

Not surprisingly, in 1931 Chaplin considered adapting Jean Weber's novel *La Vie Secrète de Napoleon,* but the project collapsed when the writer attempted to place restrictions upon the cinematic adaptation. Chaplin embraced the Napoleon subject again in 1933 after meeting a young Alistair Cooke (1908–2004). All of twenty-four, the British journalist-broadcaster was just embarking upon a lengthy career which would include his signature BBC radio series *Letter from America* (1946–2004), and later hosting PBS's *Masterpiece Theatre* (1971–1992). The witty, cultured man with the mellifluous voice immediately captured Chaplin's attention, just as he would eventually do with listeners and viewers on two continents. Cooke had come to interview the comedian for England's *Manchester Guardian,* and a friendship developed over several months. In time, Chaplin suggested that if Cooke, who was then in America on a Commonwealth Fund Fellowship, was free in the summer of 1934, the comedian would appreciate his assistance in researching and writing a Napoleon script.

In Cooke's chapter on Chaplin in *Six Men* (1977), he notes that long before the comedian asked him to be a collaborator, the subject of Napoleon had come up during a relaxing cruise on the filmmaker's yacht. After some light talk about British royalty, Chaplin asked Cooke to immediately take both still photographs and home movies of the comedian as Napoleon:

> He pulled his hair down into a ropy forelock [and] started to talk to himself, tossing in names strange to me—[Henri] Bertrand, [Charles] Montholon [two French generals close to Napoleon, though the latter is alleged to have poisoned their leader]—and [Chaplin-

Napoleon] took umbrage, flung an accusing finger at me, and, having transformed his dreamy eyes into icicles, delivered a tirade.... His face was now a hewn rock of defiance. I have it still on film, and it is still a chilling thing to see.[8]

Cooke's comments could double as a description of Chaplin in his first tirade as Hynkel-Hitler in *The Great Dictator*. On a broader level, Cooke's writing on Chaplin also reveals the comedian's "obsession with royalty" and the "need to deflate it in mimicry."[9] Thus, I would posit that Chaplin's lifelong artistic need to undercut authority figures, such as kicking the cruel customs official in *The Immigrant* (1917), naturally attracted him to the dark comedy possibilities of undercutting Napoleon ... which in the late 1930s were more timely when directed at another dictator—Hitler.

When working on the Napoleon script with Cooke, Chaplin articulated a dictatorial approach which exactly mirrors the comedian's harsher *Great Dictator* production attitude documented by Kevin Brownlow's film *The Tramp and the Dictator* (2001).[10] Cooke stated that when they began the script, the first thing Chaplin taught him

> was that you don't begin at the beginning. "We look," he said, laying down the law with a firm index finger tapping the table, "for some little incident ... that fixes the other characters. The audience must never be in any doubt about them.... Nobody cares about *their* troubles. They stay the same.... This is no different from the characters who surround 'the little fellow.'"[11]

Though this philosophy also reflects the game plan for the Tramp's world, the filmmaker's attitude when discussing both the unrealized Napoleon picture and the Hitler-inspired *Great Dictator* had an iciness more emblematic of these two dictators than a normal Chaplin set.

In another Cooke text, *Letter from America* (2004, drawn from his BBC series), the journalist knew the precise point when their Napoleon project would never eventuate:

> Mostly, [Chaplin] would stomp or slouch around the room mumbling incomprehensible dialogue [a precursor to Chaplin's Hynkel-Hitler gibberish in *Dictator*?] ... though he had a gift to look more like Napoleon than Napoleon, or ... more like any of the real people he mimicked ... [especially a certain dictator who stole Charlie's mustache].[12]

Cooke added that the official plug was pulled on their Napoleon script when Chaplin nonchalantly told him, "It's a beautiful idea—for someone else.... Nobody pays to see Chaplin do an artistic experiment. They go to see the little man [Charlie]."[13] Was this the filmmaker's first inkling that he could more readily have it both ways by playing both a contemporary dictator (Hynkel-Hitler) *and* a Jewish barber variation of his "little man" in the same picture—*The Great Dictator?*

Chaplin being Chaplin, the comedian remained interested in Napoleon and the aforementioned novel *La Vie Secrète de Napoleon,* to which he finally acquired the rights in late 1935. In quick order, a 1936 treatment was prepared by Jean de Limur, one of Chaplin's assistants from *A Woman of Paris.* The comedian rejected the treatment because of what was becoming the Josephine problem: It did not have a meaty part for the filmmaker's current leading lady–lover Paulette Goddard. Keep in mind, much of this stop-start Napoleon activity transpired while Chaplin was working on *Modern Times.* While the comedian had not been a prolific artist since the two-reeler days of the 1910s, he constantly had a project in the works.

Seemingly the last hurrah for Chaplin's Napoleon picture occurred when the comedian collaborated with the British left-wing politician-author John Strachey (1901–1963) on a script ultimately copyrighted in 1936 as *Napoleon's Return from St. Helena.* Strachey, though only thirty-four, was already a former member of the British Parliament, after previously editing the *Socialist Review,* and was then (the 1930s) one of *the* most widely read Marxist-Leninist theorists. Though elements of Chaplin's earlier Napoleon treatments remain, such as the Weber novel's use of a double to aid the emperor's escape from his St. Helena banishment, the new work is much more politically pacifist in nature. (By his own admission, Cooke was largely apolitical at that time.)

What follows is an excerpt from this final script which exemplifies its heightened pacifism. One of Napoleon's generals, the aforementioned Montholon, asks the emperor to more fully explain his new non-militaristic philosophy. Chaplin's Napoleon responds, in part, "I mean the day of war and aggression will be a thing of the past.... One can accomplish more by treaties, friendship, commercial understanding...."[14] This reads like a rough draft beginning to *The Great Dictator*'s final speech, when citizen Chaplin, via his Charlie-like Jewish barber doubling as Hynkel, makes his plea for universal peace. But how would the comedian briefly summarize this last script, which was never to be a movie?:

> Well, you see, the plot is this. Napoleon had a double. It was this double that the British sent to Elba and St. Helena. The real Napoleon then lived quietly on in Paris, tending a bookstall near the Pont de l'Alma. He became a pacifist, and gave his earnings to the widows and children of war veterans.... [When the double for Napoleon died, the body] was brought back by the British Navy, and given to the French for burial.... All Paris now turned out.... It's a great crowd scene. In fact, it is my opening [movie] scene.... The real Napoleon ... is busy as usual at that bookstall of his; business was very good that day. As the [funeral] barge on the Seine slowly sails by—pan for close-up—he murmurs, "The news of my death is killing me!"[15]

This Chaplin overview comes from James P. O'Donnell's *Encounter* article "Charlie Chaplin, Adolf Hitler & Napoleon" (1978), which was inspired by the author's late 1950s attempt to get an interview with the comedian. O'Donnell (1917–1990) was a popular American author and journalist who had a long tenure at *Newsweek*; his other accomplishments ranged from work as a State Department advisor on Berlin, to being a leading authority on the death of Hitler (see his 1975 book *The Bunker*). O'Donnell's perspective on the subject at hand was very basic: "The origin of Chaplin's *The Great Dictator* was an earlier [the Strachey collaboration] Napoleon script on which Chaplin had been working—and brooding—for at least twenty years."[16] While the remainder of this chapter will suggest this view is too narrow, there is no doubting the *huge* significance Chaplin's ongoing fascination with Napoleon (even including collecting artifacts connected to the emperor) had on the making of *The Great Dictator*. If the unproduced Napoleon script contained nothing more than the look-alike factor, it would still merit being the starting point for any study of Chaplin's dark comedy take on Hitler. Add in the genre's "man as beast" component in the Chaplin as Napoleon amateur film by Cooke, and the pacifism influence of Strachey so central to *Dictator*'s close, and the emperor's shadow looms large over the comedian's creation of Hynkel. Fittingly, *after* Chaplin had completed the *Dictator* he would confess:

> I tried to make [Hynkel] a composite of all dictators.... [E]very actor has a yearning to play [the megalomaniac] Napoleon. I've [now] got it out of my system. I've now played Napoleon and Hitler and the mad [Russian] Czar Paul all rolled into one.[17]

Yet Chaplin will go back and forth on the origins of Hynkel for the rest of his life.

After using Napoleon as a basic foundation for *Dictator,* however, what were the direct Hitler-Hynkel links to the film? In Chaplin's memoir he suggests British producer Alexander Korda first suggested to him a Hitler-Tramp mistaken identity picture in 1937.[18] Yet there are assorted earlier links, such as Chaplin's friend Ivor Montagu sending him the anti–Semitic text *The Jews Are Looking at You* (1934, see Chapter 6), in which the comedian is defamed. Prior to these dates, in Lillian Ross' short reminiscence about her friend, *Moments with Chaplin* (1980), she includes:

> Charlie Chaplin making a confession about the origins of *The Great Dictator:* "When I first saw Hitler [presumably during the comedian's 1931 visit to Berlin], with that little mustache, I thought he was copying *me,* taking advantage of my success. I was that ego-tistical.[19]

Also prior to World War II (1939–1945), the Jews who suffered most at the hands of Hitler often used Chaplin's Tramp as a survivor's indispensable laughter resource against the dictator. In Steve Lipman's provocative study *Laughter in Hell: The Use of Humor During the Holocaust* (1991), one finds jokes like:

> Charlie Chaplin is indignant. "I don't complain that Hitler has my small beard [sic], it's all the same to me that [Nazi propaganda minister Joseph] Goebbels imitates my [duck] walk, but it makes me very angry that the [fat Lufwaffe–air force commander Herman] Goering gets more laughs than I do.[20]

During the period between the World Wars there had always been speculation that the dictator copied the popular toothbrush mustache of the comedian. For instance, in Richard Attenborough's *Chaplin* (1992), a biography based upon the comedian's memoir, and David Robinson's *Chaplin: His Life and Art* (1985), Charles' best friend Douglas Fairbanks (Kevin Kline) even kids the comedian, "I think he stole your act [the mustache] ... Adolf, I mean." Moreover, as the 1930s progressed, it was not unusual for political newspaper cartoonists to have fun with the look-alike nature of the duo.

For the record, history's funniest man first wore the undersized mustache when he began appearing as Charlie in 1914. History's scariest man assumed the style shortly after the First World War in 1919. What would have been the motive of the then wannabe leader, had he consciously borrowed Charlie's "cookie duster?" One assumes it would have been the hope that some of the Tramp's fame would have rubbed off on him. After all, to paraphrase gifted period humorist Will Rogers, "Charlie is better known in Zululand than Greta Garbo is in Arkansas." Along less amusing lines, some historians have suggested that Hitler's appropriation of Charlie's mustache caused period leaders to initially underestimate the dictator. For instance, Ron Rosenbaum argues:

> Chaplin's mustache became a *lens* through which to look at Hitler. A glass in which Hitler became *merely* Chaplinesque: a figure to be mocked more than feared, a comic villain whose pretensions would collapse of his own disproportionate weight like the Little Tramp collapsing on his cane. Someone to be ridiculed rather than be resisted.[21]

Be that as it may, there are several almost perverse dark-comic links between Chaplin and Hitler, many of which are showcased in Brownlow's *The Tramp and the Dictator.* The ties would include having European births a mere four days apart in 1889, having alcoholic fathers but mothers they worshipped, surviving childhood poverty, and fears of family histories with insanity. Most telling, both men were control freaks easily reduced to childish behavior if things did not go their way—situations often minimized by surrounding themselves with yes men. Plus, while Chaplin was an actor whose art often had political overtones, Hitler was a politician who took acting lessons to better sell his politics. And both men had a natural gift for mimicry. Like Chaplin, Hitler was fascinated by film and utilized arguably cinema's greatest

Another telling parallel between Hitler and Chaplin was ego. Here the comedian sits for a sculpture (circa 1925), years before a comparable Hynkel-Hitler scene appears in *The Great Dictator*.

woman director, Leni Riefenstahl, to celebrate Nazi Germany in the acclaimed documentaries *Triumph of the Will* (1935, chronicling the 1934 Nazi Party Convention at Nuremberg) and *Olympia* (1938, covering the 1936 Berlin Olympic Games).

Fortuitously, the sniper-like detail of Jürgen Trimborn's definitive Riefenstahl biography provides a window into Chaplin's period thoughts on *Triumph of the Will*. In the late 1930s, Spanish surrealist director Luis Buñuel, a Chaplin friend then living in the United States, was commissioned by New York's Museum of Modern Art to display the propaganda power of Riefenstahl's pictures. His task was to make several abridged films from *Will*, in order to demonstrate Riefenstahl's various cinematic political techniques. Buñuel later recalled that celebrated French filmmaker René Clair and Chaplin

> saw [the *Will* shorts] and had totally opposite reactions. Clair was horrified by the effectiveness of the films and said to me: 'Don't show them to anyone, or we're lost!' Chaplin, on the other hand, laughed like a crazy man. He even fell off his chair laughing. Why? Was it because of *The Great Dictator*? I don't to this day understand it.[22]

Given that Buñuel's first film *Andalusian Dog* (1928, in collaboration with Salvador Dali) was a pioneering surrealistic-dark comedy which features an eye being sliced for comic shock effect, one would assume the Spanish filmmaker would be prepared for any audience reaction. That being said, Chaplin's response to Riefenstahl's work would certainly qualify as unusual for the time. For example, when Frank Capra first saw *Will*, after the United States government assigned him to produce a seven-part series of propaganda films for America (what became the 1942–1945 *Why We Fight* documentaries), his response was along René Clair lines:

> The film was the ominous prelude of Hitler's holocaust of hate. Satan couldn't have devised a more blood-chilling super-spectacle.... The film's opening was a master stroke of god-building [Hitler seemed to descend without a plane.] The Nuremberg Congress of supermen had opened! A hundred thousand storm troopers—booted, armed, swastika-draped—stood rigid row on row, as Hate walked alone to his altar of microphones.[23]

Clair's forte was farce and fantasy, like *The Ghost Goes West* (1936) and *I Married a Witch* (1942), while Capra's whole oeuvre is often referred to as a "fantasy of goodwill," from the metaphorical variety like *Mr. Smith Goes to Washington* (1939), to the real fantasy deal, *It's a Wonderful Life* (1946).[24] In contrast, Chaplin's response to *Will* further demonstrates the filmmaker's inherent dark comedy base—though as this text has already begun to demonstrate, Chaplin's position on the genre was forever evolving. Moreover, Trimborn's Riefenstahl biography provides an answer for Clair's paper lion of a set-up question—why Chaplin fell out of his chair with laughter:

> Chaplin saw the exaggerated staging of Riefenstahl's film and the theoretical, studied look of Hitler's gesturing, his rolling eyes, and the way his voice cracked as something funny. Riefenstahl's film, which [Chaplin] watched over and over again while preparing *The Great Dictator,* allowed him to study Hitler's poses and behavior....[25]

For a darkly comic satirist like Chaplin, any pompously overstated cinema scene was an invitation to comically prick it, just as he does Hynkel's balloon globe. *The Tramp and the Dictator* also documents, via an interview with Chaplin's son Sydney, that his father loved visiting a Hollywood theater which only showed documentaries and newsreel films, giving Chaplin further time to study his darkly comic *target* subject—Hitler.

Whatever series of events led to Chaplin making *The Great Dictator,* one might now assume it was a no-brainer for the comedian to take on the Nazi leader. Yet, given the overwhelmingly isolationist sentiment in America during the late 1930s, Chaplin's production was an act of artistic bravery. Couple this with the sad scenario that there was also a great deal of anti–Semitism in America; the celebrated comedian actually received death threats over his decision to shish kebab the dictator. Controversy associated with *Dictator,* besides the aforementioned pioneer dark comedy status of the film, also involved something of a rarity for a 1930s movie star—being in the public doghouse for taking *any* political position. Embracing a stand on topical issues is now common in filmland, but it was a rare animal (notwithstanding Will Rogers) in 1930s Hollywood. The phenomenon might be compared to the mainstream movie industry's long-standing axiom against the problem film genre during the same time: "If you want to send a message, use Western Union" (attributed to countless movie producers).

For the 1940s public, however, the most dicey aspect of *Dictator* still came down to the picture's watershed dark comedy—even overshadowing the much-publicized fact that this was Chaplin's first "talkie." Yet, unlike *Shoulder Arms'* less controversial use of the genre, for a war in which most people then believed, *Dictator* assumes a posture first expounded upon by Chaplin in *Modern Times:* The individual was directly threatened by society's new norms. Yet *Dictator* gave this threat a face (Hitler-Hynkel), and by moving from the abstract problem-solution dilemma of a world economic crisis, *á la Modern Times,* to the more obviously immediate pressing dangers of world conflict, Chaplin was better able to display society's conscious threat to the individual.

One of dark comedy's seminal traits, man as beast, had frequently been present in Chaplin cinema, be it the abusive big top proprietor of *The Circus,* or the slave-driving factory owner in *Modern Times.* However, Chaplin's *Dictator* title character had no mitigating circumstances, such as creating a better performance (the circus owner), or increasing production in the *Modern Times* factory. No, the introduction to Chaplin's dictator is simply about a national leader wishing to liquidate a race of people.

The comedian made his new evolving twist on dark comedy more palatable, yet more disturbing, by casting himself against type as Hynkel, the perpetuator of this genocide. Chaplin further warped our emotions into topsy-turvydom (a dark comedy basic) by having the focus victim suffering these horrific crimes against humanity be played by cinema's most beloved figure, the Tramp in the guise of the Jewish barber (also played by Chaplin). This contrasting Chaplin dichotomy would be as if in *Shoulder Arms* he had played both Charlie the soldier *and the Kaiser,* forcing himself into an application of dark comedy for which neither the filmmaker nor the public was yet prepared. In fact, over twenty years later many viewers were still not capable of appreciating what Chaplin accomplished along black humor lines by playing Hynkel and Hitler. However, for *Dictator* fans, the effective manner in which the comedian inspiringly applies the picture's dark comedy is by employing the age-old technique of dual focus narrative, though it was then new for a cinematic application of this genre.

An archetypal example of dual focus narrative from another medium is a typical stained glass window from the Middle Ages. The upper portion of the window depicts Jesus, God and several signature figures from His heavenly court; the bottom half highlights Hell's Lucifer and an equal number of fallen angels—with each domain having a one-to-one correlating opposite character. Thus, one has a simplified visual storyline—know one figure, and the viewer immediately understands the other. An opposite type of dual focus also exists, where two individuals represent variations of the same character—something in which Chaplin was well-versed. For example, the youth, vitality and spontaneity of *Modern Times'* gamine (Paulette Goddard) is the first and only Chaplin heroine created in the quasi-image of the Tramp. Moreover, the situation is reminiscent of the dual focus narrative found in *The Kid* (1921), in which Chaplin's delightful diminutive co-star and title character (child star Jackie Coogan) is simply a miniature version of Charlie. Such satellite characters reinforce the comedy of the central clown. Regardless, though Chaplin uses dual focus of opposites in *Dictator,* enough of Charlie remains in Hynkel, such as his ballet-like interaction with the world-balloon, that the viewer is reluctantly drawn in, and thus implicated in what he stands for. Such mixed emotions, like life, is another aspect of dark comedy: Events can create conflicting emotions.

Though this variety of dual focus is without satellite characters, there are frequently supporting players who baldly state what the star figure is about. In *Dictator* the amusingly plump Field Marshal Herring (Billy Gilbert) is that individual. No one addresses dark comedy's use of death with more enthusiastic joy than Gilbert. He is forever bursting into Hynkel's chambers with the latest instrument of war, which inevitably means death. His most fanatically funny entrance has him breathlessly and happily announcing the creation of a wonderful poison gas: "It will kill *everybody!*" Though intended for the picture's enemy soldiers, this comically macabre statement foreshadows the Nazi "final solution" of concentration camps. Plus, Herring's gung-ho eagerness to share a blanket endorsement of death is consistent with black humor's shock effect ... which plays even more darkly today.

Again, using such a popular comedy-related character as Gilbert (a period regular in

Laurel & Hardy films and the voice of "Sneezy" in Walk Disney's *Snow White and the Seven Dwarfs*, 1937) also produces a nervously comic shock value effect. One simply does not expect it of his persona; in laughing, the viewer might also feel implicated in evil. On other occasions, Gilbert acts as a deathly dark comedy set-up man for Chaplin's Hynkel. For example, Herring interrupts the dictator so a bulletproof suit can be demonstrated. The inventor steps forward and Hynkel tests it by shooting him. The man drops dead and the dictator nonchalantly remarks, "Far from perfect." On another occasion, Gilbert's character brings in the inventor of a parachute hat. The patriotic fellow hails Hynkel (Nazi style) and jumps off the balcony. Chaplin's character and Herring momentarily lean over and watch the guinea pig's off-camera demise. The dictator then asks, "Herring, *why* do you waste my time like this?"

Such a casual demeanor in these settings is a perfect dark comedy combination of two primary components of the genre: man as beast and the everpresent yet casual treatment of death, summarized by Kurt Vonnegut's aforementioned, "So it goes." For all the comic frightfulness of an unordered universe, man has been a strong contributor to the third key component of dark comedy: absurdity. Man-made absurdity is the result of flaws as a species and its perpetuation in human institutions, *à la* Herring's application of Hynkel's beliefs. Chaplin had also suggested this in the *Modern Times* monitor sequence which inspired George Orwell's "Big Brother is watching you" mantra from *1984*. Yet Hynkel as dictator is a pioneering, blatant example of a catalyst for institutionalized absurdity—the crazed God-playing person with an *army* of willing disciples. Chaplin scholar Charles J. Maland reminds us that Hynkel is from Tomania, "a blend of the word for food poisoning and the suffix 'mania'—[for] madness."[26]

In a 1940 interview Chaplin revealed a provocatively personal view of the dangers inherent to institutionalized absurdity/man as beast/death in even the most seemingly minor of details. As briefly noted earlier, he found himself acting arrogantly abusive by merely wearing the elaborate but regimental Nazi-like uniform called for by his Hynkel part, even involving his in-costume, off-camera behavior—a fact seconded by individuals on the set.[27] To Chaplin,

> the uniform undoubtedly is a great deal to blame [for Nazi behavior]. The wearing of it often creates a false sense of being better than one's fellow man, when in most instances the reverse is the case.[28]

Though a correlation between a uniform and threatening authority might be tied to several nationalities, it is especially pertinent to Germany, a country created by the battlefield "diplomacy" of "Iron Chancellor" Otto von Bismarck (1815–1898). Born in Prussia, a North German country noted for its warlike and militaristic spirit, Bismarck united through war what had previously been a loose confederation of German states. For Bismarck the military was the state, and what was good for the military (uniform) was more important than the individual citizen. Needless to say, this view was later greatly admired by Hitler.

The power of the uniform even played itself out in twentieth century German pop culture. Chaplin and Hitler were both great fans of a 1920s film movement called German Expressionism (yet another parallel between the two). One of the most honored movies of this national cinema was *The Last Laugh* (1924), in which a doorman (Emil Jannings) bases his self-respect and importance upon a military-like hotel uniform. When he loses the position and the all-important uniform, his neighbors turn on him. Jannings' tour de force *Last Laugh* performance had critics calling him the world's greatest actor, and brought him to Hollywood. Fittingly, he would go on to win the first Best Actor Oscar for *The Way of All Flesh* (1927) and *The Last Command* (1928). Regardless, in the first half of the 20th century, it is hard to over-estimate the importance of the military uniform in German society. Or, in Chaplin's case, the importance of sideswiping military attire in one's dark comedy. (As an ironic Hitler-related addendum to Jannings' career, with the 1933 rise of the Nazi party, the actor was recruited by Josef Goebbels—Garbitsch in *Dictator*—to assist the party in propaganda. Not surprisingly, this would ultimately end his career in shame.)

Whatever one's take on the effectiveness of Chaplin's military uniform factor in his *Dictator* black humor, the comedian constantly uses such garb to subtextually skewer the Nazi party throughout the film. Examples would range from the biting use of a *double-cross* insignia in place of the Nazi swastika, to Hynkel's opening warning speech in German gibberish, "We must sacrifice, tighten der belton"—with the heavy Herring immediately rising to do so, only to have his belt split when he sits down. Comically, this sends his assorted attachments, such as his clanging dress sword, to the floor. Later in the sequence Herring accidentally butts Hynkel down a flight of stairs, and the dictator then comically strips the multiple medals from the plump one's chest. Later the bit is expanded to include buttons, and soon Herring is in his undershirt. The routine was so popular that countless variations appeared, such as Bugs Bunny doing the medal- and button-popping sketch to another German in the Warner Brothers war cartoon *Herr Meets Hare* (1945). In the early 1950s Sid Caesar's TV program *Your Show of Shows* even did a variation on the bit which harkened back to *The Last Laugh*: Caesar is a German doorman in another elaborate military-like uniform, but this time while Caesar's commands to his assistant (Howard Morris) are also in gibberish German, *à la* Chaplin's Hynkel, they involve how to *dress* this imposing doorman.

The uniform-directed humor is equally broad in one Jewish ghetto sequence which is reminiscent of the whitewashing barbershop clown sketch in *The Circus*. That is, when a *Dictator* storm trooper paints "Jew" on the Tramp-like barber's storefront window (a rare cinema use of the word in that era), the altercation which follows finds Chaplin's little Jewish barber also doing some whitewashing ... of the trooper with the German's own bucket and paintbrush. Score one for the underdog. Other military uniform–focused dark comedy would include Hynkel putting on a pompous cape that fittingly acts like more of a straitjacket (an apt metaphor on how the neo–Nazi tends to act in these uniforms), to the food fight between Hynkel and the equally uniform-obsessed Napoloni (Jack Oakie in an Oscar-nominated turn mocking Italian dictator Benito Mussolini).

On another dark comedy level of absurdity, the use of a uniform, actually two, acts as the film's ultimate turning point. On the eve of Tomania's invasion of Austerlich (Austria?), Hynkel embraces the goofy idea of going duck-hunting, with the most amusing Germanic hunting attired possible. One might christen it "the basic Tyrolean short shorts, suspenders, and feathered cap ensemble suitable for yodeling ... or scaring small children." Naturally, out of his double-cross uniform he is mistaken as the at-large barber and arrested. Conversely, the fleeing Charlie-like barber, attired in Hynkel's garb, is just as readily accepted as the dictator. The power of the uniform is further underlined by its quasi–Pied Piper effect, as deceived soldiers methodically fall in around the Hynkel-attired barber. The uniform, or its absence, has made all the difference. Indeed, is that not the danger of uniformed organizations—they often encourage a dangerous *group think*? The Marx Brothers' *Duck Soup* (1933) suggests just this concept with the team wearing a cross-section of military garb through the ages to close their anti-war picture. The power of the elaborate military uniform might even be used as a provocative explanation for the film's controversial conclusions when citizen Chaplin steps out of his barber–Charlie character dressed in the dictator's uniform to speak for peace. However, it could be argued that the uniform itself gave the little barber the sudden assertiveness to ask the world to throw down its guns.

Without trying to do so, Chaplin actually differentiated between his evolving use of dark comedy from *Shoulder Arms* to *Dictator* in a 1940 article entitled "Mr. Chaplin Answers His Critics." The comedian's immediate purpose was to defend *Dictator*'s black humor, yet note his reference to *Shoulder Arms:*

> There is a healthy thing in laughing at the grimmest thing in life, laughter at death even. *Shoulder Arms* ... had to do with men marching off to war.... Laughter is a tonic, the relief, the surcease from pain.[29]

Shoulder Arms, however, ultimately used its dark comedy to celebrate "men marching off to war"—because it was initially embraced as a just conflict. *Dictator,* conversely, ends with a passionate plea for men to *stop* marching off to war and all the movie's deployment of its black humor, from the man as beast Hynkel, to his killing machine party of the double-cross, would have accomplished Chaplin's goal for peace.

Chaplin does use the First World War of *Shoulder Arms* as an effective bridge to *Dictator* and a heightened and more disturbing altered change to his dark comedy. First, *Dictator* begins with Chaplin's Tramp-like barber as a World War I soldier, too, though now he is Tomanian (German). Like Erich Maria Remarque's novel *All Quiet on the Western Front* (1928), a sympathetic American-like German *enemy* underscores the absurdity of war much more than *Shoulder Arms*. Moreover, by making Charlie's version of a conscientious German soldier Jewish, it further accents the pointless man-as-beast absurdity of Hitler's racial hatred, since countless Jewish-German soldiers served with distinction during the First World War.

Second, while Chaplin's *Shoulder Arms* doughboy *dreams* his dark comedy war experience, *Dictator*'s counterpart lives his and tops it off with a major head injury, which, though played comically, ups the dark comedy quotient. Moreover, while our American Charlie's *sleeping* combat is merely the length of an afternoon nap, his German private is disabled for years in a convalescent facility ... and it gets darkly comic worse. Our Rip Van Winkle–like Charlie then enters a living nightmare called "Hynkel-Hitler's Germany," which he cannot understand. Moreover, this allows Chaplin to again couple dark humor in a then groundbreaking area: what would now be labeled post-traumatic stress.

Charlie's unlikely winning of the *Shoulder Arms* war by capturing the Kaiser is immediately erased at the picture's close by showing it was only a short snooze. Thus, Chaplin almost did the proverbial dark comedy exaggerated happy ending to ironically underline that this could never happen. In contrast, the controversial closing *Dictator* speech is more complex. Forget, momentarily, that Chaplin is channeling himself through the barber, who has been mistaken for Hynkel. Though not exactly a happy ending, it is a hopeful speech which freeze-frames the picture's hint of World War II. Plus, the optimism of the barber-citizen Chaplin's final lines, "We are coming out of the darkness into the light! We are coming into a new world...!" again suggests that when this genre presents an over-the-top positive conclusion, it is to be "read" as a cynical pipe dream. Yet, we know Chaplin was dead serious about stepping out of character to do some soapboxing.

Another ending the comedian filmed for *Dictator*'s close would have embraced dark comedy's standard "it's not to be believed" ending. Chaplin had initially planned, and shot, a conclusion to the speech which caused German soldiers to throw down their weapons and spontaneously go into some sort of peace folk dance. It does not get more absurd than suddenly friendly dancing storm troopers. Such an ironically upbeat close would even have topped the later satirically false happy endings of dark comedy classics like *Catch–22* (1970) and *Brazil* (1985). While Chaplin was dead serious about his *Dictator* closing, a revisionist "reading" of the sequence could still argue it was a pioneering example of the genre's tendency not to take a positive ending at face value.

Just as *Shoulder Arms*' World War I setting assisted the same war transition start to *Dictator,* Chaplin also transformed and further twisted elements of *Modern Times*' dark comedy into *Dictator*. For instance, the institutionalized group think, mechanical lock-step marching behavior of the inmates in *Modern Times*' prison sequence seems a precursor to the forced goose-stepping of the barber in *Dictator*'s concentration camp. Furthermore, it suggests the then (1940) universal prison-like state which had become the Nazi norm.

Second, the man-as-beast component is often played out in lustful quasi-sexual scenes, such as the Tramp's nervous breakdown attraction to *Modern Times*' pretty blonde in the factory setting. This lasciviously absurd behavior by the normally romantic Charlie is further suggested by his attempt to tighten the breast-high buttons of a passing matron when Charlie is running amok with his factory wrench. While it is funny and darkly comic, the viewer grants the Tramp a pass because modern society has driven him to this atypical crazy behavior. In contrast, *Dictator*'s Hynkel finds this salacious beast-like attitude (he even snorts) toward his sexy secretary as the new dark comedy norm. Moreover, in Hynkel's opening hate-filled gibberish speech about the Jews, his passionate rage seems almost sexually driven, since at one point he finds the need to pour cold water down his pants—as if only this will keep his talk on track.

Third, *Modern Times*' dark comedy opening metaphor on man being like so many animals that are almost mechanically trained and herded to their own demise (just as Charlie is swallowed by the machine and loses his sense of self), is brought home more directly and darkly by another of the barber-citizen Chaplin lines in *Dictator*'s final speech: "You are not machines, you are not cattle, you are men." (One is reminded of Stanley Kubrick's 1971 dark comedy *A Clockwork Orange*, from Anthony Burgess' novel. The title references a government being allowed to negate a citizen's free will, and reduce an individual to "a clockwork orange"—only part human.) Also, in *Dictator*'s final speech reference to the Scriptures (from the 17th Chapter of St. Luke, which states the Kingdom of God is not in one man but all men), Chaplin references machines in another way. To paraphrase his comments here, "The *people* have the power to do anything, from creating positive machines, to creating happiness and democracy. Don't give yourself to unnatural men [dictators]—machine men with machine minds and machine hearts...."

While it is most logical to tie *City Lights*' opening use of distorted sound with the *Dictator*'s Katzenjammer German (since both satirize the verbal mumbo-jumbo of political leaders), one could also link the Tramp's discombobulated verbiage of *Modern Times*' closing song to Hynkel's gibberish. The latter is more of a stretch, since Charlie's first words are in an innocent musical language of his own invention, with no agenda beyond joyful laughter. Yet one could still argue that Charlie's singing waiter's desperate theatrical need to please was also the starting point for Hitler-Hynkel, since the Nazi leader even took acting lessons in an equally desperate desire to sell his convoluted ideas.

Regardless, as herein demonstrated, the dark comedy from *Modern Times* to *Dictator* had been appreciably increased, and the genre's general application by Chaplin had been greatly altered. Even the latter picture's opening titles, in part, suggest the change about to be experienced: "This is the story of the period between two World Wars—an interim in which Insanity cut loose, Liberty took a nose dive, and Humanity was kicked around somewhat." Paradoxically, possibly the most disturbing *Dictator* demonstrations of dark comedy come from its most poetically ephemeral sequence—when Hynkel does his ballet of world conquest with a balloon-like world globe. Naturally, dark comedy is a genre which often embraces the apocalypse, real or imagined. Consequently, win or lose, Hynkel's (or any other crazed leader's) dance of death is about the ongoing threat to civilization ... by man himself.

What gives the Hynkel globe sequence an added, disturbingly poignant aura is the passionate beauty Chaplin brings to the performance. As Chaplin biographer Theodore Huff observed, "It is a scene that enthralls one, simultaneously with its wit, its fantasy, and its ballet grace."[30] Yet, despite this charm, the sequence represents a formula for destruction, a poisoned flower in the garden. Again, the viewer's enjoyment of the scene implicates him in the horror to come. Moreover, like a child playing with a ball, when this fragile globe explodes, and Hynkel is reduced to profuse tears, a fascinating parallel to, yet contrast with, the Tramp is revealed. As was suggested earlier in this text, Charlie is essentially a boy playing at being a man in his father's oversized clothing. Early in the Tramp's evolution he could be crude and rude, yet his overriding tendency even then was the idealized romanticism of a youth. In contrast, Hynkel's ultimate fearfest suggests the disturbed child as potential monster—for his *game* of ball meant death to millions. However, the Hynkel boy factor implicates the viewer anew beyond the breathtaking pleasure in witnessing his ballet. That is, there is still a momentary modicum of sympathy, because this sequence, more than any *Dictator* scene, does the least to disguise Hynkel's childish nature ... and no matter what that ultimately means, compassion for a crying youngster is a knee-jerk response for most people.

Napoleon and Hitler were at the heart of Chaplin making *Dictator*. Yet, as noted early in the text, the catalyst for this book was Russell Martin's text *Picasso's War* (2002), which examines the painter's response to the first large-scale attack against a non-military city in modern history—the German Luftwaffe's total destruction of the Basque town of Guernica during the Spanish Civil War on April 26, 1937. Spanish expatriate Pablo Picasso would immediately create a canvas expressing the world's outrage at this act of terror and bearing the city's name *Guernica*—a work immediately recognized as an inspired statement against man's abhorrence to the brutality of war.

While a single event during the Spanish Civil War (the prelude to World War II) propelled Picasso to create arguably his greatest work and one of the seminal works of art of the twentieth century, Chaplin's equally significant *Dictator* was, as thus documented, more the result of a cumulative series of events. (However, Chaplin biographer David Robinson briefly notes that the comedian had written an unpublished poem, in 1936 or 1937, about the Spanish Civil War, as well as a later short story on the killing of a Spanish Loyalist.[31]) Even without factoring in this Chaplin writing, Picasso's explanation-defense for the initially controversial *Guernica* might just as well have doubled as Chaplin's justification for the making of the equally controversial *Dictator:* "What do you think an artist is? An imbecile who has only eyes, if he is a painter [filmmaker]? ... No, painting [art] is not done to decorate apartments. It is an instrument of war [for peace]."[32] Fittingly, though Picasso's work was not anchored in dark comedy, *à la* Chaplin's, he could assume a dark comedy posture in discussing it. For instance, in the

Second World War Picasso had to face Nazi harassment during their occupation of his city, Paris. In the course of one tormenting Gestapo visit Picasso endured in his apartment, a German officer had recognized a sketch of "*Guernica* pinned to the wall of his studio and had asked him, 'Did you do that?' Picasso coldly had replied, 'No, you did.'"[33]

Movie columnist Hedda Hopper wrote in March 1940:

> As you know, there hasn't been much news on *The Dictator* because Chaplin is following the lead of neighbor David Selznick and suppressing publicity until release time. But Paulette Goddard tells me she plays a kitchen slave named Hannah in the picture.[34]

Chaplin had *always* been secretive about his projects but *Dictator* was a special case, right down to his receiving death threats. As if to make Chaplin and Hopper liars, the same issue of the *Los Angeles Times* included an anecdote about the production:

> Jack Oakie contributes an amusing story from *The Dictator* set. Seems Chaplin was lining up a scene in which his "Storm Troopers" were doing their drill. "You're at attention as the scene starts," he explained—and paused as he caught sight of bit player Tom Bennett's slouchy stance. "I said 'ATTENTION!,'" shouted Chaplin. "But I am at attention," reported Bennett. "It's this darned uniform that's at ease."[35]

Not until the following month, April, does another *Dictator* anecdote appear in the *Los Angeles Times*. The reference is to the film's early World War I sequence in which the Charlie-like barber-soldier is preparing to fire Germany's gargantuan Big Bertha cannon. A huge dud of a spinning shell will then drop out of this heavy artillery piece and comic chaos will ensue for Chaplin's character and 200 extras. All day the cast had rehearsed the scene:

> Finally, near 5 o'clock, everything was ready and the cameras started grinding. It was a perfect "take," until, suddenly, one of the Chaplin boys [Sydney], on the set to watch daddy, burst into a loud laugh. Chaplin whirled, glared, then announced, wearily, "That will be all for today. Everybody back tomorrow and we'll try it again.[36]

After revealing Sydney's scene-stopping laughter, the *Los Angeles Times* is essentially devoid of tales from the *Dictator* set until Hedda Hopper offers up a *possible* scoop in August which ultimately does not make the picture:

> [Chaplin's] finally licked the [*Dictator*] finish, Hitler's [Hynkel's] been set for an address to the world over the radio. Through some unforeseen happening, he can't make it, and Chaplin [mistaken for Hynkel] gets on and does the speech for him. He starts all right but in the middle asks the world to listen carefully, and launches into a tirade against the Führer [Hynkel]. Naturally, before he finishes, he's cut off the air and the storm troopers are closing in on him.[37]

(Sometimes *Dictator* misinformation was planted—this will be addressed in the following chapter.)

Between the aforementioned March reference, and the October press-only screening of the *Dictator*, occasional references to Chaplin would appear in the *Los Angeles Times;* but the insider material largely stops. The reader is much more likely to receive columnist conjecture about the production and/or the odd factoid. For instance, in the space of a week during late May, both Hopper and columnist Jimmie Fidler made similar prophetic (to many) statements about *The Dictator*. Hopper's came first:

> Chaplin has more than the war to worry about now. It's his million and a half [dollar] production of *The Dictator*, which everyone says is his greatest picture. But with the condition of the world at present [fighting had escalated in 1940], no one feels like laughing at any dictator. As Molly says to Fibber, "Taint funny, McGee" [from radio's popular *Fibber McGee & Molly* program].[38]

Chaplin's workaholic nature during the *Dictator* production also largely shut down his social calendar, which was the comedian's regular modus operandi. Yet, there is a telling late June exception to this norm reported by the *Los Angeles Times*:

> You would have howled at Paulette Goddard, Marlene Dietrich and Dolores del Rio all dressed and bejeweled, with Charlie Chaplin, [Mexico's premier artist] Diego Rivera, Orson Welles [romantically involved with del Rio] and [*All Quiet on the Western Front* novelist] Erich Remarque, going to look at ... Eddie Robinson's [celebrated collection of] paintings.[39]

The gathering reveals much about Chaplin, and his by-then cordially estranged relationship with third wife Goddard (they remained friends but lived separate lives). First, Goddard had probably helped pry Chaplin loose from his work because she was both a great admirer of Rivera, and earlier that month the artist had been invited to paint a mural for the Golden Gate International Exposition in San Francisco ... which would incorporate images of both Goddard and Chaplin (addressed later in the text). Second, the fact that Welles was included in the group was another example of how Chaplin did not care about Hollywood opinion. The "boy genius" Welles had often been mocked by the mainstream movie industry for the unprecedented carte blanche power RKO had given a novice filmmaker (*Citizen Kane* 1941, was yet to come). No less a name than novelist–wannabe screenwriter F. Scott Fitzgerald had punned, "All's well that ends Welles."

Third, this Chaplin social outing had also displayed his cavalier attitude towards conservative America's opinion on a much broader scale by hobnobbing with the proud-to-be-a communist Rivera. For instance, in the 1930s the painter, with his wife and fellow artist Frida Kahlo, had been instrumental in getting Mexican political asylum for Leon Trotsky, a guiding light of the Bolshevik Russian Revolution of 1917. Yet, following fellow revolutionist Vladimir Lenin's 1924 death, fellow communist revolutionary Joseph Stalin ruthlessly assumed power and exiled Trotsky, though this man without a country would continue to be an influential communist theorist and arch foe of his former comrade. (Stalin-directed agents would assassinate Trotsky in Mexico in 1940.)

The inclusion of Remarque was also most fitting, since his novel *Western Front* remains arguably the greatest of all anti-war texts; and Chaplin was just finishing his seminal anti-war film. Since the Nazi movement had essentially also exiled Remarque from Germany for the "defeatism" of his book, despite the rest of the world considering it *the* treatise on the absurdity of war, the novelist and Chaplin undoubtedly had a great deal to talk about. (As an additional note to the proceedings, much later Remarque and Goddard married, and like Chaplin and his final wife Oona O'Neill, both couples would find themselves living in Switzerland—the most neutral, anti-war of countries.)

Host Edward G. Robinson was the versatile actor most synonymous with gangster films, such as his crime boss Rico Bandello in *Little Caesar* (1931). This tough guy on the screen was the most urbane of Hollywood liberals and rapidly putting together one of the world's largest private art collections. Decades before Frida Kahlo was recognized as a major talent, Robinson purchased one of her first paintings, with an appreciatively supportive Rivera nicknaming his wife's early patron the "gangster actor." So how is this pertinent to Chaplin, besides documenting a cultured circle of acquaintances? Despite being like Chaplin in his open-minded disregard for the politics of his friends, Robinson went on to have one of the most patriotic of résumés during World War II, with regard to his active support of Allied causes. Yet, as with Chaplin and so many other liberal television and film artists, he too would be victimized by 1950s McCarthyism and the House Un-American Activities Committee.

Indeed, the reactionary seedlings were already present in America. For example, just a month before the Robinson gathering, the appointment of future two-time Oscar-winning actor Melvyn Douglas as a lieutenant colonel in the California National Guard intelligence unit was "protested" by the American Legion because "Douglas for years has been associated with radicals."[40] Arch conservatives would later have better luck sabotaging the career of his wife, actress turned politician Helen Gahagan Douglas, the first woman elected to Congress from California (in 1944). When the liberal Democrat Gahagan ran for the Senate against fellow Representative and future President Richard Nixon in 1950, she was defeated in a smear campaign in which Gahagan was falsely portrayed as a "pink" lady, and alleged "Red" sympathizer. (As a comically modest personal victory, she was the one who nicknamed him "Tricky Dick.")

Moreover, besides isolationist conservatives in the 1940s, or reactionary HUAC sorts in the 1950s, Nazi appeasement was still alive and well in the United States, close to our official involvement in the war. For instance, when the Germans were taking over Europe with victory after victory in 1940, high-profile syndicated *Los Angeles Times* columnist Jimmie Fidler could write:

> Well, it's come more quickly then I expected! [German domination in Europe].... Foolishly (I think) several studios went right ahead making anti–Nazi films.... Quoting *Variety*, the industry's leading trade journal, "[Several recent American dramas] contain slaps at Hitler and most of them have already drawn loud protests from the German embassy in Washington...." Belief is strong in some circles that Uncle Sam will crack down on American distribution of any films objectionable to Hitler....[41]

While the United States was not about to do any such thing (with President Franklin Delano Roosevelt privately even encouraging Chaplin's production of *Dictator*), most Hollywood studios *were* working closely with Los Angeles representatives of the German Embassy to edit American films so as to not upset the Nazi government!

Even amidst this gloom, however, from the expansion of the war in Europe, to industry-related individuals more interested in profit sheets them Nazi atrocities, Chaplin's studio produced some unintended humor during August of 1940. A *Los Angeles Times* article entitled "Cowboy Author Sees Chaplin but Tactics Upset Studio" reported:

> Noel Jones ... strode into the Chaplin studios dressed in a complete cowboy outfit from 10-gallon hat to spurs [and] demanded to see Chaplin about a manuscript he had sent the comedian through the mail.... [When told that] all unsolicited manuscripts ... are returned to the sender unopened ... Jones proceeded to pull all the telephone wires out of the switchboard, cutting off communications to the studio.[42]

Chaplin, attempting to get said cowboy off the lot, was soon assisted by the police, with whom the comedian shared a threatening letter he had recently received from Jones: "Believe me, brother, I am a man possessed, you had better read the enclosed manuscript."[43] The visit sounded like a cross between Chaplin's year with Mack "Keystone Cops" Sennett, and the comedian's next Hollywood boss, Essanay's Gilbert M. "Broncho Billy" Anderson; the wannabee writer Jones was eventually arrested for sending threatening letters. So at a time when Chaplin was under considerable strain making his controversial comedy, he also had to deal with a deranged cowpuncher. Still, one cannot help wondering if the comedian confronted cowboy Jones when dressed as the Führer!

Speaking of Hynkel-Hitler, that same summer Chaplin finalized the title *The Great Dic-*

7. Napoleon, Hitler and The Great Dictator 117

tator.[44] The original plan was simply to call the movie *The Dictator*, but Paramount owned the rights to that moniker dating back to a now lost 1920s Wallace Reid silent film. Instead of paying Paramount $25,000 for the rights, Chaplin went with *The Great Dictator,* though numerous publications were still referring to the picture as *The Dictator* right up until the movie's October 1940 release.

Prior to the film's premiere, *Dictator* was also receiving indirect attention by way of publicity related to Paulette Goddard's co-starring with Bob Hope in the mega-hit *The Ghost Breakers* (1940), their smash follow-up to *The Cat and the Canary* (1939). One of Hope's fondest memories was the praise he received from his boyhood comedy hero for *The Cat and the Canary*. Keep in mind, Hope's first stage experience had been as a young Charlie impersonator during the Tramp mania of the 1910s:

> Bumping into Hope at a racetrack one afternoon while *The Cat and Canary* was still in production, Chaplin said to him, "Young man, I've been watching you in the [film] rushes every night. I want you to know that you are one of the best timers of comedy I have ever seen."[45]

Los Angeles Times references to Paulette also provided a slant on what possibly helped bring Chaplin and Goddard together during the early 1930s. The standard story has them meeting at a weekend party aboard producer Joseph Schenck's yacht. The filmmaker always included several beautiful young actresses on these outings. Chaplin and the lovely Goddard immediately hit it off, assisted by the comedian providing some helpful financial advice, which rescued the

Paulette Goddard and Bob Hope in *The Ghost Breakers*.

recently divorced actress from investing her settlement in what was essentially a scam operation. So what was the hitherto unknown potential added factor about the couple's beginnings? Well, in Goddard's early Hollywood days, when she was more of an extra than an actress, the budding performer also modeled, with an artist's committee first bringing her fame "by announcing her body [the] most beautiful in Hollywood."[46] With this being no small accomplishment in la-la-land, there is not a doubt that Chaplin, quite the connoisseur of lovely ladies, would have been well aware of Goddard's recognition.

References to Goddard's goddess status kept popping up in the 1940s *Los Angeles Times*. For example, while the previous quote was simply a caption to a Goddard picture, sans article, other acknowledgments included an early review of *Breakers*: "Miss Goddard may not have 'the most beautiful body in the world' but you'll never prove it by me. Let us say it is beautiful enough."[47] Though not noted in the *Times,* its sudden plethora of references to Goddard's beauty might also have been fueled by Rivera's description of how he was using her in the aforementioned mural as "Representing American girlhood," or what the actress said symbolized "the tree of life and love."[48] Goddard's collaboration with Rivera meant the actress could bookend the decade by her work as a model, though, of course, the performer's 1930s career would forever be synonymous with Chaplin.

The *Los Angeles Times* coverage of *Ghost Breakers* also provided as excellent window into the still largely escapist world in which Chaplin would soon drop his provocative dark comedy *Dictator. Breakers* is a popular personality comedy, which also affectionately spoofs the horror genre.[49] And prior to the October opening of *Dictator,* the *Times* devoted a great deal of ink to *Breakers* and four other comedies. First, in what was turning into a breakout year for Bob Hope, the first of the Hope-Bing Crosby-Dorothy Lamour *Road* pictures appeared, destination Singapore. This film franchise would produce six more misadventures between 1941 and 1962. As with *Breakers, Road to Singapore* is a compound genre of clown comedy and parody.

A second breakout artist highlighted by the 1940s *Times* was writer turned director Preston Sturges. Unlike Hope's career, his would be meteorically brief but during the 1940s no one could write such inspired comic dialogue. A screenwriter during the 1930s, Sturges sold Paramount his original story *The Great McGinty* in 1940 for $10, with the provision he be allowed to direct.[50] The result was a critical and commercial smash, as well as an Oscar for Best Original Screenplay. The *Times* critique nicely summarized the satire by observing, "[T]his film is to the issue of politics what *She Done Him Wrong* [1933, the] early Mae West feature was to the question of sex."[51] Sturges' success would soon help other writers get the opportunity to direct their own material, such as Billy Wilder (a huge fan of Sturges' wit) and John Huston.

Speaking of West, another 1940s comedy which grabbed plenty of *Times* attention was the teaming of West and W.C. Fields in *My Little Chickadee.* Much of the period coverage addressed why the film, though funny, was not more entertaining. While 1940s pundits blamed West's domination of the story, the most amusing *Times* printed item related to the movie was Fields airing a lengthy pet peeve which concluded, "[I]t is only fair that we hams [actors] do some [negative review] writing to retaliate [since critics are] hardly to be identified as efficient [actors]."[52] Once again, *Chickadee* was another mix of personality comedy and parody ... gone West squared.

The final 1940s comedy producing numerous *Times* pieces could be coupled with *Chickadee*: the Marx Brothers' cowboy spoof *Go West.* While this parody fared better with the *Times* then the Fields-West outing, the Marxes created added attention because, unlike Chaplin's secretive *Dictator* set, Groucho and company took a rough script outline of the movie on the road. The team played a limited number of West Coast theaters to polish the material. One such *Times* "live" review stated, "[T]he Marxes behave quite as informally as they might in your drawing room. And heaven help the drawing room!"[53] Road tours of this nature had been done with great success earlier in the team's MGM career.

Maybe Chaplin should have made *The Führer Goes West,* since 1940 even found Jack Benny making an entertaining picture in cowboy land, *Buck Benny Rides Again.* One only belabors these period personality comedy parodies, whether in Singapore, or where sagebrush is the number one backdrop, to suggest that Chaplin's topical thinking person's dark comedy was going to be nothing like the delightfully escapist mind candy just described, excepting one brief W.C. Fields aside during *Chickadee.* That is, when the comedian's umbrella is bent during an introduction; when he is asked, "Almost busted it?," Fields drawls, "It can't break. It's a perfect Chamberlain." (This is a reference to then British Prime Minister Neville Chamberlain, best known for his acts of appeasement—bending—towards Hitler.) Be that as it may, the stark contrast with the 1940s fun fluff might best be summarized in a *Dictator* overview in which the *Times* cites Chaplin's description of the picture's basic theme: "the persecution of any minority is inhuman and unnatural."[54] Naturally, given the movie fare just noted, the newspaper adds,

> As to whether dictatorships are any longer a source of hilarity—if indeed, they ever were—the public will soon enough pronounce the answer. Insists the comedian himself, "We must laugh in the face of these crazy times."[55]

As the time drew closer for the New York premiere at two theaters (an unusual move for a then-unusual film), *Dictator* material became more prevalent in the *Los Angeles Times.* And there were still suggestions of traditional Chaplin comedy, such as this revelation: "so closely does the film's barber resemble the little man of the baggy pants, skimpy coat, oversized shoes, cane and mustache that he is referred to throughout the script simply as 'Charlie' ...."[56] There were also other interesting revelations:

> While casting *The Great Dictator* Charlie Chaplin's office sounded like a courtroom in the process of selecting a jury. Actors were selected not only for ability but with regard to political feelings. There's so much dynamite in the picture Charlie didn't want any civil strife while it was being shot.[57]

Not surprisingly, Chaplin was pleased with the picture, especially after showing a final print to a small, intimate circle of friends including Goddard, actor Burgess Meredith (Goddard's next husband), Mr. and Mrs. Lewis Milestone [Milestone won a directing Oscar for the first and still best adaptation of the anti-war *All Quiet on the Western Front,* 1930] and the later Oscar-winning director Anatole Litvak. According to Hedda Hopper, "The celebration after the picture went on into the night. They were all so emotional it took them hours to get back to normal."[58]

Chaplin's provocative politics were not always the first thing on West Coast minds, with the *Times* musing about the one and only press screening, "[This screening] will exemplify the first real test of Charlie Chaplin as a talking picture actor. Imagine that—considering talkies have been going in a big way for nearly 12 years."[59]

Regardless, the *Times*' later *Dictator* review of the press showing, "Chaplin Film Shows Flashes of Genius," was not quite as rosy as that title indicates.[60] Neither Chaplin nor Goddard were present, having already gone east for the New York premieres. The following chapter examines many of the multi-faceted responses to *Dictator* first demonstrated in the Los Angeles critiques, such as the soapbox speech of a conclusion, or just the subject matter itself. Still, with Hollywood being a film industry town, the *Times* piece focuses more on *Dictator*'s limitations as a modern movie than any of the East Coast critiques to come. Moreover, the next chapter also chronicles Chaplin's movement to an even more extreme, disturbing exploration of black humor. Between *Dictator* and *Monsieur Verdoux* Chaplin would have a great deal of time to ponder the merits of George M. Cohan's old observation, "Talk well of me if you can, bad if you must but don't stop talking."

An examination of the *Dictator* reviews to follow, however, makes one ponder what directions the critiques might have followed had the pundits been privy to an off-the-record remark President Franklin Roosevelt had made just prior to the 1935 assassination of Louisiana senator Huey Long. The catalyst for Roosevelt's warning was America's questioning of whether democracy could survive (versus the seemingly successful model of dictator Adolf Hitler), and Long's potential for stirring up stateside anti–Semites. Roosevelt observed, "[Behind Long] there could be more blood running in the streets of New York than in Berlin."[61]

Nevertheless, E.H. Gombrich has noted that any historian who has lived long enough "to experience what happens as the present becomes the past has a story to tell about the way the outlines change with increasing distance."[62] The horrific scale of what occurred at Guernica has been greatly eclipsed by later war atrocities, such as the Second World War fire-bombing of Dresden, Germany (February 13–15, 1945, which inspired Kurt Vonnegut's classic anti-war novel *Slaughterhouse-Five,* 1969). But *Guernica* and Chaplin's *Dictator* remain as watershed examples of art's retaliation against man's dark side.

One irony of what is to follow in this text is how the increasing scope of these war-generated tragedies push Chaplin toward an even more *now* modern twisted take on black humor.

8

After *The Great Dictator*; Before *Monsieur Verdoux*

Fittingly, dark comedy author Franz Kafka's (1893–1924) favorite film comedian, Chaplin, had represented to him a spokesman for people who "could no longer manage to do what they liked with their lives."[1]

Though Franz Kafka died long before the release of *The Great Dictator* (1940), his comments quoted above had never been more true. Moreover, a Kafka biographer would later observe that the writer's perception of his responsibilities as a black humorist "uncannily anticipated the still-to-come [greatest advocate] films of Charlie Chaplin," such as *Dictator*.[2] Kafka short stories like "The Penal Colony" foreshadow the future concentration camps ... where the writer's three sisters would one day die.

The major difference between the works of Chaplin and Kafka is that the filmmaker was a mainstream artist in a much more high-visibility medium. However, both men were dark comedy prophets sending out a warning about the precarious plight of modern men and women. While Kafka experienced none of the fame and fortune known by Chaplin for most of his adult life (little of Kafka's writing was published before his death), each artist's work has grown in stature through the years.

The mix of *Dictator* satirizing Hitler and being Chaplin's first talkie helped make the film his greatest commercial hit at over five million dollars (which translates into an excess of $100 million plus today), and this was without the box office from a Nazi-controlled mainland Europe where it was banned. There were many positive critiques in the American press, including this country's pioneering premier film critic, the *New Republic*'s Otis Ferguson, who observed:

> [A]s always where there is a Chaplin picture, there is laughter here, warmth and grace, too. I think it will do you good, just for what is there, let alone that this is still Chaplin the Great, and [even] growing at his age.[3]

Variety, America's entertainment bible, prophetically recognized the picture's watershed nature:

> Audience reaction can't help but be favorable, granting that Nazi sympathizers are not considered at all. Through the 127 minutes of the film it is virtually certain that the average customer will go out of the theater with a feeling of having thoroughly enjoyed it.[4]

However, as the *Hollywood Citizen-News* later summarized, "[W]ith [some] exceptions, the New York reviewers were what might euphemistically be called 'disappointed.'"[5] The long gestation period between the comedian becoming serious about a Hitler dark comedy in 1937 and the picture coming to fruition in 1940 (more and more a Chaplin norm), now found much of the world at war. Thus, as *New York Times* critic Bosley Crowther suggested in an otherwise positive review, for many people, "the subject of it [Hitler] is much too grim for jesting."[6] Along similar lines, John Mosher's generally positive *New Yorker* review opens with a telling overview of the then shell-shocked (over dark comedy) viewing public:

> There's a general feeling ... prevalent around the town that *The Great Dictator* is a very curious affair indeed, something distinctly odd, and certainly unique. People aren't sure that they like it, or anyhow they aren't very eloquent about why they do, or ... why they don't.[7]

Mosher goes on to say a great many laudatory things about the movie, such as calling "the dance of the dictator at play with the world ... just about as delightful a bit as Charlie Chaplin has ever given us anywhere."[8] Still, Mosher's opening time capsule take on the state of dark comedy in 1940 remains his most telling contribution to the film's literature.

Chaplin had successfully applied dark comedy to *Shoulder Arms* (1918) at a time when the United States was actively engaged *in* World War I—*22 years before*. What had changed? Granted, Hitler was undoubtedly perceived as a great threat in 1940, but recall earlier in this text the effectively over-the-top villainous depictions of the Kaiser during the First World War. Yes, part of the 1940s' public deer-in-the-headlights shock response to *Dictator* was about dark comedy. If done effectively, that is the genre's impact on *most* eras. What had made more of a difference in 1940, however, was that many viewers felt awkward filtering the enemy through Chaplin as Hynkel-Hitler. A similarly uneasy public response would undoubtedly have attached itself to *Shoulder Arms* if the comedian had played both a sometimes entertaining Kaiser (in an expanded part) *and* Charlie the doughboy. Chaplin had only semi-successfully (for the time) pushed the envelope on what sort of character the public could laugh at ... even if it involved the world's favorite clown.

Granted, Chaplin had also provided a partial entertainment safety net for the audience and artist alike by playing a sympathetic Jewish barber-like Tramp, too. With a Charlie figure present in whatever was Chaplin's latest picture—throughout his career to this point—the comedian seemed capable of weathering assorted controversies, from sexual and political scandals, to even a groundbreaking narrative, *à la Dictator*. However, with the emphasis of the last picture on the disturbing title character, Chaplin had clearly reached a career tipping point on what his core audience would find acceptable in his ever-evolving exploration of dark comedy. (As examined in the next chapter, the lack of a winsome Charlie balancing factor would contribute to the initial American rejection of *Monsieur Verdoux* in 1947.)

A second reason for the iffy American acceptance of *Dictator* as a whole (versus hosannas for individual parts like the globe ballet) was that Chaplin was not just rocking the comedy boat about a belligerent dictator (*Time* magazine's 1938 Man of the Year); the filmmaker was also subtextually attacking more broadly controversial subjects, such as the anti–Semitisms which existed in the United States. For example, the American Nazi Party was holding rallies in venues as prominent as New York's Madison Square Garden as late as 1940—the year the *Dictator* was released.[9] Even some conservative German-Americans were offended by *Dictator*. For example, when Mexico's celebrated painter Diego Rivera was invited to San Francisco in 1940 to paint a ten-panel mural for the city's Golden Gate International Exposition, he included both a scene from *Dictator* and a portrait of Chaplin's wife Paulette Goddard in his work "Pan American Unity" (completed late that year). Goddard was a friend and patron, while Chaplin had long been an artistic hero to Rivera. (Years before, Rivera and Picasso had formed a Chaplin fan club in Paris.) In Rivera's autobiography he stated:

> Soon after the showing of this mural, a storm arose over the scene from *The Great Dictator*. As most people will recall, this movie was detested by reactionaries. The ladies of the Century Club, many of whom belonged to the influential German-American families, publicly denounced the composition, and to insure my knowing their opinion, they sent a delegation of the oldest and most respectable members to berate me personally.[10]

Though this group was overruled, their actions undoubtedly contributed to the mural not finding a permanent home (at San Francisco City College) until the late 1950s. Ironically, when Chaplin was later attacked for being a communist, his friendship with leftist artists like the controversial communist Rivera would be used as more evidence that the comedian was a Red. Regardless, right up until the Japanese attack on Pearl Harbor on December 7, 1941, America was largely an isolationist country. Chaplin's politicized art, therefore, was upsetting to many U.S. citizens, especially if they were anti–Semitic and/or of a conservative German heritage.

By contrast, the propaganda barrage against Germany and the Kaiser had been so effective during the First World War that Chaplin's conservative approach to dark comedy in *Shoulder Arms* did not approach *Dictator*'s multi-faceted controversy. (Tragically, this earlier, perverted propaganda image of the Kaiser as a "beast"—but not in Chaplin sources—contributed to later Americans not always believing the odious Hitler stories coming out of 1930s Europe.)

Another explanation for why *Dictator*'s evolved take on dark comedy was more controversial than *Shoulder Arms* again involved a politicized movie card in two diverse ways. First, many prominent American Jewish leaders were afraid the film would inflame Nazi action even more in Europe. But to paraphrase an exasperated defense by Chaplin, "How much worse can it get?"[11] Such concerns, however, went beyond U.S. Jewish kingpins. In 1937 and '38 when it first became a distinct possibility that Chaplin would make *Dictator,* Britain—still in its appeasement period—threatened to ban the picture for fear of further upsetting Hitler. (Ironically, the movie was later warmly received in Britain after the start of the war.) Second, many Hollywood powerbrokers feared that the film would cause the Führer himself to do the banning, if he was upset by *Dictator.* That is, Hitler might prohibit all American films from continental Europe, creating a financial fear (loss of box office) which would sadly trump legitimate concerns over human rights.

Given that Chaplin co-owned his own studio (United Artists), was using his own money, and was the most driven of artists, once he committed to the project, there was little chance of the comedian backing away from it. Yet, there was enough pressure on him not to go through with the film that President Franklin Delano Roosevelt made it known through private channels that he wanted—that the country needed—said picture, and promised his support. Though the president later groused that the finished film could cause the United States some propaganda problems in Fascist-leaning South America (where many former Nazis would go into hiding after the war), *Dictator* suited the FDR administration's mission to encourage America's support of a Nazi-beleaguered Britain.

Chaplin's approach to dark comedy in *Shoulder Arms* was groundbreaking, but the time and conditions were right for a breakthrough. Plus, the entertainer had built a mountain of goodwill with his World War I bond tour. Yet if the genre were a poker game, with Chaplin upping the ante on *Dictator,* not to mention his activities in the years following its release, there was an increased potential for a negative backlash. First, starting with the most hated figure in the Western World as a *comic* title character, the reviews were often mixed, especially concerning Chaplin's normally stalwart status among New York critics. In fact, Chaplin's disappointment here is often cited as the controversial cause of his refusing the New York Film Critics' Best Actor award for 1940. Another Chaplin explanation was that one does not accept awards for necessary humanitarian acts. Whatever the reason, his action did not seem to impact the Academy Award nominations that year, the first time sealed envelopes were used to keep the winners' names secret following the fiasco of leaked Oscar champions in 1939. Though *Dictator* took home no statuettes, it received nominations in five categories: Best Picture, Best Actor (Chaplin), Best Supporting Actor (Jack Oakie), Best Original Screenplay (Chaplin), and Best Original Score (Meredith Willson). As an addendum to the last nomination, Willson, later best known as the creator of the hit Broadway musical *The Music Man* (1957), would write:

> I've seen Chaplin take a soundtrack and cut it all up and paste it back together and come up with some of the dangedest effects you ever heard—effects a composer would never think of. Don't kid yourself about that one. He would have been great at anything—music, law, ballet dancing, or painting—house, sign, or portrait. I got the screen credit for *The Great Dictator* music score but the best parts of it were all Chaplin's ideas, like using the *Lohengrin* "Prelude" in the famous [globe] balloon-dance scene.[12]

What post-release developments, beyond the reviews, impacted both *Dictator* and Chaplin's future career? Most obviously, with much of the world already at war, from Germany's death grip on Europe, to Japan's equally atrocity-laden domination of Asia, Chaplin was unable to go on one of his beloved post-release world tours (which also doubled as pioneering press junkets for his current picture). Of course, for Chaplin, maybe this was just as well; with the film being his most expensive to make, the longest in both production and total length, he deserved a more conventional rest period.

Once the United States was in the war, Chaplin was almost unique among Hollywood stars in *not* entertaining the troops in some manner, either at American military bases or near actual war zones. This did not register well with the public. (For more on the war-related work of other entertainers see the author's biography of Joe E. Brown—who even topped the legendary efforts of Bob Hope.[13])

Chaplin had his reasons, starting with all the effort that had gone into his "stop the insanity" dark comedy epic *Dictator*. After all, he had risked a fortune for the cause, or as the comedian was fond of joking, the picture cost more than two million dollars: "And that isn't a publicity figure. It came out of the bank."[14] More seriously, Chaplin had passionately confessed the "why" behind his distinct contribution to the war effort shortly before *Dictator*'s release:

> Pessimists say I may fail—that dictators aren't funny any more, that the evil is too serious. That is wrong. If there is one thing I know, it is that power can always be made ridiculous. The bigger that fellow gets, the harder my laughter will hit him.[15]

Certainly part of Chaplin's frustration over the shortsightedness of reviewers not providing a complete critical embrace of *Dictator*'s use of dark comedy can be found in a much later *New York Times* positive play review of *Work on a Special Day,* which also addresses Hitler prior to America's entry into the war: "Part of the point ... is that imagination is a necessary bulwark against totalitarianism, or, more darkly, the only refuge."[16] Not surprisingly, Chaplin's position had received total vindication well before Kevin Brownlow's documentary *The Tramp and the Dictator* (2001) and the companion text, *Chaplin: The Dictator and the Tramp* (2004).[17]

Still, much of this critical *Dictator* fallout has focused upon these reviews from New York; how did the film fare with Chaplin's major home turf newspaper, the *Los Angeles Times*? Though he had screened the movie privately for friends, as well as a critics-only peek at the picture, prior to its extravaganza dual New York premieres it did not officially open in Hollywood until November 14, 1940—approximately three weeks after its Gotham City blowout. Even prior to its West Coast premiere (*sans* Chaplin), *Los Angeles Times* columnists and critics were struggling with *Dictator*, bolstered by an early viewing. Hedda Hopper took the harshest perspective: After calling some parts of the movie "riotous," she added that the climactic speech "left me colder than an icicle. It was so over-rehearsed that all the [movie's] feeling was squeezed out."[18] *Times* critic Philip K. Scheuer also keyed upon *Dictator*'s close:

> The best that could result from it is the coming of the better, kindlier world for which it pleads: the worst, that it will prove Charlie Chaplin's swan song as the world's funniest man.[19]

Then Scheuer obliviously stumbles upon the closest period definition of dark comedy. He suggests Chaplin has gone beyond satire, an insight which embraces the future mantra, "the message of black humor is there is no message."[20] Again, looking towards a future possibly more predisposed to this new age genre, Scheuer states:

> Chaplin's comedy on Hitlerism and the Jews ... is also so many other things that only posterity can give it its proper rank. The emotionally violent changes from humor to hate ... would seem to make it a picture of great [contrasting] movements....[21]

Similar critical comments were later made about a seminal scene in Arthur Penn's groundbreaking dark comedy *Bonnie and Clyde* (1967).[22] Penn's initially slapstick sequence begins with the bank robbery escape of the duo (Warren Beatty and Faye Dunaway) when their ditzy driver (Michael J. Pollard) cannot extricate the getaway car from its parking place. After much comic banging of fenders with those of other parked automobiles, juxtaposed with the stunned looks of absurdity planted upon the faces of the desperately waiting Bonnie and Clyde, a careening Keystone Cop–like exit ensues. All will seemingly soon be comically all right for these bumbling bank robbers. Yet, the parking place delay has allowed an angry victimized bank employee the time to suddenly jump on the getaway car's running board. The likable but panicked Clyde impulsively shoots said banker at point-blank range in the face; and Scheuer's earlier *Dictator* comment about a humor scene abruptly capable of "emotionally violent changes" would be right at home here. Moreover, unlike the Chaplin-damning Hopper, Scheuer closes his piece by observing, "As for Chaplin the actor, the mime—the word is still 'genius.'"[23]

Los Angeles Times critic Edwin Schallert skirted much of the *Dictator* controversy by also, like Scheuer, anticipating a future cinematic critical stance. Yet, instead of only focusing upon dark comedy, Schallert flirts with what will soon be called *auteurism*, in which one discerns ongoing patterns in a director's oeuvre. Consequently, he keys upon *Dictator*'s ballet-like balloon globe scene, and compares it to another non-traditional example of Chaplin comic choreography, *The Gold Rush*'s (1925) dance of the dinner rolls. The latter sequence has a seated Charlie spearing two potato-like rolls with forks, and through a foreshortened medium shot, a seemingly large-headed Charlie performs the delightful "Oceana Roll" dance:

> In each instance Chaplin performed a feat of such significance that he was able to hold the attention of the audience that witnessed it by minutes at a time.... In one case it was the man [Charlie] looking toward the light [in a darkly comic world]; in the other his [Hynkel's] gaze penetrates into a Stygian blackness [towards a world of macabre humor].[24]

(One could also note the aforementioned dance-like back-and-forth fearful movement of bully Eric Campbell's street gang in *Easy Street,* 1917.) Schallert's closing comments also included the word genius: "[*Dictator* offers] moments which are alone [in their uniqueness] and outstanding, and truly reflect the breath and the life of genius."[25]

With a November 14, 1940, Los Angeles opening for *Dictator*, the *Times*' coverage of New York's October response to the film was a potpourri of conflicting comments showcased under

126　　　　　　　　　　Chaplin's War Trilogy

an ambiguously positive headline, "Chaplin's *Great Dictator* Has All New York Agog"[26]: "One and all unite in calling it a great film. But it was not quite what they expected and they found it disconcerting."[27]

Ironically, while some of the same New York critique complaints would surface in *Los Angeles Times* reviews, such as the closing speech and/or dated production values, the *Times'* take on *Dictator* defends the picture in a typical "industry town" manner:

Hynkel is about to begin his acclaimed balloon globe ballet in *The Great Dictator*.

8. *After* The Great Dictator; *Before* Monsieur Verdoux

> [N]early everybody was expecting it to be "like" the standard films of [today's] stand-by filmmakers who keep us going from one year to the next. *The Great Dictator* has no truck with the method which produce such films; it is ... old-fashioned and a work of genius.[28]

As Los Angeles' *Dictator* opening grew closer, entertaining and/or revealing *Times* references and articles about the film began to regularly appear. An early November Hedda Hopper column coyly hinted at the communist label which would soon be linked to all things Chaplin:

> While Jack Oakie [*Dictator*'s Napaloni-Mussolini figure] was dining at the [Brown] Derby last night, a guy in the next booth, who had been lifting the elbow, evidently had seen Jack's performance in *The Great Dictator* and started to pick on Jack because he was wearing a red [as in communism] tie. Jack ... never lifted a finger—but it made him so nervous that he went out and bought a punching bag and set it up in his garage [to be prepared the next time].[29]

In a short article two days later, Chaplin wrote, "Every actor has a yearning to play Napoleon. In *The Great Dictator* I've gotten it all out of my system. I've played Napoleon and Hitler and the mad Czar Paul, all rolled up into one."[30] A short *Times* piece the following day managed to get a negative jab in among some *Dictator*-related numbers. After noting it was "Chaplin's 83rd picture" and cost "$2,200,000 of his own money," the dark comedy was described as "the most pretentious and costly one the comedian ever has attempted."[31]

A November 7, 1940, *Times* article announced "Notables Will Attend [*Dictator*] Premiere," yet no stars outside of such cast members as Paulette Goddard and Jack Oakie were mentioned.[32] Indeed, everyone included on the list had worked on the production, right down to assistant producer Carter de Haven. The day after this obvious PR ploy, a *Times* piece entitled "Chaplin Plans Attendance at Premiere Event" revealed that the Los Angeles opening was supposed to draw him home from New York, where he had been enjoying himself since *Dictator*'s Gotham premiere in October.[33] The day after the "Chaplin Plans Attendance" piece, yet another *Times* article announced:

> Success scored by Charlie Chaplin's *The Great Dictator* in New York and other eastern cities has caused United Artists to arrange for a second local run of the comedy [at the United Artists theater] along with that of the Carthy Circle [theater]."[34]

The picture had gone from the periodic "pretentious" label to the diplomatic "Chaplin Opus," as in the *Los Angeles Times* headline: "Dual Run Set for Chaplin Opus."[35]

One often neglected PR plus for *Dictator* was that Chaplin's co-star wife Paulette Goddard was blossoming into a film star on her own. Because of Chapin's increasingly slow gestation period for each film, followed by lengthy post-production work, Goddard had been able to star in several critical and commercial hits prior to the *Dictator*'s release, such as the aforementioned *The Ghost Breakers*. Just days before the Los Angeles premiere of Chaplin's dark comedy, Goddard was garnering great reviews for Cecil B. DeMille's first film in Technicolor, *North West Mounted Police* (1940). The *Los Angeles Times* observed, "Playing what is possibly her best role, Paulette Goddard appears as a fiery half-breed...."[36] She had come a long way from *Modern Times*' (1936) Gamin; now she was yet another asset for *Dictator*.

Though there were last-minute hints that Chaplin would not make *Dictator*'s West Coast opening, which would prove true, the *Times* belonged to him the day of the premiere.[37] On November 14, 1940, section 4 of the newspaper might better have been called "Everything You Want to Know About Charlie's New Picture." No less than *twenty-one* articles, short and long, were devoted to *Dictator;* this does not include *all* ads having a Chaplin connection. For example, "Everybody Is Cheering Chaplin on the Screen.... And HUDSON [automobiles] on the Highway!"[38] There were even several "soft sell" Chaplin ads, such as "Congratulations to CHARLIE CHAPLIN in *The GREAT DICTATOR*, Hollywood Typewriter Shop."[39]

Even more significant than taking over a complete section of a major newspaper, is that the Chaplin barrage was obviously choreographed to downplay the film's dark comedy nature. The first major piece, "Charlie Chaplin Is BACK!," largely skirts past *Dictator* controversies by concentrating on the film's production, Chaplin's career to this point, and that the comedian finally speaks.[40]

In the article "Satire Added Slapstick in Departure from Precedent," the unsigned writer says this is the first time Chaplin has played "an unsympathetic character."[41] Yet, s/he defuses any black humor controversy with two points. First, by noting that the comedian also plays his Charlie-like barber, Chaplin has merely found a new way to present his traditional formula of a bully and the bullied. Second, the essay provides a further soft landing for seriousness by simply likening the barber-dictator dichotomy to a children's Punch and Judy puppeteer program in which Hynkel-Hitler as Judy is merely "an unpleasant individual whose unpleasantness is made laughably ridiculous...!"[42] Even more of a dark comedy smoke screen is provided by the title of another article: "Film Deemed FUNFEST Not Propaganda."[43] Interestingly, a reference is made to Chaplin's first dark comedy war picture, *Shoulder Arms* (1918). However, besides the essay's importance in revealing the ongoing relevance of *Shoulder Arms* in 1940, the piece stumbles over the movie's basic black comedy difference with *Dictator* by stating that Chaplin

> has been besieged with requests to re-issue *Shoulder Arms* which many a soldier in the World War often said gave him courage to go on fighting. Charlie's answer, was not *Shoulder Arms*: but *The Great Dictator*.[44]

Yes, but the dark comedy goal of *Dictator* is to have the soldiers *throw down* their weapons, *not* give them "courage to go on fighting." *Shoulder Arms*' black humor was a real backdrop to a war most Americans had come to believe in by 1917. *Dictator*'s black humor was fueled by the anti-war "Lost Generation's" "Waste Land" realization which had eventually settled over World War I—thanks to imagery like a section of the German-French Western Front being called a "cemetery of the unburied dead."[45] Thus, this last-minute public pandering for a *Dictator*-"lite" is surprising. Had the mixed New York critical reception spooked Chaplin that much? Taking a different but related tack, the remaining section 4 articles are all of a generic human interest nature, some as inane as Goddard managing to knit several sweaters for friends and *Dictator* cast members during the long production.[46]

That being said, several of these articles provide entertainingly informative material on all things *Dictator*. The best of this collection addressed Chaplin's production censorship. Through the years the comedian's tradition was to have cast and crew swear to complete story secrecy. Moreover, as a further safeguard, Chaplin was "[s]omething of a dictator himself.... Charlie did not believe in taking everybody into his confidence. He trusts his own judgment and expects his staff to trust it too."[47] (Chaplin fan Woody Allen often follows the same policy. For example, instead of getting a script, his actors might receive only their lines ... for the following day.)

Regardless, newspapers were so anxious to get a *Dictator* scoop that Chaplin had to always guard against "fifth columnist" extras (journalists). However, the most interesting insight from the piece comes courtesy of Reginald Gardiner who played Schultz, the barber's only ally in

Hynkel's army. One evening during the production Gardiner was dining with a friend who kept pumping him for *Dictator* information. He was reluctant to refuse her flatly, especially with the woman's ongoing vow of secrecy; yet he wished to honor Chaplin's privacy request. Consequently, he hit upon a compromise which would satisfy everyone and also double as an experiment in discretion. Gardiner provided the woman with a detailed account of *a* Chaplin story. "Two days later the synopsis, considerably abridged, appeared in the column of a well-known Hollywood correspondent. But Gardiner was not shot at sunrise [by Chaplin]. He had had the presence of mind to make up the story ... to his secretive friend. There wasn't a word of truth in the whole thing."[48] The previous chapter's Hedda Hopper finale "scoop" about Hynkel's storm troopers allegedly dragging away the little barber before he could finish his plea for peace, something neither shot nor otherwise noted in *Dictator* literature, would seem to be one such example of a cagey cast member ... maybe even Gardiner himself ... hoodwinking an opportunist.

Among these many human interest stories in the *Times*, two others tales are especially fascinating for the student of Chaplin, though again, there is nothing remotely connected to dark comedy. The first examines how Paulette Goddard consciously avoided the seeming jinx of being a Chaplin leading lady. Put another way, his previous heroines were never able to sustain a film career *after* working with him. The most obvious example is Edna Purviance, his co-star in nearly three dozen short subjects, as well as being the focus of Chaplin's groundbreaking feature *A Woman of Paris* (1923), which was meant to launch the solo career of his friend and one-time mistress. Other forgotten heroines would include *The Gold Rush*'s (1925) leading lady Georgia Hale, *The Circus*' (1928) Merna Kennedy, and *City Lights*' (1931) Virginia Cherrill (later briefly married to Cary Grant).

Goddard's theory on these post–Chaplin failed careers was simply typecasting: "[His] heroines are invariably wistful, tender, delicate women—children of nature whom life has somehow cheated ... [Hamlet's] Ophelia is seldom given an opportunity to play Lady Macbeth."[49] Since Chaplin had the monopoly on this type of Hollywood role, Goddard's thinking was that options for the comedian's former leading ladies were limited. Consequently, when not performing for Chaplin, she sought out roles radically different from this stereotype, like her comically spunky waiting-to-be-divorced character in the critical and commercial hit *The Women* (1939). Of course, while her *Dictator* role as the Jewish ghetto girl returned the actress to Chaplin's standard heroine, Goddard would successfully continue her rich and varied 1940s film career.

However, a backstory to the article could say that Goddard was Chaplin's best pupil but at a cost. The filmmaker was relentless in his push for perfection, repeatedly acting out every part, large or small, for each performer, with him/her then expected to try again. According to Charlie Chaplin, Jr.'s affectionate but fair-minded biography of his father, Goddard especially felt the pressure: "She had to take more drilling than anyone else in the cast—drilling at times which pushed her to the breaking point.[50] Junior felt that Chaplin was ultimately proud of her finished performance but that the filmmaker destroyed what was already a fragile marriage.

Another meritorious human interest story in the preponderance of the *Times*' November 14, 1940, *Dictator* literature is best summarized by its punning title, "Jack Oakie Hits Jackpot in Chaplin Film."[51] The piece both demonstrates the high status of being in a Chaplin film, as well as puts in joke form the legendary length of the comedian's work:

> When a capable actor who toils steadily and profitably in the Hollywood vineyards suddenly goes out of circulation, the cause is no mystery. He has either retired or gone to work in a Charlie Chaplin picture.[52]

When Chaplin had approached Oakie two years earlier, (in 1938) for a part in what was then called *Production No. 6*, Oakie was involved in a number of successful comedies and "nothing in the world could have induced him to drop [everything]. Nothing in the world, that is, but a part in a Charlie Chaplin film."[53]

The rest of the article provides a brief Oakie career overview and more on the special status of a call from Chaplin. Oakie had indeed made a wise choice, with his Mussolini takeoff becoming the most memorable role of his career and garnering him his only Oscar nomination. He lost in the Supporting Actor category to Walter Brennan in *The Westerner*.

The L.A. critical reception was as mixed as the movie's New York reviews. Ironically, the difficulty of the newspaper's chief film reviewer, Edwin Schallert, to fully absorb and assimilate the film's dark comedy is reflected in the ambiguity of his critique title, "Genius Touches Flit, Flash in *Dictator*."[54] However, as occurred earlier in a Philip K. Scheuer review noted in this chapter, an equally perplexed Schallert also stumbles onto what might pass as the beginning to a dark comedy definition: "[W]hile his film is a phenomenon, it is also a strange inharmonious anomaly in the modern realm of audible features."[55] Otherwise, he reverts to a standard period critic's take on *Dictator;* puzzled by black humor's rapid jumps from shock to slapstick and/or mime, he reverts to praise for the traditional latter:

> [T]he best moments ... stem from roots ... imbedded in the soil of the silent picture. He proves this spectacularly in a remarkable scene performed with a globe.... It might be called a kind of bubble dance.[56]

Jack Oakie (right) as Napaloni more than holds his own against Chaplin's Hynkel in *The Great Dictator*. Henry Daniell is on the left.

I am reminded that, *Guernica* or not, Picasso at times (such as in his 1927 painting *Figure*) felt monsters could have pathos. Consequently, if any *Dictator* scene would qualify along these lines, it would be Chaplin's global "bubble dance." Regardless, period Los Angeles viewers would probably have agreed with critic Schallert's reading of the scene as something from the Charlie past. For instance, Chaplin's United Artists representatives had created an audience measuring device which clocked the laughter generated by both Chaplin characters. And despite the movie's emphasis clearly being on Hynkel's title character, who was also gifted with more highlight reel material, U.A.'s "clock" device showed

> that despite the hilarity which greets Chaplin's every appearance [as Hynkel,] Chaplin's antics in the [Charlie] garb which has made him one of the best-known persons in the world drew just as great a volume of applause.[57]

Scheuer, whose *Dictator* review is referenced earlier, revisited the film in December 1940. While his initial critique was kinder than *Times* colleague Schallert's, his later mini-review is, if not more enlightened about dark comedy, even more open-minded about an artist's right to push the creative envelope. Calling *Dictator* a normal experiment, he adds:

> [W]hat its detractors have been prone to forget is that two hours with this master of comedy (even when he is being serious!) are a joy not to be matched by any other experience in the realm of the theater.[58]

Whatever one's perspective about *Dictator* in 1940, the controversial mixture of taking on Hitler and Chaplin's first talkie made the film one of the top grossers of 1940–1941.[59] Beyond the critical and commercial side of the film, how did the period's *real* dictators and world leaders feel about the film? For example, what about Hitler, an avid film fan who "routinely telephoned German motion picture studios with ideas for productions. [And] occasionally ... visited the studios, to watch scenes being filmed and have lunch with the stars."[60] (He was also very aware of how Allied propaganda pictures like *The Kaiser: The Beast of Berlin* had aided the Allies during World War I.) Regardless, German records have Hitler seeing the *Dictator* twice.[61] There is no record of how he felt about the picture; but a repeat viewing suggests some fascination. When later informed that Hitler sat through two screenings, Chaplin essentially said he would have given anything to know what he thought about it. In contrast, the views of Hitler's ally but later bitter enemy, the Soviet Union's premier Joseph Stalin, are known. Shortly after Chaplin's 1977 death, the most interesting of letters turned up in the *New York Times*. Nougzar Sharia, a former American embassy employee in Moscow, revealed that a copy of *Dictator* was received in 1940. Because Chaplin's *Modern Times* (1936) had been such a Moscow hit, a Kremlin gala screening was organized for *Dictator*. The elite of both Soviet film society and the communist party attended, which occurred *before* Hitler's 1940 invasion of the Soviet Union:

> Stalin was seated in front of all invited guests and enjoyed Chaplin's performance tremendously, laughing like a child all through the first part of the film. However, when at the end Chaplin began to criticize all dictatorships, Stalin stopped the performance [screening] with a sweeping gesture, announcing, "[W]e don't need Chaplin here."[62]

Ironically, here was a criticism of *Dictator*'s close which had *nothing* to do with aesthetics!

On the Allied side, as previously noted, President Franklin Delano Roosevelt's behind-the-scenes support was instrumental in getting *Dictator* made and released. However, he could not be overly demonstrative upon its opening, given that the controversial film premiered just weeks before a 1940 election in which isolationism was still a major issue, especially given the appeasement voices of such prominent American anti–Semites as Charles Lindbergh, Henry Ford, and Joseph Kennedy. Still, Roosevelt found a masterful way to endorse the movie with wording which would be difficult to condemn. When the subject of Chaplin and *Dictator* came up at a September press conference, the president read aloud a telegram he had received from an alleged Senator whose identity he could not then reveal:

> Have just been reading book called the holy Bible. Has large circulation. Written entirely by foreign born, mostly Jews. First part full of warmongering propaganda. Second part condemned isolationism with story about a good Samaritan. Should be added to your list and suppressed.[63]

Moreover, as critic-editor Jacob Heilbrunn has stated, "Now that it is 'the good war,' the ferocity of the disputes over entering World War II has largely been forgotten."[64] Indeed, just shortly before *Dictator*, opened Lindbergh sounded like a mouthpiece for Hitler. In a September 1940 speech in Des Moines, Iowa, he announced that the era's real enemy was domestic and Jewish: "[T]heir greatest danger lies in their large ownership and influence in our motion pictures, our press, our radio and our government."[65] Celebrated novelist Philip Roth was so disturbed by Lindbergh's rhetoric that he was later moved to write *The Plot Against America* (2004), pondering what would have happened had the famous fascist-like flyer been elected president in 1940. (Besides his anti–Semitic beliefs, Lindbergh had a great affinity for Germany's attention to detail in all walks of life. This was perfectly demonstrated in their construction of the Jewish death camps.) Strangely, a dark comedy paradox to Lindbergh's Des Moines comments exist in such later studies as Thomas Doherty's *Hollywood and Hitler: 1933–1939* (2013), which documents how major studios, save Warner Brothers, were barely short of being Nazi fifth communists.[66] Via a Los Angeles' German consultant, Hollywood movies were routinely re-edited so as not to risk losing the business of the Third Reich. Thus, as noted by Doherty,

> in an irony better appreciated in retrospect, even as Nazi bellicosity and violence towards the Jews in Germany escalated, the trademark product of Jews in America remained up on marquees throughout the Third Reich.[67]

Today the 1940s breadth of America's anti–Semitism is still almost unfathomable. In parts of the country it actually *increased* after the onset of war, including the introduction of many discriminatory laws. Moreover, when a *Boston Globe* article from mid–1942 verified the mass murders of over 700,000 Jews in Poland, the piece was tucked "away at the foot of page 12."[68] Page 12 for one of the largest mass slaughters in modern history? While the numbing number would eventually rise to *six million* Jews killed by the Nazis, one still must ask, page 12? Tragically, Lindbergh was not alone among many Americans in his warped thinking. When Roosevelt and his Secretary of Interior, Harold L. Ickes, attempted to get around the United States' low Jewish immigration quota with a strange but intriguing proposal, they had to couch their plan in economic-development language rather than humanitarian relief. That is, with the assistance of Undersecretary Harold Slattery, a proposition was put forward titled "The Problem of Alaskan Development," later referred to as the Slattery Report. The strategy was to resettle German Jews in Sitka, Alaska. This fascinating effort to circumvent American anti–Semitism did not come to pass; but it demonstrates the lengths to which humanism had to be disguised to fight prejudice *at home*. (Pulitzer Prize–winning author Michael Chabon wrote a novel anchored in the idea this settlement had come to pass, *The Yiddish Policemen's Union*, in 2007.)

Roosevelt was attempting to be a "third termite" by bucking the two-term precedent for presidents established by George Washington; and his Republican opponent was the popular liberal businessman Wendell Willkie. (Willkie's campaign inspired the hit Broadway play *State of the Union* [1945–1947], which Frank Capra successfully adapted to the screen in 1948 to cash in on another presidential election. Affable and articulate, Willkie was an internationalist similar enough to the president to be called "the rich man's Roosevelt."[69] With Willkie's most effective attack line being that the president would take the country to war, Roosevelt had to tread lightly about his admiration for *Dictator,* especially with the "New Deal" also long nicknamed by anti–Semitics as the "Jew Deal," given that several of Roosevelt's advisors were Jewish. Though Roosevelt would go on to win, the Willkie race would remain his closest presidential contest (including yet another victory in 1944 over Thomas Dewey).

Finally, how did Roosevelt's British counterpart, Prime Minister Winston Churchill, feel about *Dictator?* Unlike the other leaders, Churchill and Chaplin had a friendship which went back to the comedian's visit to London for the 1921 premiere of *The Kid.* Each one would make a point of visiting the other in their travels, including Chaplin staying with Churchill in 1937, during the comedian's around-the-world trip following the release of *Modern Times* (1936). Moreover, as noted earlier in the text, Churchill had even written a celebratory 1930s essay about cinema's most iconic figure. Not surprisingly, the prime minister enjoyed *Dictator* at a private screening in late 1940. The setting was his regular weekend retreat, Ditchley Home Park, the estate of Ronald Tree, a friend and member of Parliament. Ditchley, located south of London, was deemed safer from German air raids than Churchill's own country manor. The prime minister so liked *Dictator* that a story, probably hyperbole, has circulated about events surrounding Churchill's second viewing of it. It allegedly occurred in 1941, the weekend Herman Hess, Deputy Führer to Hitler, parachuted into Scotland and was immediately arrested, on an unsanctioned-by-Germany peace mission. Despite the possible importance of this unorthodox, even delusional act, Churchill was said to have delayed any action until the completion of *Dictator.* Whether true or not, the ongoing popularity of the tale speaks to Churchill's fondness for the film.[70]

Though Churchill could be more publicly positive about *Dictator,* Chaplin loyally supported President Roosevelt, whom he greatly admired, and accompanied a Hollywood delegation to the January 1941 inauguration celebrating FDR's unprecedented third election. Chaplin was part of the program, broadcasting the final speech of *Dictator* to a national radio audience of millions. Other than a temporary glitch in mid-speech, when a dry throat made his voice break, the film's concluding plea—so artistically controversial for *Dictator*—was a hit during the inauguration festivities. And Chaplin would periodically be requested to repeat the speech at other patriotic functions during the war. Ironically, early on, the political right felt the speech, especially its reference to "comrades," sounded communistic. When Chaplin would later give speeches for leftist organizations supporting a "second front" for the Soviet Union against the invading Nazis (the Russians lost well over twenty million lives in this conflict, far exceeding any other World War II nation), American conservatives had their proof that Chaplin was a "Red."

Prior to America's December 1941 entry into the Second World War, after the Japanese surprise attack on Pearl Harbor, much of Chaplin's time was taken up with preparation for a sound reissuing of *The Gold Rush.* The comedian wrote a new musical accompaniment, with a Chaplin voice-over which replaced the titles. Some silent comedy purists much prefer the original, feeling the voice-over is an unnecessary, obtrusive affront to the original. Yet, to hear Chaplin's own voice describing his greatest story is a wonderful treat, not unlike an inspired DVD audio commentary of a director's cut of one's favorite film. I am a college professor alternating between the two versions in various classes; the 1942 reissue is invariably the student favorite.

The catalyst for Chaplin's 1942 version was his disappointment that *Dictator* had not received universal acclaim despite many critical hosannas and monster box office returns. This was Chaplin's indirect acknowledgment that whenever the public found fault with him (usually involving scandal in his private life), he often righted the ship by putting Charlie or, as he described his alter ego in *The Gold Rush*'s voice-over, "the little fellow"—back on the screen and all was forgiven. By the 1940s, silent films were starting to be artistically acknowledged again, after years of literally being destroyed or allowed to deteriorate. Still, film historians sadly estimate that over 80 percent of all silent films are forever lost. Chaplin's updated *Gold Rush* was warmly received by fans and critics alike.

Unfortunately, the other most memorable event to occur during this period was Chaplin's early 1940 ties to a beautiful young redhead wannabe actress named Joan Barry. To paraphrase an old vaudeville joke for Chaplin, "The trouble for him was not in the chase but in the catching." Ironically, for once he did not marry the young woman, his normal M.O., which would probably have eliminated the problems to come. For once, maybe another old show business gag had kicked in for the comedian: "To avoid domestic strife, don't marry in January ... or the rest of the months either." The Barry entanglement would eventually involve the comedian in two sex scandals. One would produce lurid headlines for years, while the other was soon recognized by Hollywood insiders as the perfect love story that Chaplin and his former screen alter ego, Charlie, had long been seeking. The first scandal waiting to happen was an outgrowth of his affair with Barry during 1941 and 1942. (Chaplin and third wife Paulette Goddard had essentially led separate lives since the late 1930s, but their 1942 Mexican divorce was just as vague as their earlier marriage claims. In fact, the *New York Times* reported, "[S]o secretive was the action that an entry of the decree had been ordered removed from the record by the jurist who issued it."[71])

Chaplin met "party girl" Barry at a function put on by oil millionaire J. Paul Getty. After a few more encounters at private gatherings, at which Barry actively pursued the comedian, an affair ensued. At this time, Chaplin was interested in adapting to film Paul Vincent Carroll's 1937 Irish play *Shadow and Substance*. The story keys upon an innocent young girl who sees visions of a saint and helps bring the various ramifications of several more sophisticated church members back to a basic faith; it was the winner of the New York Drama Critics' award for Best Foreign Play in 1938. Chaplin felt the Irish-looking, red-haired Barry would be a perfect fit for the girl.

Chaplin's lovers frequently became candidates for potential film projects; such was the case with Barry. After giving her a screen test to guarantee that she registered well on film, he also enrolled her in some acting classes in preparation for the adaptation. Ironically, the instability one might associate with a vision-seeing character was also part of Barry's character—which Chaplin would discover only too soon. When the filmmaker ended his contact with her in 1942 over a lack of professionalism (drinking, missing classes, etc.), Barry began to harass him, doing everything from shattering windows in his house to actually breaking in and holding him at gunpoint.

In 1943, Barry named Chaplin in a paternity suit, which was followed in 1944 by a federal grand jury indictment of the comedian for violation of the Mann Act (the transfer of a woman across a state line for sexual intentions). The latter accusation, involving Barry, was soon shown to be ludicrous, and the charge was dropped. Yet the paternity suit was upheld in court through the slanderous melodramatics of Barry's lawyer—effectively recreated by James Woods, working from original transcripts, in Richard Attenborough's film *Chaplin* (1992). At one point in this miscarriage of justice, though not included in the Attenborough picture, an emotionally overwhelmed Chaplin inadvertently told the judge he was not a "monster." Of course, the whole paternity trial—which Chaplin lost—was a sham, because blood tests proved conclusively that Chaplin could not have been the father. (Blood tests were not then accepted as positive proof in California court cases ... but this specific injustice would eventually be instrumental in helping change the law.)

The second "scandal" would normally not have been pigeonholed as such, but it became inevitable because of its timing and Chaplin's proven fondness for young women. A few months after the paternity suit was filed in December 1942, the comedian married eighteen-year-old Oona O'Neill, daughter of playwright Eugene O'Neill. Chaplin was fifty-four. And though this fourth marriage would become *the* success of his private life, lasting until his 1977 death and producing a family of Victorian size (eight children), the union only intensified the ballyhoo against him in the mid–1940s ... and for years to come. Things had certainly changed since his war bond tour of 1918, when every community, big or small, had received him like the proverbial conquering hero. As if thinking along these lines, Chaplin would later confess, "Occasionally I would sink into a deep depression, feeling that I had the acrimony and the hate of a whole nation upon me and that my film career was lost."[72]

As Yankee Hall of Fame catcher Yogi Berra once observed, "Even if the world were perfect ... it wouldn't be." Besides the controversial sex scandals dogging Chaplin during World War II, his aforementioned continued proclivity for "second front" talks alienated many conservative American patriots despite the Soviet Union now being an ally. The phenomenon essentially began with a May 1942 speech for the American Committee for Russian War Relief. Chaplin was a last-minute replacement for an ill Joseph E. Davies, America's former ambassador to the Soviet Union (from 1936 to 1938) and the author of the bestselling *Mission to Moscow* (1941). (In both the book and its 1943 film adaptation, America's ally is depicted in an unrealistically positive manner, even justifying Stalin's purges.) The movie, made at the request of President Roosevelt to assist in the war effort, would later be famously targeted by the House Committee on Un-American Activities as evidence of communism's infiltration of Hollywood. Yet even in 1943 the picture had opened to mixed reviews and poor box office.

Throughout the war, many Americans still distrusted the Soviet Union, a fear anchored in the short-lived Nazi-Soviet Non-Aggression Pact of 1939, which had allowed Germany to attack Poland without Russian intervention. Thus began World War II in Europe, with Germany allowing the Soviets to occupy a "sphere of influence" in eastern Poland, too. Of course, all this changed with the Germans' surprise attack upon the Soviet Union in June 1942, giving the United States and Britain the most unlikely of allies. While the Soviets were absorbing at great cost the might of the Nazi war machine—giving the United States and Britain invaluable time to better prepare for the prolonged conflict—most American and British citizens were only too happy to allow fascism (the Nazis) and communism (the Soviets) to simply kill each other off ... with no rush for a second front.

Consequently, at a time when most Americans were tepid at best about the Soviets, Chaplin's replacement speech for Ambassador Davies was overly enthusiastic, as was the comedian's nature (remember his World War I bond rally tour). Thus, the pep rally nature of his speech began with the controversial word one—"Comrades!"—and was peppered with demands for a second front in Europe and calling upon the crowd of eight thousand to send telegrams on just this point to President Roosevelt. (The second front would not occur until June 1944, D-Day, with the Germans long in retreat from the Soviets.)

Chaplin's Russian War Relief address was considered brave even for period leftists. In the fall of 1942 he would give a similar rousing stump speech at Carnegie Hall for the "Artists Front to Win the War," which was considered "a dangerously leftist organization."[73] The comedian's oldest child, Charles. Jr., recalled the night:

> As usual, my father prepared his speech with a great deal of care and anxiety. [Then] he was attacked by his usual state of nerves and ... had to throw up. [Losing his notes, he made an impromptu speech,] holding his audience so spellbound you could have heard a pin drop....
> [The Artists Front was] considered a pink organization. Whether it was, or not, Dad himself was never a communist. He did sincerely admire Russia for her stand against Germany and

Chaplin (kneeling with Marie Dressler) first met Franklin Roosevelt (far left) during the World War I Liberty Loan Bond Drive, when the president was assistant secretary of the Navy. Other individuals in this April 14, 1918, Washington, D.C., photograph include Douglas Fairbanks and Mary Pickford (behind Chaplin) and future president Herbert Hoover, then head of the U.S. Food Administration (directly behind Pickford).

felt not only that she should have help but that a second front would win the war more quickly for us all.[74]

Though Chaplin shared the platform that night with other high-profile personalities and artists, ranging from Orson Welles to Pearl Buck, it was the comedian's well-received speech which got the most negative attention from the political right. Several more such addresses would follow, including a talk entitled "Salute to Our Russian Ally" at Chicago's Orchestra Hall in November 1942, and a speech to Russia recorded at the office of the Soviet consul in February 1943. American conservative press smears tied to his second front addresses increased tenfold during the Cold War, which almost immediately followed the end of the Second World War in 1945. Such things would turn many post-war conservatives, at least as it applied to Chaplin, into so many wannabe junior age Machiavellis (1469–1527).

Beyond "pinko" slurs and morality attacks, the reactionary right also began pummeling Chaplin for never having become a United States citizen, despite living here for thirty-plus years. Yet there was nothing unusual about this in the international artistic community. For example, Stan Laurel of Laurel & Hardy fame "proudly retained his British passport from his arrival in California in 1910 to his death there in 1965, was never accused of "failure" to become a United States citizen, and it irked him considerably to read the press attack Chaplin in this respect."[75]

Mary "America's Sweetheart" Pickford, who teamed with Chaplin and Douglas Fairbanks to sell so many war bonds during the First World War, was a Canadian citizen at the time. Though she eventually became a United States citizen, later in her life she made arrangements with America's Department of Citizenship to regain her Canadian status. There were no attacks about the "failure" to become and/or remain a U.S. citizen for "America's Sweetheart."

Like Pickford, Chaplin had also raised millions of dollars for America's World War I effort, donated a small fortune himself, made two morale-boosting movies (at his own expense) about each conflict (*Shoulder Arms* and *The Great Dictator*), and had met with and followed the requests of Democratic Presidents Woodrow Wilson and Franklin Roosevelt. In fact, his political connections stretched back to a 1918 war bond rally with Roosevelt, when the future president was assistant secretary of the Navy. Plus, both of Chaplin's grown boys, Charles, Jr., and Sydney, served in the military during World War II. And though Chaplin had played a more active patriotic part during the First World War, he had done what he felt was his patriotic duty with the second front addresses, as well as donating a portion of the proceeds for one of the *Dictator* premieres to the families of American servicemen.

Paradoxically, however, as has been shown regarding his leftist speeches during World War II, the enthusiastically progressive ideas with which they were imbued did further damage to his patriotic standing among conservatives. Moreover, in the spirit of Roosevelt's dream of a functioning United Nations (a reworking of Wilson's failed League of Nations) during the turbulent Cold War days of the late 1940s, Chaplin was also fond of calling himself an "international citizen," versus being tied to any one nation. This did not play well with many Americans, conservatives or not. For instance, even the aforementioned Meredith Willson, a professional colleague and Chaplin fan, could not wrap his head around the concept of an international citizenship:

> [Chaplin] is a real genius ... though he does some awfully strange things for a genius, like not becoming a citizen. I read his explanation of that in the paper. He said he was an international citizen. Didn't belong to any one country. And that remark hit me like a nightmare. Imagine

standing in the middle of the world like in a [surrealistic Salvador] Dali painting as an international citizen.[76]

If a quasi-friend and co-worker, who had essentially credited his Oscar nomination for Best Original Score to Chaplin, could not fathom his politics, it did not bode well for the comedian's position among average citizens. Yet maybe the greatest hypocrisy was simply that it was *Chaplin* calling himself an "international citizen." The same year, 1948, that Meredith Willson expressed his reservations about this concept, Frank Capra directed the critical and commercial hit movie *State of the Union*—where another of his populist characters (played by the quintessential American actor Spencer Tracy) strongly advocated a single international "United States of the World" citizenship. And this movie was adapted from Russel Crouse and Howard Lindsay's *Pulitzer Prize–winning* drama. In the play the pitch for international citizenship is implied in the central character's observation, "We've got to move on to something [the world has] never had before"—a United States of the World. In fact, the sense of an "international citizen" had existed in *many* celebrated works of art prior to this. For example, in G. Chevallier's *Fear* (1930), a bitter French soldier of World War I takes a different tack:

> My country? ... You want to know what "my country" really is? Nothing more or less than a gathering of shareholders.... Think about all the people in your country whom you wouldn't go near, and you'll see that the ties that are supposed to bind us all together don't go very deep....[77]

It was into this hypercritical and/or negative conservative American mindset that Chaplin would launch his next sinister "study" on dark comedy. And a *personal* study he very well knew it to be, simply because Chaplin was aware that many critics would be "reviewing" his ever more controversial life, instead of the film itself. Once again, as with the second front addresses, he was, as described by critic-historian Richard Schickel:

> being a very brave man.... [T]he idea of making a piece sympathetic in its way to an immoralist, symbolically throwing his own dubious sexual reputation back in the face of his critics, he found irresistible.[78]

One also assumes that his tarnished sexual reputation was what made Orson Welles first approach Chaplin with the idea which eventually became *Monsieur Verdoux*. Despite Chaplin's "brave" act in making the movie, the comedian's oldest son recalls his father confessing major fears about the project. After co-star Martha Raye shared her nervousness about working with someone she considered the "God" of comedy, Chaplin said:

> "I'm bloody nervous myself," and went on to tell her that *Monsieur Verdoux* was an altogether new experience for him. He missed his talisman, the Little Tramp, who had walked out of *The Great Dictator* for good. He missed those familiar baggy pants, the derby and mustache. In their place was this strange, even repulsive character, a French Bluebeard. Out of his gruesome life he had somehow to construct a comedy and manage to keep it balanced dexterously on the borderline not only of tragedy but of the downright macabre.[79]

The following chapter examines how Chaplin was able to get beyond his "bloody nervous" self.

9

Monsieur Verdoux, Without His "Talisman" Charlie

> Dad told me he kept the Little Tramp in [*The Great Dictator,* 1940] as a talisman, because throughout his life he had brought him luck, wealth and fame. Dad had had a lot of laughs out of him, too, Dad and millions of people the world around.[1]—Charlie Chaplin, Jr.

Monsieur Verdoux (1947) not only had Chaplin pushing his dark comedy evolution even further, he was finally reworking the genre without his eternal good luck constant, Charlie. So what made the comedian go *so far* off the dark comedy reservation at this time? From a personal standpoint, and a stroking of the proverbial imaginary beard, I would recycle a comment from novelist Ferrell Sam: "If you lose your sense of the ridiculous, you've fallen into a terrible pit. The only thing that's worse is never to have either."[2] Thus, with or without his talisman, Chaplin felt the need to bravely push on his black humor experiment. Moreover, he did this despite *not* following the age-old wisdom of novelist Gustave Flaubert (1821–1880): "Be regular and orderly in your life, like bourgeois, so that you may be violent and original in your art"—an axiom followed by artists as diverse as filmmaker Robert Wise and novelist William Styron.[3] Chaplin's further black comedy breakthrough with *Verdoux* was not always about inventing the new so much as rearranging the known. However, before addressing this fact, his namesake son provides as insightful overview of *Verdoux* as representing an amalgamation of all things macabre which had fascinated his father since Chaplin's Victorian childhood—an era often drawn to such subject matter. (See Chapter 1, which also includes additional corroboration from the comedian's son Michael about Chaplin's dark side.[4]) Chaplin, Jr., wrote:

> *Verdoux* was more than a mission with my father.... [T]his picture served to objectify for him all the mingled fascination and horror he had felt throughout his life towards violence and the macabre—the gruesome newspaper story ... suicide and madness and the drama that precedes an execution, the condemned man's last meal and words and actions.[5]

Like *The Great Dictator* (1940), *Verdoux* was also inspired by an actual person: Henri Landru (1869–1922), who murdered ten potential wives (and a child), after he romantically obtained access to the women's valuables. After killing them, he would dismember their bodies and burn them in his stove. He was guillotined for his crimes in early 1922, after a high-profile trial and appeal. Chaplin's film maintains several parallels with the serial killer, beyond gaining the victims' trust through romantic seductions. *Henri* Verdoux, like *Henri* Landru, also disposes of the bodies by burning, which had an added macabre mid–1940s twist since the film's release followed the revelations about the Nazi concentration camp ovens. Like Landru, Verdoux also used a second-hand furniture shop as a cover. Since neither story left any bodies for evidence—no corpus delicti—the ultimate guilty verdicts were through the persistent activities of victims' families. And Landru's bemused audacity during the trial sometimes produced a sense of comedy, upon which Chaplin's Verdoux would greatly expand.

Given the ugliness of the Joan Barry case, many Chaplin biographers have suggested the vindictiveness of the unstable woman might have been an added catalyst for making a movie like *Verdoux,* with its working title *Lady Killer.* Certainly it would hardly have dampened the idea, especially when one also adds the especially ugly 1920s Lita Grey divorce, which gave the comedian a nervous breakdown. Yet, like many Chaplin films, there was seemingly a long gestation period for *Verdoux.* Well before the Barry scandal, the *Hollywood Reporter* carried a front page story on the proposed picture, noting:

> Charlie Chaplin is apparently serious about playing Landru, the French Bluebeard, in his next picture, and towards that end has grown a Van Dyke beard, and is mugging in the mirror and getting the opinion of friends on how he'd photograph minus his trademark midget mustache.[6]

The comedian eventually decided against the beard, and went with more of a pencil-thin dandy's mustache.

Beyond Chaplin's well-documented fascination with all things macabre, the comedian was also a huge fan of pulp fiction detective stories and murder mysteries, which his son Charlie, Jr., remembers always being stacked beside his father's bed.[7] The genre, frequently laced with dark comedy, was particularly popular during the early 1940s. For instance, period critic and dark comedy essayist Will Cuppy edited three such anthologies between 1943 and 1946, with the most evocative title being *Murder Without Tears: An Anthology of Crime.*[8] Thus, a case could also be made for *Verdoux* simply being an exploration of a genre Chaplin enjoyed reading in his leisure time. One even has a period precedent with another popular funnyman whose work Chaplin admired: Bob Hope was also fan of detective stories and murder mysteries, and he chose as his first independent production *My Favorite Brunette* (1947, the same year as *Verdoux*) an affectionate spoof of film noir—the budding genre mix of murder mysteries and tough guy detectives.[9] Of course, Hope did not make himself the murderer ... though the picture begins with him on Death Row.

Along related lines, when Chaplin traveled, he was more likely to visit a prison than a museum. This is best demonstrated in the comedian's *My Trip Abroad* (1922), which chronicles his trip to Europe upon the completion of *The Kid* (1921). Back in the United States, he goes on at length about New York's Sing Sing prison:

Chaplin as Verdoux.

> The big gray stone buildings seem to me like an outcry against civilization. The huge gray monster with its thousand staring eyes. We are in the visiting room.... All of them ... crossed out of faces by lines of suffering and life's penalties. Tragedy and sadness.... The men looked resigned. Their spirit is gone. What is it that happens behind these gray walls that kills so completely? ... Why are sinners always so loved? Why do sinners make such wonderful lovers? Perhaps it is compensation as they call it.... Human nature improves but the tragedy remains just as dramatic. The cells where they sleep are old fashioned, built by a monster or a maniac.... Until [new prisons are built] these poor wretches must endure these awful cells. I'd go mad there.[10]

Like Dickens, who also had an obsession with civilization's (so-called) dark corridors, Chaplin's fascination with such places throughout his writing runs the gamut from sympathy for prison reform, to curiosity about the power of civil discourse.

Fittingly, for the subject of *Verdoux*, this same trip to Europe nearly paralleled the trial of Henri Landru, a subject which murder mystery junkie Chaplin must have found intriguing. Thus, my hypothesis on the credit Chaplin later gave Orson Welles for *Verdoux* is that the creator of *Citizen Kane* (1941) had merely *reawakened* Chaplin's interest in a trial from decades earlier. Plus, since the most high-profile comedian in history was frequently sued for plagiarism once his pictures opened, he did not want a similar fate to befall him from Hollywood's then-current boy wonder. Consequently, Welles received both $5,000 and the screen credit: "Idea suggested by Orson Welles."

When Welles had originally suggested doing a series of docu-dramas about Landru starring Chaplin, the comedian noted he was well aware of the "celebrated French murderer."[11] There is no way of knowing how closely Chaplin would have followed the Landru case, despite both his interest in the subject, and being in France shortly before the pre-trial hullabaloo began. Yet it does seem unlikely a singular element of the French prosecutor's final summation could have been missed by the comedian, especially since Chaplin employed a clipping service (any journalistic reference to a subject was saved; at this time, New York's dozen-plus newspapers were a primary focus). Also, keep in mind that during Landru's trial the condemned man's demeanor had produced a certain degree of amusement in the courtroom.[12] Consequently, what follows is the portion of the prosecutor's final comments which seemingly foreshadow a Landru/Verdoux movie: "He sought at the outset to warn the jury against regarding Landru as a comic figure, as 'the Charlie Chaplin of the cinema of crime, the genial Guignal [the main character in a French puppet show], tricking the police and checking the Magistrate.'"[13]

With this foundation of the subject matter for *Verdoux*, how does Chaplin take the film to an even more macabre dark comedy level? First, as noted in the chapter opening references, unlike *Shoulder Arms* (1918) and *The Great Dictator*, *Verdoux* provides the viewer with no sympathetic Charlie figure to root for and/or with whom to identify. In the previous chapter, Charlie Chaplin, Jr., recalled his father's fear of going forward on *Verdoux* without Charlie. Yet, long before this time, Chaplin had expressed fears about pure dark comedy in the contemporary entertainment scene. For instance, in a conversation with his friend and multifaceted writer Max Eastman more than a decade before *Verdoux*, Chaplin confessed:

> Modern humor [dark comedy] frightens me a little. The Marx Brothers are frightening.... They say, "All right, this is how we live and we'll live that way." They go in for being crazy. It's a soul-destroying thing. They say, "All right, you're insane, we'll appeal to your insanity." ... Annihilating everything.[14]

Thus, while this text has documented how dark comedy had always been a component in Chaplin's art, it seems to have forever been a trial for him, even when he had the mainstream protection of his talisman Tramp. Consequently, as he went forward with the genre without Charlie the safety valve, *Verdoux* is the one film in his war trilogy that makes no attempt to disguise its dark comedy foundation. Even *Dictator* begins with an extensive World War I Charlie prologue which could be mistaken for quality outtakes from *Shoulder Arms*. Third, just as *Verdoux* quickly announces itself as a dark comedy, it immediately establishes what will become traditional patterns for the genre. Thus, the picture begins with the now standard dysfunctional family at the center of so many later dark comedies (society's primal misleading "institution"), which then often puts the genre into crash mode against the hypocrisy of "civilization's" many other comfortably misleading institutions. For instance, *Verdoux* leads the way for a later classic dark comedy like *Harold and Maude* (1972). That film also begins with a dysfunctional family, and then methodically demonstrates the falsehood of such seemingly pivotal institutions-establishments as the church, the military and medicine (psychiatry).

Immediately after *Verdoux* establishes its dark comedy dysfunctional family underpinnings, the movie quickly moves to the genre's three primary themes: man as beast (Verdoux), the omnipresence of death (the burning body of his latest victim producing billowing black smoke from his crematorium), and the unbelievable absurdity of the whole scenario. Yet, like so much black humor, the absurdity is based in truth ... and even then, the frightening facts are usually more disturbing than the cinematic interpretation. Point in fact, Landru was guillotined for the murder of eleven people, though the real number seems to have been closer to 300. *Verdoux* does not even come remotely close to the figure eleven.

Among related lines, Chaplin, the pioneering yet struggling standard-bearer of dark comedy, was frequently on record as saying he would *not* have made *Dictator* had he known the horrors of Hitler's atrocities. But while the full extent of Hitler's crimes against humanity were largely unknown at the time of *Dictator*'s 1940 release, the Nazis did not implement their so-called "Final Solution," the extermination of all Jews, until 1941. Consequently, *Dictator* was based upon the mere beginnings of what would prove to be the most infamous crime against humanity in recorded history, and Chaplin's film has actually become an even more extreme example of this shock genre since the facts of the Holocaust have become known. Still, as with *Verdoux*, *Dictator*'s study in dark comedy horror pales in comparison to reality.

Another way in which Chaplin escalates the profile of dark comedy, with a completely unsympathetic character, is that he still asks the viewer (as do all entertainers), "Love me." And because Verdoux retains some of the Tramp's basic characteristics, a certain charm and physical gracefulness, the viewer struggles *not* to be drawn to him like another victim. Rare has casting against type been utilized so effectively. One could also argue that in the burgeoning postmodernism of that era—what often passes as today's artistic *norm*—Chaplin's *Verdoux* is now an exercise in contemporary comic self-referential absurdity-parody. That is, being aware of the Tramp in Verdoux reinforces the viewer's skeptical and paradoxical view of any product of human culture ... inviting one to take a radical reappraisal of Chaplin's Charlie. For example, how far is the Tramp's casual sniper in *Shoulder Arms* from Verdoux? Also, as Robert Warshow writes, "Verdoux, despite his pretensions, was still basically a figure of absurdity, clearly unable to understand how one must get along; in his way he was just as 'innocent' as the Tramp."[15] (Of course, Charlie's struggling "innocence" is that of a child, while Verdoux's "innocence" is more along the lines of those Leopold and Loeb "boys.")

Another take on *Verdoux*'s significance as pushing dark comedy to a new provocative high came from the critic and multi-faceted writer James Agee, the best (and nearly only) American period champion of *Verdoux:*

> At a time when many people have regained their faith in war under certain conditions and in free enterprise under any conditions whatever, [Chaplin] has ventured to insist, as bitterly as he knows how, that there are considerable elements of criminality implicit in both.[16]

Not surprisingly, after *Modern Times'* (1936) machine society and *Dictator's* war ethos literally threatened Charlie's existence, *Verdoux* is the logical evolution—kill or be killed. Warshow encapsulated the transition thusly: "[W]ith Verdoux, the opposition between the [formerly good] individual and [the now threatening] society has lost its old [live and let live] simplicity. The [now lethal] society has flowed into the individual...."[17] For the Charlie who morphed into Verdoux, what could be more of a profitable safeguard then embracing a dealership of death? As Chaplin observed at the time, "Things are in just as much of a mess now [as during World War II] and I could hardly come on [screen] again in baggy pants [and my Charlie costume], pretending that life is still all Santa Claus."[18] The year after *Verdoux,* even a Frank "Capra-corn" picture, *State of the Union* (1948), made a similar statement when Angela Lansbury's character said, "Life is war, don't count the casualties!"

Along similar roots-in-*Verdoux* lines, flash forward to a later hallmark of dark comedy, the Paddy Chayefsky–written *Network* (1976), where a television mogul states, "There is no America, no democracy, there is only [corporation after corporation]. Those are the nations of the world." As if the metaphor needed further expansion, he adds, "The world is a business; it has been since man crawled out of the slime." Yet, whereas *Network* was a critical and commercial smash in American, with a multitude of Oscars (including one for Chayefsky's script), *Verdoux* was ahead of its time and unappreciated.

One more reason for the ease with which *Verdoux* pushed dark comedy even further could be tied to a post-war period when a sort of shadowland zeitgeist descended upon much of Western cinema. For example, playing upon the previously noted Capra reference, the always provocatively engaging critic David Thomson said of this populist director's best-loved picture:

> In America I "discovered" the uneasy depths of *It's a Wonderful Life* ... bringing good cheer without quite letting us forget a vision of dread. For happiness here was pursued by the hounds of hell; the American dream was so close to the nightmare. The film that [commercially] failed in 1947 had become a token of uplifting fellowship, yet it was a film noir full of regret, self-pity, and the temptation of suicide.[19]

Through Thomson's modus operandi is to challenge the status quo, there is insight in his American dream rubbing shoulders with a nightmare comment. Poor George Bailey (James Stewart) can never quite follow his dreams out of town. He might just as well be Truman Burbank (Jim Carrey) in *The Truman Show* (1998), forever trapped under an invisible glass bubble in another seemingly tranquil small town. As writer-director John Cassavetes once observed, "Maybe there really wasn't an America; maybe it was only Frank Capra."

Regardless, in the post-war, post-modernism world of the later noirish 1940s, one might have assumed, even with Chaplin's recent scandals and the jettisoning of the Tramp, that *Verdoux* would have found more critical and commercial success in an America growing cynical about absolute truth. Yet, to paraphrase an axiom from Raymond Chandler, one of film noir's seminal architects, "To exceed the limits of a [genre] formula without destroying it is the dream of every successful artist." But the eventually celebrated-in-America *Verdoux* had exceeded

1940s' "limits" on the dark comedy film genre Chaplin had been instrumental in creating. For example, Robert Warshow stated:

> Complex and sustained irony is a rare thing in literature and rarer still in the movies. Probably the closest analogy to *Monsieur Verdoux* is [Jonathan] Swift's *Modest Proposal* [1729]; one can never quite get to the bottom of the irony. Just as there have been people who could see nothing funny about eating babies [a dark comedy suggestion that absentee English landowners would treat the Irish better if they saw them as a food source—you don't abuse your cattle or hogs], so there are people who can see nothing funny about [Verdoux's] mass murder of women [despite being a metaphor for life as a war in general.].[20]

For that time period, Chaplin had not thrown viewers a sympathetic character to latch on to. By comparison, Capra's unusual decision to adapt Joseph Kesselring's dark comedy lite *Arsenic and Old Lace* (1944) gave audiences two delightfully dotty old ladies who poison lonely elderly callers (their daffy Brooklyn version of euthanasia). In a further demonstration of what Chaplin was up against, the year after *Verdoux,* Alfred Hitchcock directed the now much praised black humor film *Rope* (1948), loosely based upon the Leopold and Loeb case—a murder just for the Nietzsche superior thrill of it. Despite being masterfully produced, as well as Hitchcock's first foray into color, the movie opened to mixed reviews and disappointing box office returns. Thus, even with no off-putting Hitchcock personal scandals, *á la* Chaplin, period audiences

A stunned Cary Grant and pretty Priscilla Lane, with one crazy aunt (Jean Adair) behind them and another (Josephine Hull) to the right in *Arsenic and Old Lace.*

9. Monsieur Verdoux, Without His "Talisman" Charlie

In *Monsieur Verdoux* Chaplin finds a more chilling way to apply his trademark use of flowers as a symbol of life and love's fragility: Now flowers help him troll for victims (with Barbara Slater as a florist).

were *not* drawn to this sinisterly detached dark comedy which, like *Verdoux,* was inspired by real events.

We can compare a signature scene from each film of Chaplin's dark comedy war trilogy and chart the escalation. *Shoulder Arms* is best exemplified by Charlie soldier's blasé use of the bullets constantly whizzing over the trenches to perform the most mundane tasks, such as opening a bottle or lighting a cigarette. "The" *Dictator* sequence is Hynkel's ballet-like routine with the balloon globe—simultaneously enchanting, yet metaphorically horrific for what it foretells. However, the most blatantly revealing dark comedy scene of all, as well as ironically being *Verdoux*'s funniest sequence, is when Chaplin's title character moistens his fingers and counts thousands of francs like a bank teller on speed. No need here for a metaphor of potential "conquest"—Verdoux is already counting the profits of yet another deadly *past tense* conquest. To pun badly, this "money shot" bears Verdoux's message of murder as business, or business being like murder. As with many pivotal movie sequences, Chaplin underlines its significance by performing a variation of it later in the film. For Verdoux, civilian life is definitely *not* a demilitarized zone.

Chaplin's *Verdoux* also advances his dark comedy recipe by mixing his unsympathetic central character with an army of even less pleasant potential victims—victims the viewer will not miss. Once again, similar-minded audience members are implicated in the temptation to murder. This is best represented by Martha Raye's Annabelle Bonheur, the only wife Verdoux fails to kill. A Chaplin biographer deliciously described her as "the vulgarian with the braying voice."[21] Even a critically negative opening review of *Verdoux* in the *Hollywood Reporter* added, "Featured in support of the star is Martha Raye, at her best in rowdy and boisterous moments, such as the boat ride when she narrowly escapes being drowned [by Verdoux]."[22]

This "boat ride" is another *Verdoux* sequence which pushes Chaplin's dark comedy to new levels. One of the genre basics the film firmly established was *not* to display the comic villain killing his victim, thereby making the odious task more palatable and laughable. The boat scene comes closest to breaking that rule, right down to having an anchored noose around Raye's neck. Chaplin seemingly has the audience prepped for this outcome by making Raye's cartoon character behave at her obnoxious best-worst, while murderous Verdoux is, more than at any other time in the movie, like his original Charlie. However, the Chaplin tease stops here, because even this artistically brave filmmaker was aware of some period dark comedy limits ... though he was seemingly making the genre up as he went along.

Such an on-screen snuffing would have been entertaining fun for the dark comedy connoisseur, even though the genre now serves up this dish on a regular basis. Yet, the almost big pay-off is not without other dark comedy bonuses. Chaplin is sometimes criticized for overusing soapbox speeches once he finally went over to sound, but the sudden brake on the pedal which keeps Raye breathing is a brilliantly economical use of off-screen sound, followed by some equally efficient subtextually dark comedy dialogue. Just as Raye's character is going to double as an anchor, one hears (but never sees) an off-screen yodeler. A disappointed Annabelle declares that "ruins everything"—meaning it is the end to their romantically private fishing party. Verdoux concurs immediately for what Mike Nichols describes as "the secrets that aren't in the lines": Once again Verdoux's murder of the seemingly indestructible Annabelle is thwarted.[23]

With the possible exception of Chaplin's casting of Jack Oakie as Napoloni-Mussolini in *Dictator,* Raye remains the comedian's greatest comic co-star. (One wants to also add Buster Keaton in the mix for *Limelight,* 1952, but his sequence is little more than a cameo.) Besides Raye almost stealing every *Verdoux* scene in which Annabelle appears, she winningly provides needed broad comedy at a time when Chaplin is playing the sophisticatedly toned-down Verdoux.

A dark comedy game changer for *Verdoux* involved focusing upon the genre's "man as beast" theme as moving beyond simply undercutting any concept of human dignity by way of finding humor in war and/or death. As briefly touched upon in Chapter 1, dark comedy often derails giving any lasting significance to man's lofty ideals when serious subjects are displaced by sex. Though period censorship put limits on what the work of any 1940s filmmaker could reveal, Chaplin's *widow*-shopping Verdoux was playing a sexual card in preying upon lonely older women of means. Undoubtedly against their better judgments, they literally got in bed with their executioner. *Shoulder Arms* and *Dictator* minimize the sexual aspect of dark comedy. Yet later revisionist criticism on *Verdoux* sometimes finds this phenomenon to be the film's highlight. For example, while Andrew Sarris later suggested that Chaplin's dark comedy attacks on war and capitalism were "mundane matters for Chaplin's genius ... he rises with the angels ... in the self-revelation of his sexual relationships, particularly with man-eating Martha Raye...."[24]

While Chaplin's man-as-beast sexually in *Verdoux* was groundbreaking for the genre, with Sarris' *angelic* praise also doubling as darkly comic criticism, Chaplin's long preparation period on the project allowed Alfred Hitchcock to steal some of the comedian's thunder. That is, Hitchcock's noirish thriller *Shadow of a Doubt* (1943) had another Merry Widow murderer (Joseph Cotten). However, viewers are not meant to identify with him but rather with his favored niece (Teresa Wright), who is endangered by her uncle when she uncovers his murders. Plus, Hitchcock is neither playing the picture for dark comedy (beyond character actor Hume Cronyn's nosy pulp-fiction expert never realizing he is rubbing shoulders with a real murderer), nor does Hitchcock ever suggest his tale is a philosophical indictment of the murderous hypocrisy of society, *à la* Chaplin's *Verdoux*. Moreover, *Shadow* is without the thought-provoking "theater" of Verdoux's closing courtroom scene; it settles for an entertaining mind-candy conclusion.

Just as *Dictator* has *Shoulder Arms* ties with the First World War, so does *Verdoux;* but the latter are subtle. While Chaplin felt that worldwide audiences' love of *The Kid*'s (1921) title character (Jackie Coogan) was based, in part, upon all the First World War orphans, Verdoux-Landru anchor his murders in a fact of life-and-death following that conflict. Landru trolled for his victims by advertising in lonely hearts sections of Paris newspapers as a widower with a comfortable income wanting to meet a widow hoping for marriage. Sadly, with the First World War's multiple millions of casualties, Landru had a huge market of potential partners-victims from which to choose.

Moreover, Landru's calculated ability to draw upon lonely widows during and after the war (he was executed in 1922) brings one to the odd chronology of Chaplin's trilogy. *Verdoux* comes last, yet while its extreme dark comedy message-mindset is clearly based upon the horrific developments of World War II, from concentration camps to the atomic bomb, its ending vaguely appears sometime during the 1930s Depression and the rise of fascist leaders Hitler and Mussolini, who are briefly seen in *Verdoux* newsreel footage. Thus, the First World War, and its aftermath, seem to be a constant link for Chaplin's trilogy. Even though Chaplin was neither shy about his dislike of the extreme Allied jingoism of World War I, nor his later passionate anti-war position in *Dictator, Verdoux*'s very embracing of a personal war as a business philosophy still demonstrates the conflict's varied but ongoing impact upon his artistry. Moreover, he is still suggesting that while a murder is specified and killers discovered, empirical solutions are not enough to displace the thought that a general dark comedy atmospheric menace now loomed over the modern world.

Another manner in which *Verdoux* ratchets up dark comedy's parameters involves the genre's fixation on death. Thus far, this Chaplin trilogy has focused on death by either the traditional varieties associated with war, from combat to the persecutions of the victims which accompany such conflicts, or the philosophy that business and murder are often one and the same. *Verdoux* also plays dark comedy's tragic trump card of death: suicide. How paradoxically approximate; the individual negates himself. Verdoux's "suicide" comes in the form of surrender to the police and certain death.

His personal and professional travail even before assuming his career as a Bluebeard, and escalating thereafter, ultimately results in his ceasing to care about anything. Consequently, Verdoux observes just before giving himself up, "Despair is narcotic; it lulls the mind into indifference." Naturally, one recalls the theme song to the later classic dark comedy *MASH* (1970), "Suicide Is Painless." In contrast, *Shoulder Arms*' Charlie willingly risks death for an absurd cause—"the war to end wars," which before a number was needed to differentiate it from the next coming-soon conflict, was ironically called "The Great War." In *Dictator* a Jewish barber masquerading as Hynkel-Hitler masquerading as a passionate private citizen-filmmaker risks death to stop the insanity of another global conflict. Finally, even world-weary Verdoux's macabre self-defense mechanism of creating his own "Murder, Incorporated" business ultimately fails, and he is as anxious to kill himself as Charlie the soldier is to live.

Because Verdoux makes no attempts to deny the murder charges, the courtroom scenes become suicide as theatre, with an end result as obvious as the title of Tom Stoppard's dark comedy *Rosencrantz and Guildenstern Are Dead* (staged in 1966, filmed in 1990). However, unlike the *Laurel & Hardy Meet Hamlet* tone of Stoppard's absurdist play, Verdoux is the all-controlling puppeteer in his courtroom drama. While Chaplin's later pontificating slows the still moving memoir-like *Limelight* (1952) and sometimes derails *A King in New York* (1957), Verdoux's comments represent a wonderful crystallization of the film's dark comedy, such as his observation, "War, conflict—it's all business. One murder makes a villain, millions a hero. Numbers sanctify, my good fellow." (Earlier he had told a young friend, "Business is a ruthless business.") And his last words to the court after being found guilty are ever so appropriate for a genre fixated upon death:

> However remiss the prosecutor has been ... he at least admits that I have brains.... And for thirty-five years I used them honestly. After that, nobody wanted them. So I was forced to go into business for myself. As for being a mass killer, does not the world encourage it? Is it not building weapons of destruction for the sole purpose of mass killing? Has it not blown unsuspecting women and little children to pieces? And done it very scientifically? As a mass killer, I am an amateur by comparison. However, I do not to wish to lose my temper, because very shortly, I shall lose my head. Nevertheless, upon leaving this spark of earthly existence, I have to say, I shall see you *all* very soon ... very soon.

Despite *Verdoux*'s initial lack of critical and commercial success in the United States (abroad it was hailed as a masterpiece), the movie did garner an Academy Award nomination for Best Original Screenplay.

Since *Verdoux* is an equal opportunity dark comedy, the screenplay lays waste, as any representative picture of the genre would do, to any and all seminal institutes of man, including religion, thus explaining the sarcastic comments by Chaplin's character to the priest who visits him in prison. After the holy emissary uttered the proverbial, "May the Lord have mercy on your soul," Verdoux replies, "Why not? After all it belongs to him." In the long run, however, Verdoux's "war" was with hypocrisy on Earth: "I have made my peace with God, my conflict is with man."

Chaplin's namesake son suggested that *Verdoux* represented an amalgamation of all the macabre things which fascinated his father. Yet, given Chaplin's messy post-war personal and professional life, his retirement of "Charlie," and the provocative nature of the *Verdoux* story, would not the comedian have had more reasons to proceed with such an iffy project? One could suggest several additional hypotheses, starting with Chaplin's need to yet again put forward a message, regardless of the consequences—a factor which had driven his work since *Modern Times*. Chaplin had been planning to retire with *City Lights* (1931), anticipating a later comment by Susan Sontag: "By silence [ending one's career, an artist] frees himself from service bondage to the [entertainment expectations of] the world."[25] It was just that global events—the Great Depression, World War II, and the ugly post-war road to McCarthyism—kept dragging Chaplin back to the cinema. Thus, just after *Verdoux*'s opening, the comedian said that as one "gets older we are not satisfied to go along with the same [thing]. We have to get excited by something before we can arouse our energy to do something ... so I suppose [*Verdoux*] is one of my indulgences."[26]

Chaplin had never known an American critical and commercials failure of any picture in which he starred ... quite the record for an always provocative personality whose career began in 1914. Who would doubt Chaplin feeling Teflon-tough? The French's perverse fascination with the comedic calm of Henri Landru during the original 1921 murder trial might have emboldened Chaplin's hopes for his cinematic take on the man in *Verdoux*. Certainly there are several detailed comic links between Landru and Verdoux, beyond the basic serial killer story. For example, the press coverage of Landru's trial often had dark comedy fun with how such an unattractive man could be so romantically successful:

> France has [found] amusement in the ease with which the ugly, rather uninteresting middle-aged man won hundreds of women and induced many to come and live with him and hand over all [their] little treasures....[27]

Flash-forward to Chaplin's film and the introduction of Verdoux, via a photograph of the Bluebeard a victimized family has obtained. In studying the Verdoux picture, one member of the household observes, "Funny-looking bird, isn't he?" To this assessment another relative replies, "Must be a pretty good salesman to sell anything with a face like that." Art imitates life here, just as another Landru article could be describing the later unruffled courtroom Verdoux, as well as even suggesting and encouraging theatrical-cinema possibilities:

> Through the [prosecutor's] whole four-hour speech [the audience] watched not the speaker but Landru, and he never flinched. With quiet indifference he entered the court, and with as quiet [an] indifference he left it. He might have been watching a play. Even policemen beside him could not maintain so detached an air, and once one of them turned and looked at his charge with incredulous eyes.[28]

Though Landru spoke little in court, and maintained his innocence, his attitude during the trial once again could be describing Verdoux: "The whole demeanor of Landru [for weeks] has furnished infinite amusement [for the courtroom audience], some laughs, a few gasps of astonishment at his audacity and any number of thrills."[29] As the trial wound down, another press overview sounded more like the review of a lowbrow farce: "Always the public has been unable to see anything but a burlesque in the comical Lothario of several hundred fiancées, the seducer of stout cooks, the wooer of lonely widows."[30] Certainly, such reporting might have later lulled Chaplin into a false sense of solid box office for *Verdoux*. Yet, as the title of Preston Sturges' final (1955) film, a French production no less, later warned, *The French, They Are a Funny Race*. Of course, in fairness, *Verdoux* was a critical and commercial hit upon its initial release in France and throughout Europe.

If Chaplin had been watching for potential warnings about puritanical Americans and movie comedians, he might have looked closer to home. Ironically, the Landru proceedings paralleled the first of three San Francisco trials for the popular 300-pound screen clown "Fatty" Arbuckle on manslaughter charges. It was alleged that his sexual assault of an actress at a party led to her death. The first two trials resulted in hung juries, with Arbuckle eventually being acquitted; an apologetic court fully exonerated him. But by then his movie career was ruined. There was not farcical fun, *à la* France, for even an *innocent* man in America, only tragedy. The Americans, they are a funny race.

Chaplin's wealth and part-ownership of United Artists meant another potential incentive for him to make *Verdoux*—simply that he could. Though the McCarthy era was still in the wings, *Verdoux* appeared at a time when the opportunities for openly liberal filmmakers were quickly closing. Later that year (1947) the first systematic Hollywood blacklist was instituted with the "Waldorf Agreement," in which a group of studio executives fired ten leftist writers and directors (soon known as the "Hollywood Ten"). This occurred the day after the ten were cited for contempt of Congress for refusing to give testimony to the House Un-American Activities Committee. In being asked to name their political affiliation—what essentially boiled down to the crucial question, "Are you now or have you ever been a member of the Communist Party?"—the ten rightfully refused, citing their First Amendment rights to freedom of speech and assembly. (The Communist Party was at that time a legal organization.) An ever-expanding blacklist was about to descend and begin a tragic period in Hollywood history. Chaplin's later film *A King in New York* would satirically attack this sorry era ... which even then (1957) had not yet ended.

One receives a sneak preview–like sense of the HUAC world to come when revisiting Chaplin's humiliating New York press conference for *Verdoux* on April 12, 1947 (the day after its premiere). The transcript of the proceedings reads like a scenario on how to conduct a witch hunt. The inquisition was in a packed ballroom of the Gotham Hotel, near Fifth Avenue at 55th Street, and also followed the picture's early mainly negative reviews. Based upon Chaplin's brief opening attempt at some levity, "Bring on the butchery," the comedian thought he knew what was coming. He had no idea. The ambush was of epic proportions. The philistine American press, save for James Agee, savaged Chaplin on his politics and patriotism, or his lack thereof. The attack ranged from more criticism of his "citizen of the world" views, to the ancient knock that he shirked his British soldiering duties during World War I by selling American bonds. *Verdoux* was almost an afterthought.

The only civilized spot in this new age witch hunt occurred when the angry, trembling voice of now celebrated critic-author James Agee voiced a Chaplin defense via an ironically rhetorical question of just what having a free country meant. Addressing this slanderous Chaplin treatment, Agee asked:

> What are people who care a damn about freedom—who really care for it—[to] think of a country and the people in it, who congratulate themselves upon this country as [the] finest on earth and as a "free country," when so many of the people in this country pry into what a man's citizenship is, try to tell him his business from hour to hour and from day to day and exert a public moral blackmail against him for not becoming on American citizen—for his political views and for not entertaining troops in the manner—in the way that they think he should. What is to be thought of general country where these people are well thought of?[31]

A very appreciative Chaplin thoughtfully but tactfully acknowledged Agee's kindness without opening himself up to further barbs from the political right: "Thank you very much—but I have nothing to say to that question." (One is reminded of Nathanael West's 1939 novel *The Day of the Locust*, a filmland satire on how the public enjoys both embracing its cinematic heroes *and* destroying them.) Agee would go on to write a passionate three-part celebration of *Verdoux* in *The Nation*, shortly to be addressed. As an Agee biographer later wrote, "He became [*Verdoux*'s] self-appointed champion and defended [it] as vehemently as if he himself had made it."[32] In Chaplin's 1964 memoir he fondly remembered Agee's "kinds words," but the comedian's memories of the ugly press conference essentially end at this point.[33]

Chaplin's civility throughout this public grilling represented, in its own way, another elegant *defense* of a maligned artist. Sometimes he even managed to slip in some humor, such as the comedian's response to his politics—was he a Communist?:

> [It] is very difficult [today] to define anything politically ... if you step off the curb with your left foot, they accuse you of being a Communist. But ... I've never belonged to any political party in my life.³⁴

Most significantly for this text, however, was a Chaplin answer to two questions which actually remained on target (*Verdoux*) though posited in a condescending manner: Was this title character meant to be sympathetic, and should there not be someone in a film for whom the public has sympathy? The comedian's response, without mentioning dark comedy by name, gets to the heart of *Verdoux*'s more virulent variety of the genre:

> As sympathy, I think—unless I'm mistaken—I intended that the feeling should be that you have sympathy for the whole human race.... [U]nder certain drastic circumstances ... conditions bring out the worst in humanity and I've been intensifying that in this picture.... My motive—if there is any sympathy for Verdoux, it is to understand crime and the nature of crime. I'd sooner understand it and the nature of it than condemn it.³⁵

For Chaplin those "drastic circumstances" were now the new *permanent* norm. Dark comedy—and the "whole human race"—deserved sympathy, for as the previously noted cartoon character Pogo once observed, with black humor conciseness, "We have met the enemy, and he is us."

Chaplin's sympathy for, yet angry frustration with, the seemingly ongoing march of humanity towards these "drastic circumstances" which makes all of us potential Verdouxs might best be embellished by two diverse yet related commentaries about the wars which drove this Chaplin trilogy. The first comes from British World War I vet Harry Patch's memoir *The Last Fighting Tommy: The Life of Harry Patch, Last Veteran of the Trenches, 1898–2009*. Eighty-nine years after the conflict ended, a still bitter Patch wrote,

> By the time I was [demobilized] I was thoroughly disillusioned. I could never understand why my country would call me from a peacetime job and train me to go out to France and try to kill a man I never knew. Why did we fight? I asked myself that many times. At the end of the war, the peace was settled 'round a table, so why the hell couldn't they do that at the start without losing millions of men? I left the army with my faith in the Church ... shattered [and my religious] belief didn't come [back].³⁶

Couple Patch's remarks with those of Nobel Peace Prize–winning author and Auschwitz survivor Elie Wiesel, who wrote nearly seven decades after the end of World War II with more learned hopelessness:

> [W]e were convinced that after Auschwitz there would be no more anti–Semitism. We were wrong. This produced a feeling close to despair. For if Auschwitz could not cure mankind of racism, was there any chance of success ever? The fact is, the world has learned nothing.³⁷

Keep in mind that the Armenian Holocaust during and after World War I, in what constitutes the present-day Republic of Turkey, resulted in the "genocide" (the word itself was actually coined to describe this event) of well over a million people. After the Holocaust of World War II, this massacre, also known as the Great Crime, is the second most studied example of genocide in world history, making Wiesel's words all the more chillingly prophetic. And while none of Chaplin's war trilogy dark comedy commentaries were created with the same weighted distance in time as the observations of Wiesel and Patch, the horrific message culminating in *Verdoux* remains the same: Man is not so much at the end of his tether, as released from it.

Yet Chaplin "said" these things via *Verdoux* too early, and it is often most fortuitous to be only slightly ahead of the times, as was the dark comedy of *Shoulder Arms*. Plus, if one factors in the comedian's previously documented controversial life, *Verdoux* hardly stood a chance in the America of 1947. In 1964, seventeen years after the volatile period when Chaplin released the culmination film of his dark comedy war trilogy, *New York Times* critic Bosley Crowther said *Verdoux*'s initial appearance had resulted in "the most antagonistic critical and public reception ever accorded a Chaplin film."[38] This is called understatement. In 1947 the entertainment bible, *Variety,* opined, "Comedy based on the characterization of a modern Parisian Bluebeard treads dangerous shoals ... Chaplin generates little sympathy."[39] The *Hollywood Reporter*'s negative reviewer added, "Only confusion results from his injecting [black humor] 'messages' and pseudo-political observations into the comedy."[40] The title for this review was even more succinctly negative: "*M. Verdoux* Disappointing."[41]

A few reviewers struggled to be positive about *Verdoux*. For instance, the *New York Post*'s Archer Winsten felt *Verdoux*'s soapbox ending was an emotional and intellectual downer, yet there are "acts of comic creation no one but Chaplin could give us. They make it a picture to be seen."[42] The *New York Mirror* even called *Verdoux* an "uneven but continuously interesting film. Though it's not off Chaplin's top shelf, it comes from a higher perch than more of the pictures you will enjoy in a season."[43]

In the United States, however, the critical reputation of *Verdoux* was kept alive until a time when such extreme black humor was more acceptable, and the public could better separate the work from an artist's life, largely because of the tragically short-lived James Agee's (1910–1955) three-part championing of the film in *The Nation*. The critic's first *Verdoux* essay focused upon various complaints about the movie, from it not being funny, to the retirement of the Tramp. One might summarize this piece with the critic's combatively bald comment:

> Disregard virtually everything you may have read about the film. It is of interest but chiefly as a definitive measure of the difference between the thing a man of genius puts before the world and the things the [provincial] world is equipped to see it in.[44]

Agee's second *Verdoux* essay tackles the key thrust of the film, what the critic felt was Chaplin's "greatest" and darkest theme thus far: "the bare problem of surviving at all in such a world as this."[45] Yet Agee's insightful vision of the comedian's Verdoux as a "metaphor for the modern personality" is a frightfully fitting take on the evolution of Chaplin's darkening persona.[46] Yet, just as the game plan for survival had radically changed by 1947, the scenario for the safety of the individual in Verdoux's world had further deteriorated, necessitating the citizen now assume the macabre tactics of the state.

The third Agee *Nation* piece on *Verdoux* further explores why this character became a murderer. Moving beyond Verdoux as a "mentor for the modern personality," even Agee finds some faults with the picture—wishing Chaplin had also embellished on some basic "bottom causes" for criminality.[47] Make no mistake, while Agee continues to call the movie "one of the few indispensible works of our time," he implies that the comedian might also have suggested that such nefarious activity would be grounded in fundamental weakness, exasperated by Verdoux's desperate need to support an invalid wife and young child.[48] Of course, given Chaplin's already documented fascination with murder mysteries, the comedian might simply have assumed this was a given in a movie of this nature. However, Agee's lengthy run-on sentence close also posits the stimulating idea that if the artist's Bluebeard figure had fully embraced his beloved handicapped wife (in support of whom he kills) in a marriage of equals, Verdoux might have been content to live in a milieu of Charlie the Tramp poverty. Thus, a more contented relationship, *sans* murder, could and would have evolved.

Agee's insight into what Chaplin had accomplished with *Verdoux*, as well as his sense of human decency over the foul treatment accorded the comedian at the United Artists press conference, were the catalysts for his inspired series of essays on the film. As a footnote to his passionate defense of *Verdoux*, Agee might also have had a special interest in the macabre, and/or simply been unusually impressed by the picture. This is because one of the two Agee screenplays produced during his later brief sojourn as a scriptwriter was an adaptation of a Davis Grubb novel for the Charles Laughton–directed *The Night of the Hunter* (1955). What was the connection to *Verdoux*? Set in the same time period, *Hunter*'s character (Robert Mitchum) marries and murders women for their money. Though more of an atmospheric allegorical thriller than a dark comedy, *Hunter* has other *Verdoux* embellishments, such as an opening in which a desperate, out-of-work father (Peter Graves) murders, like Chaplin's character, in order to take care of family. Plus, both figures calmly go to their executions. As a final ironic link, while *Hunter* is now an acclaimed American classic like *Verdoux*, it also went unappreciated when initially released in the United States, though it too garnered immediate critical acclaim abroad. (*Hunter*'s lack of box office success kept first-time director Laughton from ever megaphoning again, and Agee died of a heart attack before the film's release.)

While *Verdoux* was soon withdrawn from distribution in the United States, given the backlash against Chaplin, the movie had a much more rewarding reception in Europe. There, where no Agee-like defense was necessary, the celebrated French theorist and critic André Bazin provided the most thought-provoking analysis of *Verdoux*. Though Bazin was a realist like Agee, his writing on Chaplin focuses on the myth of Charlie—how an international audience relates to him as a twentieth-century Ulysses.[49] Bazin's thesis is most provocative when it is applied to movies in which the comedian did *not* play the archetypal Charlie, such as the iconoclastic *Verdoux*, discussed in the theorist's essay "The Myth of Monsieur Verdoux."[50] By pushing this cult of a comic myth into the darkest of Chaplin territory, Bazin provides an explanation for why there might be viewer identification with a Bluebeard, 1947 America notwithstanding: "It is the character [of Charlie in *Verdoux*] that we love, not his qualities or defects. The audience's sympathy for Verdoux is focused on the myth [of Charlie], not on what he stands for morally."[51] Plus, without actually using the phrase "dark comedy," Bazin also suggests the ludicrousness of trying to attach any ethical standard to a genre and central character tied to absurdity and the notion of man as beast.

One might also take Bazin's implied links between the sometimes similar physical shtick of Charlie and Verdoux a step further. For example, there is another dual focus narrative taking place here, but one more ephemeral than Charlie and title character Jackie Coogan in *The Kid*, or Paulette Goddard's gamin and the Tramp in *Modern Times*. The alter ego of the occasionally Charlie-like Verdoux is the figure only known as "The Girl" (Marilyn Nash) in the movie's credits. She is a prostitute Verdoux picks up on a rainy night in order to test a new, seemingly untraceable poison. He takes her to his nearby residence in the city, and they discuss her hard-knock life, including jail time for a minor theft. Knowing that she has little time to live, he acts the ironically perfect host, seemingly assuring her, "Nothing is permanent in this world—not even our troubles." With that he prepares her a last supper, some scrambled eggs and poisoned red wine. Noticing that the Girl is reading a book by German philosopher Arthur Schopenhauer (1788–1860), Verdoux turns the conversation towards that scholar's thoughts on suicide. For Verdoux, since the girl's life has been sad and is about to end soon anyway, the viewer assumes this Bluebeard plans to make her a collaborator, of sorts, on her impending death.

Yet Chaplin's use of Schopenhauer enriches the scene. First, while the philosopher did not promote the idea of suicide, he was passionate in his belief that it was neither a religious sin nor anyone else's business More specifically, Schopenhauer wrote:

> They tell us that suicide is the greatest piece of cowardice ... and other insipidities of the same kind; or else they make the nonsensical remark that suicide is *wrong,* when it is quite obvious that there is nothing in the world to which every man has a more unassailable title than to his own life and person.[52]

Thus, Chaplin is documenting one of the seminal themes of dark comedy—the omnipresence of death, often by suicide. Also, as a ladykiller using marriage as his MO, Verdoux has respect neither for women nor for the marital state. Again, Schopenhauer is just the man for Verdoux: "[W]omen are defective in the powers of reasoning and deliberation.... [T]o marry means to half one's rights and double one's duties."[53] Another significant reason for Schopenhauer to be referenced in this *Verdoux* sequence is that, like Chaplin, the philosopher also has some dark comedy fun with the subject of suicide:

> Suicide may also be regarded as an experiment—a question which man puts to Nature, trying to force her to answer.... What change will death produce in man's existence and in his insight into the nature of things? It is a clumsy experiment to make, for it involves the destruction of the very consciousness which puts the question and awaits the answer.[54]

Chaplin had to love this macabre levity. Moreover, the Schopenhauer passage nicely anticipates the mock suicide "experiment" in the later dark comedy gem *MASH* (1970), in which Duke Forrest (Tom Skerritt) describes a potential suicide as merely going on a "little [deathly] reconnaissance" trip for the unit.

Still, when Verdoux plays his Schopenhauer "life is negative" card, the Girl surprises him by observing, "Yet life is wonderful [too] ... music, art, love...." This last revelation (love) further takes Verdoux aback, and he discovers she had been fiercely devoted to her late handicapped veteran husband (another tie to World War I). The verbally innocent coup de grace which saves her life occurs when she passionately utters, "I'd have killed for him [her husband]!" Since that was precisely what Verdoux's murderous mercenary marriages were about—to care for his real invalid wife—he immediately "sees that [the girl] is his philosophical twin," and spares her life.[55] They will meet twice more in the picture, and the bond between them is further sealed on their last visit, when the girl's newfound wealth and secure life is based upon a loveless marriage to a war munitions tycoon. For survival, she, like Verdoux, has applied the policies of state to the individual. Verdoux even admits the munitions racket is something he might have looked into. Fittingly, for Chaplin's ultimate dark comedy, this is his blackest dual focus narrative. And to come full circle back to the suicide theme initially discussed at their first encounter, following the final meeting—after a meal she has provided for him—Verdoux commits voluntary suicide by allowing himself to be caught by the police. (As a footnote to Chaplin's use of Schopenhauer and suicide being "nobody's business but my own," a safe bet would be that the comedian first came to this perspective by way of the later American writer-orator Robert Ingersoll, 1833–1899. Ingersoll's Schopenhauer-like perspectives had a profound influence upon Chaplin as a young adult. Yet, by the time of *Monsieur Verdoux,* Ingersoll had largely fallen through the cracks of time, and Chaplin undoubtedly went with the more high-profile Schopenhauer for an intellectual viewing audience.)

9. Monsieur Verdoux, Without His "Talisman" Charlie

The Verdoux murder trial which follows deserves one final addendum. Verdoux's calmly caustic comments merit comparison to the controversial speech which closes *Dictator*. While Chaplin as Verdoux does not obviously step out of character as does the Tramp-barber mistaken for Hynkel, Verdoux's extended remarks in court are the most blatant platform of the film for citizen Chaplin to express his disappointment/disgust with "modern times." This difference accents *Verdoux*'s status as Chaplin's ultimate dark comedy, since *Dictator*'s compassionate plea for peace is the mirror opposite of *Verdoux*'s pungent accusation of hypocrisy on a murderous global scale. Citizen Chaplin is as disillusioned as Verdoux, because now all that drives his creative efforts are ever-darker personal commentaries—"like a Socrates."[56] Just two years after Verdoux's controversial argument for the individual's right to appropriate the murderous model of governments, the darkly comic noir villain Harry Lime (Orson Welles) of the Graham Greene–scripted *The Third Man* (1949), observes of his killing ways: "In these days, old man, nobody thinks in terms of human beings. Governments don't, so why should we?... They have their five-year plans so have I." Is Verdoux a Harry Lime or a New Age Socrates?

Whether one accepts Bazin's provocative Chaplin as Socrates-like or not, I would only modestly differ with the theorist on the opening to the essay from which it comes, the aforementioned "Myth of Monsieur Verdoux." Being that *Verdoux* is based upon famous French serial killer Henri Landru, it is most appropriate that his fellow countryman critic begins the essay by discussing the actual case. Bazin states that Landru's conviction was largely based upon the Bluebeard's meticulously maintained account book. That is, Landru would record *every* transaction, including the cost of train tickets to the country home where the murders took place. His account book had all these notations for two tickets there, but only one was a round-trip ticket! With the thoroughness of the Nazis, who recorded their every horrific act, Landru's own attention to detail brought him down. Bazin's point on this subject is that while there were many parallels between Verdoux and Chaplin's Tramp, such particularness would not apply to Charlie.

I disagree. The Tramp might not have kept books, yet he always seemed prepared for every situation. For instance, in *Shoulder Arms,* soldier Charlie comes equipped to the trenches with a rattrap in his pack. In *The Idle Class* (1921), his meager supplies include a golf bag—hardly expected of a Tramp. Yet, sure enough, he finds a course, and when he prepares his first tee shot, in the days when sand propped up the ball, Charlie does not like the quality of sand provided by the course. Not to worry; he calmly reaches into his pocket and pulls out his own special blend of sand. In *The Circus* (1928) Charlie prepares an impromptu breakfast from a tin cup over a campfire. Needing a spoon to stir his concoction, he fishes one out of a pocket; deciding some sugar is necessary, he dips some from a vest pocket. Later in the same film, the Tramp ruins a William Tell sketch by eating part of the apple placed as a target upon his head; he then attempts to calm the frustrated comic archer (Chaplin company regular Henry Bergman) by producing a banana from another pocket—though a much harder target to hit on one's head. (I'm convinced that Charlie scenes such as these were the later inspiration for Chaplin fan Harpo Marx's surreal magic pockets in any number of pictures, such as the blowtorch Harpo pulls from a pocket in *Duck Soup,* 1933.[57]) My difference with Bazin on this subject merely reinforces the theorist's overall perspective: So much of the Charlie persona remains in the Verdoux character that the viewer relates to the Bluebeard despite himself.

In addition to Bazin and other French critics, Britain was also full of period praise for *Verdoux* at the highest level. For example, in 1948 the British Film Institute published a pamphlet on the picture insightfully linking its dark comedy to Chaplin's other political films:

> The frustrations, paradoxes, inconsistencies and incomprehensibilities of modern industrial society appears as too big to handle in *Modern Times,* the machines run riot; in *The Great Dictator* statesmanship [runs riot], and in *Monsieur Verdoux* it is in his economic life that man loses his footing [and kills].[58]

The same pamphlet had the BFI strongly stating that any Chaplin film "should be examined not on its own merits alone but in a context of individual artistic development."[59]

Verdoux is the culmination of Chaplin's ever-darker evolution of his black humor war trilogy, and the axiom that one "can not go home again" eventually did not apply to Chaplin's most controversial film. The picture which chased him out of Gotham in 1947 was suddenly golden upon its limited reissue in 1964. The *New York Times* both praised and apologized for what had occurred years earlier:

> The engagement now permits all these people who did not get to see it … years ago and all those who had been hearing about it as one of the great Chaplin films through all the years to see for themselves what a superior sardonic comedy it is—and also to estimate how unjust was the bitter discrimination against it.[60]

Some additional revisionist comments bear noting, such as the shock of the *New York Post*'s aforementioned Archer Winsten, one of the rare American critics to praise *Verdoux* in 1947: "Seeing the picture again [in 1964] with crowds agog with enthusiasm, [and] lining up for a block outside the theatre, is a strange and sobering experience."[61] The title of his piece said it all: "Rages and Outrages."[62] *Newsweek*'s 1964 *Verdoux* essay fine-tuned the "Outrages": "This is all exactly as it was—the work of a comic genius. Nothing in the film has changed.... What has changed … is the atmosphere. Chaplin is no longer a villain."[63]

There were also excellent new insights in all this revisionism. For instance, Andrew Sarris observed in one of his *Village Voice* essays on the film:

> The [*Verdoux*] hilarity I found richest and deepest was inspired … by that fantastic surprise when Chaplin comes dancing into Isobel Elsom's apartment [a potential victim whose appearance he has forgotten] to embrace Miss Elsom's fat, ugly housekeeper before discovering his mistake. The rest of the scene is drowned out by the convulsed audience as Chaplin [Verdoux] commits a second gaffe with Miss Elsom's lady friend and then pauses in perplexity for Miss Elsom herself. Beneath the laughter is the most incisive expression of pathos and tragedy of Don Juanism I have ever encountered.[64]

Such is the *business* of dark comedy's "man as beast" use of sexuality. Yet, *New York Herald* critic Judith Crist's 1964 review was the most poetically succinct in finally crowning *Verdoux* the seminal status for this genre: "[The] prototype of the lovable-murder [dark] comedy."[65] In 2008, *New York Times* author J. Hoberman said of this Chaplin dark comedy, "No star ever took a greater risk with his public image or more directly challenged his audience."[66]

10

Monsieur Verdoux to *Limelight*: From "The Little Tramp" to "The Little Red"

> There's something about working the streets [as a musician] I like. It's the Tramp in me, I suppose.—Chaplin as Calvero in *Limelight* (1952)

Artists seldom retire, and so it was with Chaplin. Moreover, as this quote from his first film after *Monsieur Verdoux* (1947) suggests, the sense of Charlie the Tramp was still lurking in his work. However, with few exceptions, such as critic James Agee's passionate defense of *Verdoux*, America's critical and commercial response to this Tramp-less movie had been a crushing disappointment to the comedian. Though his films had only been appearing intermittently since the 1920s, Chaplin had largely held the keys to the Hollywood Kingdom as a cinema icon until the 1940s.

Chaplin was not yet done with dark comedy, as his less successful *A King in New York* (1957) will demonstrate. Yet, his ever more provocative application of the genre in his war trilogy of *Shoulder Arms* (1918), *The Great Dictator* (1940), and *Verdoux* remains a watershed foundation for black humor. The visceral American rejection he had suffered from *Verdoux* brings to mind a short defense mechanism penned by Elie Wiesel in his book *Open Heart* (2011): "To chase [away] this onset of anxiety, I let my thoughts take me back to a distant past [of my childhood]."[1] This perfectly describes the next project Chaplin threw himself into almost immediately after the *Verdoux* debacle: *Limelight*.

Limelight goes back in time to the London of his youth, 1914, also the year his Tramp first appeared on the screen. Chaplin plays Calvero, a stage clown who has lost his audience, not unlike the comedian's position with the American public in the 1950s. The film opens with Calvero coming home to his flat (in the Kennington slums of Chaplin's youth) pleasantly plastered. Noting an odd odor in the hall, he smells his cigar, and checks his shoes, *à la* a crude Keystone dog-dropping bit. Suddenly, the washed-up entertainer realizes he smells gas. He breaks through the door of a boarding house neighbor and saves from suicide a young ballerina (Claire Bloom), who through an illness has succumbed to a psychological disorder making her believe her legs are paralyzed.

Calvero turns his quarters into a platonic nursing arrangement with Bloom's character Terry. Within the movie the aging clown winningly describes the scenario with the aphorism, "When you reach my age, a platonic friendship can be maintained on the highest platonic level." The situation also works as an understated in-joke, given Chaplin's Lothario-like reputation with young girls, especially with his leading lady (Bloom) bearing such a striking resemblance to his fourth wife Oona O'Neill—only five years older than Bloom and already the mother of four Chaplin children. (Three of them, Geraldine, Michael and Josephine, appear in cameos at the beginning of *Limelight*.) The lookalike effect of Bloom and O'Neill is actually acknowledged in the film by Mrs. Chaplin (also a former ballerina) doubling for Bloom in a scene.

The casting of Bloom as Terry, as well as the nuances of the part, reflected the beauty and the haunting vulnerability of both Chaplin's mother and the comedian's first love, Hetty Kelly. The young British comic fell hard for the teenage performer, but his first trip to America for the Karno comedy stage troupe separated the young lovers just as a relationship was beginning. Then his popularity in America, first in vaudeville and later in the movies, doomed *the* love which was not to be. A second-chance friendship was denied when she then died young during the Spanish influenza epidemic which engulfed the globe following World War I. Until Chaplin's marriage to Oona in 1942, many aficionados of the comedian felt the iconic star's loss of Kelly drove his obsession, on-screen and off, to find the perfect young heroine. In Bloom's 1982 memoir *Limelight and After*, whose very title both denotes the importance of Chaplin's film to his public, and her career, she delicately describes the complexity of the part she was asked to play:

> [Chaplin and I] went to a theatrical costumer to outfit me for the [*Limelight* screen] test. Chaplin had already decided upon every last detail of every garment I was to wear. He remembered the way his mother had worn such a dress, and the way his first girlfriend [Kelly] had worn such a shawl, and I quickly realized, then, that some composite young woman, lost to him in the past, was what he wanted to bring to life.[2]

(Chaplin had lost Kelly through death and he had lost his beloved mother through insanity.)

Given that Chaplin's style was to act out every part for each performer, and for them to follow his directions *exactly,* one would assume Bloom's "composite" Terry greatly reflected every important shading of the real women who occupied this densely populated character. For instance, here is Bloom's take on Chaplin's directing:

> I was close to panic [about the screen test] until I saw that Chaplin intended to give me every inflection and every gesture exactly as he had during rehearsal. This didn't accord with my high creative aspirations but in the circumstances [young, anxious to embrace the break of a lifetime, and in awe of this artist] it was just fine. I couldn't have been happier—nor did I have any choice. Gradually, imitating Chaplin, I gained my confidence, and by the time we came to the actual filming I was enjoying myself rather like some little monkey in the zoo being put through the paces by a clever, playful drillmaster.[3]

Without belaboring *Limelight* ties to the comedian's youth, several more links merit noting. For example, in the novel *Footlights* which Chaplin wrote and pared down to the *Limelight* screenplay, he provides some important Calvero details which are missing from the film. For instance, a key to Calvero's alcoholic decline as a performer was tied to the infidelity of an earlier, never-seen wife. As noted in Chapter 2, a young Chaplin had resented being largely abandoned by his hard-drinking popular stage entertainer father but, through the years his view of Chaplin, Sr., had softened, given that a contributing factor to his father's drinking himself to death before the age of forty was probably to his wife's promiscuity. A first-page description of Calvero from *Footlights* was equally true of Chaplin: "Calvero was not gregarious. He was shy and reserved and difficult to know. At times [he was] melancholy and austere."[4]

Another connection between Chaplin's youth and *Limelight* is tied to his 1910 Karno trip to America. During the tour Chaplin was mesmerized by one of the era's key Broadway and vaudeville headliners, Frank Tinney (1878–1940). Tinney's masterful timing and delivery squeezed big laughs out of old material, such as the following question and response: "How about lending me a dollar for a week, old man?" [Pause] "Who's the weak old man you want it for?"[5] (So causally slick was Tinney's routine that a later London engagement paid him $2,250 a week—breaking then-current records for an American solo act.[6]) One would not be amiss in making a possible connection between Tinney's ability to "sell" old comic chestnuts with Calvero's confident poise in successfully presenting his corny but charmingly entertaining flea act in *Limelight*. Indeed, Chaplin originally wrote the flea sketch during Tinney's heyday, and never got around to utilizing it in a film until *Limelight*. Much later Chaplin was shocked by an aging Tinney performance without any of the monologist's original comedy gifts. Again, as the old axiom states, "Success has many fathers." That is, years after *Limelight*'s release, Chaplin said Tinney's fall from comedy grace by way of age and lost confidence had also been a factor in making the film.[7] Of course, this story might have been the result of a now elderly Chaplin rewriting his own life—not wanting to confess just how close he had felt to the forgotten Calvero.

Barry Anthony's *Chaplin's Music Hall: The Chaplins and Their Circle in Limelight* (2012) makes a case for Calvero being drawn, at least in part, from the once popular British stage performer Lee Dryden (1863–1939), the father of Chaplin's half-brother Wheeler Dryden (1892–1957).[8] Like Calvero, Dryden had once been a 19th century stage star, only later to find his fame so faded he too was reduced to working as a street musician. Also like Calvero, the senior Dryden enjoyed a late-in-life final triumph at a benefit in his honor. Chaplin would have been well aware of these things, both from his childhood career paralleling that of Dryden, and from the fact that Chaplin reconnected with the younger Wheeler when they were adults. (Wheeler was eventually employed by the Chaplin studio; his tasks included working as an assistant director on *Dictator* and a producer on *Limelight*.)

While much of *Limelight* was a visit to Chaplin's past, the picture was also something of a family home movie of yesterday *and* today (1952). Besides the aforementioned brief appearances by wife Oona and three of their young children, Chaplin's two oldest sons (Charles Jr., and Sydney) from his union with Lita Grey were part of the cast, and the previously noted half-brother Dryden was one of the film's producers. Moreover, Sydney plays a prominent (fourth-billed) part as Terry's (Bloom) ultimate love interest. Also, the family "home movie" slant should not merely be taken as simple nepotism. Throughout Chaplin's private life he genuinely enjoyed making and/or appearing with friends and family in actual home movies. In fact, one such 1920s amateur production documents the roots of *The Great Dictator*'s balloon-like globe scene years *before* Hitler even came to power.[9]

In addition, like most auteurs, great or otherwise, Chaplin was most comfortable directing and performing when surrounded by people he knew and/or had worked with before. With regard to the latter, two former Chaplin regulars from the silent era, Snub Pollard (1893–1962) and Loyal Underwood (1893–1966), were cast in minor *Limelight* parts. Pollard's Chaplin ties went back to the Essanay Films of 1915—though here Pollard's later signature walrus mustache was a work in progress. Underwood had frequently worked with Chaplin between 1916 and 1923, most notably in *Easy Street* (1917). In this sometime dark comedy, the diminutive Underwood's huge brood of children so impresses Charlie's neighborhood cop character, that he briefly decorates the undersized father for unexpected virility by pinning his police badge on Underwood's coat. Ironically, the mere presence of these actors would have reinforced a pivotal theme of the picture: the transitory nature of fame.

In *Limelight*, Chaplin (right) and Buster Keaton, silent comedy's greatest duo, were teamed at last.

Paradoxically, Buster Keaton's (1895–1966) casting is an even more spot-on examination of *Limelight*'s heart. Keaton had been one of the pantheon comedians of the silent era—Chaplin's only serious artistic rival. Though never as commercially successful as Chaplin and Harold Lloyd (1893–1971), Keaton's "Great Stone Face" minimalism in a chaotic world now makes his persona more existentialistically relevant with each passing year. But Keaton's significance had long been forgotten because of a number of factors—the coming of sound, loss of artistic control to parent studio MGM, an ugly divorce, and alcoholism. Yet, by the late 1940s, thanks in part to a seminal cinema essay by James Agee, "Comedy's Greatest Era," Keaton's fortunes were beginning to improve.[10] Early television appearances by Keaton, including a brief but influential local Los Angeles program of his own, had also assisted the revival of his career. Teaming with Chaplin in *Limelight*'s funniest sketch—a zany duet with Calvero on the violin and his nearsighted partner (Keaton) struggling to play the piano while maintaining control of his ever tumbling sheet music—marked the high point of Keaton's comeback. Serendipitous or not, the neglected Calvero-Chaplin satellite characters played by Keaton, Pollard, and Underwood ratcheted up the real poignancy of the story. (Agee, the defender of *Verdoux* and the resurrectionist Keaton essayist, also assisted Chaplin in editing the massive *Footlight* novel into a manageable *Limelight* screenplay.)

Before examining *Limelight* in detail, however, one needs to briefly examine what else was going on in Chaplin's life during the five years between the picture's completion and the previous *Verdoux*—besides the prolonged writing of *Footlights*. Once again, the comedian's political activity got him in hot water. Despite the disastrous *Verdoux* press conference during the spring of 1947, after which the picture was quickly pulled from release in the United States, Chaplin still had hopes of reissuing the movie in the fall. A special ad campaign would stress that Verdoux was a new Chaplin persona—something that was, indeed, stated in the poster art for *Verdoux* in Brazil and South America.[11]

Chaplin felt that when what essentially became the "Hollywood Ten" testified before HUAC in the fall of 1947, with many Hollywood liberals (including John Huston, Humphrey Bogart, Lauren Becall, Gene Kelly, Danny Kaye, Frank Sinatra, Judy Garland, and Chaplin's previous wife, Paulette Goddard) flying to Washington, D.C., to support these artists under the flag of an ad hoc Committee for First Amendment rights, the time would be ripe for reissuing *Verdoux*. Yet, these unfriendly witnesses went on the offensive (questioning Congress' right to even call them), and the proceedings became a messy theater of the real. This legitimate but controversial game plan alienated many Americans, including the aforementioned First Amendment committee. Support for the Hollywood Ten began to disappear, and Chaplin's hope for a new liberal autumn launching pad for *Verdoux* faded. Yet, given that he was still the celebrated Chaplin, that *Verdoux* had a generated some positive notices (*Time* magazine called it one of the most notable films of the year), and the fact that controversy invariable generates curiosity, some theater chains still wanted to book the picture.[12] However, threatening boycotting and picketing actions by conservative organization like the American Legion ultimately led to potential *Verdoux* bookings being dropped. An even better measure of the sheer hatred of Chaplin and *Verdoux* was generated by the extreme political right, and can be boiled down to Hollywood columnist Hedda Hopper begging FBI director J. Edgar Hoover in April 1947 for an opportunity to attack Chaplin: "You give me the material and I'll blast!"[13]

Chaplin, moreover, was pulled into several additional controversies at the time, from the likelihood he would be called before the HUAC committee, to his 1947 attempts to thwart the deportation of composer Hans Eisler, who had first arrived in the United States to escape Nazi persecution during World War II. Eisler's politics were undoubtedly of a communist nature but the naïve apolitical Chaplin knew him as only a friend and a talented musician. The comedian went so far as to cable Pablo Picasso to organize French artists to protest this action at the United States Embassy in Paris. For conservative Americans, already upset over Chaplin never becoming a United States citizen, such actions were next to some sort of oddball treason—a non–American citizen encouraging foreign opposition against the red, white, and blue. Moreover, in 1948 Chaplin had strongly supported Democratic splinter party candidate Henry A. Wallace for president. This liberal innocent and former vice-president under Franklin Delano Roosevelt ran a campaign hurt by its open support from the American Communist Party.

If Chaplin had any sense of politics, one might apply to him the comically well-worn description "limousine liberal." The Hollywood powerbroker status acquired from his inspired talent, not to mention the affection the Tramp had produced worldwide, made the comedian feel (even after *Verdoux*) like Teflon. For decades he had always done as he pleased. Chaplin was a prisoner of his poses as well as his principles. Put another way, outside Chaplin's area of expertise, a creative genius can be a car wreck.

The comedian had played the comic provocateur from the earliest days of his fame. For instance, when the Chaplin FBI files were eventually opened to the public, one of the earliest allegations against him was the claim he had held a 1919 fund rally for the radical activist William Z. Foster, later the chairman of the American Communist Party.[14] (During Chaplin's long residency in the United States, ending in 1952, it was never illegal to belong to the communist party.) Regardless, anonymous 1919 sources also said Chaplin had donated $1,000 to Foster, as if either act was anyone's business. Yet, in Chaplin's ultimately 2,060-page FBI file covering a 50-plus–year period, there was *no* evidence the comedian had ever been a member of the controversial communist party.[15] In point of fact, Chaplin had held a reception for Foster in 1919. Yet, what follows is a typical comic example of Chaplin's so-called "radical" comments to Foster:

> "We [Hollywood people] are against any kind [of] censorship, and particularly against Presbyterian censorship." Laughing, [Chaplin] led Foster to the men's toilet and pointed out a pennant with the words WELCOME WILL HAYS [the Hollywood censorship czar] that was tacked to the door.[16]

Hays' name was also to be found at the bottom of the toilets, too. This was the extent of Chaplin as *anarchist!*

Naïve or not, Chaplin was just one of many post–World War II liberals victimized by the growing right wing paranoia fueled by HUAC which then segued into the McCarthy witch-hunting and blacklisting of the early 1950s. In 1954 a cowed Congress passed the Communist Control Act which criminalized involvement in the party and was signed into law by President Dwight D. Eisenhower, yet another example of his "reluctance to engage himself [directly] in the McCarthy issue."[17] This Control Act as of 2013 has neither been repealed nor enforced. Plus, the Supreme Court has not addressed its legality, and the American Communist Party continues to exist. These bipolar politics actually began that same year with a series of televised Army-McCarthy hearings which finally revealed to America the bullying demigod nature of Senator Joe McCarthy. Later in 1954 the Senate decisively censored him. "His death in 1957 merely ratified his [being a] political demigod."[18]

Eisenhower's questionable decision to sign the Control Act, in order to show (because of McCarthy) he was also tough on communism, had been foreshadowed two years earlier (1952) when Chaplin's re-entry visa to America was revoked. That is, President Harry Truman's attorney general, James P. McGranery, "decided to beat ... Joe McCarthy at his own game [being America's self-appointed communist witch-hunter] by barring Chaplin's re-entry to the United States."[19] In 1964 famed auteur critic Andrew Sarris sardonically stated:

> The late [anti–McCarthy news reporter] Elmer Davis remarked at the time that the resourceful attorney general would go down in history as the man who kept Chaplin out of America. Davis was wrong. No one remembers J.P. McGranery, whose name I had to look up in a *World Almanac*.[20]

Before expanding upon the events leading to Chaplin being so unceremoniously bounced from the country, it is time to return to *Limelight*: Its London premiere was the catalyst for the Chaplin family to leave the country and make themselves vulnerable to McGranery's actions. The heart of the comedian's film anticipates a signature poster ad line for the future British picture *Education Rita* (1983): "Sometimes students make the best teachers."[21] That is, the rescue of Claire Bloom's suicidal ballerina by Chaplin's Calvero ultimately results in *his* own rebirth. The young dancer's love, devotion and appreciation for this unlikely fatherly mentor bring back Calvero from a loss of faith in himself and life in general. It also represents a nice narrative twist, because the movie begins like so many Chaplin pictures, with the Tramp as a caretaker.

The tragic comedy *Limelight* story allows the once famous but now forgotten Calvero a second chance (a benefit show triumph) before dying in the wings as his protégé dancer Terry is on stage in a tour de force ballet performance—as movingly sentimental as "the show must go on," or as poignantly appropriate as two saved souls helping each other achieve their dreams. Given that Chaplin had always wanted to play Jesus on-screen, his choice of the name Calvero, so close to the place where Jesus was crucified (Calvary), suggests, given the neglected Calvero's miracle-like role in the rebirth of Terry, that Chaplin had finally created a scenario in which he could flirt with playing Jesus. Granted, it is an egotistical act for an artist's work to portray his death; yet other than Bob Fosse's staging his own demise in *All That Jazz* (1979), Calvero-Chaplin's *Limelight* passing is a unique movie moment which goes beyond ego. For example, one can play with the concept of dark comedy, in a film which does not readily bring that genre to mind. Calvary is the Latin word for "the skull." No one knows for sure why the place where Jesus was crucified was known as "the skull," beyond the knee-jerk explanation that it was an execution site, since "the skull" is a widely recognized symbol for death. Yet *Limelight*'s end presents the increasingly dark comic dilemma that while ones close to the deceased feel that the world should stop and the sun be blotted out, life goes on. Calvero has also again shown Terry that life and death should be natural and not wasted in suicide.

The volatile nature of Chaplin's presence in Hollywood during the period between *Verdoux* and *Limelight* can be "read" in two diametrically opposed ways. From a positive perspective, Chaplin greatly enjoyed revisiting the English music hall tradition of his youth in preparing for the production of *Limelight*. He was also well aware of the fact that some reviews panning *Verdoux* were simply based upon a dislike of dark comedy and not a personal vendetta. For instance, John Beaufort's negative *Christian Science Monitor* critique closes with the sympathetic observation: "One can perhaps be forgiven for hoping that Mr. Chaplin will revive the baggy pants, the bowler, and the cane, and will give us more of the old, wise and wonderful foolishness [of Charlie]."[22] As if in direct response to citizens such as these, Chaplin revived *City Lights* on Broadway in April of 1950, and while he feared demonstrations and picket lines, the film wiped away "any possible bad taste by *Verdoux*, confounded the Chaplin detractors [and] *Life* magazine proclaimed the twenty-year-old film 'the best picture of the year.'"[23] Quite possibly this remarkable reverse from *Verdoux* further encouraged his softer reminiscent perspective in the writing of *Footlights-Limelight*.

Life further encouraged the revival of Chaplin in a 1952 feature pictorial article just prior to the completion of *Limelight*, "Chaplin at Work: He Reveals His Movie-Making Secrets":

> Today, at 63, Chaplin is a small, graceful, white-haired man who still walks with the mincing gait of the universal tramp, still uses the familiar gestures of the early pantomime. His work schedule, his stubborn, tempestuous and infinitely exacting methods wear out men far younger than he.[24]

What is now often forgotten is that the original American reviews of *Limelight*, which were largely limited to a relatively brief New York run, with few bookings outside of Gotham after the comedian's re-entry visa was revoked, were generally superlative. For instance, Alton Cook's *New York World Telegram* critique said it all in the title, "Chaplin's *Limelight* a Film Masterpiese."[25] Archer Winsten's *New York Post* review called *Limelight* "the fitfully glowing twilight of a true motion picture genius [and] the power is still there."[26] Otis L. Guernsey Jr.'s *New York Herald Tribune* review stated:

> [T]he sense of longing that [Chaplin] has established throughout *Limelight* hangs over [any] flaws like a luminous cloud of sympathetic genius, in a haunting movie experience.... [I]ts camera work is often imaginative and its music [which later won a delayed Oscar for Best Original Score, co-written by Chaplin] seems to ache right along with the sensibilities of the characters. In it Chaplin's brilliance is visibly and palpably at work....[27]

The *New York Times*' Bosley Crowther called *Limelight*

> a brilliant wearing of comic and tragic strands, eloquent, tearful and beguiling with supreme virtuosity.... [T]he brilliance of *Limelight* [lies most] in the artistry of Mr. Chaplin in the use of his supple, mobile person as a positive instrument for the capture of thoughts and moods.[28]

Variety's New York reporter's prediction was also very positive: "*Limelight* is Chaplin all the way. It's deserving of stout b.o."[29] The only consistent complaint of reviewers was that Calvero often has too much to say; *Variety* countered:

> Some of the dialogue is brilliant, almost like fine prose writing than celluloid wordage. For example: "We're all amateurs; none of us lives long enough to be anything else." And "I hate the sight of blood but it's in my veins."[30]

The time leading up to *Limelight*'s New York opening had not been without additional Chaplin positives. His marriage to Oona continued to flourish, and with it the joy of an ever-expanding family: Geraldine (born 1944, the future star of such memorable movies as *Doctor Zhivago,* 1965, and *Nashville,* 1975), Michael (born 1946, who would co-star with his father in *A King in New York,* 1957), Josephine (born 1949, a future actress), and Victoria (born 1951, a circus performer intended for the lead in *The Freak,* an unrealized Chaplin film). Thus, Oona was happily orchestrating a renovation and expansion at their home, and while their Los Angeles house was no longer a mecca for many old movie friends, there were now new regulars, such as critic turned screenwriter James Agee. The reviewer who had so fiercely defended *Verdoux* even attempted to pen a return for Charlie in a script later entitled *The Tramp's New World,* to be set in a post–atomic war world. Agee wrote, "The film alternates and combines, and collides, two kinds of comedy—the icy [black comedy] ... bitterness of Verdoux, and the humanistic comedy of the Tramp."[31] Nothing came of the project.

It was Oona who had changed the tenor of the social life at Los Angeles' Summit Drive home:

> [She] demonstrated an ability to make people feel welcome and relaxed ... and, more crucial, in the presence of her illustrious husband.... In the past Chaplin's friends had gathered ... on Sunday afternoons for quiet English teas, but by the time Oona came into his life Charlie's passion for the game of tennis had accelerated and the staid tea ceremonies were superseded by lively tennis parties. Chaplin grew increasingly sociable, and intimates believed that Oona, not tennis, was the source of this new gregariousness.[32]

Chaplin's passion for tennis was anchored in the sport's ballet-like grace. Paradoxically, while he felt the beauty of tennis' form and movement was the seminal attraction (beyond even striking the ball), he *always* was driven to win. *New Yorker* writer Lillian Ross recalled spending many "pleasant hours on the Chaplin's tennis court," adding her own description of the comedian's Sunday gatherings as like a

> refuge from the Hollywood frenzy, a very nice refuge ... which [Charlie and Oona] shared graciously with other refugees of all kinds, both foreign and domestic. It was great fun for me ... to talk in a relaxed way with guests like Jean Renoir, James Agee, and Carol Matthau [child-

hood friend of Oona, wife of Walter, and whose witty personality was the later inspiration for Truman Capote's Holly Golightly character in the novella *Breakfast at Tiffany's*].[33]

Ross also recalled an amusing domestic moment from 1950 when Chaplin and Oona were fussing over a leg of lamb with their small children about. Food was very important to the comedian because

> as he used to explain, he had been so often deprived of it when he was a child. On this day [the comedian had] a chef's big white apron tied around his waist, a big spoon in his left hand, and giving the lamb his full concentration, with a Charlie Chaplin pursing of the lips ... "I baste and baste," Chaplin said to me, with authority. "Baste and baste and baste."[34]

If, to paraphrase Jonathan Freedland, the primary task of biography is to create a man who leaps off the page, this "baste and baste and baste" image of a chef-attired Chaplin would arguably bear inclusion with the Tramp basting his boot in *The Gold Rush* (1925).[35]

Besides starting a second family, Chaplin was doing some further bonding with his two sons from his marriage to Lita Grey, Charlie, Jr., and Sydney. This especially involved Chaplin donating time to the Circle, a noncommercial Hollywood theater in which Sydney was very involved. Always after reality in entertainment, Chaplin invariably imparted his most repeated directing tip about *not* acting; rather, "Give the audience the feeling that they're looking through the keyhole."

Chaplin had lived so long with the threat of being called before HUAC, that he sometimes kidded about the situation. His favorite hyperbole was to suggest he might appear in the garb of the Tramp, an appropriately comic response to a ludicrously comic committee (though given his treatment during these years, Chaplin might better have arrived as Verdoux). Some of the unfriendly witnesses (witnesses refusing to name names) managed to create a sort of comedy of the real rebuttal to HUAC. For example in Eric Bentley's play-like satire of the committee, *Are You Now or Have You Ever Been* (1972), he edits together actual commentary from the hearings which entertainly demonstrate the ridiculousness of the situation. The two most winsome examples would best start with excerpts from character actor Lionel Stander's 1953 comments:

> I'm shocked by your cutting me off. I am not a dupe, or a dope, or a moe [idiot], or a schmo, and I'm not ashamed of anything I said in public or private.... [But] by using psychopaths [against me] and I have the letter here giving the mental history of Marc Lawrence [one informer against him], who came from a mental institution ... and you used that psychopath and this [second informer] Leech, who the district attorney and the grand jury didn't believe and they cleared me [in 1940] ... I don't want to be responsible for a whole stable of informers, stool pigeons, psychopaths, and ex-political heretics who came in here beating their breasts and saying, "I'm awfully sorry, I didn't know what I was doing, please, I want *absolution,* get me back into pictures!" They will do anything *to get back into pictures.* They will mention names! They will name *anybody*![36]

From this Marx Brothers–like verbal slapstick, a more Chaplinesque response to HUAC comes from actor-comedian-painter Zero Mostel, best known for his delightful comic character in Mel Brooks' *The Producers,* 1968). When asked in 1955 if he attended a meeting which had been partially subsidized by a legal American communist party during a period (World War II) when the Soviet Union was the United States' ally, Mostel responded:

> Maybe it is unwise and impolitic for me to say this. [Pause] *If* I appeared there, what if I did an imitation of a butterfly at rest? There is no crime in making anybody laugh. [Responding

when HUAC said this was still wrong if it involved communists, Mostel said,] Suppose I [merely] had the *urge* to do the butterfly at rest somewhere?[37]

Not surprisingly, political jesters Stander and Mostel remained blacklisted. But they were true to Lillian Hellman's eloquent comment about this sorry chapter in American history: "I cannot and will not cut my conscience to fit this year's fashions...."[38]

One might also note two final positive events in the days before that fateful one-way ocean voyage: First, while the previously quoted critical raves for *Limelight* had appeared after his exit from America, Chaplin had held a private Hollywood preview on August 4, 1952, and it was attended by such well-known screen luminaries as Humphrey Bogart, Ronald Colman, and producer David (*Gone with the Wind*) Selznick. When the film ended the comedian attempted to make a short speech thanking them for coming. However, he was interrupted by first one and then another "Thank you!" "Thank you!" from the audience. Eventually "the cry was taken up by everyone until the room rang.... [I]t was such an electric demonstration that columnist Sidney Skolsky described it as 'the most exciting night I had ever spent in a projection room.'"[39]

The second gratifying example is more modest but no less moving. It is simply Lillian Ross chronicling a lengthy walking tour of New York she had taken with a very happy Chaplin the day before his boat sailed.[40] Ross was subbing for Oona, who still had blisters from her recent walkathon with Chaplin in Chicago. (At this point in his life, the comedian preferred train travel over flying.) Throughout his walk with Ross, he affectionately reminisced about New York and acted as sort of a tour guide of the past and present.

Chaplin's upbeat walk with Ross around the changing New York of his youth hardly suggests an individual on the eve of exile. Yet, there are many other details during this witch-hunting period which suggest that the action taken by Attorney General McGranery might not have been surprising. For example, the question of a re-entry visa had occurred as early as 1947, when Chaplin had flirted with the idea of shooting his next movie in Great Britain.

The sluggish British film industry had received a government assist in the tax laws, making it advantageous for foreign filmmakers to produce films in England. Since Chaplin's *Limelight* was set in London, he could save money by actually shooting there; the comedian naturally looked into making this happen. Plus, he had recently finished *Verdoux,* and Chaplin invariably had wanderlust after completing a movie; for example, he took a trip to Asia following *Modern Times* (1936).

For all these reasons, Chaplin considered a trip to Great Britain in early 1948. As a resident alien he needed to apply for a permit assuring his right to re-enter the United States. For the first time during his long residency here, he was subjected to a special federal interview. The questions covered everything from adultery to associations with different communist-backed organizations. Keep in mind that this occurred almost exactly a year after Congressman John T. Rankin, a member of HUAC, demanded upon the House floor that President Truman's first attorney general Tom Clark "institute proceedings to deport Charlie Chaplin...."[41] Thus, the 1952 re-entry hullabaloo might have occurred during the comedian's proposed 1948 trip.

Chaplin ultimately cancelled these travel plans for other reasons. He had standing disputes with the IRS, and their demand that he post over a million dollars before he left suddenly cooled the comedian's ardor for this trip. Not surprisingly, starting in late 1947 Chaplin periodically talked of "his plans to leave the United States...."[42] Chaplin confessed that Oona's renovations to their home were pointless, since "I know I shall never see the day when I shall live in it."[43]

Ongoing financial problems with United Artists continued to be a stress point with the comedian. Moreover, in the post-war era Chaplin had even lost faith in the production side of Hollywood, feeling that the movies were becoming too standardized. Add to this Chaplin's continued outspokenness about any and all controversial topics, and he continued to give conservatives more fodder with which to demonize him. For instance, in 1950 there was a false rumor that Chaplin planned to apply for United States citizenship. Instead of just letting it quietly blow over, the comedian again felt compelled to reiterate his provocative one world global citizenship stance. Many of Chaplin's friends and associates, such as his longtime cameraman Roland Totheroh, felt that while the comedian had been mistreated by the press and the government, he often egged on a situation. In his defense, one could say the filmmaker embraced what Italian journalist Misha Stille called "la forza delle cose," meaning "the force of things."⁴⁴ The comedian's passion knew no restrictions on the importance of a subject, big or small. While the trait served him well professionally, it was often the bane of his private life.

Chaplin biographer Joyce Milton states that in the spring of 1952, at the same time he was telling friends he was considering a move to Jamaica, the comedian was "quietly transferring his stock in United Artists to Oona, an indication that he was reorganizing his finances in preparation for [possible] exile."⁴⁵ Adding Oona's name to his bank accounts and giving her power of attorney also suggests that Chaplin was preparing for the worst. That is, with money in the name of a resident alien (Chaplin), his assets could be frozen after leaving the country; with Oona being an American citizen, however, all was safe and accessible. Still, Chaplin was somewhat surprised that, at this time, after granting him a reentry visa, the United States would almost immediately renege on it; he was *not* unprepared for such a development.

For someone who was not above having his fortune told as a young man, or sharing premonitions about not remaining long enough in Los Angeles to enjoy Oona's house renovations, Chaplin might have taken the 1950s departure from his home of Welsh poet Dylan Thomas (1914–1953) as a bad omen. Following a birthday gathering for the comedian in the house that doubled as an artistic refuge for "refugees of all kinds," the mellifluously voiced alcoholic icon "pissed on Charlie Chaplin's door as he made an early exit from [said] party...."⁴⁶ Of course, for someone (Thomas) who would observe "Cold Beer Is Bottled God," this might have been standard etiquette.⁴⁷

Regardless, in presenting two distinctive Chaplin perspectives on the period between *Verdoux* and *Limelight,* the text is merely addressing Paul Murray Kendall's observation:

> The biographer can only answer that biographical truth is not and can never be absolute truth. He knows too well the fallibility of himself and his materials, and what he engages to tell is the best truth he can find....⁴⁸

For this biographer, the "best truth" for Chaplin in the time frame, despite his periodic bluster about leaving the United States, was that he wanted to stay, despite all the reactionaries. But he was a proud man, and Attorney General McGranery's action was one insult too many; being prepared for this event, he simply chose to begin a new chapter of his life. In becoming a voluntary exile (the universal view now is that he could have successfully attained a reentry resident alien visa), Chaplin was metaphorically doing to McGranery what the Tramp had done to a *reel* custom official in *The Immigrant* (1917), when, ironically, he was trying to *enter* the country: give him a kick in the backside.

11

Two Bitter Kings, Dark Comedy Reality, and a Lesson from *Monsieur Verdoux*

At the opening of *A King in New York* (1957), Chaplin inserted this title: "One of the minor annoyances of modern life is a revolution."

Chaplin's understated sarcasm with the above statement is dual focus in nature. First, it applies to his title character in *A King in New York,* Shahdov, the deposed king of the fictional European country of Estrovia. Chaplin borrowed from a popular personality comedian trend of early 1930s Hollywood, when the film capital was awash with goofy mythical European kingdoms. For instance, Wheeler and Woolsey vied for control of El Dorania in *Cracked Nuts* (1931). Will Rogers found himself in Sylvania as the title character of *Ambassador Bill* (1931), and Groucho Marx, was president of Freedonia in *Duck Soup* (1933). However, in Chaplin's picture, the United States is more sinisterly strange than the pretend Estrovia, since it is America that is under comic attack. Chaplin's second example of this understated sarcasm masquerading as a dual focus narrative from *A King in New York* is its reminder that Hollywood (another mythological-like land) also had deposed its king (Chaplin). Yet, most importantly, neither King Shahdov nor King Charlie ever took this usurping of power as a "minor annoyance." The dark comedy catalyst for the anti–HUAC *A King in New York* can best be examined first by a detailed examination of what transpired between the time Chaplin and his family embarked from New York (September 17, 1952) on the *Queen Elizabeth,* bound for the London premiere of *Limelight* (1952), and Chaplin's official break (April 10, 1953) with the United States. Along the way, this press coverage also showcases bonus black humor insights directly related to the comedian's use of the genre.

The central themes of black comedy—the inherent absurdity of life, man as beast, and the omnipresence of death—are right at home here. The most pervasive of the components to be applied to this small Chaplin window of time is absurdity. Two days after Chaplin and his family left for England, United States Attorney General James P. McGranery ordered Immigration authorities "to determine whether the famous comedian should be readmitted."[1] The métier of absurdity on why this action was being taken involved Section 137 of the United States Aliens and Citizenship Code: "'This paragraph is aimed at persons who advocate the overthrow of the Government,' with a Justice Department spokesman adding, 'I would say that we have a pretty good case.'"[2] Yet, as if this absurdity-squared accusation was not enough, the *New York Times* coverage of the situation suggested that beyond any Chaplin communist ties, McGranery was most "incensed at Mr. Chaplin over the latter's involvement in a paternity case Joan Barry brought ... against him [Chaplin]."[3] The comedian lost that 1942 case, but as previously noted, blood tests at the time proved the child could *not* have been his ... except such a test was not then admissible as evidence. This nonsense soon led to a landmark change in California state law. Regardless, this hardly suggests that Chaplin's plan was to "overthrow" the government.

The *London Observer* quickly addressed this official action: "[To revoke a re-entry permit] because of random imputations and not on the basis of [a] judicial verdict ... would be acting within their [USA] rights but rather shabbily and with little sense of logic."[4] The same article also included the most fitting of tributes to Chaplin from Sir Michael Balcon, head of Ealing Studios, which had been heavily influenced by *Monsieur Verdoux* (1947) and which went on to produce such dark comedy classics as *Kind Hearts and Coronets* (1949) and *The Lavender Hill Mob* (1951). Indeed, a later watershed example of Ealing black humor would merely pluralize the working title of *Verdoux*—*The Ladykillers* (1935). Balcon stated: "Chaplin is perhaps the only genius the screen has produced. He is most definitely welcome by the industry here and I hope he will stay and make pictures."[5]

Like Balcon's comments drawing indirect attention to *Verdoux,* one of Chaplin's first responses brought to mind another of the comedian's pivotal dark comedies, *The Great Dictator* (1940): "I am not a super-patriot. I think super-patriotism leads to Hitlerism and we have had our lesson from that. I assume that in a democracy one has a right to a private opinion."[6] This same interview ended with Chaplin returning to the balderdash nature of the situation, with an implied dash of man as beast (McGranery and company) factored in, too:

> Three months ago I applied for a re-entry permit in the proper way. Three months later I received a re-entry permit. The immigration authorities treated me with great courtesy and even wished me "bon voyage." ... [A]fter leaving New York I heard about the [revoking] statement. They had three months to investigate me. That's all I have to say.[7]

The most entertaining slant on this absurdity came from the editorial page of the *New York Times:*

> We hold no brief for Mr. Chaplin's private life or public views, but there is something just a little ridiculous in the United States of American indicating it is frightened of Charles Chaplin.[8]

Critic Bosley Crowther's defense of Chaplin was also a combination of inconceivability and the man as beast component. With regard to the former perspective, Crowther poignantly struck a position reminiscent of the comedian's world citizen stance, when he observed that despite Chaplin maintaining his British passport, "his 'little tramp,' though a universal favorite, is as native and important in this land and in our great homely, popular culture as [a] Alger hero

Alec Guinness as one of the eight victims he plays in the *Monsieur Verdoux*–influenced *Kind Hearts and Coronets.*

or Huckleberry Finn."⁹ Crowther then broadened the man-as-beast perspective beyond the comedian's victimization:

> Chaplin's experience is not dissimilar to that of many people in Hollywood whose names have been mentioned in the hearings of the House-Un-American group ... against whom no charges have been proved. And yet many of these people, on account of the suspicion that have been raised ... have not been able to get work.¹⁰

Crowther's point on HUAC victimization takes one to dark comedy's third component, the omnipresence of death. Chaplin had the money and moxie to continue making movies, here or abroad. Yet, for many this McCarthy-HUAC–directed movie ban not only killed careers, it killed people, sometimes referenced as a "disease called the blacklist." Many of these victims simply killed themselves. The definitive face of such suicide deaths was gifted stage, screen and television actor Philip Loeb (1891–1955), who was also a sought-after acting coach to such stars as Kirk Douglas and Rosalind Russell. The false accusation that Loeb was a communist made the work stop; the depressed artist checked into New York's Taft Hotel under an assumed name and took an overdose of sleeping pills. His tragedy was immortalized in the later film about blacklisting, *The Front* (1976). The picture included many former blacklisted friends of Loeb, including the picture's director Martin Ritt, its screenwriter Walter Bernstein, and actor-painter Zero Mostel, with the latter's character of Hecky Brown closely patterned upon Loeb, right down to a hotel suicide.

Other HUAC victims, like pioneering Method actor John Garfield (1913–1952), took their lives in a more veiled matter. Garfield, already suffering from long-term heart problems, was stressed out over the heart attack deaths of acting friends Canada Lee (1907–1952, dying just before being called by HUAC) and J. Edward Bromberg (1903–1951, dying shortly after his HUAC appearance). When Garfield's own HUAC testimony was being reviewed for possible perjury charges, he went against his doctor's orders by engaging in strenuously dangerous physical activity and keeping late hours, inducing heart attack–like symptoms. Refusing a friend's attempt to get medical attention, he, too, died of a heart attack.

Chaplin's formal rejection of this deadly madness occurred when he "surrendered his re-entry permit to State Department officials in Geneva, Switzerland" on April 10, 1953.¹¹ Chaplin had no comment, but a week later in a bitterly worded statement during a London press conference at the Savoy Hotel, just across the Thames from his birthplace, he stated:

> It is not easy to uproot myself and my family from a country where I have lived for forty years without a feeling of sadness. But since the end of the last World War, I have been the object of lies and propaganda by powerful reactionary groups who by their influence and by aid of America's yellow press have created an unhealthy atmosphere in which liberal-minded individuals can be singled out and persecuted. Under these conditions I find it virtually impossible to continue my motion picture work, and I have therefore given up my residence in the United States.¹²

Oona Chaplin's best friend, Carol Matthau, describes the comedian's lingering bitterness in her memoir, with the most fitting of titles given this situation: *Among the Porcupines:*

> It was truly unbelievable that [the USA] would do this to the greatest artist in what had become the greatest medium of our time. Charlie was a communist like I am Madame Chiang Kai-shek. Charlie couldn't believe it himself, and though he and Oona ended up in a beautiful house in Switzerland, his exile destroyed him. He would rant on and on for years to come about what he would have said to the House Un-American Activities Committee.¹³

Like Chaplin's Verdoux, and the prostitute on whom he intends to test a new untraceable poison, Matthau is much taken with Arthur Schopenhauer, which inspired her memoir title. She opens her autobiography with a long, darkly comic quote from the philosopher anthropomorphically using porcupines to describe the difficulty with which humans must interact for survival. That is, a group of porcupines huddle together during winter for the mutual warmth of survival. Yet, those quills soon force them apart. But then the cold repeatedly tosses the porcupines back and forth between two types of suffering ... until a tolerable survival distance is discovered:

> Thus the need for company, born of the emptiness and monotony inside them, drives men together but their many revolting qualities and intolerable faults repel them again. The medium distance that they finally discover and that makes association possible is politeness and good manners. But whoever possesses much inner warmth of his own will prefer to avoid company lest he cause or suffer annoyance.[14]

One could metaphorically suggest that Chaplin's prickly "inner warmth" allowed him to "avoid [HUAC] company lest he ... suffer [further] annoyance." More importantly, however, Matthau's use of Schopenhauer, as in Chaplin's *Verdoux,* also encourages one to re-examine how life imitated art in the aforementioned period between when the comedian re-entry visa was revoked and his later surrender of said documentation in Geneva. That is, *Verdoux* is a film in which the title character attempts to survive by applying the conniving practices of vindictive governments. Chaplin's actions even before the revoking of his re-entry permit demonstrate the comedian using subterfuge, too.

First, Chaplin hoped to stay in America yet, as previously cited, his distrust of the government had him transferring all his assets to the safety of his wife, a United States citizen, before they left for England. Then, if the country reneged on its promise, which it did, America could not touch his wealth. Second, when Chaplin's fears were realized, a possible plan to exit America went into action. To avoid further tricks by the United States, he gave his greatest sustained acting performance. Despite the earlier documentation of how bitter he was about this miscarriage of justice, he showed no hint of planning permanently to leave the U.S., no anger at his first European press conference:

> Charlie Chaplin, in a jovial, holiday mood, said today threats to bar him from the United States had not altered his plans to return there in about six months.... Laughing and smiling, Mr. Chaplin told reporters: "I am not political. I have never been political. I don't want to create any revolutions. I just want to create a few more films."[15]

Chaplin continued this deception for months, until giving up his re-entry visa. For example, when the comedian first met with the London press he described himself as "a very conservative person" and denied that he was or ever had been a Communist, joking that the whole affair was like "the $64 question."[16] Certainly the warm reception he immediately received in his native England would only have reinforced the decision to stay in Europe:

> When the Chaplins' car drove out of [London's] Waterloo Station at a walking pace several hundred fans surged around it. As Mr. Chaplin leaned forward and waved, his wife, the former Miss Oona O'Neill, said, "It's wonderful. It's wonderful. I had no idea it would be like this. It's really marvelous."[17]

While Chaplin's English hosannas seemed to escalate in the following weeks, as the comedian gave his wife a tour of his youth, the United States Department of Justice also was sifting through his past; so much for the smoking gun it claimed to have had when his visa was lifted.

For instance, in early October, Justice "ordered immigration agents to check on Paulette Goddard's [June 1942] divorce from Charlie Chaplin to determine whether any moral turpitude was involved in either their marriage or divorce."[18] Justice was digging for ethics infractions from over a decade before Chaplin's visa was lifted for allegedly supporting organizations trying to overthrow the government?

Simultaneously to this probe, Chaplin revisited a stance that had *always* helped him in past occasions of public controversy: The comedian untethered his ace in the hole, the Tramp. Thus, when honored at a London luncheon by British film critics, he spoke of reviving Charlie. Yet, as before, he would not rob him of his silent universality: "To give [the Tramp] a voice would take away the strength of the symbol that is essentially a figure of the dance."[19] (As noted before, a jealous W.C. Fields was once fond of describing Charlie as a "God-damn ballet dancer."[20])

Soon, with the European premieres of *Limelight,* Chaplin did not have to play Verdoux's strategy of subterfuge. The celebration of both the film and the artist acted as its own smokescreen. One headline noted, "London Cheers Premiere of Chaplin Film":

> Thousands of admirers gave Charlie Chaplin round after round of applause tonight.... The cheers were as loud as those for Princess Margaret, who was in the audience.... More than 200 mounted and foot police linked arms to check crowds outside, who shouted, "We want Charlie!"[21]

The *London Times* also covered Princess Margaret's first night attendance at *Limelight* and being presented to Chaplin.[22] The article added that 4,000 people gathered outside the Odeon Cinema; when Chaplin arrived with his wife and two of their children, he walked out into the road "within two or three feet of the crowd, smiled and waved to them and blew kisses in all directions."[23] Those in attendance included such notable performers as playwright-actor Noël Coward, Douglas Fairbanks, Jr. (the actor son of Chaplin's most beloved friend, the late actor-producer Douglas Fairbanks), performer John Mills, and actress-singer Frances Day.

Again, with more ironic timing, almost to the late October day (1952) on which Attorney General McGranery stated that Chaplin could re-enter the country if he "can prove his worth and right to enter the country" (meaning Justice had nothing new on the comedian), the filmmaker was in Paris to be made an officer of the Legion of Honor, the highest distinction France can confer on an alien citizen in peacetime.[24] Thousands of fans waited to greet the comedian, who flew in from London. Moreover, this special French decoration, coupled with the announcement that President Vincent Aurial would greet Chaplin personally,

> were regarded as an implied rebuke to American officials who have indicated that the British-born actor may not be allowed to re-enter the United States.[25]

But forget politics. For the French, *Limelight* was simply an instant masterpiece. France's greatest critic-theorist André Bazin describes a pre-public screening for a who's who of their country's cinema elite:

> [T]he whole French cinema world wept at the sight of the death of Molière—that is to say, of Calvero, alias Chaplin. [Both Molière and Calvero die after a lead stage performance.] When I say I wept, I am not exaggerating. As the lights went up, they revealed four hundred directors, screenwriters, and critics choked with emotion, their eyes as red as tomatoes. There is only one word to describe the note struck by this film, and we must first restore it to its full classical meaning—sublime.[26]

French Premier Antoine Pinay attended the Paris premiere of *Limelight,* while President Aurial helped arrange a private preview at Elyseé Palace. One almost needed a scorecard to keep up with the honors being bestowed upon Chaplin. For instance, the comedian was nominated for that year's Nobel literature prize "by Olof Lagercrantz, [the] outstanding Swedish literary critic."[27] And shortly after Chaplin was decorated with Italy's Legion of Merit, he received "three more honors today [December 22, 1952], from the National Syndicate of Cinema Writers, the Italian film industry, and the University of Rome."[28]

With such acclaim, this treasure of cinema (Chaplin) could hardly question his *Verdoux*-like, still-secret decision to thumb his nose, *à la* the opening of *City Lights,* at officialdom. That is, in November 1952 Oona Chaplin left Great Britain by air for the United States to allegedly "attend a meeting of a film company of which she is an executive."[29] In reality, she later told a friend,

> following Charlie's instructions she had gathered up the [Chaplin] funds, turned everything into thousand-dollar bills, and had the money sewn into the lining of her mink coat. With the fur draped nonchalantly over her arm, she boarded her transatlantic flight and flew back to England.[30]

Yet the ongoing cover for the Chaplins remained the same: The family would return to the United States "next spring, she said."[31] Oona could play actress, too.

While Chaplin had already orchestrated his exit from America plan, public opinion—from large organizations to individuals—was beginning to suggest that the comedian could successfully have fought any ban on re-entering the country. For example, in December 1952 the fifth annual conference of the American Committee for Protection of Foreign Born passed a resolution protesting the Justice Department's treatment of Chaplin "and demanded that he be permitted to return to the United States with his family."[32] Along similar lines, one editorial with the haunting title, "Is 'Charlot' [France's term for Charlie] a Menace," movingly closed by stating:

> [T]hose who have followed [Chaplin] through the years cannot easily regard him as a dangerous person. No political situation, no international menace can destroy the fact that he is a great artist who has given infinite pleasure to many millions.... Unless there is far more evidence against him than is at the moment visible [nothing new *ever* came forward], the Department of State will not dignify itself or increase the national security if it sends him into exile.[33]

By far the most poetic, thought-provoking letter to an editor on the subject came from Corporal Hugh Namias of Fort Mammoth, New York:

> [T]he American cinema has acquired prestige and respect as a result of Mr. Chaplin's artistry.... Moreover, I should think this country should somehow feel proud that he has ignored the country of his birth and turned to us instead. His long stay here has given a touch of art to the American cinema. This alone is actually England's loss. The question as to where one should belong is really in the heart of Charlie Chaplin. Why not leave it that way?[34]

Unfortunately, Chaplin's heart had already been made up—or should one say broken? The family would purchase a Swiss chateau, just outside the village of Vevey, in January 1953, though still saying they would come back to America.[35] (After all, wealthy people are always buying multiple houses.) This chateau would remain home for the remainder of Chaplin's life; he died there Christmas Day 1977. The comedian's bitterness about the events surrounding his 1952 exit from the United States would linger for years, but his royal reception in Europe

Chaplin in happier days (circa 1935), with Douglas Fairbanks on the right, and Harold Lloyd on the left.

had eased the transition. It was reminiscent of his triumphant tour of the American south selling bonds during World War I. Still, just as the subterfuge of *Verdoux* served as a model for getting his assets out of the U.S. (not to mention all the other real-life examples of dark comedy occurring during this 1952–1953 period), the era was still rife with additional theater-of-the-real instances of absurdity.

For instance, Chaplin had been constantly on record as stating he was a one-world international citizen. This was his explanation for never becoming a U.S. citizen. Yet no one, including the comedian, made reference to a high-profile line from his *Dictator*-ending speech, in which citizen Chaplin steps out of character to plead for peace. For this reason, it was initially considered artistically controversial. Yet, as this text has documented, during World War II Chaplin frequently was asked to repeat said speech, with great success, to various patriot audiences. So what was the highlighted *Dictator* line which was immensely pertinent to Chaplin's later HUAC problems, after the speech had been so popular a decade earlier? "Let us fight to free the world—to do away with national barriers—to do away with greed, with hate and intolerance." (As a historic addendum to the subject, even one of America's key founding fathers, *Common Sense* author Thomas Paine, came to believe that the hope of the future was universal citizenship.)

Second, despite all the attacks upon Chaplin because of his unproven ties to communism, the general consensus now is that losing his re-entry permit was most tied to the comedian's sexual scandals—particularly the Joan Barry case. Yet, for all of Chaplin's admittedly questionable escapades, there is great irony in the fact he was metaphorically crucified for the one act in which then inadmissible blood tests proved he was innocent. It is reminiscent of the *Verdoux*-like antihero of *Kind Hearts and Coronets,* and a Bluebeard convicted for the one murder he did *not* commit.

A third example of Chaplin-related absurdity during this 1952–1953 window of time involves two radically different performers, film comedian Harold Lloyd (1893–1971) and singer-actor-activist-athlete Paul Robeson (1898–1976). Chaplin silent comedy rival Lloyd was given an honorary Academy Award at the ceremony on March 19, 1953. Though this special statuette was not underserved, the timing and the wording on Lloyd's citation was a darkly comic dig at Chaplin: It was presented for Lloyd being a "master comedian and good citizen." In contrast, African-American Robeson was blacklisted during the 1950s for his pioneering outspokenness on civil rights issues and his ongoing support of pro–Soviet Union policies, which he saw as being non-racist. In 1952 he was even awarded the International Stalin Prize by the USSR. Yet Robeson was not allowed to accept the award in Moscow because he was denied a passport by the State Department. Thus, at the same time a controversial U.S. citizen (Robeson) could not leave the country, another controversial U.S. resident alien (Chaplin) was not allowed to re-enter it. Such was the period's whirling dervish of HUAC absurdity.

Is it any wonder, therefore, that the often politically driven Chaplin would respond with a cinematic attack on his former adopted land? Moreover, just as this chapter has chronicled how *real world* dark comedy derailed his early 1950s life, it also provided him with a basic blueprint for a payback movie. That is, start with the unquestioned "king" of comedy (Chaplin) being banished by U.S. reactionaries upon leaving New York. Once in Europe, he is celebrated as if he really were a king. Chaplin's cinematic revenge reverses the situation with *A King in New York*: A European monarch is forced from his country by another extreme political group, and upon his Gotham arrival he too is suddenly the most lionized of figures—again, radical change with a mere trip across the Atlantic.

One should hasten to add that, Chaplin being Chaplin, other options were briefly considered, from the early 1940s idea to adapt *Shadow and Substance,* to resurrecting either a Verdoux-like character, or the signature Tramp himself. Yet, the foundation for what eventually became *A King in New York* was further reinforced simply by settling into his new home: Switzerland seemed to be crawling with banished royalty, including the former kings and/or queens of Italy, Spain, Yugoslavia, Bulgaria and Albania. This scenario made for some unintentionally funny social events, since various forms of protocol remained in place, from non-stop bowing and curtsying, to the highest ranking monarch in attendance needing to set a precedent for even mundane activities. For instance, at its most ludicrous, one non-smoking ex-queen had to mime lighting a cigarette *before* party guests could indulge themselves with real tobacco. Fittingly, Chaplin's original title for the production was *The Ex-King.* Inexplicably, Chaplin never fully mined this goofy rich potential of arcane royal protocol possibilities, something Woody Allen later entertainingly taps into with *Love and Death* (1975).

Before examining *A King in New York*, one should set the scene for its 1957 release. Because of bitter Chaplin comments about America, the first of which was noted earlier, many felt the comedian would again fully embrace dark comedy *à la* his war trilogy. Other factors fed into this belief. First, the film had a lengthy birthing period, opening in Europe almost five years to the day from when Chaplin's re-entry visa was revoked. Second, at the time it was widely reported that besides *King*, "Chaplin has said he does not want any of his films shown in this country (USA) and during the past few years none has been...."[36] Third, as noted by American print humorist Art Buchwald:

> Because of the secrecy involved in the making of the picture, as well as its [alleged] controversial subject matter, a great deal of interest has been stirred up. Although [Chaplin] denies it, many people have called it "Charlot's Revenge" [Charlot being Frence's name for Charlie the Tramp].[37]

While many viewers were expecting *Monsieur Verdoux II*, *A King in New York* is soft satire which is funny but with a laugh quotient below Chaplin standards. The fun portions of the picture are derailed when he feels the need for his corrosive attacks, however deserving, upon HUAC. The *London Daily Telegraph and Morning Post* critic Campbell Dixon best described such moments: "[Chaplin] is, in a word sincere. Alas, that leads us ... to [Oscar] Wilde's conclusion ... that in art little sincerity is a dangerous thing, and a great deal of it is absolutely fatal."[38] This author's take upon *King* would mirror the *London Daily Herald*'s Margaret Hinxman: "[I]t is not by any means his funniest but the least of Chaplin is comparable with the best of almost anybody else."[39]

The picture's mild satire (even in 1957) clearly differentiates it from Chaplin's final evolution of dark comedy in *Monsieur Verdoux*. That is, with black humor's absurdity, the point is that there is no point, whereas satire offers the possibility of change. Be that as it may, Chaplin's King Shahdov's New York arrival soon finds his character short of funds. This necessitates his working with the attractive advertising agent Ann Kay (Dawn Addams). Just as he is interested in her sexually, she sees him as a TV commercial cash cow. Thus, Kay initially tricks the king to reveal his marketing potential by televising (unbeknownst to him) his appearance at a posh dinner party.

This scenario represents a double satirical whammy, though it is so affectionately funny it plays more like a parody. That is, Ann Kay's scam kids two popular period TV series. The first is *Person to Person* (1953–1961), the pioneering celebrity interview program hosted by Edward R. Murrow. The second is Allen Funt's *Candid Camera* (1948–1967), which comically snooped upon unsuspecting citizens—a precursor to today's reality shows. (This would have necessitated some research by Chaplin, since TVs were always verboten in his homes.) Regardless, the unprompted King Shahdov could do no wrong for his new American audience, just as "King" Chaplin once had the same power in the U.S. Shahdov is soon inundated with commercial offers. He is reluctant to become a pitchman for products with which he is unfamiliar, but monetary needs and the enticing Addams character soon have him before the TV cameras. This results in the film's funniest scene, a whiskey commercial in which he first tastes the alcohol on live television and spontaneously spits out the horrid brew. The public assumes this is an inspired spoof of the product; both Chaplin's King and the whiskey become even more in demand, which represents more satire by way of the public's gullibility.

Much of the movie's first half is focused upon funny but less then hard-hitting jabs at American pop culture, such as kidding rock 'n' roll, commercialism, instant celebrities, and cinema's various new wide-screen effects. In fact, Shahdov goes to a movie and visualizes in his film within a film a popular joke then making the rounds in Hollywood: The ideal leading man for wide-screen movies would be a snake! Chaplin also satires low-budget cult movies when Shahdov sees a preview for *Man or Woman?*, a takeoff on Ed Wood's grade Z campy picture *Glen or Glenda* (1953, originally entitled *I Changed My Sex!*). Chaplin selected a great satirical topic, since the film is now considered one of the worst movies ever made, topped only by cross-dressing Wood's *Plan 9 from Outer Space* (1959). In addition, Chaplin's king also zeroes in on subjects like plastic surgery, which are even more relevant in today's "nip-tuck" society. While Chaplin might have succumbed occasionally to the earlier warning about bitterness, *à la* Oscar Wilde, the funny plastic surgery sequences Addams' character has Chaplin take might have been inspired by Wilde's novel *The Picture of Dorian Gray* (1890), in which an obsession with a youthful appearance becomes more timely with each passing year.

The plastic surgery scenes in *King in New York* work on two levels. The first involves makeup which gives Chaplin's "new" Shahdov a comic pig man look one might have expected to see in one of that era's science fiction films. The second related sequence is when the king goes to a nightclub with the express warning *not* to laugh, or his return-to-normal stitching will come out. Naturally, the floor show entertainment includes a Laurel & Hardy–like duo, and with predictable but amusing results, Shahdov fails to fight off the laughter. Consequently, in both cases Chaplin has successfully managed to include silent comedy visual humor in a sound film.

A final example merits special attention and rivals the surprising sight gag of spitting out the low-grade whiskey as the picture's funniest sequence. It also appears in the aforementioned nightclub, and Chaplin creatively establishes a legitimate reason for his classic pantomime which also doubles as more satire of contemporary America. That is, the club's overly loud modern music necessitates that the comedian must mime his order for caviar and turtle soup, and briefly he brings back the glory days of *The Gold Rush* (1925) and *City Lights* (1931).

Though the mime is at a minimum, one later story development allows him to briefly return to Mack Sennett days when he accidently hoses down members of HUAC. This latter twist is a rare slapstick scene in the serious message portion of the picture. To expand upon this scenario, Chaplin's King Shahdov's celebrity status has him visiting one of New York's "progressive schools" where he meets a boy prodigy-wannabe anarchist named Rupert (played by Chaplin's son Michael). The child, acting as his father's mouthpiece, rejects all forms of modern government in such a programmed manner, he might be one of Jean Renoir's mechanical singing birds in *Rules of the Game* (1939). Yet, Renoir's machine-like creatures gently symbolize a brittle dying aristocracy, while Chaplin's preachy quasi-ventriloquism of Rupert is more like a miniature Verdoux. Still, the king takes a liking to the boy (after all, he created Rupert-Michael, to paraphrase a line from *Verdoux*) and affectionately baits the boy into some stimulating discussion in the vacuous U.S. world of rock 'n' roll, widescreen pictures, TV celebrities, and wall-to-wall commercialization.

To be fair to Michael's Rupert, when he is not required to be robotic, he is a charming child with an equally believable screen persona. Regardless, because of Shahdov's friendship with Rupert, whose parents are communists, the king is called before HUAC. However, the only thing they get from Chaplin is fire hose wet. During the boy's HUAC appearance he is tricked into naming names of family friends of his already jailed parents. Not surprisingly, the boy is broken, as were so many other real HUAC witnesses, both unfriendly and even "friendly" (such as the forever remorseful actors Sterling Hayden and Larry Parks). Shahdov next sees the angst-ridden boy when he is presented to the king as a patriot. Chaplin's character comforts the boy, telling him, "This madness [HUAC] won't go on forever. There's no reason for despair." He also invites Rupert and his parents to eventually visit him in Paris, once the king leaves America.

As with so many blacklisted artists, like Chaplin's Oscar-winning close friend Donald Ogden Stewart (1894–1980), Shahdov has had enough of America, and is voluntarily relocating to Europe. And the king's parental-like concern for Rupert, especially at the close, is reminiscent of the conclusion to *The Kid* (1921), in which title character Jackie Coogan is also traumatized by society. Yet, while little Coogan's dilemma is both localized and quickly resolved, the psychological damage to Rupert's inner self many never be undone, just as HUAC's national malaise would continue to linger for years. Chaplin was well aware that the best card to play when showcasing an injustice of a society was to have the victim be the most vulnerable ... a child.

Ironically, in Buchwald's aforementioned mini-critique of *King,* he implies it is not appropriate to have put Rupert before HUAC, since in reality children had yet to be called. However, besides applying the universal justification of an artist's creative license, one must say the blacklisting results of HUAC *were* harming children. For example, Christopher Trumbo, the son of outspoken "Hollywood 10" writer Dalton Trumbo (1905–1976), documents just that fact in *Trumbo: Red, White and Blacklisted* (2003), a play composed of letters his father had written during this period. This off–Broadway hit was adapted to the screen by its director Peter Askin and Christopher Trumbo as the documentary *Trumbo* (2007). From this amazing collections of letters (read by a who's who of film actors), Askin and Trumbo's son also intertwine a collage of contemporary interviews and period newsreels to create an angry, poignant, often funny window into the life of Dalton Trumbo. Beyond the many shattered families and children, *Trumbo* focuses especially upon the direct and indirect bullying of Christopher's younger sister Mitzi. Her elementary education and Blue Bird membership, of all things, resulted in verbal abuse from children of conservative parents which necessitated Mitzi to both leave school and begin counseling. (The bullying often began from birth, with the children of liberals often being mocked as "red-diapered babies.") In later years, Mitzi could kid about some comically absurd elements attached to growing up in a blacklisted household. For instance, *Trumbo* also documents that because her father used so many aliases, at home Mitzi felt there was no such thing as a wrong number phone call! And one is reminded of another bittersweet story from Joe Gilford, whose parents Jack and Madeline Gilford were also blacklisted. Joe recalled, "The joke in our family was that our first three words were 'Mama ... Papa ... Fifth Amendment.'"[40] Though this dark comedy resiliency is admirable, like Mitzi's brother, Joe Gilford was also driven to write a play about this stain on American history: *Finks* (2013, named for those who informed to HUAC). Interestingly, during this same blacklist period, two other children (fictionalized children "Scout" and "Jem" Finch, from Harper Lee's Pulitzer Prize–winning 1960 novel *To Kill a Mockingbird*), also have to endure taunts and slanders against their principled father. Though Lee's story was set in the 1930s, she told it from a 1950s perspective where racism and HUAC-fueled conflict rained its narrow-mindedness down on children, too.

For the Trumbos and Gilfords, all this grief was merely the result of leftist fathers who first flirted with Communism when the Soviet Union was still an ally of the United States. Trumbo was such a "threat" that during his blacklisted period he would anonymously win two writing Oscars for such "controversial" (so-called) stories as a bullfighting picture entitled *The*

Brave One (1956, under pseudonym Robert Rich and the first uncollected statuette in Hollywood history, which he finally received in 1975) and the romantic comedy *Roman Holiday* (1953, which was not posthumously awarded to Trumbo until 1998, after Ian McLellan Hunter had fronted for him). As an added bit of hypocrisy, here is how Hollywood columnist Hedda Hopper, the queen of filmland's McCarthy witch-hunting era, would describe a Trumbo script at a time when the writer was allegedly undermining American values: His "story embodies the ideals of democracy..." (*Los Angeles Times,* March 26, 1940).

What was the general European critical response to this gentle satire (not unlike the sketch comedy from that era's classic TV program *Your Show of Shows,* 1950–1954), when spliced together with Chaplin's rather bludgeoning attack on HUAC? The best overview can be gleaned from the title of a September 18, 1957, *Variety* article: "Chaplin's [*King* Received] Good Press in Britain in Contrast to Raves in France."[41] The New York newspapers were reluctant to offer up any praise of the pictures. For example, the *New York World Telegram and Sun* headlined its article "Chaplin Film So-So in London," while a *New York Times* piece entitled "Chaplin's *King* Bows" described a "generally unenthusiastic reception from the [London] critics...."[42] Yet, even in such skewered perspectives, positive comments were confessed. For example, in "Chaplin's *King* Bows," critic Leonard Ingalls added:

> Even some of the British critics who found [Chaplin's] latest effort "puzzling" ... had to admit that large parts were "hilariously funny" ... [and the film] is doing good business here ... London audiences do not usually applaud at the end of films. But they have been doing that at the conclusion of each showing of the new Chaplin feature.[43]

Yet, this "puzzling" comment is puzzling, when so many London critics were full of praise. Harold Conway of the *London Daily Sketch* considered the satire restrained, amiable but never vicious and thought that Chaplin "had disciplined his revenge into mellow good humor."[44] The *London Times* opined:

> Chaplin amidst all the gags is insisting ... that to force a man to inform against his friends is wrong, and to bring up children in the belief that betrayal is praiseworthy is bad for them. I cannot see that this is an unreasonable thing to say.[45]

The *London Daily Mirror*'s Donald Zec rated the film "superbly funny."[46]

There were some London critics who were either critical of the "heavy-handed treatment of the [film's] politi-

Though this is the stereotype which persists, Chaplin as the angry *King in New York,* the film more often plays as a combination of light parody and mild satire.

cal message," or felt that *King* was not as polished as a standard Chaplin picture.[47] (Shooting at England's Shepperton Studios, the comedian was away from the comfort zone of his own Hollywood studio and a familiar, supportive crew.) Yet even these mixed reviews often found provocatively positive aspects to what some might have called *King* negatives. For example, Kenneth Tynan's diplomatically neutral *London Observer* critique opined:

> Nobody has subjected the script to "a polishing job," which is the film industry's euphemism for the process whereby rough edges are planed away and sharp teeth blunted. The result, in the fullest sense of the phrase, is "free cinema," in which anything ... can happen. In every shot Chaplin speaks his mind, but its naked outspokenness is preferable, any day, to a smooth fettered one.[48]

To better appreciate Tynan's comments, one must place them in the context of period British theater and cinema. If not otherwise obvious, Tyson even employed two phrases which point in this direction: the review's title, "Looking Back in Anger," and the critique's reference to "free cinema." John Osborne's seminal play *Look Back in Anger* (1956) reinvented British theater with a ranting young Jimmy Porter, an angry post-war anti-class anti-hero who made J.D. Salinger's Holden Caulfield (*Catcher in the Rye,* 1951) sound like a church mouse, though an admittedly witty one. Paralleling Osborne's groundbreaking play, English stage and screen director-critic Lindsay Anderson used the phrase "Free Cinema" to describe the movies he organized and screened for the British Film Institute between 1956 and 1959. Comprised of both documentaries and mainstream commercial pictures like Jack Clayton's groundbreaking international hit *Room at the Top* (1958), this movement also embraced Porter's anger at status quo society. Brits like Osborne and Anderson celebrated blue collar types who neither sounded like Lord Laurence Olivier nor had anything to do with the *polite* society comedies of a Noël Coward. This British new wave was often referenced as the "angry young man" school.[49]

Consequently, Tynan's praise of *King*'s "rough edges" makes perfect sense. Ironically, despite the old complaint that Chaplin's production values were increasingly old-fashioned, he suddenly and unexpectedly found *King* praised for its parallels with Britain's new cutting edge cinema. "Free cinema" was fundamentally about a realism which revealed basic truths in the too-often-ignored everyday world around us. The *special effects* were the *settings,* whether blunt and ugly, or a neglected backdrop which poignantly mirrored the rhythms of life. Chaplin indirectly addressed this philosophy in a 1967 interview:

> I'm not afraid of doing a cliché, if it's right. We don't wade through our existence with any sort of originality. We all live and die and eat three meals a day, and fall in and out of love, and the rest of it.... In avoiding clichés I think one can become dull....[50]

Chaplin might also have been addressing Italian neo-realism, a precursor to this British new wave realism, especially the work of Vittorio De Sica and his inseparable scriptwriter Cesare Zavattini who were so pivotal in founding the movement. One is especially reminded of a simple scene in their *Umberto D* (1952) in which the housemaid (Maria-Pia Casilio) rises early to begin her kitchen chores. Her duties embrace all the repetitive blue-collar clichés of a young working girl. Yet there is a neglected beauty in recording this repetitive activity, not unlike one of Edgar Degas' (1834–1917) paintings of a Parisian laundress at work. (As an addendum to this Italian film and Chaplin's *King* is the fact that *Umberto D* chronicles the life of an elderly man so poor he is about to be forced into the streets, with only his mongrel dog to comfort him. The picture could have been a fascinating blueprint for bringing back Chaplin's Tramp as an old man—a sort of late sequel to 1918s *A Dog's Life*, where Charlie's loyal companion is the mut Scraps.)

So how does one now close the book on *King*? As Roger Ebert bluntly wrote decades after the film's original release, the initial ugly U.S. rumors stating that *King* was overly "bitter" turned "out to be a lot of baloney."[51] Moreover, when *King* finally went into general American release in the early 1970s, the reviews were positive. However, the uniqueness of Chaplin's lone filmmaker attack upon the HUAC blacklisting during its heyday still took an American back seat to satire so gentle it almost bordered upon parody. Stanley Kauffman's *New Republic* critique stated that the one consistency in *King*

> is that most of the seeming disasters turn out to be advantageous. Shahdov is trapped by a hidden camera into making a TV spectacle of himself, and it transforms him into a celebrity. He "blows" a TV commercial by coughing, and it makes him a comedy hit. The implication—that nothing is too ridiculous for American success if only sufficiently "exposed"—is much better satire than any of the political stuff.[52]

However one "reads" the Chaplin bitter meter on *King*, the film still merits kudos for its head-on period attacks on HUAC. Plus, while the five years since *Limelight* undoubtedly softened the satire, one must still balance this actuality with Chaplin's refusal to allow the picture to be released into the 1957 U.S. market. The latter point is no small item; if the comedian unofficially embraced any "ism," it was capitalism. To voluntarily turn away the millions of dollars represented by American theater chains suggests some bitterness lingered.

Still, a softer *King* fairly guaranteed that Chaplin's evolving look at dark comedy and war had stopped with *Verdoux*. That is, there had always been the chance, however remote, that the comedian might have revisited James Agee's aforementioned unfinished script *The Tramp's New World,* about Charlie in a post–nuclear apocalyptic New York. Of course, such a picture would have been a fitting finale to the comedian's excursions into dark comedy and war—with the closing trial in *Verdoux* almost pointing to humanity's mushroom conclusion. Yet *King* had seemed to close Chaplin's creative attack on HUAC; the remaining years of the comedian's life bore this out. The following chapter examines this period of almost exactly two decades which remained after *King,* and his *Limelight*-like tendency to creatively look back at the times of Charles and Charlie. Naturally, he could not rest; for artists as for most people, life is in the work.

12

Coming Full Circle: Chaplin's Last Years, an Unrealized Darkly Comic Project, and a Final Macabre Twist

"There's nothing more present tense than a movie star. You can only talk to them about the future."—Movie agent Sue Mengers (Bette Midler) in Josh Logan's play *I'll Eat You Last* (2013)

This darkly comic observation is the embodiment of the twenty years between the release of Chaplin's *A King in New York* (1957) and his death on Christmas Day 1977. Yet, as only the truly gifted ones manage, the comedian's multifaceted new projects involved visiting the past, including his first signature dark comedy, *Shoulder Arms* (1918). That is, while *King* was a qualified critical and commercial success in Europe, Chaplin's decision *not* to release the picture in America drastically reduced its potential for large box office returns.

Chaplin addressed his hollow victory by returning to basics. He composed music for *A Dog's Life* (1918), *Shoulder Arms,* and *The Pilgrim* (1922) and released the package as *The Chaplin Review* in 1959. The feature-length compilation also included a prologue of sorts: It opens with footage originally shot for an aborted short subject entitled *How to Make Movies* (1917–1918). Consequently, Chaplin had not only brought back the Tramp, he gifted the public (via the documentary footage) with a metaphorical look at his alter ego's growing years. The introductory footage also was given added black humor bite, as it pertained to the groundbreaking *Shoulder Arms,* by including some actual documentary footage of World War I.

For the remainder of Chaplin's life he would both tweak and compose new music for his earlier Tramp films. For instance, in 1971 he wrote a new score for *The Circus* (1928), as well as penning a charming theme song, "Swing, Little Girl," which the comedian credibly sang over the opening credits. (The aforementioned *Pilgrim,* sometimes referenced as "The Chaplin Western," had also included another theme song composed by the comedian, "Bound for Texas," sung by Matt Muno.) And in 1971, at 82 years of age, Chaplin wrote new scores for *The Kid* (1921) and *The Idle Class* (1921), which were revised as a package. The comedian had previously set a personal precedent for such work, after his 1942 reworking and re-releasing of 1925's *The Gold Rush* following the controversial reception given *The Great Dictator* (1940). The Tramp forever remained his return-to talisman.

With the mix of dark comedy and war becoming more mainstream and acceptable by the 1960s, particularly with Stanley Kubrick's *Dr. Strangelove or: How I Learned to Stop Worrying and Love the Bomb* (1964), Chaplin's pioneering work in the genre was becoming both more visible and celebrated at the perfect time, especially as the U.S. was then plunging into yet another unnecessary war—Vietnam. Moreover, with the Cold War still in full swing, the black comedy absurdity of *Monsieur Verdoux* (1947) became all the more relevant, just as it is today in America's ongoing war on terror in the Middle East. That is, the realpolitik (practical over ethic values) of all those conflicts raises the age-old philosophical question: If one adopts the negative tactics of the enemy—stooping to their level—has one not already lost the war by becoming the enemy? For *Verdoux,* aping the underhanded antics of the government was merely one man playing for survival. Yet, when countries practice it as standard policy, "civilization" revisits the Dark Ages.

Still, citizen-artist Chaplin had finally escaped the love-hate phenomenon of being a controversial spokesman. For example, in real undercover intelligence there is an ideal go-to figure known as " 'the traditional gray man,' who can blend in anywhere, who is 'so inconspicuous that he can never catch the waiter's eye in a restaurant.'"[1] Chaplin had revealed these ugly truths about governments early and without any gray cloak of anonymity, and had been unfairly chastised for it. Now, what had once passed for "love it or leave it" blasphemy was shown to be the absurdly dark comic truth ... and the U.S. had yet to reach the government vilification on steroids known as Watergate. As CBS journalist Edward R. Murrow had so sagely observed in the 1954 *See It Now* broadcast which signaled the beginning of the end for Joe McCarthy:

> We must not confuse dissent with disloyalty. We must remember always that accusation is not proof and that conviction depends upon evidence and due process of law. We will not walk in fear, one of another. We will not be driven by fear into an age of unreason, if we dig deep in history and remember that we are not descended from fearful men.[2]

As a comedian once observed, "love it or leave it" makes as much sense as "my mother, drunk or sober." Yet, Chaplin was forced out of the U.S. and spent his remaining years on a mountain in Switzerland. Lingering bitterness can be somewhat placated by living in a palatial estate on a continent which admires both you and your work. Yet, the real tragedy of the revoked re-entry visa was three-fold, besides Chaplin's travail and the global black eye it gave the U.S. First, the greatness of *Limelight* (1952) was largely lost upon American period audiences, since it was soon pulled from U.S. distribution, despite glowing stateside reviews, all because of the hullabaloo caused by the actions of the attorney general. When the picture finally went into limited American release in 1972, it was still capable of generating passionate critical raves, including the following comments by longtime *New York Daily News* film critic Kathleen Carroll:

> "Did you cry?" asked a friend as we walked out of *Limelight*, the Charles Chaplin film Howard Hughes once threatened to ban. I nodded happily, blinking away the tears. It felt good, that cry. For months now, we had been feeling nothing, a sense of numbness settling down over us after each new [mediocre] movie ... [Chaplin's] film is an exquisitely lyrical tribute to humanity and as such it touches a responsive chord in all of us.[3]

The second Chaplin tragedy linked to the forced 1952 exit was moving his production base to England, away from the safety net familiarity of his Hollywood studio home. Whatever positive revisionist spin is placed upon *A King in New York,* it suffers from a rushed production schedule (dictated by pricey rental space in a foreign studio) and the absence of his normal staff. Third, had there not been the ugly disconnect with the U.S., and its accompanying bitterness, who is to say what other thought-provoking themes of self-discovery this cinema pioneer might have further mined from his past? Though *Limelight* is an inspired subtextual exploration and exorcism of Chaplin past and present, he might also have moved on to a contemporary scenario of self, always with the freedom to backtrack via nightmares, daydreams, and all forms of memory to share his movie journey. Such a tale might have played like Ingmar

Bergman's *Wild Strawberries* (1957, the same year as *King*), in which a grouchy, stubborn, yet egotistically funny old professor plumbs his past on a road trip to receive an honorary degree. Like life, the award means little; it is all about the journey. But all this is not merely the wishful conjecture of an admiring biographer; ironically, just prior to leaving America in 1952, the comedian had flirted with making a picture celebrating the U.S. immigrant experience. And whose story, besides Chaplin's, is any more emblematic of the rags-to-riches possibilities of just such an American tale? As it was, Chaplin's last years call to mind the opening tagline to a popular American TV program of that era, "the thrill of victory ... and the agony of defeat."[4]

On the plus side, Chaplin had a huge commercial success with his memoir *My Autobiography* (1964).[5] Years in the making, as was his tradition, and after spending hundreds of writing hours in his library, the self-educated 75-year-old comedian had reached that difficult process of facing one's self. The first 150 pages

> are remarkable for their incomparably vivid impressions of poverty in turn-of-the century London in which both Dickensian vitality and Dickensian misery persisted side by side; they recapture, too, the exhilaration experienced in first discovering and exploring those rich talents which were to take him so far from the unpromising origins.[6]

Though the succeeding book is not without interest, much of this big, elbow-straining memoir (500-plus pages) succumbs to a litany of important "who's who" people the comedian met during his lifetime. Consequently, one gets further and further away from the specifics of comedian Charlie Chaplin and must meet Renaissance man *Charles* Chaplin, who talks socialism with H.G. Wells, economics with John Maynard Keyes, the plight of India with Gandhi, and so on. And whereas a Hitchcock film movement from specific to general helps an audience relate to a character, Chaplin's potpourri of generalities threatens to alienate. In an autobiography of film's greatest clown, the reader wants to stay focused on that specific clown.

It is therefore necessary to look deeper into the memoir, once the poignantly written early childhood chapters are past. Certain patterns soon emerge that in and of themselves seem inconsequential but when considered in total, represent an even more strongly Victorian value system than has previously been linked to Chaplin.

To start with, there is the comedian's propensity for name-dropping. Is this merely the wish fulfillment of a poor, neglected boy who has become rich and famous? While this is certainly part of it, Chaplin literature has neglected how much Victorian culture was obsessed with hero worship. Walter E. Houghton, in his seminal *The Victorian Mind* (1957), makes the point that for the Victorian,

> in actual life to meet a great man, or look on anything he possessed, was an overwhelming experience. "One man is so little," a lecturer told his audience, "that you see him a thousand times without caring to ask his name; another man is so great, that if you have exchanged a word with him while living or possess 'a hair of him' when dead, it is something of which you are proud.[7]

This statement captures Chaplin's sense of awe at meeting the famous. For example, while socializing with actor Sir Herbert Beerbohm Tree (1852–1917), a towering London theatrical figure of Chaplin's youth, the comedian confessed, "I never thought of you existing offstage. You were a legend. And to be dining with you tonight in Los Angeles overwhelms me."[8] Ironically, as film historian Arthur Knight notes, "it never seems to occur to him that the people he has met were, in all probability, no less impressed at having met the great Charlie Chaplin."[9]

If Chaplin's interest in the famous can be linked to this Victorian characteristic, it was certainly fueled by Chaplin's mother Hannah, the most influential force in his young life. As Chaplin himself notes, she had had a life-sized painting of Nell Gwyn (the English actress and mistress of Charles II) in their sitting room and was wont to do imitations of everyone from Gwyn and Napoleon to the famous of fiction. (That his mother was a promiscuous actress of the Victorian era, too, gives a provocative twist to her deification of Gwyn.) And though Hannah often brought parody to her mimicry, there was also a balance of respect; for instance, this was Chaplin's description of her rendition of Wilson Barrett in *The Sign of the Cross:* "She acted with a suspicion of humor but not without an appreciation of Barrett's talents."[10]

An extension of Victorian hero worship can be seen in the period's interest in self-development, to become all that is possible. Chaplin notes that after he read Emerson's essay "Self-Reliance," "I felt I had been handed a golden birthright."[11] (Other comedy contemporaries who followed this same Victorian self-development included W.C. Fields and Eddie Cantor.[12]) Thus, Chaplin's dropping literary titles therefore joins that of famous names, a characteristic that was surfacing as early as his 1922 book *My Trip Abroad*.[13] Chaplin's autobiography constantly finds him haunting bookstores. And when his comedic fame allowed him to converse with some of the very authors he was reading, it is hardly surprising that he should dwell on— even celebrate—such a metamorphosis.

Further encouragement for this infatuation of the famous no doubt came from the fact that Victorian society did not place that much significance on comedy. For example, America's greatest humorist Mark Twain died believing one of his pivotal books was the sentimentally serious biography of Victorian heroine Joan of Arc. Chaplin mirrors this in his autobiography by seldom talking about comedy and the nuts-and-bolts construction of his films. Apparently he started to link comedy with a second-class identity as early as 1922, when the article "Charlie Chaplin, as a Comedian, Contemplates Suicide" reported his preference for tragedy.[14]

He did, however, have time for a Victorian fascination with the macabre, such as the Donner Party, which earlier chapters in the text have addressed. This frontier cannibalism served as the inspiration for the boot-eating scene in *The Gold Rush* (1925), not to mention his film partner Mack Swain periodically hallucinating that the Tramp is a man-sized chicken. Moreover, the text has also documented how Chaplin's interest in twisted Victorian tales was the catalyst for some rather grisly bedtime stories for his children with both Lita Gray and Oona O'Neill. Unfortunately, he spends little time on how his "Grimm" tales so easily mixed with his comedy. Still, this 1964 memoir's frequent Victorian fixation on the macabre demonstrates how, unlike *Monsieur Verdoux,* the timing of the man who invented the dark comedy war film with *Shoulder Arms* was back on track again.

Until *Verdoux,* the Chaplin heroine was usually the idealized Victorian woman; even in this picture his Bluebeard activities are to support an invalid wife. In fact, his memoir even has him describing a brief romance as "like the last chapter of a Victorian novel."[15] The book in hand has also documented his fixation on the lost love of young Hetty Kelly, the girl he put on a pedestal, higher than the one on which F. Scott Fitzgerald's Gatsby foolishly placed Daisy; in neither case could either woman equal the ideal. Poor Hetty even seems to follow the scenario of that classic Victorian poem canonizing the divine woman, Dante Gabriel Rossetti's "The Blessed Damozel." As with Rossetti's heroine, Chaplin's Hetty dies young, before their love can be consummated. This idyllic dream of Hetty continued to haunt him through the years."[16]

Chaplin's second wife, Lita Gray, notes in her *My Life with Chaplin* (1966) that he often remarked that she reminded him of the girl in the *Age of Innocence*.[17] Eventually, Chaplin had a company artist paint a likeness of her "in the *Age of Innocence* pose."[18] The 1778 Sir Joshua Reynolds painting is a touchingly romantic rendering of a young girl by an artist more often associated with the classical tradition. The hardback editions of Gray's memoir include a photograph of her posing for the *Age of Innocence*–inspired portrait, in which she is remarkably similar to the girl of Reynolds' original. It makes it all the more believable that at the height of their romance Chaplin should tell her, "There are many things attractive about you, Lita, but the most appealing is your virginal innocence."[19] Yet, this child bride mother of his first two children does not even make the index of Chaplin's memoir.

More than one reviewer of the autobiography was surprised at the relative silence of Chaplin on his many amours.[20] Yet this is also consistent with a Victorian perspective on glorified womanhood: Women were heavenly symbols meant for worship, not for the debasement of sexuality, at least not in print. As Victorian scholar Walter E. Houghton suggests, the male of this period had to constantly fight the sexual "tempest of passion," or else be reduced to a "wild beast."[21] After all, that is why he put the female on the proverbial pedestal.

Chaplin suffered from more than a modicum of this duality, as the telling juxtapositioning of his heavenly screen romances and the messy sex scandals of his private life so vividly demonstrate. Though Chaplin avoids commenting on this Victorian male duality in his autobiography, there is an almost provocative tongue-in-cheek reference to it in his later *My Life in Pictures* (1974). Midway in the volume is a beautiful full-page picture of his first child bride Mildred Harris, which faces a far from complimentary matching full-page photo of an unshaven, completely disheveled Chaplin. He labeled the pictures "Beauty and the Beast."[22]

Regardless, the best part of the Chaplin memoir played upon his childhood, or negation of one. With a father dead from drink and a mother institutionalized for insanity, his early years embraced another Victorian interest: the cult of the child. Thus, as with his friend and silent star contemporary from World War I bond drive days, Mary Pickford, their careers often pivoted upon an earlier era's enchantment with the cherub and/or the urchin. Consequently, while Pickford never escaped her spunky young girl persona (even as late as 1926's *Sparrows*), Chaplin was equally tied to his childlike Tramp, though both sometimes doubled as caretakers of the young, as in Chaplin's *The Kid* (1921) and Pickford's *Sparrows*.

Between the movingly revealing early portions of Chaplin's memoir, and a somewhat more sociological Victorian "reading" of the remainder of the book, the diligent student of the comedian can still gain valuable insight into cinema's most iconic figure. Otherwise, Brendon Gill's ironic observation about Chaplin and the Tramp could be applied to the filmmaker's whole life, as described in his autobiography: "Having read elsewhere of the tradition of the Tramp ... we appear to know more about the Tramp than Chaplin himself knows."[23]

If the grand success of Chaplin's memoir was his greatest late-in-life achievement, his final film *A Countess from Hong Kong* (1967) would be the rock bottom. This quasi-screwball comedy was a reworking of his 1930s screenplay for *Stowaway,* which Chaplin had originally written for third wife Paulette Goddard while the couple vacationed in the East. The plot in a nutshell finds a beautiful but poor title character (Sophia Loren) so desperate to leave Hong Kong (ironically, another exile) that she stows away in the luxury liner suite of American millionaire diplomat Ogden Mars (Marlon Brando). Now set shortly after World War II, the plot is still traditional Depression era farce: This often picaresque genre, sometimes referred to as "caviar comedy" for its wealthy escapist backdrop, follows the spoofingly madcap romance of an "implosive couple"—one rich, one poor.[24]

Chaplin, who lived only to work, had been struggling with new story ideas after *A King in New York* and finally decided to rehash this earlier script; the comedian first announced the project at a late 1965 London press conference. One of Loren's biographers states that the actress and her husband, producer Carlo Ponti, were the catalyst for the production:

> Perhaps [Loren] takes particular pride [in *Countess*] because the idea of teaming Brando, Chaplin, and Loren originated with Ponti. And a dinner meeting of Sophia with Chaplin at his home in Vevey, Switzerland, during the filming of [the 1965 Loren comedy] *Lady L* had inspired the master to dust off and update a twenty-five-year-old [plus] script of his....[25]

The production often proved difficult, especially the relationship between Chaplin and Brando. The actor was such a fan of the comedian that he had accepted the part script unseen. But besides the fact that Brando was totally miscast for a farce, the working styles of the two men were a constant source of friction. Chaplin's old school approach to directing continued to be orchestrating every move and gesture of his cast. This was the antithesis of Brando's Method acting, in which the performer attempts to almost channel the character by drawing upon personal experience and exploring the motivation for each action. Years later, Robin Williams would kiddingly describe the Method approach of Al Pacino in a Broadway production, when an audience member complained, "I can't understand him," only to be shouted down by another playgoer, "Shut up, he feels it!" Needless to say, Brando *never* felt his part in *Countess*. The actor also believed that Chaplin took this directing style to a "sadistic" level with his co-star Sydney Chaplin, the comedian's son: "He was vicious to him."[26] But then again, Brando had little that was positive to say about *Countess,* even complaining about Loren's "bad breath."[27]

Period critics often savaged *Countess*; Bosley Crowther's blunt *New York Times* pocket summary was, "[S]o the dismal truth is it is awful."[28] The overriding complaint was that the genre was outdated, or as the *New York Daily News*' Kathleen Carroll opened her review, "Why has Charles Chaplin waited over ten years to make a movie 30 years too late?"[29] Carroll also had issues with Brando's casting, describing him as "like a bull in a china shop when it comes to comedy."[30] Still, Carroll gives the film two and one-half stars and rightly praises both Patrick Cargill's screwball Jeeves-like valet (*à la* the comic character from the high society stories of P.G. Wodehouse) and Sydney Chaplin's Tony Randall–like friend to Brando. (Peter Sellers had lobbied for the Cargill part, but Chaplin felt the film already had enough star power.)

Though Chaplin had a brief walk-on as an old steward, with unbilled daughters Geraldine and Josephine also having cameos, the single short scene which steals the movie belongs to Dame Margaret Rutherford. Her magnificent but too brief appearance as a zany old lady confined to her bed mumbling complaints about her stuffed panda crowding her, and flowers which "take up all the oxygen," goes by much too quickly. (It seems appropriate that Chaplin's last screen appearance has his steward being either drunk or seasick, since the comedian's drunk act is what originally got him into the movies.)

Newsday's kind panning of the picture included an overview which is even more true today:

> There is something missing in *Countess* and I think that something is Chaplin.... As a *Pillow Talk* kind of casual comedy, the film does have some charm with its predictable [farce] predicaments.... You will enjoy *Countess* enormously, if you forget who made it and who stars in it and what it should have been. But if, like me, you expect [more] from a Chaplin film, you will be sorely disappointed.[31]

The disappointment of *Newsday* critic Joseph Gelmis would only have been heightened as 1967 went on to be arguably *the* year of New American Cinema, with such game-changing pictures as *Bonnie and Clyde, The Graduate,* and *In the Heat of the Night.*

The *Variety* reviewer of *Countess* attempted an upbeat opening by suggesting the names Chaplin, Loren, and Brando "should stimulate enough activity at the wickets to make this a box- office success," yet he also eventually confesses that the movie is "surprisingly and disappointingly, a pedestrian job...."[32] British critiques followed the same negative pattern, though the ever loyal French often praised the picture. For example, *Paris-Match* described the farce as "a charming comedy [which] did not deserve the severity of the British Press."[33]

Regardless, it was a difficult failure for Chaplin to accept after such a lionized career. Paradoxically, however, he must have had received a certain balm from the equally old-fashioned instrumental theme song he had composed for *Countess,* "This Is My Song." Pop star singer-actress Petula Clark, who had a home in Switzerland near Chaplin's residence, recorded the song late in 1966. Released a month after the January premiere of *Countess,* the 45 single "This Is My Song" became a monster international hit, selling over two million copies worldwide, including a million in the United States alone. Recorded in several languages, it was number one on pop charts in numerous countries, including Clark and Chaplin's native England. This was quite the coup for the duo in a decade dominated by the Beatles. Ironically, Clark, whose signature song is "Downtown," had been reluctant to record Chaplin's composition because she felt the lyrics were not modern enough! Thus, Chaplin was still capable of composing pop standards in his late 70s, with this even being arguably his best single after the haunting "Smile."

What if Clark's rendition of the theme song had been prominently featured throughout the movie, and Brando's character had been played by someone better suited for farce, such as David Niven? Adding the multi-faceted comedy of Sellers could not have hurt. *Countess* still would not have been a classic Chaplin film, dripping with the seemingly effortless greatness of his best work, but period audiences might have found it more palatable. As it is, the years have been kind to *Countess.* By no longer looking at it through the lens of a specific time period but simply comparing it to screwball comedies of all ages, the film receives modestly passing grades for the genre.

Though this last quarter century of Chaplin's self-imposed exile produced only two lesser features, he still kept busy with rewarding work, from composing new music for old classics, to the aforementioned bestselling memoir. There was also Chaplin's ever growing family. Prior to their sudden exit to Europe, Oona and the comedian had had four children: Geraldine (1944), Michael (1946), Joseph Hannah (1949), and Victoria (1951). After their relocation to Switzerland, Oona would give birth to four more youngsters: Eugene (1953, named for Oona's Nobel Prize-winning playwright father), Jane (1957), Annette (1959) and Christopher (1962, when the comedian was 73). To paraphrase a Billy Crystal comic line from the period, "Chaplin was still making babies even when he couldn't lift them." (Though Oona and her father had been estranged for most of her adult life, especially after she had married a man O'Neill's age, there had been signs of a thaw at the time of his death; thus, her son born that year was named Eugene.)

Chaplin was now a better father, or at least a more available parent, than to his first children, Charles Jr. and Sydney. Yet, even in his later years, he remained a workaholic and often spent long hours isolated in his study. Moreover, though Oona dearly loved the children, her relationship with Chaplin was so close and increasingly needy in his final years, that the children were always secondary to their mother's devotion to Chaplin. When I spoke with Geraldine at the University of Paris' international celebration of Chaplin's 100th birthday (1889–1989), she shared warm memories of her father and confessed that until he suffered some minor strokes in his 80s, his amazing energy level kept them from ever thinking about him dying.[34] (She revealed the added detail that some of the aforementioned darkly comic stories with which Chaplin entertained his children were drawn from Luis Buñuel films!)

Throughout his twenty-year American exile, from the revoked re-entry visa, to the return for a special honorary Oscar, the comedian still had the ability to ruffle American conservative feathers. Two such instances occurred during 1954. In May, Chaplin accepted the Communist World Peace Prize Award, and in July he lunched with the Communist Chinese Premier

Geraldine Chaplin and the author at the University of Paris in 1989 during the centennial celebration of her father's birth.

Chou-en-Lai who was attending a Geneva conference. Though one would expect a provocative self-described "peacemonger," who always accepted tributes with the word "peace" in the title, to gracefully accept that award, Chaplin the successful capitalist was probably more than happy to also receive the roughly $10,000 which went with this prize. And with regard to the premier, Chaplin inevitably enjoyed meeting new and interesting people, regardless of their politics (not to mention his previously noted Victorian tendency for hero worship).

The small Swiss village of Vevey was hardly Hollywood, so for the Chaplins there were often trips throughout Europe and even an African adventure. London's Savoy Hotel was their most frequent home away from home. A taste of Southern California was created at their Swiss home by the building of a swimming pool and a tennis court—with the dance-like nature of tennis making it Chaplin's favorite sport. Though the comedian claimed tennis' graceful form always trumped winning, he was a very competitive player. Like many successful people, losing at anything was difficult for him.

With Chaplin being arguably cinema's most iconic figure, one could recycle the old axiom, "If Mohammed will not go to the mountain, the mountain must come to Mohammed." That is, a veritable who's who forever visited the comedian. Yet, no guests were more important than Chaplin's beloved brother Sydney and his wife Gypsy, who lived in Nice. Each summer the couple would come to Vevey for an extended stay. While Sydney had always doubled as Charlie's best friend, savvy business adviser, and sometimes co-star, he and Gypsy were also great favorites of Chaplin's youngsters. Sydney, with no children of his own, was the perfect uncle, with non-stop jokes and gags and equally inspired humorous letters to the older children throughout the years. He never wrote his own memoir, though in Lisa K. Stein's beguiling biography of Sydney she quotes from a provocative letter he wrote to his journalist-playwright friend R.J. Minney:

> If I had the energy and desire, I could make a lot of money by writing the true history of the Chaplin family. It would be so startling that the [groundbreaking 18th century tell-all autobiography the] *Confessions of Rousseau* and [the graphic sexual adventures of Frank] Harris' *My Private Life and Loves* [1931] would read like children's primers alongside of it. Nearly everything I have read concerning my brother and I in newspapers, etc., has been mainly bunk....[35]

Consequently, one has another possible explanation for Chaplin's love of his brother: Sydney knew where all the proverbial bodies were buried but took all the secrets to his grave.

Oona was always aware that her husband's happiness depended on being immersed in some creative project—a trait she forever encouraged even though it often meant less time together. Yet, in the years after the *Countess from Hong Kong* debacle, she became more and more protective of her husband's increasingly fragile health, starting with a broken ankle which occurred during the production of *Countess*. Moreover, she had specific concerns about Chaplin's next film proposal, *The Freak*. His unfinished script was about a young girl who suddenly sprouts a pair of wings, only to be kidnapped in order that her captors can pawn her off as an angel. She manages to escape but then is arrested and dehumanized by standing trial to determine whether she is human. It provocatively sounds like Dickens meets Kafka, with a pinch of sci-fi HUAC. The script also vaguely brings to mind Robert Altman's dark comedy *Brewster McCloud* (1970), in which the ambition of a character played by young, owlish Bud Cort (the co-star of 1970s *Harold and Maude*) is to make wings and learn to fly in the Houston Astrodome. Living in a nuclear age fallout shelter at the stadium, he is assisted by his fairy godmother (Sally Kellerman).

Altman's bizarre picture is now considered a cult classic, and one wonders what Chaplin might have accomplished with a similarly dark comic scenario. Chaplin's plan was to have his third daughter Victoria play this winged character, since he felt she was the child who had most inherited his inspired comedy gift. Yet here several complications set in. After two years of preparation, teenage Victoria suddenly left home to join and eventually marry actor Jean-Baptiste Thiérrée, with whom she created an intimate traveling circus. This setback was compounded by the difficulty Chaplin's assistant, Jerry Epstein, had in raising money for the project. The *coup de grâce* for the film came from Chaplin's concerned wife. According to the definitive biography of the woman, *Oona: Living in the Shadows* (1998), she finally stepped out from the shadows and said "no..."—but not to Chaplin. Epstein finally found backers for the picture after the company Chaplin had co-founded, United Artists, turned him down. He happily returned to Vevey with the good news but Oona interceded before Epstein could speak to Chaplin:

> "There's no picture," she forcefully told an amazed Epstein. "I have to make a decision. He'll never survive this picture. If *The Freak* was an easy film I would let it go ahead. But you know how impatient Charlie is on the set. Can you imagine what he [an octogenarian] would be like waiting for the special effects people to get the flying right[?] ... [T]his picture would kill him."[36]

It was a bittersweet decision. To paraphrase her mantra during Chaplin's declining years, "He took care of me when I was young, and I'll take care of him in old age." Still, the *Freaks* project was something he obsessed about until the end of his life. For example, one of Oona's low stress "let's keep Charlie engaged" projects was a book entitled *Charlie Chaplin: My Life in Pictures* (1974), a fascinating and invaluable visual peek at his life and career, with the comedian coining the captions.[37] Yet here is Chaplin's final heartbreaking quote, describing a contemporary still of himself:

> In my study at Vevey, reading my latest film script, *The Freak*. It's about a girl who was born with wings. I wrote it for my daughter Victoria and we began to rehearse it—then she left home to get married. But I mean to make it one day.[38]

It is painful to know he *could* have made and/or attempted the movie. It might even have prolonged his life. One could draw an analogy with the aforementioned Robert Altman. This maverick filmmaker had a heart transplant a decade before his death but kept making excellent movies. Indeed, his last film, and one of his most endearing dark comedies, *A Prairie Home Companion* (2006, from the year he died), found him in such poor health that the director Paul Thomas Anderson was hired to shadow Altman, in case the filmmaker could not complete the movie. (Anderson would later dedicate his much-praised 2007 dark comedy *There Will Be Blood* to Altman.) Yet, 81-year-old Altman had very publicly gone on doing what made him happy. One should respect Oona's gut-wrenching decision—she wanted to keep the much older (35 years) love of her life with her as long as possible. Yet others might have embraced a different decision. One is always selfishly obsessed by the "what if" projects of artists forever lost to their public, be it the unfinished films of Orson Welles, or F. Scott Fitzgerd's uncompleted novel *The Last Tycoon*. Moreover, even if *The Freak* had proved to be a lesser work, one last Chaplin film would still have been a gift.

Oona was assisted in keeping the senior Chaplin busy and happy by merely helping him sort through all the many career capstone awards coming his way. Of course, receiving special recognition was nothing new to the comedian, dating back to his honorary Oscar for *The Circus* (1928). Yet, in his final years Chaplin seemed to receive every award possible. Besides the aforementioned honors received upon leaving the United States in 1952, and an honorary Oxford degree in 1962, the 1970s were awash with the awards for the comedian. The Cannes Film Festival made him the Commander of the National Order of the Legion of Honor in 1971. The following year the Venice Film Festival gave him its special lifetime achievement Golden Lion Award. That same year there were a litany of additional honors: a Lincoln Center Lifetime Achievement Award which now bears his name, another honorary Oscar, and a star on Hollywood's Walk of Fame. The topper was being knighted by Queen Elizabeth in 1975. For an Englishman, this most cherished of achievement would have occurred back in the McCarthy 1950s, but the U.S. had put pressure on Britain not to so honor this then-controversial artists. Since *Limelight* had not originally opened in Los Angeles during 1952, twenty years later Chaplin even *won* (with Raymond Rasch and Larry Russell) an Academy Award for the film's Original Dramatic Score!

For history's sake, Chaplin's second honorary Oscar, presented on April 10, 1972, was *the* award—America's belated apology to its most pivotal pioneering star:

> The Academy announced that no other honorary awards would be given to make Chaplin's all the more special. [Producer] Howard Koch said the show would be "nostalgic and glamorous"

and the actresses were asked "to wear black, white or silver to comply with the theme, a salute to nostalgia, and to complement the noncolor [homage to silent cinema] background sets."[39]

The standing ovation Chaplin received after the playing of a Tramp highlight reel still remains the most sustained applause ever accorded an Academy guest or performer. The comedian's deeply moved appreciation was then played out in the most fitting way: He performed a "thank you" trick with his old Charlie derby, which Jack Lemmon had brought out. He said in an interview,

> Last night ... was a terrific thing. My god, the affection of the people. So sweet. Like children after they've been slapped down [by the government] and they're sorry they've done something. The kindness that came through. [I] thought I was going to blubber like a big kid. I cannot cope with emotion any more. It's very hard to respond to affection....[40]

Fittingly for the provocative Chaplin, there was some controversy connected to the Oscar show, but it did not involve the comedian—but the hullabaloo somehow seemed appropriate, given Chaplin's pioneering status in dark comedy. Several seminal performers, including Barbra Streisand, refused an offer to present the Best Pictures statuette that year because Stanley Kubrick's X-rated adaptation of Anthony Burgess' dark comedy novel *A Clockwork Orange* was nominated. The other nominees were *Fiddler on the Roof*, *The Last Picture Show*, *Nicholas and Alexandra*, and the ultimate winner, *The French Connection*. Perennial bad boy Jack Nicholson was only to happy to present the Best Picture award to *The French Connection*.

Chaplin would live five more years, with the comedian's last jaunt from his Swiss manor a short one to the nearby village of Vevey. The family attended a performance of the local Circus Knie, a tradition for the Chaplins since moving to Switzerland. Roughly two months later, early Christmas morning 1977, the beloved symbol of cinema passed away in his sleep surrounded by his family. Always the provocateur, however, even late in life, his explanation for wearing an overcoat on the hottest day was this: "It's the vigors of age. I hope I go to the hot place when I die. I can't ever seem to keep warm."[41]

Ironically, Chaplin had always claimed to detest Christmas, based upon its overt commercialization, though there are several amusing Christmas stories connected to him, such as an aforementioned holiday party to which surrealist filmmaker Luis Buñuel had been invited in 1940s Hollywood. Host Chaplin's only request was that each guest bring an unmarked gift for a general exchange. Buñuel, true to his surreal philosophy, "gifted" the gathering by destroying the tree and assorted presents. Chaplin's bemused response is usually chronicled as an open-minded liberal response from one artist to another. Yet, just to play devil's advocate, maybe Buñuel's performance art-like crushing of Christmas festivity was closer to Chaplin's real feelings. Moreover, even Chaplin was capable of a little tongue-in-cheek holiday commercialization. The first Christmas following the publication of his memoir resulted in the Chaplins' annual holiday card being a family portrait of the comedian's sizable brood ... each reading a copy of the book, often in a foreign edition.

For the superstitious there is an old wives' tale that states that dying on Christmas guarantee one's admittance into Heaven. I'm reminded of a curious parallel he had with one of his comedy contemporaries, W.C. Fields. The story goes that late in Fields' life a friend visited the less-than-religious comedian, also an apt description of Chaplin, and found him doing the most atypical of things—leafing through a Bible. When asked what was the gag, Fields responded, "I'm looking for loopholes." Interestingly, when "The Man in the Bright Nightgown," Fields' euphemism for death, came for the red-nosed hero to all blue-nose victims, he came on Christmas, too.[42]

Through the magic of movies, neither comedian has really ever left. Fields, like Chaplin, invariably brought a dark comedy twist (or is that "twisted?") long shot view to the human comedy, which remains forever relevant. Early on, Chaplin himself had inadvertently stumbled onto this when he noted, "I am not a bit funny, really. I am just a little nickel comedian trying to make people laugh. They act as though I were the king of England."[43] For most people, he represented much more.

Paradoxically, or maybe not so paradoxically, for a pioneering auteur of dark comedy, Chaplin's story could not simply end with a Christmas death and an unpretentious burial in Vevey two days later. Like another bizarre unrealized Chaplin project *à la The Freak,* on March 2, 1978, the comedian's grave was found open, and the coffin was gone. Weird speculation immediately became the topic of the day, including the screwy scenario that neo–Nazis had taken the body for a *very* delayed revenge against the *Great Dictator*. As with most budding conspiracy theories, the simplest explanation usually provides the answer. In this case, two bumbling local mechanics, best characterized by Stan Laurel's description of Laurel & Hardy, "two minds without a single thought," had stolen the coffin for ransom in order to buy a garage![44] The two men were eventually caught and tried, and Chaplin's undamaged coffin and remains were re-interred ... under *many* feet of concrete. In the decades since then, reality and black humor, with or without war, seem ever more intertwined. Once again, Vonnegut says it best: "And so it goes."

Epilogue

Kurt Vonnegut described his anti-war novel *Slaughterhouse-Five* (1969) "as so short and jumbled ... because there is nothing intelligent to say about a massacre [war]."[1]

Thomas Maeder observed in his "Afterword" to dark comedy author Will Cuppy's book *The Decline and Fall of Practically Everybody* (1950) that when World War II ended, Cuppy "said he felt that he had died, as though one of the bombs had killed him.... [H]e began to say he had written all he knew how to write, and that he was unable to do any more."[2]

The born-again nihilism of dark comedy makes it less than a user-friendly genre, especially when wrapped around the insanity of war. The seeming pointlessness of a genre defined by absurdity, death and man as beast might, for argument's sake, still be used as a rallying cry for a change, if enough of a war-related shock value is present. Yet conscientious artists who apply their gifts to such a cause sometimes end up as war victims, too. For example, after writing the cathartic *Slaughterhouse-Five* and stumbling into a bestseller, a guilty Vonnegut attempted suicide; Cuppy succeeded.[3] The genre forces one to examine life (especially during the blatant absurdity of war) as some sort of runaway train with no apparent destination other than death. Even without war, the train metaphor inspired Carl Sandburg's darkly comic poem "Limited" (1916). The poet's narrator contemplates the transitory nature of life among rushing commuters. Predictably, Sandburg's figure eventually meets an unthinking wall; When asked his (philosophical) destination, a fellow traveler replies "Omaha."[4]

Regardless, it seems most appropriate that Francis Ford Coppola adapted Joseph Conrad's 1902 novella about traders in Africa, *The Heart of Darkness*, into an anti-war film about Vietnam, *Apocalypse Now* (1979), if for no other reason than to repeat the dying words of the missing man Kurtz, "The horror; the horror." There it is, the nakedly haunting realization that even death provides no objective truth about the hypocrisy of humanity. The confident resiliency of Chaplin fortunately made him up to the task of wrestling with his dark comedy war trilogy, though like Vonnegut after *Slaughterhouse-Five,* his later lesser work seemed drained by the effort. (Interestingly, also like Chaplin, Vonnegut also wrote an anti–Joseph McCarthy work, the 1965 novel *God Bless You, Mr. Rosewater*.[5]) Still, Chaplin's evolving thoughts about the genre, via the trilogy, anticipate America's eventual dark comedy transition, too. For example, *Cue* critic William Wolf wrote the year after the comedian's death:

> A major element of Chaplin's genius was a knack for being ahead of his time. Not only was *Monsieur Verdoux* (1947) released when political hostility raged against him, but it was also a black comedy made long before that genre was appreciated.[6]

Like Pablo Picasso's painting *Guernica*, which helped both inspire this book and make a direct link for me to Chaplin's *The Great Dictator* (1940), drastic events in society provoke drastic events in art. Creativity does not spring from a vacuum. "T.S. Eliot said that the emergence of a new ... form always occasions a revolution in consciousness."[7] Sad to say, the artistic effect of this domino effect often takes time. Thus, a brave iconoclast like Chaplin risked losing his audience by ever increasing the dark comedy quotient in his trilogy. Viewers much prefer embracing mind candy to being reminded of the harsh "horror" of a reality which once would have pigeonholed any surreal nightmare as merely an exercise in avant-garde art, *à la* Luis Buñcel and Salvador Dali's *Andalusian Dog* (1928).

Since dark comedy is that rare genre which risks thumbing its nose at the audience, those artists who embrace and survive often have a sort of absurdist moxie themselves. For example, Nobel Prize–winning dark comedy author Saul Bellow once described to his oldest son an unnamed cinematic example of the genre which applied equally to the "what the hell" attitude of both the senior Bellow and Chaplin. Fittingly, for dark comedy, the tale was also the most random of addenda to an already disjointed conversation. Moreover, for a purely coincidental Chaplin link, it involves a silent comedian with whom the Tramp's creator had worked:

> Your old pal Oscar Tarcov thought Ben Turpin was a very funny man. In a brief film sketch about moving into a new apartment, Turpin carried furniture up several flights and carefully arranged it. Turpin's redecorating concluded when he threw a couch through the living room window, shattering the glass. Asked why he did not open the window first, he answered, "I'm an artist. I can't be bothered."[8]

Moxie or not, World War II had had a profound impact upon Charlie's perception of dark comedy. One might paraphrase the earlier description of Cuppy's post-war feelings and apply them to Chaplin: "The conflict had, if not killed, at least further qualified his belief in comedy's ability to change the world's evils." For example, before the release of *The Great Dictator*, Chaplin made a statement in a *New York Times* interview which is incompatible with a man who could make *Monsieur Verdoux:* "Behind [*Dictator*] is the belief that laughter may help check the ... the ... the bad behavior in the world."[9] Though *Dictator* proved controversial, even then many others only half-heartedly bought into the premise. For instance, *Picturegoer and Film Weekly* critic Wm. H. Mooring penned "An Open Letter to Charlie Chaplin" in August of 1940:

> But, Charlie, the war cannot be halted: the struggle for democracy and freedom will not wait. The people who are fighting the dictators cannot stop in their tracks, nor can the broken victims of the dictators of Europe wait for the sustenance and now courage which they hope to find in the warmth of living friendships on this happier side of the Atlantic which you once crossed as a Tramp. If you genuinely wish to caricature the dirty deeds of the painter from Hofbrau [Hitler] and his bedaggered friend [Mussolini], it seems they must have gone quite far enough by this time to provide you with a "meaty" screenplay.... We know that you have completed filming on "Production Number 6" [*Dictator*] many months ago and that your very closest friends declared it was your best picture ever.... What are you waiting for? The end of the war and the "New Order?"
> Impatiently yours,
> Wm. H. Mooring[10]

The writing and passion for peace which Chaplin brings to his stepping-out-of-character close to *Dictator* not only stops the picture cold, it undercuts the dark comedy thrust of the movie. Earlier chapters herein have discussed the modern revisionist justifications for that close, which are entirely legitimate ... but the ending still derails the nature of the two hours of dark comedy which proceed it: Life is absurd, bad people continue to exist, and death is forever around us. Paradoxically, Chaplin's previously cited *New York Times* interview perhaps provides an insight into this dark comedy dilemma—call it "the people factor":

> I laugh at the dictators—but they are not inhuman, really, in [*Dictator*].... [A]t one point as the dictator I do a dance with the world [where the balloon globe ultimately explodes].... And there the poor madman is something else than ridiculous: [H]e is one little man with the whole wide, vast unconquerable world, and he thinks the world is his.[11]

Yet, Hitler and Joseph Stalin made excellent "little man" attempts at conquering the world, with the latter even changing teams (more absurdity) during the Second World War. The point is, to paraphrase Stanley Kubrick's modern mantra for the genre, "If people are involved, the project is always fated to fail," be it the "perfectly planned" robbery (*The Killing,* 1956), the ultimate "safeguard" doomsday device (*Dr. Strangelove,* 1964), the "flawless" computer Hal (*2001: A Space Odyssey,* 1968), the most "progressive" therapy to prevent antisocial behavior (*A Clockwork Orange,* 1971), and "so it goes." Dark comedy is about *not* getting humanity together; it is a race to a Darwinian extinction. One might liken it to a darker variation of Woody Allen's gag about nature merely being a giant restaurant, with each creature eating the next animal up the food chain. The logical conclusion to that thinking-joking is man destroying man.

Chaplin's personal plea to close *Dictator* is not unlike the ending to H.G. Wells' anti-utopian novella *The Time Machine* (1895). The time traveler has seen the far distant future and realizes it is all but hopeless; Earth is ruled by subterranean monster men called Morlocks, feeding upon another line of mankind named the Eloi. The latter are essentially fatted cattle living on the surface purely as prey for the Morlocks. (When *Machine* was written the victimized Eloi also doubled as a subtextual suggestion that modern man was becoming too decadent.) Regardless, the traveler visits this future hell and somehow pinballs back to the civilized safety of the 1890s. Yet even then, after experiencing the Darwinian proof he had always imagined coming true, he goes back to the future, attempting to make a difference, simply because it is the right thing to do.

One could posit the same justification for the controversial close to *Dictator*. It needed to be done, and done earlier, but did the comedian really think his words would stop war? Just as Don Delillo called the assassination of President John F. Kennedy "the seven seconds that broke the back of the American century," the almost seven years of World War II could be said to have further broken/darkened Chaplin's perspective on comedy.[12] One might liken his sense of betrayed idealism to the mushrooming popularity of dark comedy in the 1960s. As black humor historian Douglas M. Davis has suggested, maybe American's affinity for the genre is an outgrowth of the nation's fundamental ties to the populism of anything-is-possible: "These beliefs do not stay the course [like the early promise of the 1960s going unfulfilled]. [Many core values] are rigid and break when they fall. Therein lies an invitation for black comedy."[13] Japanese scholar Kōji Numasawa assumes the same pose in his essay "Black Humor: An American Aspect."[14]

A similar disillusionment is at the heart of Chaplin reversing his application of dark comedy with *Monsieur Verdoux,* just as it drew the genre to 1960s center stage. Of Chaplin's black humor trilogy, *Verdoux*'s final installment took a forever listing genre to a zone which could never be listless again. That is, in *Shoulder Arms* (1918), Charlie the soldier merely treats dark comedy as an occupational hazard of war. With few exceptions, such as Charlie's sniper sequence, the genre is even day-to-day handy, such as opening a bottle of wine by merely putting its top above the trench so as to have it shot off by the enemy. *Dictator* essentially pushed the dark comedy genre further by having the title character based upon Hitler. However, with a variation of the Tramp available as the barber, and the "final solution" (the Nazi plan to exterminate all Jews a year away), the Hitler the world saw in 1940 is not remotely close to our collective vision of him *now*. One is reminded of the opening to L.P. Hartley's novel *The Go-Between* (1953): "The past is a foreign country; they do things differently there." Indeed, Chaplin frequently stated after the Second World War that he would not have produced *Dictator* had he known what the Nazis were doing, but the stereotypical concentration death camps of which the filmmaker spoke were not yet in place upon the film's release. *Dictator* is that rare dark comedy that became darker with the passing years, once the Nazi atrocities of 1941 to 1945 were revealed.

The documentary *50 Children: The Rescue Mission of Mr. and Mrs. Kraus* (2013), about an American couple's success in saving these Jewish youngsters from 1939 Nazi Europe, reveals the most gut-wrenching of details about what might have been. At this point Germany would have been content to just have all Jews leave their growing empire. But country after country, including the United States, had orchestrated small anti–Semitic immigration quotas which turned away countless Jews. One of the Krauses' lucky 50 would later tragically reveal: "What people don't understand is at the beginning, [Jews] could get out. Everybody could get out. Nobody would let us *in*. Everybody could have been saved. Everyone."[15]

Consequently, many people besides Hitler had blood on their hands, such as the pioneering American automobile manufacturer Henry Ford. His inflammatory anti–Semitic book *The International Jew* (1920, ghostwritten but with his approval), as well as Ford's endorsement of a patently false document, *The Protocols of the Learned Elders of Zion* (an alleged plot for Jewish world domination), continue to poison minds today. Not surprisingly, Hitler was a major fan, with Ford being the *only* American mentioned in the dictator's later memoir–ideology outline *Mein Kampf* (*My Struggle,* 1925–1926).[16] Ford's definitive biographer, Vincent Curcio, states in his largely positive Oxford-published text:

> It is fair to say that next to Hitler, Ford was the most influential Anti-Semite ever, with the possible exception of Martin Luther ... though Ford never advocated violence toward Jews, much less genocide ... Ford's view were based in part on the myth that Jews were providing money for armaments to promote the violence and destruction of war.[17]

As late as 1938, the year of the infamous "Cristal Night" (the horrific evening when the Nazis razed synagogues, pillaged Jewish stores, and beat and killed countless Jews), the Ford company was assisting in building truck companies in Germany, all in the name of profit—the very sin the car manufacturer held against the Jews. Moreover, beyond this hypocritical blind eye towards the anti–Semitic horrors unfolding in Europe, a further sickening paradox was now in the making. Many of these German-Ford trucks would soon be adapted for military use against the Allies in 1939, when World War II began in Europe.

An additional twist on this tangential Chaplin-Ford link would take one back to an earlier chapter's examination of *Modern Times* (1936). Ford's invention of the assembly line, which reduced workers to quasi-robots without a craft, so helped inspired *Times* that Chaplin footnoted Ford in the film by casting actor Allan Garcia, who resembled the industrialist, as the company boss.[18] Given both Chaplin's fierce pride in having people think he was Jewish (not true, but his beloved half-brother Sydney was), and later risking his career on a controversial film (*Dictator*) in the Jews' defense, is it not possible that Ford's highly anti–Semitic beliefs might have also contributed to the comedian casting a "twin" to the tycoon in *Modern Times*? Speculation or not, period assembly line workers got the message. For example, Ford biographer Curcio noted that when *Modern Times* scenes showing

Charlie at the mercy of mechanical routines of the modern plant [were] first shown in Pittsburgh to audiences of steelworkers, nobody laughed. It was simply too true to be funny. In essence, this endless repetition of one single task had little to differentiate it from the work of machines ... in part because there were not yet machines that could do them.[19]

From the beginning of Chaplin's watershed trilogy of dark comedy, he was aware that governments stoked fear as a smokescreen for their own devices. Indeed, Chaplin was part of the program in his war bond tours of 1918. Yet, even then, and in his first installment of the trilogy *Shoulder Arms,* he attempted to play down the evil German stereotype so prevalent during World War I. Of course, the great critical and commercial success of that groundbreaking dark comedy, not to mention how Chaplin was feted like an American Caesar on that bond tour, undoubtedly contributed to the sense that he could do no wrong. Link this sentiment to that dangerous artistic belief one can either read the public's pulse or point it in the right direction, and a filmmaker often pushes a watershed movie past the embrace of a mainstream audience. Such was definitely the case for *Monsieur Verdoux,* though fissures in the public's embrace of Chaplin had already occurred with *Dictator.*

Even without Chaplin's messy personal life, which helped derail *Verdoux,* one can find a similar period problem with the genre by way of the popular writer-director Preston Sturges. For example, Sturges' satirical skewering of the Capra world via screwball comedy in *The Miracle of Morgan's Creek* (1944), was the *piece de resistance* of his many hit 1940s pictures. Yet, when Sturges made the now celebrated dark comedy *Unfaithfully Yours* (1948), the public was equally appalled over just the possible ways an imaginative husband (Rex Harrison) *might* murder a potentially cheating spouse (Linda Darnell). How could two such gifted artists consistently succeed with the American public, only to crash and burn when they pushed the comedy envelope into pure dark comedy, with no mitigating Tramp? Answers might include: being *too* far ahead of the times, the lack of someone with whom to identify, and a pinch of artistic megalomania.

Though this newspaper cartoon defense of Chaplin first appeared after a 1920s controversy, it better serves his mistreatment during the McCarthy witch-hunting 1950s (by permission of the estate of Rollin Kirby Post).

Paradoxically, playwright Bertolt Brecht (1898–1956), a Chaplin friend and fellow artist also victimized by McCarthy, had written and produced a play, *The Caucasian Chalk Circle* (1948), which assumed a radically different perspective. Consider this seminal axiom from *Circle*'s narrator: "Terrible is the temptation to do good!"[20] This is a double irony, since Brecht's normal *oeuvre* is closer to dark comedy, at least in the sense that humanity is less than positive. Yet, in Brecht's *Circle,* good manages to triumph. For Chaplin's *Verdoux* and most dark comedies, just the opposite maxim is true: "Terrible is the temptation to do evil." Of course, neither outlook helped either artist, since both individuals were politically forced from the U.S. by the early 1950s.

Period success with black humor was best tied to that new popular movie genre *film noir*. While the movies *Double Indemnity* (1944), *The Big Sleep* (1946), *Out of the Past* (1947) and others like them fairly oozed dark comedy, the component was sublimated to noir's fresh take on the mainstream mystery–tough guy detective story. *Verdoux* and *Unfaithfully Yours* are not without some noir characteristics; yet neither one gives the viewer someone with whom to relate, other than any lingering vestiges of the Tramp in *Verdoux*.

A final take on Chaplin's changing perspective on dark comedy through *Shoulder Arms, Dictator,* and *Verdoux* might "read" along the following lines. First, while *Arms* was a groundbreaking example of the genre, discouraged by the Hollywood film industry save for Chaplin's best friend Douglas Fairbanks, the rabid hatred for the Kaiser was such that Chaplin could showcase a restrained version of black humor without alienating the public. Somewhat the same principle applied to Hitler and *Dictator,* though the leader hardly hit the negative factor of the 1918 Kaiser. Moreover, who could have imagined Hitler would soon implement his "final solution" towards the Jews? Next, add in the extreme American isolationism which still existed. And then, sad to say, factor in America's own rampant anti–Semitism. Because of these factors, *Dictator* would receive mixed reviews. However, the controversy of attacking Hitler, this being Chaplin's first talking film, and the lingering presence of the Tramp-like barber made *Dictator* the comedian's top-grossing picture. Seven years later, *Verdoux* was Chaplin without a Charlie net. It was pure dark comedy, asking a 1940s audience to accept and laugh at a quasi-biography of a real Bluebeard. Even without Chaplin's scandals, its negative U.S. reception is no more surprising than the failure of Sturges' brilliant *Unfaithfully Yours*.

What made Americans increasingly embrace dark comedy from the 1960s on, as well as more fully appreciate during this decade Chaplin's evolving evolution of the genre, was a growing distrust of government. This was driven by America's first full TV coverage of a war (Vietnam, an unpopular U.S.-manufactured war), followed by the equally reported Watergate scandal. Of course, governments have been letting the U.S. down since 1776, but the transparency factor has increasingly gone steroid. With the ever-expanding social media phenomenon, everyone is a potential whistle-blower. Perhaps the future will present us with fewer Gulf of Tonkin–type lies, which made the Vietnam War possible. But still, dark comedy has never been more relevant.

Chaplin's 1940s black humor message of how easily all governments manipulate citizens was also articulately explained during this same period by one of the Nazi masters of the process, high-ranking German leader Hermann Göring. Convicted of war crimes by the Nuremberg tribunal in 1946, he cheated the hangman by committing suicide. What follows is Göring's breezy explanation of how easy it is to dupe the public—any public—into war:

> Why, of course, the people don't want war. Why would some poor slob on a farm want to risk his life in a war when the best he can get out of it is to come back to his farm in one piece? Naturally, the common people don't want war, neither in Russia nor in England, nor in America, nor in Germany. That is understood. But after all, it is the leaders of the country who determine the policy and it is always a simple matter to drag the people along, whether it is a democracy or a Fascist dictatorship or a parliament or a Communist dictatorship. The people can always be brought to the bidding of the leaders. That is easy. All you have to do is to tell them they are being attacked and denounce the pacifists for lack of patriotism and exposing the country to danger. It works the same way in any country.[21]

It is still all too typical that the public tends to want to kill the messenger. For instance, if *Verdoux* disturbed the viewer, ultimately the same was true of Chaplin, since in shedding Charlie he revealed "what he must have thought [was] a more serious and in that sense more 'real' aspect of himself."[22] And since the picture was essentially rejected in the U.S., so was Chaplin. This might be pigeonholed as the aforementioned phenomenon of "artistic megalomania," in which a filmmaker feels he can do no wrong and pushes his ideas beyond his audience. Yet, at the time (1947) Chaplin had a more logical explanation for the Charlie breakout with *Verdoux,* besides a dark comedy morality tale. As noted in Chapter 9, increasing age encourages an artist to do something new.[23]

Coming full circle to this text's beginning, why not say that Chaplin was simply geared to the dark side? In a candid interview two decades after *Verdoux* he confessed:

> I've never been obsessed with friendship.... One's friends die or they drop out of one's life and, it's an awful thing to say but one doesn't miss them.... In the first place I'm shy. In the next place I'm busy. People usually think I'm very sad, but I'm not sad. I am not a bit sad.[24]

For anyone, who might take this confession as a pure Chaplin negative, one can easily say that the comedian was just the opposite of what the 1970s Tom Wolfe satirized as "radical chic."[25] The phrase came out of a gathering Leonard Bernstein put together for the Black Panther Party, a study in absurdism in which one lampoons social elites who endorse leftist groups to affect both worldliness and garner prestige ... even if the cause is incongruous to their traditional power positions. In contrast, Chaplin at times acted with a degree of political naiveté, yet his motives were honest and loyal, even when his position was *not* garnering anything remotely connected to prestige. Indeed, the conservative right was crucifying him for his steadfastness to unpopular causes. For Chaplin, it was prestige be damned, whatever the cost.

Chaplin was also implying, do *not* fall into that hollow trap of old men sending the young off to fight in war, and think they are doing them a favor. As Kurt Vonnegut said in his last book, 2005's *A Man Without a Country* (a title which echoes Chaplin's belief in being an international citizen), "When I got home from the Second World War, my Uncle Dan clapped me on the back, and he said, 'You're a man now.' So I killed him. Not really but I certainly felt like doing it."[26] (These thoughts are not dissimilar from those of the young German soldier on his last furlough home in the novel *All Quiet on the Western Front,* when his father and the other old men see only macho glory in war, any war.)

Regardless of how one interprets Chaplin and/or his game-changing dark comedies, my favorite summation of the man and his movies comes in a subtextual joke from the comedian's palmy days in Hollywood. Cleverly covering his ego *and* his liberal politics, the story tells of Chaplin responding to an actor asking how he should play a scene: "Behind me and to the left."[27]

Filmography

1918 (October 20) *Shoulder Arms* **(First National, 4 reels).**
Script-Producer-Director: Charles Chaplin. Photography: Roland H. Totheroh. Cast: Chaplin (Tramp/soldier), Edna Purviance (French girl), Sydney Chaplin (soldier/Kaiser Wilhelm), Henry Bergman (Heavy German Sergeant/Field Marshal von Hindenburg/Bartender), Albert Austin (American soldier/German soldier/Kaiser's chauffeur), Tom Wilson (Training camp sergeant), Jack Wilson (German crown prince), John Rand, Park Jones (American soldiers), Loyal Underwood (small German officer).

1940 (October 15) *The Great Dictator* **(United Artists, 126 minutes).**
Script-Producer-Director: Charles Chaplin. Photography: Roland H. Totheroh, Karl Struss. Assistant Directors: Dan James, Robert Meltzer, Wheeler Dryden. Music: Chaplin, including paraphrasing of Wagner, Brahms. Musical Director: Meredith Wilson and an uncredited Chaplin. Arrangers: Edward Powell, David Raksin. Musical Director: Alfred Newman. Art Director: J. Russell Spencer. Editor: Willard Nico. Sound: Percy Townsend, Glenn Rominger. Coordinator: Henry Bergman. Cast: Chaplin (Adenoid Hynkel/Jewish German Tramp–like soldier-barber), Paulette Goddard (Hannah), Jack Oakie (Benzino Napaloni), Henry Daniell (Garbitsch), Reginald Gardiner (Schultz), Billy Gilbert (Herring), Maurice Moskovick (Mr. Jaeckel), Emma Dunn (Mrs. Jaeckel), Bernard Gorcey (Mr. Mann), Paul Weigel (Mr. Agar), Grace Hayle (Madame Napaloni), Carter DeHaven (Ambassador), Chester Conklin (barber shop customer), Hank Mann, Eddie Gribbon, Richard Alexander (storm troopers), Leo White (Hynkel's barber), Lucien Prival (officer).

1947 (April 11) *Monsieur Verdoux* **(United Artists, 122 minutes).**
Script-Producer-Director: Charles Chaplin. Photography: Roland Totheroh, Curt Courant. Cameraman: Wallace Chewning. Associate Directors: Robert Florey, Wheeler Dryden. Assistant Director: Rex Bailey. Art Director: John Beckman. Editor: Willard Nico. Music: Chaplin. Musical Director: Rudolph Schrager. Sound: James T. Corrigan. Costumes: Drew Tetrick. Makeup: William Knight. Hair stylist: Hedvig M. Jornd (and an uncredited Chaplin). Cast: Charles Chaplin (Monsieur Henri Verdoux/Narrator), Martha Raye (Annabella Bonheur), Isobel Elsom (Marie Grosnay), Marilyn Nash (the girl), Robert Lewis (Monsieur Bottello), Ada-May (Annette), Marjorie Bennett (maid), Helen High (Yvonne), Margaret Hoffman (Lydia Floray), Irving Bacon (Pierre Couvais), Edwin Mills (Jean Couvais), Virginia Brissac (Carlotte Couvais), Almira Sessions (Lena Couvais), Edna Morgan (Phoebe Couvais), Bernard J. Nedell (Prefect), Charles Evans (Detective Morrow), Arthur Hohl (estate agent), John Harmon (Joe Darwin), Vera Marshe (Mrs. Darwin), William Frawley (Jean La Salle), Fritz Leiber (priest), Fred Karna, Jr. (Mr. Karno), Barry Norton (guest), Pierre Watkin (attorney), Cyril Delevanti (postman), Charles Wagenheim, James Craven (friends), Addison Richards (M. Miller), Franklin Farnum (victim), Herb Vigran (reporter), Boyd Irwin (warder), Paul Newland (guest), Joseph Crehan (broker) Wheaton Chambers (druggist), Frank Reicher (doctor), Wheeler Dryden (salesman), Julius Cramer (executioner), Barbara Slater (flower girl).

Chapter Notes

Preface and Acknowledgments

1. Foster Hirsch, *The Dark Side of the Screen: Film Noir* (New York: A. S. Barnes, 1981), 78.
2. See the author's *Robert Wise: Shadowlands* (Indianapolis: Indiana Historical Society Press, 2012).
3. E.H. Gombrich, *The Story of Art* (London: Phaidon, 1972), 470.
4. See the author's *Screwball Comedy: A Genre of Madcap Romance* (Westport, CT: Greenwood, 1986); *Romantic vs. Screwball Comedy* (Lanham, MD: Scarecrow, 2002).
5. Russell Martin, *PICASSO'S WAR: The Destruction of Guernica, and the Masterpiece That Changed the World* (New York: Dutton, 2002), i.
6. Bill Russell, with Alan Steinberg, *Red and Me: My Coach, My Lifelong Friend* (New York: HarperCollins, 2009), 145.
7. Graham Greene, *A Sort of Life* (1971; rpt. New York: Pocket Books, 1973), 18.
8. William Kelleher Storey, *Writing History* (1996; rpt. New York: Oxford University Press, 2004), 1.

Prologue

1. Ingrid Schaffner, *The Essential Pablo Picasso* (New York: Harry N. Abrams, 1998), 101.
2. Russell Martin, *PICASSO'S WAR: The Destruction of Guernica, and the Masterpiece That Changed the World* (New York: Dutton, 2002).
3. See the author's *American Dark Comedy: Beyond Satire* (Westport, Connecticut: Greenwood, 1996).
4. Julian Smith, *Chaplin* (Boston: Twayne, 1984), 88.
5. Earl Wilson, "It Happened Last Night: Paulette Recalls Charlie," *New York Post*, December 26, 1977, 30.

Chapter 1

1. See the author's *American Dark Comedy: Beyond Satire* (Westport, CT: Greenwood, 1996).
2. Hennig Cohen, "Introduction to Melville," *The Confidence Man* (1857; rpt. New York: Holt, Rinehart and Winston, 1964).
3. Alfredo Bonadeo, *Mark of the Beast: Death and Degradation in the Literature of the Great War* (Lexington: University of Kentucky Press, 1989), 101.
4. Anne Frank, *Anne Frank: The Diary of a Young Girl* (1947; rpt. New York: Pocket Books, 1958), 257.
5. Victor E. Frankl, *Man's Search for Meaning* (1946; rpt. Boston: Beacon, 1992), 54.
6. Ibid., 29.
7. Tadeusz Borowski, *This Way for the Gas, Ladies and Gentleman* (1959; rpt. New York: Penguin, 1986).
8. Steve Lipman, *Laughter in Hell: The Use of Humor During the Holocaust* (1991; rpt. Northvale, NJ: Jason Aronson, 1993).
9. Charlie Chaplin, *My Autobiography* (1964; rpt. New York: Pocket Books, 1966), 33.
10. Charles Chaplin, Jr., with N. Rau and M. Rau, *My Father, Charlie Chaplin* (New York: Random House, 1960), 93.
11. Ibid., 94.
12. Ibid., 196.
13. Chaplin, *My Autobiography,* 209.
14. Michael Chaplin, *I Couldn't Smoke the Grass on My Father's Lawn* (New York: G. P. Putnam's Sons, 1966). 47.
15. Chaplin, *My Autobiography,* 327.
16. Carl Sandburg, "Carl Sandburg Says Chaplin Could Play Serious Drama," in *Authors on Film*, ed. Harry M. Geduld (Bloomington: Indiana University Press, 1972), 264. Originally in *Chicago Daily News*, April 16, 1921, 13.
17. Used periodically in Kurt Vonnegut's classic *Slaughterhouse-Five* (1969; rpt. New York: Dell, 1974).
18. See the author's *American Dark Comedy: Beyond Satire.*
19. See the author's *Groucho & W. C. Fields: Huckster Comedians* (Jackson: University Press of Mississippi, 1994); *Forties Film Funnymen: The Decade's Great Comedians at Work in the Shadow of War* (Jefferson, NC: McFarland, 2010); *W. C. Fields: A Bio-Bibliography* (Westport, CT: Greenwood, 1984).
20. "The Black Humorists," *Time*, February 12, 1965, 94–96.
21. Quoted by Barry Gewen in his "Staying Power" review, *The New York Times,* September 2, 2012, "Book Review" section, 11.
22. Luis Buñuel (trans. Abigail Israel), *My Last Sigh* (1982; rpt. New York: Random House, 1984).

Chapter 2

1. Terry Ramsaye, *A Million and One Nights: A History of the Motion Pictures Through 1925,* 2 vols. (1926; rpt., in vol. 1; New York: Simon and Schuster, 1964), 648–649.
2. Denis Gifford, *Chaplin* (Garden City, NY: Doubleday, 1974), 11.
3. The author's collection, for example F & J. Smith's

Glasgow mixture cigarettes (Great Britain and Ireland), "Cinema Stars No. 4: Charlie Chaplin," circa early 1920s.
   4. R. J. Minney, *Chaplin: The Immortal Tramp* (London: George Newness, 1954), 6.
   5. See both Stephen M. Weissman's essay, "Charlie Chaplin's Film Heroines," *Film History* (Indiana University Press), vol. 8, No. 4, as well as Weissman's book *Chaplin: A Life* (New York: Arcade Publishing, 2008), which includes an Introduction by the comedian's daughter, Geraldine Chaplin.
   6. Weissman, "Charlie Chaplin's Film Heroines," 75.
   7. David Robinson, *Chaplin: His Life and Art* (New York: McGraw-Hill, 1985), 22.
   8. John McCabe, *Charlie Chaplin* (Garden City, NY: Doubleday, 1978), 29.
   9. John McCabe, *Mr. Laurel & Mr. Hardy* (1961; rpt. New York: Signet, 1966), 23.
   10. George De Coulteray, *Sadism in the Movies,* trans. Steve Hult (New York: Medical Press, 1965), 163–177.
   11. See the author's *Charlie Chaplin: A Bio-Bibliography* (Westport, CT: Greenwood, 1983).
   12. McCabe, *Charlie Chaplin,* 39.
   13. Theodore Huff, *Charlie Chaplin* (1951; rpt. New York: Arno Press and the *New York Times,* 1972), 19.
   14. Robinson, *Chaplin: His Life and Art,* 78.
   15. Mack Sennett, as told to Cameron Shipp, *King of Comedy* (1954; rpt. New York: Pinnacle, 1975), 148.
   16. Frank "Kin" Hubbard, *Back Country Folks* (Indianapolis: Abe Martin, 1913), 45.
   17. David Robinson, *The Great Funnies: A History of Film Comedy* (London: Dutton Pictureback, 1969), 43.
   18. Sennett, *King of Comedy,* 29.
   19. Walter Kerr, *The Silent Clowns* (New York: Alfred A. Knopf, 1975), 51.
   20. See the author's "John Bunny: America's First Important Film Comedian," *Literature/Film Quarterly,* vol. 23, No. 2 (1995).
   21. "Death of John Bunny," *London Times,* April 29, 1915, 5-d.
   22. Henry Wysham Lamier, "The Coquelin of the Movies," *World's Work,* March 1915, 577.
   23. James Agee, *A Death in the Family* (1957; rpt. New York: Bantam, 1972), 20.
   24. Louis Delluc, "Max Linder's and Elsie Codd's Views on the Working Method" (1922), in *Focus on Chaplin,* Donald W. McCaffrey, ed. (Englewood Cliffs, NJ: Prentice-Hall, 1971), 55.
   25. Charlie Chaplin, *My Autobiography* (1964; rpt. New York: Pocket Books, 1966), 148.
   26. Charles Chaplin, Jr., with N. Rau and M. Rau, *My Father, Charlie Chaplin* (New York: Random House, 1960), 23.
   27. Charlie Chaplin, "What People Laugh At," *American Magazine* No. 86 (November 1918), 134–137.
   28. Budd Schulberg, *The Disenchanted* (New York: Random House, 1950), 212.
   29. Isabel Quigly, *Charlie Chaplin: Early Comedies* (London: Dutton Pictureback, 1968), 20.
   30. Huff, *Charlie Chaplin,* 50.
   31. Denis Gifford, *Chaplin: The Movie Makers* (Garden City, NY: Doubleday, 1974), 75.
   32. David Robinson, *Charlie Chaplin: Comic Genius* (New York: Harry N. Abrams, 1996), 42.
   33. Peter Cotes and Thelma Niklaus, *The Little Fellow: The Life and Work of Charles Chaplin* (1951; rpt. New York: Citadel, 1965), 106.
   34. Chaplin, *My Autobiography,* 198.
   35. Chaplin, "What People Laugh At," 134–137.
   36. Cotes and Niklaus, *The Little Fellow,* 107.
   37. See the author's *W.C. Fields: A Bio-Bibliography* (Westport, CT: Greenwood, 1984), and *Groucho & W. C. Fields: Huckster Comedians* (Jackson: University Press of Mississippi, 1994).
   38. Chaplin, *My Autobiography,* 461.
   39. A paper on this subject, entitled "Charlie Chaplin and the Progressive Era: The Neglected Politics of a Clown," was presented by the author at the Second International Conference on Humor," Los Angeles, August 25, 1979. It was published in the autumn 1981 issue of *Indiana Social Studies Quarterly,* 10–18.

Chapter 3

   1. "Fairbanks and Chaplin Wall St. Hosts," *New York Sun,* April 9, 1918, 16.
   2. Richard Schickel, "Introduction: The Tramp Transformed," in *The Essential Chaplin: Perspectives on the Life and Art of the Great Comedian,* ed. Richard Schickel (Chicago: Ivan R. Dee, 2006), 6.
   3. Ibid., 14.
   4. Philip Norman, *John Lennon: The Life* (New York: HarperCollins, 2008), 348.
   5. Roger Manvell, *Chaplin* (Boston: Little, Brown, 1974), 159.
   6. Isabel Quigly, *Charlie Chaplin: Early Comedies* (London: Dutto Pictureback, 1968), 8.
   7. Kevin Brownlow, *The War, the West, and the Wilderness* (London: Secker & Warburg, 1978), 39.
   8. Ibid., 40.
   9. Clement F. Chandler, "Max Linder Comes Back!," *Motion Picture,* February and March, 1917; Rhea Irene Kimball, "Max Linder, Soldier, Actor, Gentleman," *Motion Picture Classic,* April 4, 1917.
   10. Robert F. Moss, *Charlie Chaplin* (1975; rpt. New York: Harvest Books, 1977), 65.
   11. "Charlie Chaplin Will Soon Don Khaki [Army] Garb," *Los Angeles Times,* April 15, 1918 Part 2:1.
   12. Ibid.
   13. Quoted in Charles J. Maland's *Chaplin and American Culture* (Princeton, NJ: Princeton University Press, 1989), 37.
   14. Raoul Sobel and David Francis, *Chaplin: Genesis of a Clown* (London: Quartet Books, 1977), 155.
   15. Julian Johnson, "Charles, Not Charlie," *Photoplay,* September 1918, 117.
   16. William Dodgson Bowman, *Charlie Chaplin: His Life and Art* (1931; rpt. New York: Haskell House, 1974), 74.
   17. "'We Must Count on Three More Years of War,' Says Taft," *New York Herald Tribune,* April 25, 1918, 10.
   18. "Roosevelt Boosts for Liberty Bonds," *Los Angeles Times,* April 3, 1918, 1.

19. "Mob Resents Disloyal Remarks and Finds Recourse in a Rope," *Los Angeles Times*, April 5, 1918, 1.
20. "Mobs Try to Hang 3 in Comden for Disparaging [War Bond] Loan Drive," *New York Herald*, April 21, 1918, Section 1:5; "'Ku Klux Klan' of Birmingham Begins Drive...," *New Orleans Times-Picayune*, May 1, 1918, 1.
21. "Tarred for Refusing to Buy Liberty Bonds," *Atlanta Constitution*, April 28, 1918.
22. "Teaching of Enemy Speech in American Schools Roundly Denounced," *Los Angeles Times*, April 4, 1918, Section 1:2.
23. "German Propagandists Attack Liberty Loan," *Los Angeles Times*, April 18, 1918, Section 2:1.
24. Heywood Brown, "New Midnight Frolic Proves to Be the Best of the Series," *New York Tribune*, April 26, 1918, 11.
25. For instance, see "*The Kaiser: 'The Beast of Berlin*'" ad in the *Raleigh News and Observer*, April 14, 1918, 6.
26. "Wham" cartoon, *Raleigh News and Observer*, April 16, 1918, 4; "Pouring In!" cartoon, *Atlanta Constitution*, April 28, 1918, 1.
27. "CAN Vegetables, Fruit & the Kaiser, Too," National War Garden Commission, 1918 (collection of the author).
28. Ibid.
29. "Mob Lynches Negro in Courthouse Yard," and "Negro Lynched in Louisiana," in the *Atlanta Constitution*, April 23, 1918, Section 1:1.
30. "'Birth of a Nation' Here All Next Week at Rialto Theatre, "*Atlanta Constitution*, April 14, 1918, Section F:12.
31. Grace Kingsley, "Chaplin Departs: Doctor Said He Must't [sic] But He Did," *Los Angeles Times*, April 2, 1918, Section 2:3.
32. Ibid.
33. David Robinson, *Chaplin: His Life and Art* (New York: McGraw-Hill, 1985), 229.
34. Mary E. Porte, "Charlie Chaplin, Cheerful Comedian," *Picture-Play Weekly*, April 1915, 1–4.
35. Ray W. Frohman, "Charlie Chaplin," *Los Angeles Herald*, December 2, 1919.
36. "Fairbanks and Chaplin Thrill Wall St. Hosts," *New York Sun*, April 9, 1918, 16.
37. "Street Rallies Coax Crowds to Buy War Bonds," *New York Telegram*, April 8, 1918, 1.
38. "[Chaplin War Bond Coverage]," *New York Herald Tribune*, April 9, 1918.
39. "Billions in Bonds Now Aim for City," *New York American*, April 9, 1918, 3.
40. "Liberty Loan Rally," *Wall Street Journal*, April 9, 1918, 10.
41. "20,000 Throng Wall St. to Hear Movie Stars Tell How to Win War," *New York Tribune*, April 9, 1918, 8.
42. "Fairbanks and Chaplin Thrill Wall St. Hosts."
43. Ibid.
44. Ibid.
45. Ibid.
46. Grace Kingsley, "Illiteracy, Note," *Los Angeles Times*, April 12, 1918, Section 2:3.
47. "Mary Pickford Convinces 20,000 in Wall St. Loan Should Succeed," *New York Tribune*, April 12, 1918, 6.
48. Ibid.
49. "Mary Pickford 'Innocent Thing' Says Boy Seized at Loan Rally," *New York Herald*, April 14, 1918, Section 1:2.
50. "Booklet of Hate Issued to Help Americans Win," *New York Tribune*, April 19, 1918, 4.
51. "Myron T. Herrick, 'Pat' O'Brien and Marie Dressler Sell Bonds," *New York Tribune*, April 11, 1918, 6.
52. "Bill Hart at Kinema," *Los Angeles Times*, April 11, 1918, Section 2:3.
53. "Mary Pickford Holds Up a Stage Coach," *Los Angeles Times*, April 17, 1918, Section 3:15; "Kings of Movies Raise $787,000 for Loan Bonds," *New York Tribune*, April 18, 1918, 9.
54. "...Actresses and Actors Doing Remarkable Work to Aid Uncle Sam," *New Orleans Times-Picayune*, April 21, 1918, C-10.
55. "Charlie Chaplin Puts 'Pep' in Crowd of 4,000," *Richmond Times-Dispatch*, April 12, 1918, 1–2.
56. "Kings of Movies Raise $787,000 for Loan Bonds."
57. Mary Pickford, "The 'Movies' in War Time" (syndicated), *Raleigh News and Observer* (North Carolina), April 28, 1918, 4.
58. Brownlow, *The War, the West, and the Wilderness*, 3.
59. "Thousand Pulpits Urge Liberty Loan," *New York Sun*, April 8, 1918, 3.
60. Harriette Underhill, "Capturing Charlie Chaplin," *New York Tribune*, May 12, 1918, Section 4:5.
61. Ibid.
62. "Charlie Chaplin Comes on Friday," *Raleigh News and Observer*, April 11, 1918, 1.
63. "Charlie and His Acrobatics Sell $227,000 Bonds," *New Orleans Times-Picayune*, April 24, 1918, 7.
64. "Chaplin Parade to Boom Liberty Loan Called Off," *New Orleans Times-Picayune*, April 23, 1918, 1, 4.
65. "Charlie Chaplin Puts 'Pep' in Crowd of 4,000," 1.
66. "Chaplin's First Speech In State at Rocky Mt. [and Wilson]," *Raleigh News and Observer*, April 14, 1918, Section 1:8.
67. "Liberty Loan Goes Beyond Half Way Point in Raleigh," *Raleigh News and Observer*, April 13, 1918, 1–2.
68. Ibid.
69. Ibid.
70. "Big Demonstration at Rocky Mt. Friday," *Raleigh News and Observer*, April 18, 1918, 5.
71. "Chaplin Traveled the Freight Elevator," *Raleigh News and Observer*, April 14, 1918, Section 1:11.
72. Ibid.
73. "8,000 People Buy Bonds from Charlie Chaplin," *Atlanta Constitution*, April 18, 1918, 1.
74. Ibid.
75. "Charlie Chaplin Coming Tuesday for Great Rally," *New Orleans Times-Picayune*, April 22, 1918, 1.
76. "Chaplin and His Acrobatics Sell $227,000 Bonds," *New Orleans Times-Picayune*, April 24, 1918, 1.
77. Ibid.

78. "Charlie Chaplin Coming Tuesday for Great Rally," 1.
79. Ibid.
80. "Chaplin Parade to Boom Liberty Loan Called Off," 1.
81. Ibid., 4.
82. "Chaplin and His Acrobatics Sell $227,000 Bonds," 7.
83. Ibid.
84. Ibid.
85. Kingsley, "Chaplin Departs: Doctors Said He Must'[sic] But He Did."
86. Underhill, "Capturing Charlie Chaplin."
87. Theodore Huff, *Charlie Chaplin* (1951; rpt. New York: Arno Press and the *New York Times*, 1972), 87; David Robinson, *Chaplin: His Life and Art* (New York: McGraw-Hill, 1985), 238.
88. Underhill, "Capturing Charlie Chaplin."
89. Ibid.
90. "[Chaplin departure piece]," *Moving Picture World*, May 18, 1918.
91. "Chaplin Sells Liberty Bonds," *Nashville Banner*, April 19, 1918, 7.
92. "Charlie Chaplin Is Welcomed by Monster Crowd," *Nashville Tennessean and American*, April 19, 1918, 5.

Chapter 4

1. Kevin Brownlow, *The War, the West, and the Wilderness* (London: Secker & Warburg, 1978), 42.
2. *Hearts of the World* ad, *New York Tribune*, April 21, 1918, Section 4:7.
3. Richard Schickel, *D.W. Griffith: An American Life* (New York: Simon and Schuster, 1984), 343.
4. William K. Everson, *American Silent Film* (New York: Oxford University Press, 1978), 98.
5. Grace Kingsley, "Griffith Returns," *Los Angeles Times*, April 19, 1918, Section 2:3.
6. Lillian Gish, conversation with the author, "The Movies: D.W. Griffith and Lillian Gish: Broken Blossoms" (Bloomington, Indiana: Indiana University Auditorium Program, March 15, 1981).
7. *The Kaiser, the Beast of Lon Berlin* ad, *New York Tribune* April 1, 1918, 11.
8. Michael F. Blake, *The Films of Lon Chaney* (1998; rpt. New York: Madison Books, 2001), 83.
9. "Great Picture Still Turning Away Thousands in New York," *Atlanta Constitution*, April 7, 1918, B-14.
10. "Life of Kaiser Shows at Tulane [Theatre]," *New Orleans Times-Picayune*, April 14, 1918, C-8.
11. Charlie Chaplin, *My Autobiography* (1964; rpt. New York: Pocket Books, 1966), 227.
12. "On the Screen," *New York Tribune*. April 29, 1918, 9.
13. "Mary Pickford at Globe [Theatre]," *New Orleans Times-Picayune*, April 14, 1918, C-9.
14. "Fairbanks Brings Joy to the Strand," *New Orleans Times-Picayune*, April 28, 1918, C-11; "Douglas Fairbanks Still the Athlete in New Picture, 'Mr. Fix-It,'" *New York Tribune*, April 22, 1918, 11.
15. "Douglas Fairbanks at Forsyth Theatre," *Atlanta Constitution*, April 28, 1918, F-2.

16. "Mary Is Honored: Picture Star Lunches with Country's Head," *Los Angeles Times*, April 9, 1918, Section 2:3.
17. "Not Fair, Says Mrs. Fairbanks," *Los Angeles Times*, April 13, 1918, Section 1:3.
18. "Owen Moore Says He'll Act in Own Protection," *Los Angeles Times*, April 14, 1918, Section 2:1.
19. Ibid.
20. "Not Fair, Says Mrs. Fairbanks."
21. "Charlie Chaplin's Antics Interest Spectators," *New York Herald*, April 15, 1918, Section 2:9.
22. "Big Twin Program Showing at Strand," *New Orleans Times-Picayune*, May 12, 1918, PC-11.
23. David Robinson, *Chaplin: His Life and Art* (New York: McGraw-Hill, 1985), 229.
24. Ibid.
25. "Chaplin Soon," *Los Angeles Times*, April 14, 1918, Section 3:1.
26. "Dog Gone, Sad Story of Grief," *New Orleans Times-Picayune*, May 19, 1918, C-10; see also Harriette Underhill, "Capturing Charlie Chaplin," *New York Tribune*, May 12, 1918, Section 4:5.
27. Paul Fussell, *The Great War and Modern Memory* (1975; rpt. New York: Oxford University Press, 1977), 313.
28. By a Y.M.C.A. Worker, "[Cigarette] Dog Scorns Shells to Help Soldiers," *Richmond Times Dispatch*, October 29, 1918, 3.
29. Kurt Vonnegut, *Slaughterhouse-Five* (1969; rpt. New York: Dell, 1974), 27.
30. Theodore Huff, *Charlie Chaplin* (1951; rpt. New York: Arno Press and the *New York Times*, 1972), 105.
31. *Shoulder Arms* review, *Variety*, October 25, 1918.
32. "Charlie Chaplin Surpassed All Former Fun Making Marks in 'Shoulder Arms,'" *New York Tribune*, October 22, 1918, 7.
33. "Charlie Chaplin in *Shoulder Arms*," *Richmond Times-Dispatch*, November 10, 1918, Section 3:6.
34. See the author's *The Marx Brothers: A Bio-Bibliography* (Westport, CT: Greenwood, 1987); *Groucho & W.C. Fields: Huckster Comedians* (Jackson: University of Mississippi Press, 1994); and *Leo McCarey: From Marx to McCarthy* (Lanham, MD: Scarecrow, 2005).
35. See the author's *Laurel & Hardy: A Bio-Bibliography* (Westport, CT: Greenwood, 1990).
36. Robert F. Moss, *Charlie Chaplin* (1977; rpt. New York: Harvest Book, 1975), 65.
37. See the author's *Film Clowns of the Depression: Twelve Defining Comic Performances*. Jefferson, NC: McFarland, 2007.
38. Chaplin, *My Autobiography*, 234.
39. Lisa K. Stein, *Syd Chaplin: A Biography* (Jefferson, NC: McFarland, 2011), 78.
40. *Charlie Chaplin in the Army* (Chicago: M.A. Donahue & Co., by an arrangement between J. Keeley and Essanay, 1917).
41. *Charlie Chaplin Up in the Air* (Chicago: M.A. Donohue, by an arrangement between J. Keelyey and Essanay, 1917).
42. "Charlie Chaplin Surpassed All Former Fun Making Marks in 'Shoulder Arms,'" *New York Tribune*, October 22, 1918, 7.

43. Ibid.
44. *Shoulder Arms* review, *Variety.*
45. "Chaplin in 'Shoulder Arms,'" *New York American,* October 21, 1918, 12.
46. Kenneth Macgowan, "Charlie Chaplin and the Pure Idea," *New York Tribune,* November 17, 1918, Section 4:5.
47. Ibid.
48. Chaplin, *My Autobiography,* 233.

Chapter 5

1. Richard Meryman, "Chaplin: Ageless Master's Anatomy of Comedy," *Life,* March 10, 1967, 94.
2. Denis Gifford, *Chaplin* (Garden City, NY: Doubleday, 1974), 11.
3. Ricky Moody, "The Girl in the Blue Dress," *New York Times,* November 11, 2012, Book Review Section: 54.
4. Joint movie ad for *Shoulder Arms* and *Borrowed Clothes, New York Sun,* November 17, 1918, 3.
5. David Robinson, *Chaplin: His Life and Art* (New York: McGraw-Hill, 1985), 247.
6. Ibid., 248.
7. Frank "Kin" Hubbard, *Abe Martin the Joker on Facts* (Indianapolis: Abe Martin, 1920), 64.
8. See the author's "Kin Hubbard's Abe Martin: A Figure of Transition in America. Humor," *Indiana Magazine of History,* March 1982, 26.
9. See the author's *W. C. Fields: A Bio-Bibliography* (Westport, CT: Greenwood, 1984), 38.
10. Robinson, *Chaplin: His Life and Art,* 250.
11. Neil A. Grauer, *Remember Laughter: A Life of James Thurber* (Lincoln: University of Nebraska Press, 1995), 48–49.
12. Julian Smith, *Chaplin* (Boston: Twayne, 1984), 53.
13. Lita Grey Chaplin, with Morton Cooper, *My Life with Chaplin* (New York: Dell, 1966), 31–32.
14. Stephen Weissman, *Chaplin: A Life* (New York: Arcade, 2008), 52–53.
15. *The Kid* review, *Exceptional Photoplays,* January/February, 1921.
16. Francis Hackett, *The Kid* review, *New Republic,* March 30, 1921.
17. Robinson, *Chaplin: His Life and Art,* 265.
18. Carl Sandburg, "Visit with Chaplin," *Chicago Daily News,* April 16, 1921.
19. Richard Schickel, *D. W. Griffith: An American Life* (New York: Simon and Schuster, 1984), 215.
20. "Millions in Bonds Are Sold by Women: Chaplin Coming Today," *Memphis Commercial-Appeal,* April 20, 1918, 1.
21. John M. Blum, "Retreat from Responsibility," in *The National Experience: A History of the United States,* Blum, ed. (New York: Harcourt Brace, 1968), 617.
22. George and Willene Hendrick, "Introduction," in Carl Sandburg's *Billy Sunday and Other Poems,* eds. Hendrick and Hendrick (New York: Harcourt Brace, 1993), xviii.
23. Charlie Chaplin, *My Trip Abroad* (New York: Harper and Brothers, 1922), 2.
24. Charlie Chaplin, *My Autobiography* (1964; rpt: New York: Pocket Books, 1966), 284.
25. Chaplin, *My Trip Abroad,* 3.
26. Ibid., 8.
27. Ibid., 5.
28. *Shoulder Arms* program notes, 1922, in the *Shoulder Arms* file, Lincoln Center Performing Arts Library, New York; see also, the *Shoulder Arms* ad, *New York American,* July 19, 1922, 8.
29. Roger Manvell, *Chaplin* (Boston: Little, Brown, 1974), 162.
30. Multiple sources; see the author's *Charlie Chaplin: A Bio-Bibliography* (Westport, CT, 1983).
31. André Bazin, "The Grandeur of Limelight," in *What Is Cinema?,* vol. 2, selected and trans. Hugh Gray (1971; rpt. Los Angeles: University of California Press, 1972), 136.
32. Theodore Huff, *Charlie Chaplin* (1951; rpt. New York: Arno Press and the *New York Times,* 1972), 167.
33. Jean Renoir, *My Life and My Films* (New York: Atheneum, 1974), 43, 205.
34. Ibid., 159.
35. Leo Braudy, *Jean Renoir: The World of His Films* (Garden City, NY: Anchor Books, 1972), 172.
36. Scott Eyman, *Ernst Lubitsch: Laughter in Paradise* (New York: Simon & Schuster, 1993), 103.
37. Huff, *Charlie Chaplin,* 174–175.
38. Herman G. Weinberg, *The Lubitsch Touch: A Critical Study* (1968; rpt. New York: E. P. Dutton, 1971), 56.
39. Eyman, *Ernst Lubitsch: Laughter in Paradise,* 104.
40. Ibid.
41. Weinberg, *The Lubitsch Touch: A Critical Study,* 56.
42. Sergei M. Eisenstein, *The Film Sense,* trans. and ed. Jay Leyda (1942; rpt. New York: Harcourt, Brace & World, 1947), 23.
43. Eyman, *Ernst Lubitsch: Laughter in Paradise,* 104.
44. Robinson, *Chaplin: His Life and Art,* 320.
45. Josef von Sternberg, *Fun in a Chinese Laundry* (1965; rpt. New York: Collier, 1973), 32.
46. Robinson, *Chaplin: His Life and Art,* 385.
47. See the author's *The Marx Brothers: A Bio-Bibliography* (Westport, CT, 1987); and *Groucho & W. C. Fields: Huckster Comedians* (Jackson: University Press of Mississippi, 1994).
48. Cobbett Steinberg, *Reel Facts: The Movie Book of Records* (New York: Vintage Books, 1978), 368.
49. *The Gold Rush* review, *Variety,* July 1, 1925.
50. Mordaunt Hall, *The Gold Rush* review, *New York Times,* August 17, 1925.
51. Chaplin, *My Autobiography,* 327.
52. Will Rogers, "Out for the Jack" (May 18, 1924, syndicated weekly newspaper article), in *Will Rogers' Weekly Articles,* vol. 1, *The Harding/Coolidge Years: 1922–1925,* ed. James M. Smallwood (Stillwater: Oklahoma State University Press, 1980), 235.
53. *The Gold Rush* review, *Variety.*
54. Will Rogers, "We Save Money, Egypt Loses It" (December 14, 1924, syndicated weekly newspaper article), in *Will Rogers Weekly Articles,* 333–334.

55. Manvell, *Chaplin,* 176.
56. Lita Grey Chaplin, *My Life with Chaplin,* 225.
57. Huff, *Charlie Chaplin,* 205.
58. Robinson, *Chaplin: His Life and Art,* 383.
59. J. L. Styan, *The Dark Comedy* (Cambridge, England: Cambridge University Press, 1968), 227.
60. Bruce Webber, "Frederick Neuman, Actor, Director and Interpreter of Becket, Dies at 86," *New York Times,* December 7, 2012, B-15.
61. Susan Kinsolving, "Without," in *Dailies & Rushes* (New York: Grove, 1999), 4.
62. Ibid.
63. See the author's *American Dark Comedy: Beyond Satire* (Westport, CT: Greenwood, 1996).
64. See the author's *Chaplin: A Bibliography* (Westport, CT: Greenwood, 1983); *Leo McCarey: From Marx to McCarthy* (Lanham, MD: Scarecrow Press, 2005); *Groucho & W. C. Fields: Huckster Comedians* (Jackson: University of Mississippi, 1994).
65. André Bazin, "The Virtues and Limitations of Montage," in *What Is Cinema?* vol. 1, selected and trans. Hugh Gray (1958; rpt. Los Angeles: University of California Press, 1967), 52.

Chapter 6

1. "Chaplin Sells Liberty Bonds," *Nashville Banner,* April 19, 1918, 7.
2. Adam Hochschild, *To End All Wars* (2011; rpt. New York: Mariner, 2012), 372.
3. Hew Strachan, *The First World War* (2003; rpt. New York: Penguin, 2004), xvii.
4. Deirdre Donahue, "'Truth' Wrapped in a Mystery in Postwar London," *USA Today,* August 29, 2006, 6-D.
5. Erich Maria Remarque, *All Quiet on the Western Front* (1928; rpt. New York: Crest, 1964), 102.
6. Ibid., 87.
7. Ibid.
8. Robert Graves, *Good-Bye to All That* (1929; rpt. Garden City, NY: Doubleday, 1957), 262.
9. Ernest Hemingway, *A Farewell to Arms* (1929; rpt. New York: Scribner's, 1957), 63.
10. Graves, *Good-Bye to All That,* 109–110, 138.
11. Humphrey Cobb, *Paths of Glory* (New York: Viking, 1935), 174.
12. "Charlie Chaplin Is Welcomed by Monster Crowd," *Nashville Tennessean and America*, April 19, 1918, 5.
13. Ibid.
14. "'City Lights' a Cinch for Big Money Everywhere," *Hollywood Reporter,* January 30, 1931, 3.
15. John S. Cohen, Jr., "Chaplin Triumphs Anew in *City Lights,*" *New York Sun,* February 7, 1931, 6.
16. Gerald Mast, *The Comic Mind: Comedy and the Movies* (Indianapolis: Bobbs-Merrill, 1973), 106.
17. Henri Bergson, "Laughter" (1900), in *Comedy,* ed. Wylie Sypher (Garden City, NY: Doubleday Anchor, 1956), 66–67.
18. "Chaplin Says He Just Had to Make That Speech," *New York World Telegram,* October 19, 1940, 7.
19. Ibid.
20. James Agee, "Comedy's Greatest Era," *Life,* September 3, 1949.
21. Ibid.
22. John S. Cohen, Jr., "Chaplin Triumphs Anew in *City Lights,*" *New York Sun,* February 7, 1931, 6.
23. Thornton Delehanty, "Charlie Chaplin Contributes a Generous Sample of His Genius in *City Lights,*" *New York Post,* February 7, 1931, Section 4:3.
24. James Gow, "Art Without Words," *New York World,* February 7, 1931, 11.
25. Mordaunt Hall, "Chaplin Hilarious in His *City Lights,*" *New York Times,* February 7, 1931, 1.
26. Richard Watts, Jr., "Charlie Chaplin in *City Lights,*" *New York Herald Tribune,* February 7, 1931, 8.
27. "London in Raptures at Chaplin Movie," *New York Times,* February 28, 1931, 22.
28. David Robinson, *Chaplin: His Life and Art* (New York: McGraw-Hill, 1985), 437.
29. *The Tramp and the Dictator,* a documentary film by Kevin Brownlow, 2001 (55 minutes).
30. See the Charlie Chaplin letter to Upton Sinclair, October 20, 1964, in the Lilly Library, Indiana University, Bloomington, Indiana.
31. *The Tramp and the Dictator.*
32. See the author's "Chaplin and the Progressive Era: The Neglected Politics of a Clown," *Indiana Social Studies Quarterly,* Autumn 1981, 10–18. The subject is also addressed in two books by the author: *Charlie Chaplin: A Bio-Bibliography* (Westport, CT: Greenwood, 1983 and *Film Clowns of the Depression: Twelve Defining Performances* (Jefferson, NC: McFarland, 2007).
33. Robert Warshow "Monsieur Verdoux," in *The Immediate Experience* (1962; rpt. New York: Antheneum, 1972), 208
34. "Chaplin to Direct the 'Perfect' Talkie," *Hollywood Reporter,* August 25, 1932, 1.
35. Charles Maland, *Chaplin and American Culture: The Evolution of a Star Image* (Princeton: Princeton University Press, 1989), 143–144.
36. "Chaplin Set on All Silent for Next," *Hollywood Reporter,* January 26, 1934, 1.
37. For example, see "Chaplin Will Talk in Production No. 5," *The Hollywood Reporter,* October 13, 1934, 1.
38. Robert Forsythe (Kyle Crichton), *Modern Times* review, *New Masses,* February 18, 1936.
39. Theodore Huff, *Charlie Chaplin* (1951; rpt. New York: Arno Press and the *New York Times*, 1972), 258.
40. George Orwell, *1984* (1949; rpt. New York: Signet Classics, 1961).
41. Michael Sheldon, *Orwell: The Authorized Biography* (New York: HarperCollins, 1991), 325.
42. See *The Life and Times of Hank Greenberg,* a documentary film by Aviva Kempner, 1999 (95 minutes).
43. "Chaplin: A Bewildered Little 'Feller' Bucking Modern Times," *Newsweek,* February 8, 1936, 19.
44. John McCabe, *Charlie Chaplin* (Garden City, NY: Doubleday, 1978), 182.
45. Charlie Chaplin, *My Autobiography* (1964; rpt. New York: Pocket Books, 1966), 415.
46. Kurt Vonnegut, *Kurt Vonnegut Letters,* ed. Dan Wakefield (New York: Delacorte, 2012), 293.

47. Kurt Vonnegut, *Player Piano* (1952; rpt. New York: Dell, 1974), 241.
48. Rose Pelswick, "Chaplin Returns in Old Role but Brings New Laughs and Sings to Film Fans," *New York Evening Journal,* February 6, 1936, 16.
49. Campell Dixon, "New Triumph by Chaplin," *London Daily Telegraph,* February 12, 1936.

Chapter 7

1. *The Tramp and the Dictator,* BBC, A Kevin Brownlow Documentary Film, 2001 (55 minutes).
2. Charlie Chaplin, *My Autobiography* (1964; rpt. New York: Pocket Books, 1966), 7, 14.
3. Ibid., 51.
4. Eric L. Flom, *Charlie in the Sound Era* (1997; rpt. Jefferson, NC: McFarland, 2009), 116.
5. Winston Churchill, "Everybody's Language," *Collier,* October 21, 1935, in *The Essential Chaplin,* Richard Schickel, ed. (Chicago: Iran R. Dee, 2006), 209.
6. Henri Bergson, *Laughter* (1900), in *Comedy,* George Meredith, ed. (New York: Doubleday Anchor, 1956), 94.
7. Flom, *Chaplin in the Sound Era,* 116.
8. Alistair Cooke, *Six Men* (New York: Alfred A. Knopf, 1977), 32.
9. Ibid., 31.
10. *The Tramp and the Dictator.*
11. Cooke, *Six Men,* 33.
12. Alistair Cooke, *Letter from America* (New York: Penguin, 2004), 324.
13. Ibid.
14. David Robinson, *Chaplin: His Life and Art* (New York: McGraw-Hill, 1985), 478.
15. James P. O'Donnell, "Charlie Chaplin, Adolf Hitler & Napoleon," *Encounter* (June 1978), 31.
16. Ibid., 27.
17. "The Great Dictator," *Sydney Morning Herald* (November 5, 1940), Woman's Supplement section, 7.
18. Chaplin, *My Autobiography,* 424.
19. Lillian Ross, *Moments with Chaplin* (New York: Dodd, Mead, 1980), 49.
20. Steve Lipman, *Laughter in Hell: The Use of Humor During the Holocaust* (1991; rpt. Northvale, NJ: Jason Aronson, 1993), 96.
21. Rich Cohen "Becoming Adolf," *Vanity Fair* (November 2007), 239–240.
22. Jürgen Trimborn, *Leni Riefenstahl: A Life,* trans. Edna McCowan (2002; rpt. New York: Faber and Faber, 2007), 124.
23. Frank Capra, *Frank Capra: The Name Above the Title* (New York: Macmillan, 1971), 328.
24. For more on these subjects see the author's *Populism and the Capra Legacy* (Westport, CT: Greenwood Press, 1995); *Romantic vs. Screwball Comedy: Charting the Difference* (Lanham, MD: Scarecrow, 2002).
25. Trimborn, *Leni Riefenstahl: A Life,* 124.
26. Charles J. Maland, *Chaplin and American Culture: The Evolution of a Star Image* (Princeton, NJ: Princeton University, 1989), 171.
27. *The Tramp and the Dictator.*
28. Reginald Gardiner, "The Great Dictator: Charlie Chaplin's Gift of Humor and Satire to the Totalitarian State," *New York Herald Tribune,* September 16, 1940.
29. "Mr. Chaplin Answers His Critics," *New York Times,* October 27, 1940, section 9, 5.
30. Theodore Huff, *Charlie Chaplin* (1951; rpt New York: Arno Press & *New York Times,* 1972), 272.
31. Robinson, *Chaplin: His Life and Art,* 485–486.
32. Russell Martin, *Picasso's War* (New York: Dutton, 2002), ii.
33. Ibid., 166.
34. Hedda Hopper, "Hedda Hopper's Hollywood," *Los Angeles Times,* March 20, 1940, Part 1:15.
35. Jimmie Fidler, "Jimmie Fidler in Hollywood," *Los Angeles Times,* March 20, 1940, Part 1:14.
36. Jimmie Fidler, "Jimmie Fidler in Hollywood," *Los Angeles Times,* April 3, 1940, Part 1:13.
37. Hedda Hopper, "Hedda Hopper's Hollywood," *Los Angeles Times,* August 12, 1940, Part 2:14.
38. Hedda Hopper, "Hedda Hopper's Hollywood," *Los Angeles Times,* May 23, 1940, Part 2:11; see also "Jimmy Fidler in Hollywood," *Los Angeles Times,* June 1, 1940, Part 1:7.
39. Hedda Hopper, "Hedda Hopper's Hollywood," *Los Angeles Times,* June 27, 1940, Part 1:16.
40. "Fight Opened on Douglas," *Los Angeles Times,* May 25, 1940, Part 1:1.
41. Jimmy Fidler, "Jimmy Fidler in Hollywood," *Los Angeles Times,* June 4, 1940, Part 1:13.
42. "Cowboy Author sees Chaplin but Tactics Upset Studio," *Los Angeles Times,* August 8, 1940, Part 2:12.
43. Ibid.
44. Edwin Schallert, "Drama," *Los Angeles Times,* July 29, 1940, Part 1:6.
45. Arthur Marx, *The Secret Life of Bob Hope* (New York: Barricade, 1993), 137.
46. Paulette Goddard picture caption, *Los Angeles Times,* May 26, 1940, Part 3:3.
47. Philip K. Scheuer, "Bob Hope Wisecracks at Zombies," *Los Angeles Times,* June 28, 1940, Part 1:16.
48. Diego Rivera, with Gladys March, *My Art, My Life* (1960; rpt. New York: Publications, 1991), 152.
49. See the author's *Personality Comedians as Genre: Selected Players* (Westport, CT: Greenwood, 1997); *Parody as Film Genre: "Never Give a Saga an Even Break"* (Westport, CT: Greenwood, 1999).
50. "'McGinty' Sold for $10," *Los Angeles Times,* August 1, 1940, Part 2:10.
51. "'Great McGinty' Boisterous Tale of Crooked Politics," *Los Angeles Times,* July 20, 1940, 1:7.
52. Edwin Schallert, "While the *Films* Reel By," *Los Angeles Times,* February 18, 1940, Part 3:3.
53. Philip K. Scheuer, "Marxmen Clown in 'Go West,'" *Los Angeles Times,* May 22, 1940, Part 2:8.
54. Philip K. Scheuer, "Town Called Hollywood," *Los Angeles Times,* August 18, 1940, Part 3:3.
55. Ibid.
56. Ibid., Part 3:4.
57. Hedda Hopper, "Hedda Hopper's Hollywood," *Los Angeles Times,* October 6, 1940, Part 3:3.
58. Hedda Hopper, "Hedda Hopper's Hollywood," *Los Angeles Times,* September 4, 1940, Part 1:14.
59. Edwin Schallert, "While the *Films* Reel By," *Los Angeles Times,* October 13, 1940, Part 3:3.

60. Edwin Schallert, "Chaplin Film Shows Flashes of Genius," *Los Angeles Times,* October 15, 1940, Part 1:15.
61. Michael Beschloss, "A Triumph Over Hate Speech," *New York Times,* July 26, 2014, 8–9.
62. E. H. Gombrich, *The Story of Art* (1950; rpt. London: Phaidon, 1975), 476.

Chapter 8

1. Deborah Crawford, *Franz Kafka: Man Out of Step* (New York: Crown, 1973), 99.
2. Ibid., 72–73.
3. Otis Ferguson, *The Great Dictator* review, *New Republic,* November 4, 1940.
4. *The Great Dictator* review, *Variety,* October 16, 1940.
5. Carl Combs, "'The Great Dictator' in Carthay Première," *Hollywood Citizen-News,* November 15, 1940.
6. Bosley Crowther, "In 'The Great Dictator' Charlie Chaplin Reveals Again the Greatness in Himself," *New York Times,* October 20, 1940.
7. John Mosher, "The Current Cinema: Charlie's Hitler," *The New Yorker,* October 26, 1940, 78.
8. Ibid.
9. *The Tramp and the Dictator,* BBC, A Kevin Brownlow Documentary Film, 2001 (55 minutes).
10. Diego Rivera, with Gladys March, *My Art, My Life: An Autobiography* (1960; rpt. New York: Dover, 1991), 152.
11. *The Tramp and the Dictator.*
12. Meredith Willson, *And There I Stood with My Piccolo* (1948; rpt. Minneapolis: University of Minnesota Press, 2009), 166–167.
13. Wes D. Gehring, *Joe E. Brown: Film Comedian and Baseball Buffoon* (Jefferson NC: McFarland, 2006).
14. Robert Van Gelder, "Chaplin Draws a Keen Weapon," *New York Times Magazine,* September 8, 1940, 8–9.
15. Ibid.
16. Rachel Saltz, "The Führer's Visit Can't Suppress This Friendship," *New York Times,* January 25, 2013, C-5.
17. Frank Scheide, Hooman Mehran, and Dan Kamin, eds. *Chaplin: The Dictator and the Tramp* (London: British Film Institute, 2004).
18. Hedda Hopper, "Hedda Hopper's Hollywood," *Los Angeles Times,* October 16, 1940, Part 1:17.
19. Philip K. Scheuer, "Town Called Hollywood," *Los Angeles Times,* October 20, 1940, Part 3:3.
20. See the author's *American Dark Comedy: Beyond Satire* (Westport, CT: Greenwood, 1996).
21. Scheuer, "Town Called Hollywood," *Los Angeles Times,* October 20, 1940.
22. See the author's *American Dark Comedy: Beyond Satire.*
23. Scheuer, "Town Called Hollywood," *Los Angeles Times,* October 20, 1940.
24. Edwin Schallert, "While the *Films* Reel By," *Los Angeles Times,* October 20, 1940, Part 3:4.
25. Ibid.
26. Richard Griffith, "Chaplin's 'Great Dictator' Has All New York Agog," *Los Angeles Times,* October 28, 1940, Part 1:11.
27. Ibid.
28. Ibid.
29. Hedda Hopper, "Hedda Hopper's Hollywood," *Los Angeles Times,* November 2, 1940, Part 2:7.
30. "Comic Realizes Ambition in 'Great Dictator,'" *Los Angeles Times,* November 4, 1940, Part 2:14.
31. "'Dictator' Costly Effort," *Los Angeles Times,* November 5, 1940, Part 1:11.
32. Notables Will Attend Premiere," *Los Angeles Times,* November 7, 1940, Part 1:12.
33. "Chaplin Plans Attendance at Premiere Event," *Los Angeles Times,* November 8, 1940, Part 1:16.
34. "Dual Run Set for Chaplin Opus," *Los Angeles Times,* November 9, 1940, Part 1:6.
35. Ibid.
36. "Paulette Plays Half-Breed Role in Melodrama," *Los Angeles Times,* November 11, 1940, Part 1:25.
37. Edwin Schallert, "Sundry Picture Plans Debated by Chaplin," *Los Angeles Times,* November 14, 1940, Part 1:20.
38. "Everybody Is Cheering Chaplin on the Screen.... And Hudson on the Highway" (ad), *Los Angeles Times,* November 14, 1940, Part 4:9.
39. "Congratulations to Charlie Chaplin in the Great Dictator, Hollywood Typewriter Shop" (ad), *Los Angeles Times,* November 14, 1940, Part 4:4.
40. "Charlie Chaplin Is Back!," *Los Angeles Times,* November 14, 1940, Part 4:2.
41. "Satire Added to Slapstick in Departure from Precedent," *Los Angeles Times,* November 14, 1940, Part 4:2.
42. Ibid.
43. "Film Deemed Funfest Not Propaganda," *Los Angeles Times,* November 14, 1940, Part 4:3.
44. Ibid.
45. Aïda D. Donald, *Citizen Soldier: A Life of Harry S. Truman* (New York: Basic Books, 2012), 51.
46. "Sweaters," *Los Angeles Times,* November 14, 1940, Part 4:3.
47. "Censorship Imposed When Chaplin Films Are Made," *Los Angeles Times,* November 14, 1940, Part 4:7.
48. Ibid.
49. "Paulette Goddard *Flaunts* Legendary JINX," *Lost Angeles Times,* November 14, 1940, Part 4:11.
50. Charles Chaplin, Jr., with N. Rau and M. Rau, *My Father, Charlie Chaplin* (New York: Random House, 1960), 219.
51. "Jack Oakie Hits Jackpot in Chaplin Film," *Los Angeles Times,* November 14, 1940, Part 4:9.
52. Ibid.
53. Ibid.
54. Edwin Schallert, "Genius Touches Flit, Flash in 'Dictator,'" *Los Angeles Times,* November 15, 1940, Part 1:18.
55. Ibid.
56. Ibid.
57. "Familiar Garb of Comic Still Close to Heart," *Los Angeles Times,* November 19, 1940, Part 1:16.
58. Philip K. Scheuer, "Town Called Hollywood," *Los Angeles Times,* December 22, 1940, Part 3:3.

59. Cabbett Steinberg, *Reel Facts: The Movie Book of Records* (New York: Vintage Books, 1978), 341.
60. Thomas Fuchs, *A Concise Biography of Adolf Hitler* (1990; rpt. New York: Berkley, 2000), 97.
61. *The Tramp and the Dictator*, BBC, A Kevin Brownlow Documentary Film, 2001 (55 minutes).
62. Nougzer Sharia, Letter to the editor, *New York Times*, January 6, 1978.
63. Susan Dunn, *1940: FDR, Wilkie, Lindbergh, Hitler—The Election Amid the Storm* (New Haven: Yale University Press, 2013), 299.
64. Jacob Heilbrunn, "War Torn," *New York Times*, July 28, 2013, Book Review Section: 16.
65. Ibid.
66. Thomas Doherty, *Hollywood and Hitler: 1933–1939* (New York: Columbia University Press, 2013).
67. Ibid., 317.
68. Martin Amis, "Towering Figures," *New York Times*, October 20, 2013, Book Review Section: 16.
69. Arthur M. Schlesinger, Jr., "The Shadow of War," in *The National Experience: A History of the United States*, John M. Blum, ed. (New York: Harcourt Brace, 1968), 721.
70. Professor John Gerber, "Lecture on American Humor," Iowa City: University of Iowa course on humor, 1976–1977 term.
71. Theodore Huff, *Charlie Chaplin* (1951; rpt. New York: Arno Press and the *New York Times*, 1972), 281.
72. Charles Chaplin, *My Autobiography* (1964; rpt. New York: Pocket Books, 1966), 458.
73. David Robinson, *Chaplin: His Life and Art* (New York: McGraw-Hill, 1985), 516.
74. Charles Chaplin, Jr., with N. Rau and M. Rau, *My Father, Charlie Chaplin* (New York: Random House, 1960), 262–263.
75. John McCabe, *Charlie Chaplin* (Garden City, NY: Doubleday, 1978), 203.
76. Willson, *And There I Stand with My Piccola*, 168.
77. Richard Schickel, "Introduction: The Tramp Transformed," in *The Essential Chaplin*, ed. Schickel (Chicago: Ivan R. Dee, 2006), 32.
78. Chaplin, Jr., with N. Rau and M. Rau, *My Father, Charlie Chaplin*, 316.
79. G. Chevallier, *Fear* (1930 rpt. New York: New York Review Book, 2011), 109.

Chapter 9

1. Charles Chaplin, Jr., with N. Rau and M. Rau, *My Father, Charlie Chaplin* (New York: Random House, 1960), 202.
2. William Yardley, "Ferrel Sams, 90, Doctor-Turned-Novelist," *New York Times*, February, 2, 2013, A-22.
3. See the author's *Robert Wise: Shadowlands* (Indianapolis: Indiana Historical Society Press, 2012); and Blake Bailey, "Styron Visible," *New York Times*, January 13, 2013, "Book Review" section, 14.
4. Michael Chaplin, *I Couldn't Smoke the Grass on My Father's Lawn* (New York: G. P. Putnam's Sons, 1966).
5. Chaplin, Jr., with N. Rau and M. Rau, *My Father, Charlie Chaplin*, 312.
6. "Chaplin Spouting 'Landru Spinach [beard],'" *Hollywood Reporter*, December 8, 1941, 1.
7. Chaplin, Jr., with N. Rau and M. Rau, *My Father, Charlie Chaplin*, 71.
8. Will Cuppy, ed., *Murder Without Tears: An Anthology of Crime* (New York: Sheridan House, 1946); also see the author's *Will Cuppy, American Satirist* (Jefferson, NC: McFarland, 2013).
9. See the author's *Forties Film Funnymen: The Decade's Great Comedians at Work in the Shadow of War* (Jefferson, NC: McFarland, 2010).
10. Charlie Chaplin, *My Trip Abroad* (New York: Harper & Brothers, 1922), 150–151.
11. Charlie Chaplin, *My Autobiography* (1964; rpt. New York: Pocket Books, 1966), 454.
12. For example, see "Trial of Landru Enters Final Week," *New York Times*, November 28, 1921, 28.
13. "Demands Extreme Penalty for Landru," *New York Times*, November 29, 1921, 5.
14. Max Eastman, "Chaplin at Mid-Passage," in *The Essential Chaplin*, Richard Schickel, ed. (Chicago: Ivan R. Dee, 2006), 217.
15. Robert Warshow, *The Immediate Experience* (1952; rpt. New York: Atheneum, 1972), 230.
16. Quoted in Andrew Sarris' "Monsieur Verdoux," in *The Essential Chaplin*, 262.
17. Warshow, *The Immediate Experience*, 211.
18. Theodore Huff, *Charlie Chaplin* (1951; rpt. New York: Arno Press & *The New York Times*, 1972), 296.
19. David Thomson, "Frank Capra," in *The New Biographical Dictionary of Film* (1976; rpt/revised. New York: Alfred A. Knopf, 2010), 133.
20. Warshow, *The Immediate Experience*, 212.
21. Kenneth S. Lyon, *Charlie Chaplin and His Times* (New York: Simon & Schuster, 1997), 454.
22. "'M. Verdoux' Disappointing," *Hollywood Reporter*, April 14, 1947, 3, 9.
23. Mark Harris, *Pictures at a Revolution* (New York: Penguin, 2008), 48.
24. Andrew Sarris, "Monsieur Verdoux," in *The Essential Chaplin*, 265.
25. David Derby, "The Last Picture Show," *The New Yorker*, February 11 and 18, 2013, 115.
26. George Wallach, transcriber, "Charlie Chaplin's [1947] *Monsieur Verdoux* Press Interview," in *Charlie Chaplin Interviews*, Kevin J. Hayes, ed. (Jackson: University Press of Mississippi, 2005), 112.
27. "Trial of Landru Enters Final Week," *New York Times*.
28. "Demands Extreme Penalty for Landru," *New York Times*.
29. "Trial of Landru Enters Final Week," *New York Times*.
30. "'Bluebeard' [Finally] Quails Under Accusations," *New York Times*, November 30, 1921.
31. "Charlie Chaplin's *Monsieur Verdoux* [1947] Press Conference," *Film Comment*, Winter 1969, 39.
32. Geneviève Moreau, *The Restless Journey of James Agee* (New York: William Morrow, 1977), 216.
33. Chaplin, *My Autobiography*, 490.

34. George Wallach, transcriber, "Charlie Chaplin's [1947] *Monsieur Verdoux* Press Conference," 105.
35. Ibid., 108.
36. Harry Patch, with Richard Van Emden, *The Last Fighting Tommy: The Life of Harry Patch, Last Veteran of the [First World War] Trenches, 1898–2009* (2007; rpt. New York: Bloomsbury, 2009), 137.
37. Elie Wiesel, *Open Heart* (2011; rpt. New York: Alfred A. Knopf, 2012), 50–51.
38. Bosley Crowther, *Monsieur Verdoux* revisionist review, *New York Times*, July 4, 1964, 8.
39. "*M. Verdoux* review," *Variety*, April 16, 1947.
40. "'M. Verdoux' Disappointing," *Hollywood Reporter*, April 14, 1937, 3, 9.
41. Ibid.
42. Archer Winsten, *Monsieur Verdoux* review, *New York Post*, April 12, 1947.
43. *Monsieur Verdoux* review, *New York Daily Mirror*, April 12, 1947.
44. James Agee, "Monsieur Verdoux—I," *Nation*, May 31, 1947, in *Agee on Film*, Vol. 1 (1969; rpt. New York: Grossett & Dunlap, 1972), 253.
45. James Agee, "Monsieur Verdoux—I," *The Nation*, June 14, 1947, in *Agee on Film*, Vol. 1, 256.
46. Ibid.
47. Ibid.
48. Ibid., 261.
49. André Bazin, "Charlie Chaplin," in *What Is Cinema?*, vol. 1, selected and trans. Hugh Gray (1967; rpt. Los Angeles: University of California Press, 1971), 52.
50. André Bazin, "The Myth of Monsieur Verdoux," in *What Is Cinema?*, vol. 2, selected and trans. Hugh Gray (1958; rpt. Los Angeles: University of California Press, 1972), 102–103.
51. Ibid., 112.
52. Arthur Schopenhauer, "On Suicide," in *Schopenhauer Essays*, trans. T. Bailey Saunders, (London: George Allen and Unwin, 1951), 25.
53. Arthur Schopenhauer, "On Women," in *Schopenhauer Essays*, 65, 71.
54. Arthur Schopenhauer, "On Suicide," in *Schopenhauer Essays*, 29.
55. Robert F. Moss, *Charlie Chaplin* (1975; rpt. New York: Harcourt Brace Jovanovich, 1977), 119.
56. André Bazin, "The Myth of Monsieur Verdoux," 109.
57. See the author's *The Marx Brothers: A Bio-Bibliography* (Westport, CT: Greenwood, 1987.).
58. "Records of the Film: *Monsieur Verdoux*," British Film Institute publication, April 15, 1948, 3, in the "Charlie Chaplin File," Performing Arts Library, New York Public Library at Lincoln Center.
59. Ibid., 1.
60. Crowther, *Monsieur Verdoux* revisionist review, *New York Times*.
61. Archer Winsten, "Rages and Outrages," *New York Post*, July 13, 1964, 20.
62. Ibid.
63. "Charles the Great," *Newsweek*, July 27, 1964, 78–79.
64. Andrew Sarris, "I Films: Monsieur Verdoux—II," *Village Voice*, July 23, 1964.
65. Judith Crist, "Mirth and Murder," *New York Herald Tribune*, July 26, 1964, 27.
66. J. Hoberman, "When Chaplin Became the Enemy," *New York Times*, June 8, 2008, 19.

Chapter 10

1. Elie Wiesel, *Open Heart* (2011; rpt. New York: Alfred A. Knopf, 2012), 20.
2. Claire Bloom, *Limelight and After* (1982; rpt. New York: Penguin, 1983), 91.
3. Ibid., 91–92.
4. David Robinson, *Chaplin: His Life and Art* (New York: McGraw-Hill, 1985), 551.
5. Joe Franklin, *Joe Franklin's Encyclopedia of Comedians* (Secaucus, NJ: Citadel, 1979), 313.
6. Ibid.
7. Robinson, *Chaplin: His Life and Art*, 550.
8. Barry Anthony, *Chaplin's Music Hall: The Chaplins and Their Circle in Limelight* (New York: I. B. Tauris, 2012).
9. *The Tramp and the Dictator*, BBC, A Kevin Brownlow Documentary Film, 2001 (55 minutes).
10. James Agee, "Comedy's Greatest Era," *Life* magazine, September 3, 1949, in *Agee on Film*, Vol. 1 (New York: Gossett & Dunlap, 1968), 2–19.
11. *Verdoux* poster/lithograph for the 1947 Brazil ad campaign, collection of the author.
12. "Cinema: Monsieur Verdoux," *Time*, May 5, 1947.
13. J. Hoberman, "When Chaplin Became the Enemy," *New York Times*, June 8, 2008, 19.
14. Charlie Chaplin File, New York Performing Arts Library, Lincoln Center, New York.
15. Ibid.
16. Joyce Milton, *Tramp: The Life of Charlie Chaplin* (New York: HarperCollins, 1996), 202.
17. Arthur M. Schlesinger, Jr., "Chapter 31: The Cold War," in *The National Experience*, ed John M. Blum (1963; rpt. New York: Harcourt, Brace & World, 1968), 799.
18. Arthur M. Schlesinger, Jr., "Chapter 32: The Eisenhower Years," in *The National Experience*, ed. John M. Bloom, 801.
19. Andrew Sarris, "I Films: 'Limelight,'" *Village Voice*, October 1, 1964, 15.
20. Ibid.
21. *Educating Rita* (1983) full sheet poster, collection of the author.
22. John Beaufort, "An Assault from Mr. Chaplin," *Christian Science Monitor*, April 19, 1947, 8.
23. Theodore Huff, *Charlie Chaplin* (1951; rpt. New York: Arno Press and the *New York Times*, 1972), 308–309.
24. Eugene Smith, "Chaplin at Work: He Reveals His Movie-Making Secrets," *Life*, March 17, 1952, 117.
25. Alton Cook, "Chaplin's 'Limelight' a Film Masterpiece," *New York World Telegram*, October 24, 1952, 20.
26. Archer Winsten, "Chaplin's 'Limelight' Now Showing," *New York Post*, October 24, 1952, 52.
27. Otis L. Guernsey, Jr., "On the Screen: 'Lime-

light,'" *New York Herald Tribune,* October 24, 1952, 14.
28. Bosley Crowther, *Limelight* review, *New York Times,* October 24, 1952, 27.
29. *Limelight* review, *Variety,* October 8, 1952.
30. Ibid.
31. James Agee, *The Tramp's New World,* in James Wranovics' *Chaplin and Agee* (2005; rpt. New York: Palgrave Macmillan, 2006), 236.
32. Jane Scovell, *Oona: Living in the Shadows* (New York: Time Warner, 1998), 139.
33. Lillian Ross, *Moments with Chaplin* (New York: Dodd, Mead, 1980), 8.
34. Ibid., 8, 10.
35. Jonathan Freedland, "A Man of His Time," *New York Times,* March 31, 2013, Book Review section, 14.
36. Eric Bentley, *Are You or Have You Ever Been?* (New York: Harper & Row, 1972), 123, 129–130.
37. Ibid., 132.
38. Ibid., 112.
39. Charles Chaplin, Jr., with N. Rau and M. Rau, *My Father, Charlie Chaplin* (New York: Random House, 1960), 354.
40. Ross, *Moments with Chaplin,* 20–23, 32–36.
41. Robinson, *Chaplin: His Life and Art,* 545.
42. Joyce Milton, *Tramp: The Life of Charlie Chaplin* (New York: HarperCollins, 1996), 472.
43. Ibid., 483.
44. Quoted in Louisa Thomas' "When Worlds Collide," *New York Times,* March 31, 2013, Book Review section, 19.
45. Milton, *Tramp: The Life of Charlie Chaplin,* 483–484.
46. Robert Sellers, *Hellraisers* (2008; rpt. New York: Thomas Dunne Books, 2009), 159.
47. Julian Patrick, ed., *501 Great Writers* (New York: Barron's, 2008), 425.
48. Paul Murray Kendall, *The Art of Biography* (1965; rpt. New York: W. W. Norton, 1985), 130.

Chapter 11

1. Anthony Leviero, "Chaplin Is Facing Barriers to Re-entry from Abroad," *New York Times,* September 20, 1952, 1.
2. Ibid., 16.
3. Ibid.
4. Special to the *New York Times,* "British Warm to Chaplin," *New York Times,* September 22, 1952, 19.
5. Ibid.
6. "Chaplin to Return Here, He Declares," *New York Times,* September 23, 1952, 9.
7. Ibid.
8. "Mr. Chaplin Bows Out," *New York Times,* April 17, 1953, 24.
9. Bosley Crowther, "Under Suspicion," *New York Times,* September 28, 1952, Section 2, 1.
10. Ibid.
11. Special to the *New York Times,* "Chaplin Gives up Re-Entry Permit," *New York Times*, April 16, 1953, 1.
12. Special to the *New York Times,* "Chaplin Says He Will Not Return to U. S.; Charges Persecution by the 'Yellow Press,'" *New York Times,* April 18, 1953, 34.
13. Carol Matthau, *Among the Porcupines: A Memoir* (New York: Turtle Bay, 1992), 86.
14. Ibid., i.
15. "Chaplin to Return Here, He Declares."
16. Clifton Daniel, "Crowds Welcome Chaplin to London," *New York Times,* September 24, 1952, 3.
17. Ibid.
18. "Chaplin Divorce Sifted," *New York Times,* October 11, 1952, 16.
19. "Chaplin May Revise Old Charlie," *New York Times,* October 11, 1952, 17.
20. See the author's *W. C. Fields: A Bio-Bibliography* (Westport, CT: Greenwood Press, 1984); and *Groucho & W. C. Fields: Huckster Comedian* (Jackson: University Press of Mississippi, 1994).
21. "London Cheers Premiere of Chaplin Film: *Limelight,*" October 17, 1952, uncited article in the Charlie Chaplin file, New York Performing Arts Library, Lincoln Center, New York, New York.
22. "Princess Margaret at Chaplin Film Show," *London Times,* October 17, 1952, 6.
23. "London Cheers Premiere of Chaplin film: *Limelight.*"
24. "Chaplin Must Prove Case," *New York Times,* October 29, 1952, 32; "France Honors Chaplin," *New York Times,* October 30, 1952, 4.
25. "France Honors Chaplin."
26. André Bazin, "*Limelight,* or The Death of Moliére," in *What Is Cinema,* Vol. II, trans. Hugh Gray (1971; rpt. Los Angeles: University of California Press, 1972), 124.
27. "Chaplin Nobel Prize Nominee," *New York Times,* October 18, 1952, 17.
28. "Italy Decorates Chaplin," *New York Times,* December 21, 1952, Entertainment Section, 3; "Barrage Greets Chaplin," *New York Times,* December 23, 1952, 18.
29. "Mrs. Chaplin Coming to America," *New York Times,* November 18, 1952, 33.
30. Jane Scovell, *Oona: Living in the Shadows* (New York: Warner Books, 1998), 172.
31. "Mrs. Chaplin Coming to America."
32. "Alien Law Repeal Asked," *New York Times,* December 15, 1952, 9.
33. "Is 'Charlot' a Menace?," *New York Times,* September 21, 1952, Section 4, 10.
34. Corporal Hugh Namias, "Movie Opinions Culled from the Mail," *New York Times,* October 12, 1952, Section 2, 6.
35. "Chaplins to Move into Chateau," *New York Times,* January 4, 1953, 23.
36. "Cinema 16 Excursion for New Chaplin Film," *New York Herald Tribune,* September 15, 1957, Section 4, 5.
37. Art Buchwald, "Art Buchwald: Charlie Chaplin's New Film," *New York Herald Tribune,* September 15, 1957, Section 4, 1.
38. Campbell Dixon, "Chaplin—The Old Master," *London Daily Telegram and Morning Post,* September 14, 1957, 9.

39. Margaret Hinxman's *London Daily Herald* review, as quoted in David Robinson's *Chaplin: The Mirror of Opinion* (London: Martin Secker & Warburg, 1983), 159.
40. Joe Gilford, "Blacklisted, from a Child's View," *New York Times*, April 28, 2013, Arts and Leisure section, 6.
41. "Chaplin's Good Press in Britain in Contrast to Raves in France," *Variety*, September 18, 1957.
42. Alton Cook, "Chaplin Film So-So in London," *New York World Telegram and Sun*, September 22, 1957, 8; Leonard Ingalls, "Chaplin's 'King' Bows," *New York Times*, September 22, 1957.
43. Ingalls, "Chaplin's 'King' Bows."
44. As quoted in *Variety*'s "Chaplin's Good Press in Britain in Contrast to Raves in France."
45. Dilys Powell, "Charlie Chaplin and Mr. C," *London Times*, [September 1957], 23, in the Charlie Chaplin File, New York Performing Arts Library, Lincoln Center, New York.
46. As quoted in *Variety*'s "Chaplin's Good Press in Britain in Contrast to Raves in France."
47. As quoted in "Chaplin's Good Press in Britain in Contrast to Raves in France."
48. Kenneth Tynan, "Looking Back in Anger," *London Observer*, September 15, 1957, 4.
49. Jim Leach, *British Film* (Cambridge, England: Cambridge University Press, 2004), 53.
50. Richard Merryman, "Ageless Master's Anatomy of Comedy: Chaplin, an Interview," *Life*, March 10, 1967, 82+.
51. Roger Ebert, "*A King in New York* [Revisionist Review]," at http://www.rogerebert.com/reviews/a-king-in-new-york-1957.
52. Stanley Kauffman, "Stanley Kauffman on Films: 'A King in New York,'" *New Republic*, December 29, 1973, 22, 23.

Chapter 12

1. Evan Thomas, "The Gray Man," *New York Times*, May 5, 2013, Book Review section, 11.
2. Edward R. Murrow, *See It Now: A Report on Senator Joseph R. McCarthy*," CBS, March 9, 1954.
3. Kathleen Carroll, "'Limelight' Restores Faith of Critic," *New York Daily News/Sunday News*, September 10, 1972, Leisure section, 28.
4. *Wide World of Sports*, U.S. TV series (ABC, 1961–1998).
5. Charlie Chaplin, *My Autobiography* (1964; rpt. New York: Pocket Books, 1966).
6. David Robinson, *Chaplin: The Mirror of Opinion* (1983; rpt. Bloomington: Indiana University Press, 1984), 1.
7. Walter E. Houghton, *The Victorian Frame of Mind* (1957; rpt. New Haven: Yale University Press, 1970), 305.
8. Chaplin, *My Autobiography*, 212.
9. Arthur Knight, "Travel with Charlie and Friends," *Saturday Review*, October 10, 1964, 45.
10. Chaplin, *My Autobiography*, 14.
11. Ibid., 138.
12. See the author's *W.C. Fields: A Bio-Bibliography* (Westport, CT: Greenwood Press, 1984); *Groucho & W. C. Fields: Huckster Comedians* (Jackson: University Press of Mississippi, 1994); *Film Clowns of the Depression: Twelve Defining Comic Performances* (Jefferson, NC: McFarland, 2007).
13. Charlie Chaplin, *My Trip Abroad* (New York: Harper & Brothers, 1922).
14. "Charlie Chaplin, as a Comedian, Contemplates Suicide," *Current Opinion*, February 1922, 209–210.
15. Chaplin, *My Autobiography*, 35.
16. Charlie Chaplin, Jr., with N. Rau and M. Rau, *My Father, Charlie Chaplin* (New York: Random House, 1960), 29.
17. Lita Gray Chaplin, with Morton Cooper, *My Life with Chaplin* (New York: Bernard Geis, 1966), 29, 31, 33, 53.
18. Ibid., 31.
19. Ibid., 79.
20. See Brendan Gill, "Books," *The New Yorker*, October 12, 1964, 238.
21. Houghton, *The Victorian Frame of Mind*, 354.
22. Charlie Chaplin, *My Life in Pictures* (1974; rpt. New York: Grosset and Dunlap, 1975), 177.
23. Gill, "Books," 240.
24. See the author's *Screwball Comedy: A Genre of Madcap Romance* (Westport, CT: Greenwood, 1986); *Romantic vs. Screwball Comedy: Charting the Difference* (Lanham, MD: Scarecrow, 2002).
25. Alan Levy, *Forever Sophia* (New York: St. Martin's, 1986), 69.
26. Patricia Bosworth, *Marlon Brando* (New York: Viking, 2001), 152.
27. Ibid.
28. Bosley Crowther, "*A Countess from Hong Kong* review," *New York Times*, March 17, 1967, 35.
29. Kathleen Carroll, "Chaplin's 'Countess' Too Little, Too Late," *New York Daily News*, March 17, 1967, 71.
30. Ibid.
31. Joseph Gehmis, "Chaplin's 'Countess' No Laughing Matter," *Newsday*, March 17, 1967, 2A.
32. "*A Countess from Hong Kong* review," *Variety*, January 11, 1967.
33. Quoted in David Robinson's *Chaplin: His Life and Art* (New York: McGraw-Hill, 1985), 615.
34. Wes D. Gehring, conversation with Geraldine Chaplin, University of Paris, April 15, 1989.
35. Lisa K. Stein, *Syd Chaplin* (Jefferson, NC: McFarland, 2011), 3.
36. Jane Scovell, *Oona: Living in the Shadows* (New York: Warner Books, 1998), 237.
37. Chaplin, *My Life in Pictures*.
38. Ibid., 319.
39. Mason Wiley and Damien Bona, *Inside Oscar* (1986; rpt. New York: Ballantine, 1993), 461.
40. Pete Hamill, "Charlie Chaplin, 88, Takes Final Bow," *New York Daily News*, December 26, 1977, 3.
41. Earl Wilson, "It Happened Last Night," *New York Post*, December 26, 1977, 30.
42. See the author's *W. C. Fields: A Bio-Bibliography* (Westport, CT: Greenwood, 1984).
43. Lewis Jacobs, *The Rise of American Film: A Critical History* (1939; rpt. New York: Teachers College Press, 1971), 231–232.

44. See the author's *Laurel & Hardy: A Bio-Bibliography* (Westport, CT: Greenwood, 1990).

Epilogue

1. Kurt Vonnegut, *Slaughterhouse-Five* (1969; rpt. New York: Dell, 1974), 19.
2. Thomas Maeder, "Afterword," in Will Cuppy's *The Decline and Fall of Practically Everybody* (1950; Boston: Nonpareil, 1984), 241.
3. See the author's *Will Cuppy, American Satirist* (Jefferson, NC: McFarland, 2013).
4. Carl Sandburg, "Limited" (1916), in *Harvest Poems: 1910–1960* (New York: Harcourt, Brace, 1960), 38.
5. Kurt Vonnegut, *God Bless You, Mr. Rosewater* (1965; rpt. New York: Dell, 1976).
6. William Wolf, "Film Cues [Chaplin]," *Cue*, January 21–February 3, 1978, 25.
7. Gregory Tietjen, quoted in the "Introduction" to Thomas Paine's *Common Sense* (1776; rpt. New York: Fall River Press, 2013), xxiv.
8. Greg Bellow, *Saul Bellow's Heart: A Son's Memoir* (New York: Bloomsbury, 2013), 4.
9. Robert Van Gelder, "Chaplin Draws a Keen Weapon," *New York Times Magazine*, September 8, 1940, 8–9.
10. Wm. H. Mooring, "An Open Letter to Charlie Chaplin," *Picturegoer and Film Weekly*, August 24, 1940, 11.
11. Gelder, "Chaplin Draws a Keen Weapon."
12. Quoted in David Jackson's "We Get to Know JFK Again in 2013," *USA Today*, May 24, 2013, 2-A.
13. Douglas M. Davis, *The World of Black Humor: An Introductory Anthology of Selections and Criticism* (New York: E. P. Dutton, 1967), 14.
14. Kōji Numasawa, "Black Humor: An American Aspect," *Studies in English Literature* (University of Tokyo), March 1968, 177.
15. *50 Children: The Rescue Mission of Mr. and Mrs. Kraus*, written, directed and produced by Steven Pressman. HBO documentary with the U.S. Holocaust Museum, 2013.
16. Vincent Curcio, *Henry Ford* (New York: Oxford University Press, 2013), 144.
17. Ibid., 149.
18. *The Tramp and the Dictator*, a Kevin Burns Brownlow Documentary Film, BBC, 2001 (55 minutes).
19. Curcio, *Henry Ford*, 128.
20. Quoted in Charles Isherwood's "A Little Groucho, A Little King Solomon," *New York Times*, May 31, 2013, C-1.
21. Richard W. Sonnerfeldt, *Witness to Nuremberg* (2002; rpt. New York: Arcade, 2006), 30.
22. Robert Warshow, "A Feeling of Sad Dignity," in *The Essential Chaplin*, Richard Schickel, ed. (Chicago: Ivan R. Dee, 2006), 275.
23. George Wallach, transcriber, "Charlie Chaplin's *Monsieur Verdoux* Press Interview," in *Charlie Chaplin Interviews*, Keven J. Hayes, ed. (Jackson: University Press of Mississippi, 2005), 112.
24. Richard Merryman, "Ageless Master's Anatomy of Comedy, An Interview," *Life*, March 10, 1967, 82+.
25. Tom Wolfe, *Radical Chic & Mau-Mauing the Flack Catchers* (New York: Ferrar, Straus and Giroux, 1970).
26. Kurt Vonnegut, *A Man Without a Country* (New York: Seven Stories, 2008), 131.
27. Stefan Kanfer, "Exit the Tramp, Smiling: Charles Spencer Chaplin: 1889–1977," January 2, 1978, incomplete citation, Charlie Chaplin file, Performing Arts Library, New York Public Library at Lincoln Center.

Bibliography

Books

Agee, James. *A Death in the Family*. 1957; rpt. New York: Bantam, 1972.

Anthony, Barry. *Chaplin's Music Hall: The Chaplins and Their Circle in Limelight*. New York: I. B. Tauris, 2012.

Bellow, Greg. *Saul Bellow's Heart: A Son's Memoir*. New York: Bloombury, 2013.

Bentley, Eric. *Are You or Have You Ever Been?* New York: Harper & Row, 1972.

Blake, Michael F. *The Films of Lon Chaney*. 1998; rpt. New York: Madison, 2001.

Bloom, Claire. *Limelight and After*. 1982; rpt. New York: Penguin, 1983.

Bonadeo, Alfredo. *Mark of the Beast: Death and Degration in the Literature of the Great War*. Lexington: University of Kentucky Press, 1989.

Borowski, Tadeusz. *This Way for the Gas, Ladies and Gentleman*. 1959; rpt. New York: Penguin, 1986.

Bosworth, Patricia. *Marlon Brando*. New York: Viking, 2001.

Bowman, William Dodgson. *Charlie Chaplin: His Life and Art*. 1931; rpt. New York: Haskell House, 1974.

Braudy Leo. *Jean Renoir: The World of His Films*. Garden City, New York: Anchor, 1972.

Brownlow, Kevin. *The War, the West and the Wilderness*. London: Seeker & Warburg, 1978.

Buñuel, Luis (trans. Abigail). *My Last Sigh*. 1982; rpt. New York: Random House, 1984.

Chabon, Michael. *The Yiddish Policemen's Union*. New York: HarperCollins, 2007.

Chaplin, Charles, Jr. (with N. and M. Rau). *My Father, Charlie Chaplin*. New York: Random House, 1960.

Chaplin, Charles. *My Autobiography*. 1964; rpt. New York: Pocket Books, 1966.

Chaplin, Charles *My Life in Pictures*. 1974; rpt. New York: Grosset and Dunlap, 1975.

Chaplin, Charlie. *My Trip Abroad*. New York: Harper and Brothers, 1922.

Chaplin, Lita Grey (with Morton Cooper). *My Life with Chaplin*. New York: Dell, 1966.

Chaplin, Michael. *I Couldn't Smoke the Grass on My Father's Lawn*. New York: G. P. Putnam's Sons, 1966.

Chaplin: The Dictator and the Tramp, Frank Scheide, Hooman Mehran, Dan Kamin, eds. London: British Film Institute, 2004.

Charlie Chaplin in the Army. Chicago: M.A. Donahue & Co., by an arrangement between J. Keeley and Essany, 1917.

Charlie Chaplin Up in the Air. Chicago: M. A. Donohue & Co., by an arrangement between J. Keeley and Essanay, 1917.

Clark, T. J. *Picasso and Truth*. Princeton, N. J.: Princeton University Press, 2013.

Cobb, Humphrey. *Paths of Glory*. New York: Viking, 1935.

Cotes, Peter and Thelma Niklaus. *The Little Fellow: The Life and Work of Charles Chaplin*. 1951; rpt. New York: Citadel, 1965.

Crawford, Deborah. *Franz Kafka: Man Out of Step*. New York: Crown, 1973.

Cuppy, Will, ed. *Murder Without Tears: An Anthology of Crime*. New York: Sheridan House, 1946.

Curcio, Vincent. *Henry Ford*. New York: Oxford University Press, 2013.

Davis, Douglas M. *The World of Black Humor: An Introductory Anthology of Selections and Criticism*. New York: E.P. Dutton, 1967.

De Coulteray, George D. *Sadism in the Movies*. New York: Medical Press, 1965.

Doherty, Thomas. *Hollywood and Hitler: 1933–1939*. New York: Columbia Press, 2013.

Donald, Aïda D. *Citizen Soldier. A Life of Harry S Truman*. New York: Basic Books, 2012.

Dunn, Susan. *1940: FDR, Willkie, Lindbergh, Hitler—the Election Amid the Storm*. New Haven: Yale University Press, 2013.

Eisenstein, Sergei M. *The Film Sense*. (trans. and ed. Jay Leyda). 1942: New York: Harcourt, Brace, 1947.

Eisenstein, Sergei M. *The Film Touch*. (trans. and ed. Jay Leyda). 1942; rpt. New York: Harcourt, Brace, 1947.

Everson, William K. *American Silent Film*. New York: Oxford University Press, 1978.

Eyman, Scott. *Ernst Lubitsch: Laughter in Paradise*. New York: Simon & Schuster, 1993.

Frank, Anne. *Anne Frank: The Diary of a Young Girl*. 1947; rpt. New York: Pocket Books, 1958.

Frankl, Victor E. *Man's Search for Meaning*. 1946; rpt. Boston: Beacon, 1992.

Franklin, Joe. *Franklin's Encyclopedia of Comedians*. Secaucus, New Jersey: Citadel, 1979.

Fuchs, Thomas. *A Concise Biography of Adolf History*. 1990; rpt. New York: Berkley, 2000.

Fussell, Paul. *The Great War and Modern Memory*. 1975; rpt. New York: Oxford University, 1977.
Gehring, Wes D. *American Dark Comedy: Beyond Satire*. Westport, Connecticut: Greenwood, 1996.
Gehring, Wes D. *Charlie Chaplin: A Bio-Bibliography*. Westport, Connecticut: Greenwood, 1983.
Gehring, Wes D. *Film Clowns of the Depression: Twelve Defining Comic Performances*. Jefferson, North Carolina: McFarland, 2007.
Gehring, Wes D. *Forties Film Funnymen: The Decade's Great Comedians at Work in the Shadow of War*. Jefferson, North Carolina: McFarland, 2010.
Gehring, Wes D. *Groucho & W. C. Fields: Huckster Comedians*. Jackson: University Press of Mississippi, 1994.
Gehring, Wes D. *Joe E. Brown: Film Comedian and Baseball Buffoon*. Jefferson, North Carolina: McFarland, 2006.
Gehring, Wes D. *Laurel & Hardy: A Bio-Bibliography*. Westport, Connecticut: Greenwood, 1990.
Gehring, Wes D. *Leo McCarey: From Marx to McCarthy*. Lanham, Maryland: Scarecrow, 2005.
Gehring, Wes D. *The Marx Brothers: A Bio-Bibliography*. Westport, Connecticut: Greenwood Press, 1987.
Gehring, Wes D. *Robert Wise: Shadowlands*. Indianapolis: Indiana Historical Society Press, 2012.
Gehring, Wes D. *Romantic vs. Screwball Comedy*. Lanham, Maryland: Scarecrow, 2002.
Gehring, Wes D. *Screwball Comedy: A Genre of Madcap Romance*. Westport, Connecticut: Greenwood, 1986.
Gehring, Wes D. *W. C. Fields: A Bio-Bibliography*. Westport: Connecticut: Greenwood, 1984.
Gehring, Wes D. *Will Cuppy: Satirist*. Jefferson: North Carolina: McFarland, 2013.
Gifford, Dennis. *Chaplin*. Garden City, New York: Doubleday, 1974.
Gifford, Dennis. *Chaplin: The Movie Makers*. Garden City, New York: Doubleday, 1974.
Gombrich, E. H. *The Story of Art*. London: Phaidon, 1972.
Grauer, Neil A. *Remember Laughter: A Life of James Thurber*. Lincoln: University of Nebraska Press, 1995.
Graves, Robert. *Good-Bye to All That*. 1929; rpt. Garden City, New York: Doubleday, 1957.
Greene, Graham. *A Sort of Life*. 1971; rpt. New York: Pocket Books, 1973.
Hall, Mordaunt. *The Gold Rush* review. *New York Times*, August 17, 1925.
Harris, Mark. *Pictures at a Revolution*. New York: Penguin, 2008.
Hemingway, Ernest. *A Farewell to Arms*. 1929; rpt. New York: Schribners, 1957.
Hirsch, Foster. *The Dark Side of the Screen: Film Noir*. New York: A. S. Barnes, 1981.
Hochschild, Adam. *To End All Wars*. 2011; rpt. New York: Mariner, 2012.
Houghton, Walter E. *The Victoria Frame of Mind*. 1957; rpt. New Haven: Yale University Press, 1970.
Hubbard, Frank Kin. *Abe Martin the Joker on Facts*. Indianapolis: Abe Martin, 1920.
Hubbard, Frank "Kin," *Back Country Folk*. Indianapolis: Abe Martin, 1913.
Huff, Theodore. *Charlie Chaplin*. 1951; rpt. New York: Arno Press and the *New York Times*, 1972.
Jacobs, Lewis. *The Rise of American Film in Critical History*. 1939; rpt. New York: Teachers College Press, 1971.
Kendal, Paul Murray. *The Art of Biography*. 1965; rpt. New York: W. W. Norton, 1985.
Kerr, Walter. *The Silent Clowns*. New York: Alfred A. Knopf, 1975.
Leach, Jim. *British Film*. Cambridge, England: Cambridge University Press, 2004.
Levy, Alan. *Forever Sophia*. New York: St. Martin's, 1986.
Lipman, Steve. *Laughter in Hell: The Use of Humor During the Holocaust*. 1991; rpt. Northvale, N. J.: Jason Aronson, 1993.
Lyon, Kenneth S. *Charlie Chaplin and His Times*. New York: Simon & Schuster, 1997.
Maland, Charles J. *Chaplin and American Culture*. Princeton, New Jersey: Princeton University Press, 1989.
Manvell, Roger. *Chaplin*. Boston: Little, Brown, 1974.
Martin, Russell. *PICASSCO'S WAR: The Destruction of Guernica, and the Masterpiece That Changed the World*. New York: Dutton, 2002.
Mast, Gerald. *The Comic Mind: Comedy and the Movies*. Indianapolis: Bobbs-Merill, 1973.
Matthau, Carol. *Among the Porcupines: A Memoir*. New York: Turtle Bay, 1992.
McCabe, John *Charlie Chaplin*. Garden City, New York: Doubleday, 1978.
McCabe, John. *Mr. Laurel & Mr. Hardy*. 1961; rpt. New York: Signet, 1966.
Milton, Joyce. *Tramp: The Life of Charlie Chaplin*. New York: HarperCollins, 1996.
Minney, R. J. *Chaplin: The Immortal Tramp*. London: George Newness, 1954.
Moreau, Geneviève. *The Restless Journey of James Agee*. New York: William Morrow, 1977.
Moss, Robert F. *Charlie Chaplin*. 1975; rpt. New York: Harvest, 1977.
Norman, Philip. *John Lennon: The Life*. New York: HarperCollins, 2008.
Olson, Lynne. *Those Angry Days: Roosevelt, Lindbergh, and America's Fight Over World War II, 1939–1941*. New York: Random House, 2013.
Orwell, George, *1984*. 1949; rpt. New York: Signet Classic, 1961.

Patch, Harry. (with Richard Von Emden). *The Lost Fighting Tommy: The Life of Harry Patch, Last Veteran of the [First World War] Trenches, 1898–2009.* 2007; rpt. New York: Bloomsburry, 2009.

Patrick, Julian, ed. *501 Great Writers.* New York: Barron's, 2008.

Quigly, Isabel. *Charlie Chaplin: Early Comedies.* London: Dutton Pictureback, 1968.

Ramsaye, Terry. *A Million and One Nights: A History of Motion Pictures Through 1925.* 1926; rpt. 2 vols. New York: Simon and Schuster, 1964.

Remarque, Erich Maria. *All Quite On the Western Front.* 1928; rpt. New York: Crest Books, 1964.

Renoir, Jean. *My Life and My Films.* New York: Athenem, 1974.

Rivera, Diego (with Gladys March). *My Art, My Life: An Autobiography.* 1960; rpt. New York: Dover, 1991.

Robinson, David. *Chaplin: His Life and Art.* New York: McGraw-Hill, 1985.

Robinson, David. *The Great Funnies: A History of Film Comedy.* London: Dutton, 1969

Ross, Lillian. *Moments with Chaplin.* New York: Dodd, Mead, 1980.

Roth, Phillip. *The Plot Against America: A Novel.* New York: Houghton Mifflin, 2004.

Russell, Bill. (with Alan Steinberg). *Red and Me: My Coach, My Lifelong Friend.* New York: HarperCollins, 2009.

Schaffner, Ingrid. *The Essential Pablo Picasso.* New York: Harry N. Abrams, 1998.

Schickel, Richard. *D. W. Griffith: An American Life.* New York: Simon and Schuster, 1984.

Schulberg, Budd. *The Disenchanted.* New York: Random House, 1950.

Scovell, Jane. *Oona: Living in the Shadows.* New York: Time Warner, 1998.

Sellers, Robert. *Hellraisers.* 2008; rpt. New York Thomas Dunne Books, 2009.

Sennett, Mack. (as told to Cameron Shipp). *King of Comedy.* 1954; rpt. New York: Pinnacle, 1975.

Sheldon, Michael. *Orwell: The Authorized Biography.* New York: HarperCollins, 1991.

Sobel, Raoul and David Francis. *Chaplin: Genesis of a Clown.* London: Quartet Books, 1977.

Sonnerfeldt, Richard W. *Witness to Nuremberg.* 2002; rpt. New York: Arcade, 2006.

Stein, Lisa K. *Syd Chaplin: A Biography.* Jefferson, North Carolina: McFarland, 2011.

Steinberg, Cobbett. *Real Facts: The Movie Book of Records* New York: Vintage, 1978.

Storey, William Kelleher. *Writing History.* 1996; rpt. New York: Oxford University Press, 2004.

Strachan, Hew. *The First World War.* 2003; rpt. New York: Penguin, 2004.

Styan, J. L. *The Dark Comedy.* Cambridge, England: Cambridge University Press, 1968.

Vonnegut, Kurt. *God Bless You, Mr. Rosewater* 1965; rpt. New York: Dell, 1976.

Vonnegut, Kurt. *Kurt Vonnegut Letters,* ed. Dan Wakefield. New York: Delacorte, 2012.

Vonnegut, Kurt. *A Man Without a Country.* New York: Seven Stories, 2005.

Vonnegut, Kurt. *Player Piano.* 1952; rpt. New York: Dell, 1974.

Vonnegut, Kurt. *Slaughterhouse Five.* 1969; rpt. New York: Dell, 1974.

von Sternberg, Josef. *Fun in a Chinese Laundry.* 1965. rpt. New York: Collier, 1973.

Warshow, Robert. *The Immediate Experience.* 1952; rpt. New York: Atheneum, 1972.

Weinberg, Herman G. *The Lubitsch Touch: A Critical Study.* 1968; rpt. New York: E. P. Dutton, 1971.

Weismann, Stephen M. *Chaplin: A Life.* New York: Arcade, 2008. (Includes Introduction by the comedian's daughter Geraldine Chaplin.)

Wiesel, Elie. *Open Heart.* 2011; rpt. New York: Alfred A. Knopf, 2012.

Wiley, Mason, and Damien. *Inside Oscar.* 1986; rpt. New York: Ballantine, 1993.

Wilson, Meredith. *And There I Stood with My Piccolo.* 1948; rpt. Minneapolis: University of Minnesota Press, 2009.

Wolfe, Tom. *Radical Chic & Mau-Mauing the Flack Catchers.* New York: Ferrar, Straus and Giroux, 1970.

Shorter Works

"...Actresses and Actors Doing Remarkable Work to Aid Uncle Sam." *New Orleans Times-Picayune* (April 21, 1918): C-10.

Agee, James. "Comedy's Greatest Era." *Life* magazine (September 3, 1949). In *Agee on Film, Volume 1.* 1958; rpt. New York: Grossett & Dunlap, 1969.

Agee, James, "Monsieur Verdoux—1." *Nation* (May 31, 1947). In *Agee on Film Volume 1.* 1958; rpt. New York: Grossett & Dunlap, 1969.

Agee, James. "Monsieur Verdoux—III." *Nation* (June 14, 1947). In *Agee on Film Volume 1.* 1958; rpt. New York: Grossett & Dunlap, 1969.

Agee, James. The Tramp's New World." In James Wranovics' *Chaplin and Agee.* 2005; rpt. New York: Palgrave Macmillan, 2006.

"Alien Law Repeal Asked." *New York Times* (December 15, 1952): 9.

"Barrage Greets Chaplin." *New York Times* (December 23, 1952): 18.

Bazin, André. "Charlie Chaplin." In *What Is Cinema? vol. 1,* selected and trans. Hugh Gray. 1967; rpt. Los Angeles: University of California Press, 1971.

Bazin, André. "The Grandeur of Limelight." In *What Is Cinema? vol. 2,* selected and trans. Hugh Gray.

1971; rpt. Los Angeles: University of California Press, 1972.

Bazin, André. "*Limelight,* or the Death of Moliére." In *What Is Cinema vol. 2,* selected and trans. Hugh Gray. 1967; rpt. Los Angeles: University of California Press, 1971.

Bazin, André. "The Myth of Monsieur Verdoux." In *What Is Cinema?, vol. 2,* selected and trans. Hugh Gray. 1971; rpt. Los Angeles: University of California Press, 1972.

Bazin, André. "The Virtues and Limitations of Montage." In *What Is Cinema? vol. 1,* selected and trans. Hugh Gray. 1967; rpt. Los Angeles: University of California Press, 1971.

Beaufort, John. "An Assault from Mr. Chaplin." *Christian Science Monster* (April 19, 1947): 8.

Bergson, Henri. "Laughter" (1900). In *Comedy,* ed Wylie Sypher. Garden City, New York: Doubleday Anchor, 1956.

Beschloss, Michael. "A Triumph Over Hate Speech." *New York Times* (July 26, 2014): 8–9.

"Big Demonstration at Rocky Mt. Friday." *Raleigh News and Observer* (April 18, 1918) :5.

"Big Twin Program. Showing at Strand." *New Orleans-Picayune,* (May 12, 1918) :PC-11.

"Bill Hart at Cinema." *Los Angeles Times* (April 11, 1918): Section 2:3.

"Billions in Bonds Now Aim for City." *New York American,* (April 9, 1918) :3.

"'Birth of a Nation' Here All Next Week at Rialto Theatre." *Atlantic Constitution* (April 14, 1918): Section F:12.

"'Bluebeard [Finally] Quails Under Accusations." *New York Times* (November 30, 1921).

Blum, John M. "Retreat from Responsibility." In *The National Experience: A History of the United States,* Blum, ed. New York: Harcourt Brace, 1968.

"Booklet of Hate Issued to Help Americans Win." *New York Tribune* (April 19, 1918): 4.

"British Warm to Chaplin." *New York Times* (September 22, 1952): 19.

Brown, Heywood. "New Midnight Frolic Proves to Be the Best of the Series." *New york Tribune* April 26, 1918): 11.

Buchwald, Art. "Art Buchwald: Charlie Chaplin's New Film." *New York Herald Tribune* (September 15, 1957): Section 4:1.

"By a Y.M.C.A Worker, [Cigarette] Dog Scorns Shells to Help Soldiers." *Richmond Times Dispatch* (October 29, 1918): 3.

"Capturing Charlie Chaplin." *New York Tribune* (May 12, 1918): Section 4:5.

Carroll, Kathleen. "Chaplin 'Countess" Too Little, Too Late." *New York Daily News* (March 17, 1967): 71.

Carroll, Kathleen. "'Limelight Restores Faith of Critic." *New York Daily News—Sunday News* (September 10, 1972): Leisure Section: 28.

"Censorship Imposed When Chaplin Films Are Made." *Los Angeles Times* (November 14, 1940): Part 4:7.

Chandler, Clement F. "Max Linder Comes Back!" *Motion Picture* (February and March, 1917).

"Chaplin: A Bewildered 'Feller' Bucking Modern Times." *Newsweek* (February 8, 1936): 19.

"Chaplin and His Acrobatics Sell 227,000 Bonds." *New Orleans Time-Picayune* (April 24, 1918): 1.

Chaplin, Charlie. "What People Laugh At." *American Magazine* (November 1918): 134–137.

"Chaplin Divorce Sifted." *New York Times* (October 11, 1952): 16.

"Chaplin Gives Up Re-Entry Permit." *New York Times* (April 16, 1953): 1.

"Chaplin in 'Shoulder Arms.'" *New York American* (October 21, 1918): 12.

"Chaplin May Revise Old Charlie." *New York Times* (October 11, 1952): 17.

"Chaplin Must Prove Case." *New York Times* (October 29, 1952): 32.

"Chaplin Nobel Prize Nominee." *New York Times* (December 23, 1952): 18.

"Chaplin Parade to Boom Liberty Loan Called Off." *New Orleans Time-Picayune,* (April 23, 1918): 1, 4.

"Chaplin Plans Attendance at Premiere Event." *Los Angeles Times:* (November 8, 1940): Part 1:16.

"Chaplin Says He Just Had to Make That Speech." *New York World Telegram* (October 19, 1940): 7.

"Chaplin Says He Will Not Return to U. S.; Charges Persecution by the 'Yellow Press.'" *New York Times* (April 18, 1955): 34.

"Chaplin Sells Liberty Bonds." *Nashville Banner* (April 19, 1918): 17.

"Chaplin Set on All Silent for Next." *Hollywood Report* (January 26, 1934) :1.

"Chaplin Soon." *Los Angeles Times* (April 14, 1918): Section 3:1.

Chaplin Spouting 'Landra Spinach [beard]." *Hollywood Reporter* (December 8, 1941).

"Chaplin to Direct the 'Perfect' Talkie. In *Hollywood Reporter* (August 25, 1932): 1.

"Chaplins to Move Into Chateau." *New York Times* (January 4, 1953): 23.

"Chaplin to Return Here, He Declares." *New York Times* (September 23, 1952): 9.

"Chaplin Traveled the Freight Elevator." *Raleigh News and Observer* (April 14, 1918).

"[Chaplin War Bond Coverage]." *New York Herald Tribune* (April 9, 1918).

"Chaplin Will Talk in Production No. 5." *Hollywood Reporter* (October 13, 1934): 1.

"Chaplin's First Speech in State at Rocky [and Wilson]." *Raleigh News and Observer* (April 14, 1918): Section 1:8.

"Chaplin's Good Press in Britain in Contrast to Raves in France." *Variety* (September 18, 1957).

"Charlie Chaplin Antics Interest Spectator." *New York Herald* (April 15, 1918): Section 2:9.

"Charlie Chaplin, as a Comedian, Contemplates Suicide." *Current Opinion* (February 1922): 209–210.

"Charlie Chaplin Comes on Friday." *Raleigh News and Observer* (April 11, 1918): 1.

"Charlie Chaplin Coming Tuesday for Great Rally." *New Orleans Times-Picayune* (April 22, 1918): 1.

Charlie Chaplin File. New York Performing Arts Library, Lincoln Center, New York.

"Charlie Chaplin in 'Shoulder Arms.'" *Richmond Times-Dispatch* (November 10, 1918): Section 3:6.

"Charlie Chaplin Is BACK!," *Los Angeles Times* (November 14, 1940): Part 4:2.

"Charlie Chaplin Is Welcomed by Monster Crowd." *Nashville Tennessean and American* (April 19, 1918): 5.

Charlie Chaplin letter to Upton Sinclair. In the Lilly Library. Indiana University, Bloomington, Indiana.

"Charlie Chaplin Puts 'Pep' in Crowd of 4,000." *Richmond Times-Dispatch* (April 12, 1918): 1–2.

"Charlie Chaplin Surpassed All Former Fun Making Marks in Shoulder Arms." *New York Tribune,* (October 22, 1918): 1.

"Charlie Chaplin Will Soon Don Khaki [army] Garb." *Los Angeles Times* (April 15, 1918): Part 2:1.

"Charlie Chaplin's Monsieur Verdoux [1947] Press Conference" *Film Comment:* Winter 1969.

"Cinema: Monsieur Verdoux." *Time* (May 5, 1947).

"Cinema 16 Excursion for New Chaplin Film. *New York Herald Tribune* (September 15, 1957): Section 4:5.

"'City Lights' a Cinch for Big Money Everywhere." *Holly Reporter* (January 30, 1931).

Cohen, Hennig. "Introduction to Melville." In *The Confidence Man.* 1857; rpt. New York: Holt, Rinehart and Winston, 1964.

Cohen, John S., Jr. "Chaplin Triumphs Anew in City Lights." *New York Sun* (February 7, 1931): 6.

"Comic Realizes Ambition in 'Great Dictator.'" *Los Angeles Times* (November 4, 1940): Part 2:14.

"Congratulations to CHARLIE CHAPLIN in the Great Dictator" ad. *Los Angeles Times* (November 14, 1940): Part 4:4.

Cook, Alton. "Chaplin Film So-So in London." *New York World Telegram and Sun* (September 22, 1957): 8.

Cook, Alton. "Chaplin's 'Limelight' a Film Masterpiece." *New York World Telegram* (October 24, 1952): 20.

Corporal Hugh Namias. "Movie Opinions Called from the Mail." *New York Times* (October 12, 1952): Section 2:6.

"*A Countess from Hong Kong* review." *Variety* (January 11, 1967).

Crowther, Bosley." *A Countess from Hong Kong* review." *New York Times* (March 17, 1967): 35.

Crowther, Bosley. "In 'The Great Dictator' Charlie Chaplin Reveals Again the Greatness in Himself" (October 20, 1940).

Crowther, Bosley. "*Limelight* review." *New York Times* (October 24, 1952):27.

Crowther, Bosley. "Monsieur Verdoux [revisionist review]." *New York Times* (July 4, 1964): 8.

Crowther, Bosley. "Under Suspicion." *New York Times* (September 28, 1952): Section 2:1.

Daniel, Clifton "Crowds Welcome Chaplin to London." *New York Times* (September 24, 1952): 3.

"Death of John Bunny." *London Times* (April 29, 1915): 5-d.

Deirdre, Donahue. "Truth Wrapped in a Mystery in Postwar London." *USA Today* (August 29, 2005): 6-D.

Delehanty, Thornton. "Charlie Chaplin Contributes a Generous Sample of His Genius in *City Lights.*" *New York Post* (February 7, 1931): Section 4:3.

"Demand Extreme Penalty for Landru." *New York times* (November 29, 1951): 5.

Derby, David. *The New Yorker* (February 11 & 18): 11, 18, 115.

"'Dictator' Costly Effort." *Los Angeles Times* (November 5, 1940): Part 1:11.

Dixon, Campbell. "Chaplin—The Old Master." *London Daily Telegram and Morning Post* (September 14, 1957): 9.

Dixon, Campbell. "New Triumph by Chaplin." *London Daily Telegraph* (February 12, 1936).

"Dog Gone, Sad Story of Grief." *New Orleans Times-Picayune.* (May 19, 1918): C-10.

"Douglas Fairbanks at Forsyth." *Athlete Constitution* (April 28, 1918): F-2.

"Douglas Fairbanks Still the Athlete in New Picture, 'Mr. Fix-It.'" *New York Herald Tribune* (April 22, 1918): 1.

"Duel Run Set for Chaplin Opus." *Los Angeles Times* (November 9, 1940): Part 1:6.

Dulluc, Louis. "Max Linder's and Elsie Codd's Views on the Working Method" (1922). In *Focus on Chaplin,* Donald W. McCaffrey, ed. Englewood Cliffs, New Jersey: Prentice Hall, 1971.

Eastman, Max. "Chaplin at Mid-Passage." In *The Essential Chaplin,* ed. Richard Schickel. Chicago: Ivan R. Doe, 2006.

Ebert, Roger. "*A King in New York* [revisionist review]." At http:/www.rogerebert.com/reviews/a-king-in-new-york, 1957.

Educating Rita full sheet poster for the 1983 ad campaign—collection of the author.

"8,000 People Buy Bands From Charlie Chaplin." *Atlanta Constitution* (April 18, 1918): 1.

"Everybody Is Cheering Chaplin on the Screen.... and HUDSON on the Highway." Ad. *Los Angeles Times* (November 14, 1940): Part 4:9.

"Fairbanks and Chaplin 'Thrill Wall St. Hosts.'" *New York Sun* (April 9, 1918): 16.

"Fairbanks Brings Joy to the Strand." *New Orleans Times-Picayune* (April 28, 1918): C-11.

"Familiar Garb of Comic Close to Heart." *Los Angeles Times* (November 19, 1940): Part 1:16.

Ferguson, Otis. "The Great Dictator review." *New Republic* (November 4, 1940).

"Film Deemed FUNFEST Not Propaganda." *Los Angeles Times* (November 14, 1940): Part 4:3.

Forsythe, Robert (Kyle Crichton). "*Modern Times* review." *New Masses* (February 18, 1936).

"France Honors Chaplin." *New York Times* (October 30, 1952): 4.

Freedland, Jonathon. "A Man of His Time." *New York Times* (March 31, 2013): Book Review Section: 14.

Frohman, Ray W. "Charlie Chaplin." *Los Angeles Herald* (December 2, 1919).

Gehmis, Joseph. "Chaplin's 'Countess' No Laughing Matter." *Newsday* (March 17, 1967): 2A.

Gehring, Wes D. "Charlie Chaplin and the Progressive Era: The Neglected Politics of a Clown." *Indiana Social Studies Quarterly* (Autumn 1981): 10–18.

Gehring, Wes D. Conversation with Geraldine Chaplin. University of Paris (April 15, 1989).

Gehring, Wes D. "John Bunny: America's First Important Film Comedian." *Literature/Film Quarterly* (vol 23, No. 2, [1995]).

Gehring, Wes D. "Kin Hubbard Is Abe Martin: A Figure of Transition in American Humor." *Indiana Magazine of History* (March 1982).

Gerber, Professor John. "Lecture on American Humor." *Iowa City, Iowa, University of Iowa* (course on humor, 1976–1977 term).

"German Propagandists Attack Liberty Loan." *Los Angeles Times* (April 18, 1918): Section 2:1.

Gilford, Joe. "Blacklisted, from a Child's View." *New York Times* (April 28, 2013): Arts and Leisure Section: 6.

Gill, Brendan. "Books." *The New Yorker* (October 12, 1964): 238.

Gish, Lillian. Conversation with the author at "The Movies: D. W. Griffith and Lillian Gish": Bracken Blossoms. Bloomington, Indiana University Auditorium Program, March 15, 1981.

"*The Gold Rush* review." *Variety* (July 1, 1925).

Gow, James. "Art Without Words." *New York World* (February 7, 1931): 11.

The Great Dictator review. *Variety* (October 16, 1940).

"Great Picture Still Turning Away Thousands in New York." *Atlantic Constitution* (April 7 1918): 8–14.

Griffith, Richard. "Chaplin's 'Great Dictator' Has All New York Agog." *Los Angeles Times* (October 28, 1940): Part 1:11.

Guernsey, Otis L., Jr. "On the Screen: 'Limelight.'" *New York Herald Tribune* (October 24, 1952): 14.

Hackett, Francis. "*The Kid* review." *New Republic* (March 30, 1921).

Hall, Mordaunt. "Chaplin Hilarious In His City Lights." *New York Herald Times* (February 7, 1931): 1.

Hamill, Pete. "Charlie Chaplin, 88, Takes Final Bow." *New York Daily News* (December 26, 1977): 3.

Hearts of the World ad. *New York Tribune* (April 21, 1918) Section: 4:7.

Heilbrunn, Jacob. "War Torn." *New York Times* (July 28, 2013) :Book Review Section: 16.

Hendrick, George and Willene, "Introduction." In Carl Sandbury's *Billy Sunday and Other Poems,* ed. Hendrick *and* Hendrick. New York: Harcourt Brace & Company, 1993.

Herrick, Myron T. " 'Pat' O' Brien and Marie Dressler Sells Bonds." *New York Tribune* (April 11, 1918): 6.

Hinxman, Margaret, "*London Daily Herald review of A King in New York,*" as quoted in David Robinson's *Chaplin: The Mirror of Opinion*. London: Martin Seckerrt Warburg, 1983: 159.

Hoberman, J. "When Chaplin Became the Enemy." *New York Times* (June 8, 2008): 19.

Hopper, Hedda. "Hedda Hopper's Hollywood." *Los Angeles Times* (November 2, 1940): Part 2:7.

Hopper, Hedda. "Hedda Hopper's Hollywood." *Los Angeles Times* (October 16, 1940): Part 1:17.

Ingalls, Leonard. "Charlie's 'King' Bows." *New York Times* (September 22, 1957).

"Is "Charlot' a Menace?." *New York Times* (September 21, 1952): Section 4:10.

Isherwood, Charles. "A Little Groucho, A Little King Soloman." *New York Times* (May 31, 2013): C-1.

"Italy Decorates Chaplin." *New York Times* (December 21, 1952) : Entertainment Section: 3.

"Jack Oakie Hits Jackpot in Chaplin Film." *Los Angeles Times* (November 14, 1940): Part 4:9.

Jackson, David. "We Got to know JFK Again in 2013. *USA Today* (May 24, 2013): 2A.

Johnson, Julian. "Charles, Not Charlie." *Photoplay* (September 1918).

The Kaiser, the Beast of Berlin ad *New York Tribune* (April 1,): 1918, 11.

"The KAISER: 'The Beast of Berlin'" ad. In the *Raleigh News and Observer* (April 14, 1918): 6.

Kanfer, Stefan. "Exit the Tramp, Smiling: Charles Spencer Chaplin: 1889–1977." Incomplete citation (January 2, 1978): Charlie Chaplin file, Performing Arts Library, New York Public Library at Lincoln Center.

Kauffman, Stanley. "Stanley Kauffman on Films: 'A King in New York':" *New Republic* (December 29, 1973): 22, 23.

"*The Kid* review." *Exceptional Photoplay* (January/February 1921).

Kimbell, Rhea Irene. "Max Linder, Soldier, Actor, Gentleman." *Motion Picture Classic* (April 4, 1917).

"Kings of Movies Raise $787,000 for Loan Bands." *New York Tribune* (April 18, 1918): 9.

Kingsley, Grace. "CHAPLIN DEPARTS: Doctor

Said He Must't [sic] But He Did." *Los Angeles Times* (April 2, 1918): Section 2:3.

Kingsley, Grace, "Griffith Returns." *Los Angeles Times* (April 19, 1918): Section 2:3.

Kingsley, Grace. "Illiteracy, Note." *Los Angeles Times* (April 12, 1918): Section 2:3.

Kinsolving, Susan. "Without." In *Dailiest Rushes*. New York: Grove Press, 1999.

Knight, Arthur. "Travels with Charlie and Friends." *Saturday Review* (October 10, 1964):45.

"'Ku Klux Klan' of Birmingham Begins Drive...." *New Orleans Times-Picayune* (May 1, 1918): 1.

Lamier, Henry Wysham. "The Coquelin of the Movies." *Worlds Work* (March 1915).

Leviero, Anthony. "Chaplin Is Facing Barriers to Reentry from Abroad." *New York Times* (September 20, 1952): 1.

"Liberty Loan Goes Beyond Half Way Point in Raleigh." *Raleigh News and Observer* (April 13, 1918): 1–2.

"Liberty Loan Rally." *Wall Street Journal* (April 9, 1918): 10.

"Life of Kaiser Shows at Tulane [Theatre]." *New Orleans Times-Picayune* (April 14, 1918): C-8.

"*Limelight* review." *Variety* (October 8, 1952).

"London Cheers Premiere of Chaplin Film: *Limelight*." (October 17, 1952). Uncited article in the Charlie Chaplin File. New York Performing Arts Library, Lincoln Center, New York.

"London in Raptures at Chaplin Movie." *New York Times* (February 28, 1931): 22.

"'M. Verdoux' Disappointing." *Hollywood Reporter* (April 14, 1947): 3, 9.

"*M. Verdoux* review." *Variety* (April 16, 1947).

Macgowan, Kenneth. "Charlie Chaplin and the Pure Idea." *New York Tribune* (November 17, 1918): Section 4:5.

Maeder, Thomas. "Afterward." In Will Cuppy's *The Decline and Fall of Practically Everybody*. 1950; rpt. Boston: Nonpareil Books, 1984.

"Mary Is Honored: Picture Star Lunches with County's Head." *Los Angeles Times* (April 9, 1918): Section 2:3.

Mary Pickford at Globe [Theatre]." *New Orleans Times-Picayune* (April 14, 1918): 6–9.

"Mary Pickford Convinces 20,000 in Wall St. Loan Should Succeed." *New York Tribune* (April 12, 1918): 6.

"Mary Pickford Holds Up a Stage Coach." *Los Angeles Times* (April 17, 1918): Section 3:15.

"Mary Pickford 'Innocent Thing' Says Boy Seized at Loan Rally" *New York Herald* (April 14, 1918): Section 1:2.

Mary Pickford, "The 'Movies' in War Time" (syndicated). *Raleigh News and Observer* (April 28, 1918): 4.

Merryman, Richard. "Ageless Master's Anatomy of Comedy: Chaplin, an Interview." *Life* (March 10, 1967).

"Millions in Bonds Are Sold by Women: Chaplin Coming Today." *Memphis Commercial-Appeal* (April 20, 1918): 1.

"Mr. Chaplin Bows Out." *New York Times* (April 17, 1953): 24.

"Mob Lynches Negro in Courthouse Yard" and "Negro Lynched in Louisiana." In the *Atlantic Constitution* (April 23, 1918): Section 1:1.

"Mob Resents Disloyal Remarks and Finds Recourse in a Rope." *Los Angeles Times* (April 5, 1918): 1.

"Mobs Try to Hang 3 In Comden for Disparaging [War Bond] Loan Drive." *New York Herald* (April 21, 1918): Section 1:5.

"*Monsieur Verdoux* review." *New York Daily Mirror* (April 12, 1947).

Moody, Ricky. "The Girl in the Blue Dress." *New York Times* (November 11, 2012): Book Review Section: 54.

Mooring, Wm. H. "An Open Letter to Charlie Chaplin." *Picturegoer and Film Weekly* (August 24, 1940): 11.

Mosher, John. "The Current Cinema: Charlie's Hitler." *The New Yorker* (October 26, 1940): 78.

"Mrs. Chaplin Coming to America." *New York Times* (November 18, 1952): 33.

"Not Fair, Says Mrs. Fairbanks." *Los Angeles Times* (April 13, 1918): Section 1:3.

"Notables Will Attend Premiere." *Los Angeles Times* (November 7, 1940): Part 1:12.

Numasawa, Kōji. "Black Humor: An American Aspect." *Studies in English Literature,* University of Tokyo (March 1968).

"On the Screen." *New York Tribune* (April 29, 1918): 9.

Orwell, George (quote). Barry Gowen, "Staying Power." *New York Times* (September 2, 2012): Book Review Section: 11.

"Owen Moore Says He'll Act in Own Protection." *Los Angeles Times* (April 14, 1918): Section 2:1.

"Paulett Goddard *Flaunts* Legendary JINX." *Los Angeles Times* (November 14, 1940): Part 4:11.

"Paulett Plays Half-Breed in Melodrama." *Los Angeles Times* (November 11, 1940): Part 1:25.

Pelswick, Rose. "Chaplin Returns in Old Role but Brings New Laughs and Sings to Film Fans." *New York Evening Journal* (February 6, 1936): 16.

Porte, Mary E. "Charlie Chaplin, Cheerful Comedian." *Picture-Play Weekly* (April 1915): 1–4.

"Pouring In!" cartoon. *Atlantic Constitution* (April 28, 1918): 1.

Powell, Dilys. "Charlie Chaplin and Mr. C., "*London Times* [September 1957]: 23. In The Charlie Chaplin File. New York Performing Arts Library, Lincoln Center, New York.

Powell, Dilys. "The Great Dictator." In *The Essential Chaplin,* Schickel, ed. Chicago: Ivan R. Dee, 2006.

"Princess Margaret at Chaplin Film Show." *London Times* (October 17, 1952): 6.

"Records of the Film: *Monsieur Verdoux*." *British Film Institute* publication (April 15, 1948): 3. In the "Charlie Chaplin File." Performing Arts Library, New York Public Library at Lincoln Center.

Rogers, Will. "Out of Jack." In *Will Rogers Weekly Articles, The Harding/Coolidge Years: 1922–1925,* ed James M. Smallwood. Stillwater: Oklahoma State University Press, 1980.

Rogers, Will. "We Save Money, Egypt Loses It." In *Will Rogers Weekly Articles, The Harding/Coolidge Years: 1922–1925,* ed James M. Smallwood. Stillwater: Oklahoma State University Press, 1980.

"Roosevelt Boosts for Liberty Bonds." *Los Angeles Times* (April 3, 1918): 1.

Saltz, Rachel. "The Führer's Visit Can't Suppress This Friendship." *New York Times* (January 25, 2013): C-5.

Sandburg, Carl. "Carl Sandburg Says: Chaplin Could Play Serious Drama." In *Authors on Film,* ed. Harry M. Geduld. Bloomington: Indiana University Press, 1972.

Sandburg, Carl. "Limited." In *Harvest Poems: 1910–1960.* New York: Harcourt, Brace, 1960.

Sandburg, Carl. "Visit with Chaplin." *Chicago Daily News* (April 16, 1921).

Sarris, Andrew. "I Films: 'Limelight.'" *Village Voice* (October 1, 1964): 15.

Sarris, Andrew. "Monsieur Verdoux." In *The Essential Chaplin,* Richard Schickel, ed. Chicago: Ivan R. Dees, 2006.

"Satire Added to Slapstick in Departure from Precedent." *Los Angeles Times:* (November 14, 1940): Part 4:2.

Schallert, Edwin. "While the *Films* Reel By." *Los Angeles Times* (October 20, 1940): Part 3:4.

Scheuer, Philip K. "Town Called Hollywood." *Los Angeles Times* (October 20, 1940): Part 3:3.

Scheuer, Philip K. "Town Called Hollywood." *Los Angeles Times* (December 22, 1940): Part 3:3.

Schickel, Richard. "Introduction: The Tramp Transformed." In *The Essential Chaplin Perspectives on the Life and Art of the Great Comedian.* Richard Schickel, ed. Chicago: Ivan R. Dee, 2006.

Schlesinger, Arthur M., Jr. "The Cold War." In *The National Experience,* ed. John M. Blum. 1963; rpt. New York: Harcourt, Brace, 1968.

Schlesinger, Arthur M., Jr. "The Eisenhower Years." In *The National Experience,* ed. John M. Blum. 1963; rpt. New York: Harcourt, Brace, 1968.

Schlesinger, Arthur M., Jr. "The Shadow of War." In *The National Experience: A History of the United States,* John M. Blum, ed. New York: Harcourt Brace, 1968.

Schopenhauer, Arthur. "On Suicide." In *Schopenhauer Essays,* trans T. Bailey Saunders. London: George Allen and Unwin, 1951.

Schopenhauer, Arthur. "On Women." In *Schopenhauer Essays,* trans. T. Bailey Saunders. London: George Allen and Unwin LTD, 1951.

Shallert, Edwin. "Sunday Picture Plans Debated by Chaplin." *Los Angeles Times* (November 14, 1940): Part 1:20.

Sharia, Nougzer. Letter to the editor. *New York Times* (January 6, 1978).

Shoulder Arms ad. *New York American* (July 19, 1922).

Shoulder Arms program notes. In the *Shoulder Arms* file. Lincoln Center Performing Arts Library (July 19, 1922).

"*Shoulder Arms* review." *Variety* (October 25, 1918).

Smith, Eugene. "Chaplin at Work: He Reveals His Movie-Making Secrets." *Life* (March 17, 1952).

"Street Rallies Coax Crowds to Buy War Bonds." *New York Telegram* (April 8, 1918): 1.

"Sweaters." *Los Angeles Times* (November 14, 1940): Part 4:3.

"Tarred for Refusing to Buy Liberty Bonds." *Atlantic Constitution* (April 28, 1918).

"Teaching of Enemy Speech in American Schools Roundly Denounced." *Los Angeles Times* (April 4, 1918): Section 1:2.

Thomas, Evan. "The Gray Man." *New York Times* (May 5, 2013): Book Review Section: 11.

Thomas, Louisa. "When Worlds Collide." *New York Times* (March 31, 2013): Book Review Section: 19.

Thomson, David. "Frank Capra." In *The New Biographical Dictionary of Film.* 1976; rpt./revised. New York: Alfred A. Knopf, 2010.

Tietjen, Gregory. "Introduction." In Thomas Paine's *Common Sense.* 1776; rpt. New York: Fall River Press, 2013.

"Trials of Landru Enters Final Week." *New York Times* (November 28, 1921): 28.

"20,000 Throng Wall St. Hear Movie Stars Tell How to Win War." *New York Tribune* (April 9, 1918): 8.

Tynan, Kenneth. "Looking Back in Anger." *London Observer."* (September 15, 1957): 4.

Underhill, Harriette. "Capturing Charlie Chaplin." *New York Tribune* (May 12, 1918): Section 4:5.

Van Gelder, Robert. "Chaplin Draws a Keen Weapon." *New York Times Magazine* (September 8, 1940): 8–9.

Verdoux full sheet poster/lithograph for the 1947 ad campaign—collection of the author.

Wallach, George, transcriber. "Charlie Chaplin's [1947] *Monsieur Verdoux* Press Interview." In *Charlie Chaplin Interviews,* Kevin J. Hayes, ed. Jackson University Press of Mississippi, 2005.

Warshow, Robert. "A Feeling of Sad Dignity." In *The Essential Chaplin,* Richard Schickel, ed. Chicago: Ivan R. Dees, 2006.

Warshow, Robert. "Monsieur Verdoux." In *The Immediate Experience.* 1962; rpt. New York: Antheneum, 1972.

Watts, Richard, Jr. "Charlie Chaplin In *City Lights*" *New York Herald Tribune* (February 7, 1931): 8.

"'We Must Count on Three More Years of War,' Says Taft." *New York Herald Tribune* (April 25, 1918): 10.

Webber, Bruce. "Frederick Neuman: Actor, Director and Interpreter of Beckett, Dies at 86." *New York Times* (December 7, 2012).

"Wham" cartoon. *Raleigh News and Observer* (April 16, 1918): 4.

Wilson, Earl. "It Happened Last Night: Paulette Recalls Charlie." *New York Post* (December 26, 1977).

Winston, Archer. "Chaplin's 'Limelight' Now Showing." *New York Post* (October 24, 1952).

Winston, Archer. "*Monsieur Verdoux* review." *New York Post* (April 12, 1947).

Winston, Archer. "Rages and Outrages." *New York Post* (July 13, 1964): 20.

Wolf, William. "Film Cues [Chaplin]." *Cue* (January 21-February 3, 1978): 25.

Documentaries

50 Children: The Rescue Mission of Mr. and Mrs. Kraus. A Film by Steven Pressman (HBO), 2013 (63 minutes).

The Life and Times of Hank Greenberg. A film by Aviva Kempner, 1999 (95 minutes).

Night and Fog. An Alain Resnais film (Images, French), 1955 (31 minutes).

See It Now: A Report on Senator Joseph R. McCarthy. An Edward R. Murrow program (CBS), First broadcast March 9, 1954 (30 minutes).

The Tramp and the Dictator. A film by Kevin Brownlow (BBC), 2001 (55 minutes).

Triumph of the Will. A Leni Riefenstahl film (German), 1935 (110 minutes).

Index

Page numbers in ***bold italics*** indicate pages with illustrations.

Abbott & Costello 61
Abe Martin 22, 67
The Adventurer 28, 29, 43
Age of Innocence 186
Agee, James 24, 93, 143, 150, 152–153, 157, 160, 164, 181
All Quiet on the Western Front 88, 111, 115, 119, 201
All That Jazz 163
Allen, Woody 62, 99, 128, 175, 197
Altman, Robert 17, 190, 191
Andalusian Dog 106, 196
Anderson, Paul Thomas 16, 191
Anderson, Wes 16
Arbuckle, Fatty 25, 41, 69
Are You Now or Have You Ever Been 165
Aristophanes 9
Armenian Holocaust 151
Arsenic and Old Lace 13, ***144***
Ashby, Hal 16
Attenborough, Richard 29, 66, 105, 135

Bairnsfather, Bruce 63, 64
Bananas 99
The Bank 27, 28, 62
Barry, Joan 134–135, 140, 168, 175
Bazin, André 74, 76, 84, 85, 153, 172
Beatles 6, 31, 188
Beckett, Samuel 84
Behind the Screen 28, 29
Being There 16–17
Bellow, Saul 196
Benny, Jack 119
Bentley, Eric 165
Bergman, Ingmar 82, 85, 183–184
Bergson, Henri 91, 102
Berra, Yogi 135
The Better 'Ole 63, 64
Bierce, Ambrose 100
Birth of a Nation 6, 35, 49, 50, 51, 72
Black Dragon Society 100
"The Black Humorists" 14
Bloom, Claire 157–159, 162
Bogart, Humphrey 161, 166
Bogdanovich, Peter 85
Bonaparte, Napoleon 6, 95, 101–104, 113, 127, 185
Bond activity in World War I 31–48, 53, 55, 57, 62, 67, 72, 73, 79, 88, 89, 123, 135, 136, 137, 150

Bonnie and Clyde 17, 125, 188
Borowski, Tadeusz 10
Brando, Marlon 186–188
Braun, Werner von 15
The Brave One 178–179
Brazil 112
Brecht, Bertolt 200
Brewster McCloud 17, 190
British Film Institute (BFI) 155–156
Brown, Joe E. 124
Brownlow, Kevin 32, 41, 94, 96, 103, 105, 124
Buchwald, Art 176, 178
Buck, Pearl 137
Buck Benny Rides Again 119
Buck Privates 61
Bunny, John 1, 23, ***24***, 31
Buñuel, Luis 15, 106, 189, 192, 196

Caesar, Sid 110
Cantor, Eddie 35, 185
Capra, Frank 13, 106–107, 133, 138, 143, 199
Cassavetes, John 143
Catch-22 13, 17, 89, 112
Catcher in the Rye 180
Chabon, Michael 132
Chamberlain, Neville 119
Chandler, Raymond 143
Chaplin (Richard Attenborough film) 29, 66, 105, 135
Chaplin, Charles, Jr. (first child with Lita Grey) 11, 25, 129, 136–137, 138, 139, 140, 141, 148, 165, 188
Chaplin, Charles, Sr. (father) 18–20, 25, 101, 158, 186
Chaplin, Charlie ***12, 34, 38, 42, 44, 47, 56, 58, 60, 64, 71, 75, 81, 86, 97, 106, 126, 130, 136, 140, 145, 160, 174, 177, 199***; Charles Dickens and 11, 19, 31, 70, 141, 184, 190; comedy thoughts of 11, 12, 25, 26, 29, 55, 58, 63, 66, 77, 103, 119, 124, 139, 141, 149, 151, 201; metamorphosis of objects by 11, 26, 27, 57, 80; *My Autobiography* by 7, 10, 12, 22, 51–52, 65, 73, 80, 101, 104, 105, 150, 184, 185, 186, 192; *My Life in Pictures* by 186, 191; *My Trip Abroad* by 73–74, 140–141, 185; pantheon artistry

of 5, 7, 18, 19, 23, 123, 157, 170, 184, 189; youth of 1, 10, 18–21, 22, 31, 139, 157, 158–159, 166, 170, 171, 184, 185, 186
Chaplin, Geraldine (first child with Oona O'Neill) 1, 158, 164, 187, ***189***
Chaplin, Hannah (mother) 18–21, 70, 84, 101, 185, 186
Chaplin, Josephine (second daughter with Oona O'Neill) 158, 164, 187
Chaplin, Lita Grey (second wife) 11, 82, 83, 84, 101, 140, 165, 185–186
Chaplin, Michael (oldest son with Oona O'Neill) 11, 139, 158, 159, 177, 178
Chaplin, Mildred Harris (first wife) 31, 65, 66–68, 82, 186
Chaplin, Norman Spencer (first child with Mildred Harris) 67, 69
Chaplin, Oona O'Neill (fourth wife) 11, 66, 115, 135, 157–158, 159, 164, 166, 167, 170, 171, 173, 185, 188, 190–191
Chaplin, Paulette Goddard (third wife) 95, 99, 100, 103, 108, 114, 115, ***117***, 118, 119, 122, 128, 129, 134, 153, 161, 172, 186
Chaplin, Sydney (half-brother) 18, 19–21, 31, 33, 35, 57, ***58***, 59, ***60***, 61, 62, 63, 70, 73, 94, 189–190
Chaplin, Sydney (second child with Lita Grey) 107, 114, 137, 165, 187, 188
Chaplin, Victoria (third daughter with Oona O'Neill) 164, 190
The Chaplin Review 182
Chaplin: The Dictator and the Tramp 124
Charlie Chaplin in the Army 63, ***64***
Charlie Chaplin Up in the Air 63
Charlie Chaplin's Comic Capers 63
Chayefsky, Paddy 143
Chevallier, G. 89, 138
Chicago Race Riots: July 1919 73
Chinatown 14, 80
Churchill, Winston 102, 133
"Circle" theatre 165
The Circus 25, 83–85, ***86***, 87, 90, 101, 108, 110, 129, 155, 182, 191

229

Index

Citizen Kane 115, 141
City Lights 27, 84, 87, 90–94, ***93***, ***95***, 100, 102, 112, 129, 148, 163, 173, 177
Claire, René 106, 107
Clapton, Eric 71
Clark, Petula 188
Clausewitz, Karl von 5
A Clockwork Orange 16, 98, 112, 193
Cobb, Humphrey 88–89, 102
Coen Brothers 16
"Comedy's Greatest Era" 160
Communist Control Act 162
Coogan, Jackie 28, 68–72, ***71***, 74, 108, 147, 153, 178
Cooke, Alistair 102, 104
Cosby, Bill 70
Costeau, Jean 41
Coughlin, Charles E. 97
The Count 28, 29
A Countess From Hong Kong 7, 100, 186–188, 190
Coward, Noël 172, 180
Crichton, Kyle 95
"Cristal Night" 198
Crystal, Billy 188
Cuppy, Will 140, 195
The Cure 28, 29, 43

Dalí, Salvador 28, 92, 106, 138, 196
Darwin, Charles 9, 15, 197
The Day of the Locust 83, 150
A Day's Pleasure 66, 68
A Death in the Family 24
Debs, Eugene 88
The Decline and Fall of Practically Everybody 195
Degas, Edgar 180
DeMille, Cecil B. 49
The Disenchanted 25–26
Dr. Strangelove 9, 12–13, 14, 15, 16, 17, 92, 93, 197
A Dog's Life 37, 46, 47, 55–56, ***56***, 68–69, 181, 182
Dressler, Marie 41, ***136***
Dryden, Leo 19, 159
Dryden, Wheeler 19, 159
Duck Soup 27, 60, 80, 85, 110, 155, 168
"duckboards" 58
Durfee, Minta 25

Ealing Studio 7, 16, 169
Eastman, Max 141
Easy Street 12, 28–29, 61, 62, 125, 159
Eisenhower, Dwight D. 162
Eisenstein, Sergei 79, 95–96
Eisler, Hans 161
Eliot, T. S. 32, 195
Emerson, Ralph Waldo 185
Essanay 21, 26–27, 63
The Eternal Jew 94
Eyes Wide Shut 49

Fairbanks, Douglas 6, 37, 39–41, 44, 45, 52, ***53***, ***54***, 55, 67, 73, ***78***, 105, ***136***, 137, 172, ***174***, 200
A Farewell to Arms 88
Fear 89, 138
Fields, W. C. 1, 12, 13; criticism of Chaplin by 28, 29, 66, 67–68, 118, 119, 172, 185, 192–193; John Bunny and 23–24
50 Children: The Rescue Mission of Mr. and Mrs. Kraus 198
Finks 178
The Fireman 28, 29
First National 30, 73, 74, 76
Fitzgerald, F. Scott 25–26, 115, 185, 191
Flaherty, Robert 81–82
Flaubert, Gustave 139
The Floor Walker 27, 29
Footlights 158, 160, 161, 163
Ford, Henry 96–97, 132, 198–199
Fosse, Bob 163
Foster, William Z. 162
Frank, Anne 10
Frankl, Victor E. 10
The Freak 164, 190–191
"Free Cinema" 180
Freud, Sigmund 9–10
The Front 170
Fussell, Paul 55

Garfield, John 170
Gehring, Jerry 1
The General 80
German Expressionism 109
The Ghost Breakers ***117***, 118, 127
Gilbert, Billy 108–109
Gilford, Joe 178
Gish, Lillian 50
Go West 118–119
God Bless You, Mrs. Rosewater 195
Gogol, Nikolai 96
The Gold Rush 11, ***12***, 23, 79, 80, ***81***, 82, 83, 84, 85, 99, 125, 129, 133–134, 165, 177, 182, 185
Good-Bye to All That 88
Göring, Hermann 200–201
The Graduate 17, 188
Grand Illusion 75–76
Graves, Robert 88, 89
The Great Dictator 1, 3, 5, 6, 91, 92, 94, 95, 96, 100, 103, 104–120, 121–125, ***126***, 127–129, ***130***, 131–134, 139, 142, 143, 145, 146, 147, 148, 155, 156, 159, 169, 174, 193, 196; "Final Solution" and 10, 108, 142, 200; final speech of 104, 111–112, 125, 126, 131, 133, 155, 174, 196, 197; Hitler and 3, 5, 6, 14, 15, 16, 17, 49, 91, 94, 101, 103, 104, 105–106, 107–111, 113, 116, 121, 122, 123, 124, 128, 131, 132, 159, 198
Greenberg, Hank 97
Greene, Graham 4, 155

Griffith, D. W. 6, 35, 49–51, 72, 73, 85, 93
Guernica ii, iv, 1, 3, 4, 5, 113–114, 120, 131, 195
Guinness, Alec 16, ***169***

Harding, Warren 90
Harold and Maude 16, 142, 190
Hart, William S. 41
Hawks, Howard 13
Hays, Will 162
Hearst, William Randolph 101
The Heart of Darkness 195
Hearts of the World 49–50, 51
Heathers 74
Heller, Joseph 13, 61, 89
Hellman, Lillian 166
Hemingway, Ernest 88, 89
Hitchcock, Alfred 13, 144–145, 147, 184
"Hollywood Ten" 150, 161
Holocaust 10, 17, 142, 151
Hoover, J. Edgar 29, 161
Hope, Bob 46, 62, 99, ***117***, 118, 124, 140
Hopper, Edward 3
House Un-American Activities Committee (HUAC) 116, 135, 150, 161, 162, 165–166, 168, 170, 171, 174, 175–181, 190
Hubbard, Frank "Kin" 22, 67

The Idle Class 23, 63, 73, 155, 182
The Immigrant 23, 29, 167
Ingersoll, Robert 154
The International Jew 198
It's a Wonderful Life 143

Jannings, Emil 109, 110
The Jazz Singer 87
Jesus 6, 70, 101, 108, 163
The Jews Are Looking at You 94, 105
Joyce, Peggy Hopkins ***76***, 77

Kael, Pauline 68
Kafka, Franz 121, 190
Kahlo, Frida 115
The Kaiser: The Beast of Berlin 35, 50, ***51***, 62, 89, 131
Karno, Fred 20, 21, 22–26, 27, 158–159
Keaton, Buster 12, 13, 72, 80, 146, ***160***
Kelly, Hetty 66, 158, 185
Kelly, Walt 75
Kennedy, John F. 31, 197
Kennedy, Joseph 132
The Kid 11, 28, 62, 68–70, ***71***, 72–74, 80, 82, 92, 133, 140, 147, 153, 178, 182
Kid Auto Races at Venice 23, 26, 27
Kind Hearts and Coronets 16, ***169***, ***175***
A King in New York 7, 148, 150,

157, 168, 175–178, *179*, 180–182, 187
Kirby, Rollin *199*
Korda, Alexander 104
Kosinski, Jerzy 16
Kubrick, Stanley 16, 49, 98, 112, 192, 197

The Lady from Shanghai 85
The Ladykillers 16
Landru, Henri 15, 139–140, 141, 147, 149, 155
Landseer, Edwin 69
Lane, Conrad 1, 4
Lang, Fritz 3
Laughter (Bergson) 102
*Laughter in Hell: The Use of Humor During the Holocaus*t 10, 105
Laurel, Stan 21, 22, 137, 193
Laurel and Hardy 1, 12, 21, 57, 60, 71, 109, 137, 148, 177, 193
Lee, Canada 170
Lee, Harper 178
Lennon, John 31
Leone, Sergio 7
Leopold and Loeb 142, 144–145
Limelight 7, 148, 157–159, *160*, 162–164, 166, 167, 168, 172–173, 181, 183, 191
Lindbergh, Charles 132
Linder, Max 23–24, 28, 31, 32–33, 99
Little Big Man 17
Lloyd, Harold 28, 72, 87, 160, *174*, 175
Loeb, Philip 170
Look Back in Anger 180
Loren, Sophia 186–188
"Lost Generation" 6, 90, 128
Love and Death 175
Lubitsch, Ernst 13, 77, *78*, 79

Machiavelli, Niccolò 137
Maland, Charles J. 109
A Man Without a Country 201
Martin, Russell 3, 5, 113
Marx, Groucho 52, 85, 119, 168
Marx, Harpo 25, 27, 85, 155
Marx Brothers 1, 12–13, 52, 80, 110, 118–119, 141
MASH 17, 92, 147, 154
Mask 85
Matthau, Carol 164–165, 170–171
Maupassant, Guy de 11
Mayer, Louis B. 67
McCarey, Leo 3, 60–61
McCarthy, Joseph 7, 18, 29, 37, 74, 115, 148, 150, 162, 179, 183, 191, 195
McIntyre, Wallace 1
Méliès, Georges 12
Melville, Herman 9
Menken, H. L. 83
Mission to Moscow 135
Modern Times 28, 94–96, *97*, 98–100, 103, 107, 108, 112, 127, 133, 143, 148, 149, 156
Monsieur Verdoux 3, 4, 5, 6, 7, 9, 13, 14–16, 17, 20, 49, 51, 56–65, 67, 71, 120, 122, 139, *140*, *145*, 157, 161, 163, 166; war trilogy and 6, 14–15, 17, 80, 96, 98, 102, 107, 111, 112, 122, 123, 128, 137, 141, 142, 145, 146, 147, 152, 157, 197, 199, 200
Montagu, Ivor 94, 96, 105
Moonrise Kingdom 16
Mostel, Zero 165–166, 170
Murder Without Tears: An Anthology of Crime 140
Murrow, Edward R. 176, 183
Mutual film company 27–30, 32, 60, 63
My Favorite Brunette 140
My Last Sigh 15
My Little Chickadee 118, 119

Nanook of the North 81–82
Napoleon *see* Bonaparte, Napoleon
Nash, Marilyn 153–154
Nashville 17, 164
Network 143
"New American Cinema" 16, 17
Nichols, Mike 13, 146
A Night in the Show 28
The Night of the Hunter 153
Nighthawks 3
1984 96, 99, 109
Normand, Mabel 22

Oakie, Jack 93, 110, 114, 124, 127, 129, *130*, 146
"Old Bill" 63
One A.M. 28, 29
Orwell, George 14, 96, 99, 109
Osborne, John 180

Paine, Thomas 37, 174
Palmer, Mitchel A. 74
Patch, Harry 151
Paths of Glory 89, 102
The Pawnshop 28, 29
Pay Day 57, 73, 74
"The Penal Colony" 121
Penn, Arthur 17, 125
Picasso, Pablo ii, iv, 1, 3, 4, 5, 113–114, 122, 131, 161, 195
Picasso's War: The Destination of Guernica, and the Masterpiece That Changed the World 3, 5, 113
Pickford, Mary 6, 37, 39–41, 52, 53, *54*, 67, 73, *78*, *136*, 137
The Pilgrim 73, 74, *75*, 76, 182
Player Piano 98
The Plot Against America 132
Poe, Edgar Allan 9, 11, 96
Pogo 75
The Police 26
Pollard, Snub 159

Progressive Era 29
The Protocols of the Learned Elders of Zion 198
Pryor, Richard 68
Pulp Fiction 16
Purviance, Edna 26–27, 28, 43, *60*, 62, 68, 69, 70, 72, 77, 79, 101, 129

Raising Arizona 16
Ramsaye, Terry 18
Raye, Martha 15–16, 138, 146
Remarque, Erich Maria 88, 89, 111, 115
Renoir, Jean 28, 75, 164, 177
Riefenstahl, Leni 15, 106, 107
The Rink 28, 29
Rivera, Diego 115, 118, 122
Road to Singapore 118
Robeson, Paul 175
Robinson, Edward G. 115–116
Rogers, Will 35, 67, 82, 83, 105, 107, 168
Roman Holiday 179
Roosevelt, Franklin Delano 116, 120, 123, 131–132, 133, 135, *136*, 137, 161
Roosevelt, Theodore 33–34
Rope 145–156
Rosencrantz and Guildenstern Are Dead 148
Ross, Lillian 105, 164–165, 166
Rossetti, Dante Gabriel 185
Roth, Philip 132
The Royal Tenenbaums 16
Rules of the Game 28, 177
Russell, Bertrand 88
Russell, Bill 4

Safety Last 87
Salinger, J. D. 180
Sandbury, Carl 12, 71, 73, 195
Schopenhauer, Arthur 153–154, 171
Schulberg, Budd 25–26
Scorsese, Martin 3
The Sea Gull 79
Sellers, Peter 15, 16–17, 187
Sennett, Mack 12, 20, 21, 22–27, 41, 69, 70, 116, 177
The Seventh Seal 82, 85
Shadow of a Doubt 147
Shadows and Substance 134, 175
Shaw, George Bernard 94
Shoulder Arms 31, 37, *42*, 49, 51, 56–57, *58*, 59, *60*, 61–63, *64*, 65, 67, 68, 71, 74, 80, 85, 95, 122, 142, 182, 185; war trilogy and 6, 14–15, 17, 80, 98, 102, 107, 111, 112, 122, 123, 128, 137, 141, 142, 145, 146, 147, 152, 157, 197, 199, 200
The Sinking of the Lusitania 51
Slaughterhouse-Five 57, 98, 120, 195
"Smile" 188

Sontag, Susan 148
Stalin, Joseph 131, 135
Stander, Lionel 165, 166
State of the Union 133, 138, 143
Sterling, Ford 25
Sternberg, Josef von 79
Stewart, Donald Ogden 178
Stoppard, Tom 148
Stroheim, Erich von 81
Sturges, Preston 13–14, 85, 118, 149, 199
"Suicide Is Painless" 92, 147
Sunnyside 66, 68
Swain, Mack 25, 185
Swift, Jonathon 9, 144

Taft, William 33
Tarantino, Quentin 16
"Tears in Heaven" 71
There Will Be Blood 16, 191
The Third Man 155
"This Is My Song" 188
This Way for the Gas, Ladies and Gentleman 10
Thomas, Dylan 167
Thomson, David 143
Thurber, James 69
Tillie's Punctured Romance 41
Tinney, Frank 159
To Be or Not to Be 13
To Kill a Mockingbird 178

Totheroh, Roland 167
The Tramp 26–27
The Tramp and the Dictator 94, 96, 103, 105, 107, 124
The Tramp's New World 164, 181
Triumph of the Will 15, 106
Trotsky, Leon 115
The Truman Show 143
Trumbo 17
Trumbo, Christopher 178
Trumbo, Dalton 178–179
Trumbo, Mitzi 178
Trumbo: Red, White and Blacklisted 178
Turpin, Ben 196
Twain, Mark 9, 11, 91, 96, 185

Umberto D 180
Underwood, Loyal 159
Unfaithfully Yours 199
United Artists 73, 76, 123, 127, 131, 149–150, 153, 167, 190

The Vagabond 28
Vigo, Jean 62, 85
The Visitor 29
Vonnegut, Kurt 12, 57, 61, 98, 109, 120, 193, 195, 201

Waiting for Godot 84
"Waldorf Agreement" 150

Wallace, Henry A. 161
Warner Brothers 132
Warshaw, Robert 95, 142, 143, 144
"The Waste Land" 32
Welles, Orson 15, 69, 85, 115, 137, 138, 141, 155
Wellman, William 3
Wells, H. G. 73, 184, 191, 197
West, Mae 118–119
West, Nathanael 83, 150
Wheeler and Woolsey 168
Wiesel, Elie 151, 157
Wild Strawberries 184
Wilde, Oscar 11, 65, 96, 176, 177
Wilder, Billy 13, 14, 118
Williams, Robin 187
Wilson, Meredith 124, 137–138
Wilson, Woodrow 37, 39–40, 45, 53, 137
Wise, Robert 3, 87, 139
A Woman of Paris 76–80, 95, 101, 103, 129
Wood, Ed 177
Wood, Grant 3
Woollcott, Alexander 83

The Yiddish Policeman's Union 132

Zero for Conduct 62, 85

www.ingramcontent.com/pod-product-compliance
Lightning Source LLC
Chambersburg PA
CBHW081552300426
44116CB00015B/2847